ELECTRONIC MUSIC COMPOSITION

for beginners

Second Edition

Robert Train Adams
University of Massachusetts Dartmouth

Book Team

Developmental Editor *Deborah Daniel Reinbold*
Production Coordinator *Deborah Donner*

Brown & Benchmark
A Division of Wm. C. Brown Communications, Inc.

Vice President and General Manager *Thomas E. Doran*
Executive Managing Editor *Ed Bartell*
Executive Editor *Edgar J. Laube*
Director of Marketing *Kathy Law Laube*
National Sales Manager *Eric Ziegler*
Marketing Manager *Kathleen Nietzke*
Advertising Manager *Jodi Rymer*
Managing Editor, Production *Colleen A. Yonda*
Manager of Visuals and Design *Faye M. Schilling*

Production Editorial Manager *Vickie Putman Caughron*
Publishing Services Manager *Karen J. Slaght*
Permissions/Records Manager *Connie Allendorf*

WCB Wm. C. Brown Communications, Inc.

Chairman Emeritus *Wm. C. Brown*
Chairman and Chief Executive Officer *Mark C. Falb*
President and Chief Operating Officer *G. Franklin Lewis*
Corporate Vice President, Operations *Beverly Kolz*
Corporate Vice President, President of WCB Manufacturing *Roger Meyer*

Cover design by Carol V. Hall

Printed in the United States of America by Wm. C. Brown Communications, Inc., 2460 Kerper Boulevard, Dubuque, IA 52001

10 9 8 7 6 5 4 3 2

CONTENTS

ILLUSTRATIONS

v

TABLES

PREFACE

The developments in electronic technology since the 1970s have had a great impact on electronic music making. Synthesizers were once found primarily in the tape music studio. They have become the mainstay of many rock groups and can be purchased in most department stores. With the development of microcomputers, digital synthesizers, and MIDI (Musical Instrument Digital Interface), ever more sophisticated musical resources are available in smaller—and less expensive—packages.

Since the first edition of this text in 1986 there has been a tremendous outpouring of MIDI software. While there have been developments in hardware, especially in the area of digital memory, leading to samplers and other digital means of recording and manipulating sound, the developments in software far outweigh the hardware. This presents the musician with a dilemma: do you concentrate on making music, or try to learn something about what goes on behind the scenes?

This text explores beginning electronic music composition concepts using both analog and digital approaches to synthesis, with the emphasis on the MIDI studio. Basic hardware and a broad range of software options and procedures are presented. There is a focus on compositional procedures throughout the book with both structured and free exercises. In discussing equipment and software, the approach is as generic as possible.

It is expected that readers of this text will have varying degrees of formal musical training. Indeed, a formal background is sometimes a handicap to the free-wheeling, imaginative spirit of the electronic medium. This text is intended for use by both music majors and nonmajors, either in an undergraduate or community college setting.

Unfamiliar terms are **boldfaced** at their first mention, briefly defined, and included in an extensive glossary. An end-of-chapter set of review questions focuses attention on those terms and concepts that the student should know. To encourage further work, many exercises are suggested throughout the book, and suggestions for further reading are provided in an appendix.

ORGANIZATION OF THIS BOOK

There are four parts to this text. Part I presents background material. Basic information on sound and typical studio equipment is presented, along with a primer on MIDI.

Part II discusses basic analog modules and their digital counterparts, along with sampling. A three-phase approach to work in the studio is presented. The three phases—

Instrument Design, Score Construction, and Rehearsal/Performance—are interrelated and provide a model for studio work.

Part III offers a look at traditional and contemporary notational practices, along with an introduction to recording. Notation and transcription software is discussed, and the uses of peripheral equipment and classic tape studio techniques are explored.

Part IV places an emphasis on compositional considerations. Sequencing software and compositional strategies are presented. Several programs that can participate in the compositional process are also discussed. The book closes with a set of 65 exercises exploring some of the creative aspects of sequencing.

THE LEARNING PROGRESSION

It is intended that this book be used flexibly, and not in the strictly linear fashion dictated by pages and binding. Following chapters one and two with four, five, and ten gives a basic introduction that moves from analog toward digital. Moving from part I directly to part IV concentrates on using the studio without worrying how sounds are constructed. Moving from chapters one and two to chapters seven, eight, ten, and eleven enhances traditional compositional studies. Following the progression of chapters as it is given presents a solid foundation that moves from hardware to software. In most cases, portions of part IV may easily be used in conjunction with material in earlier chapters.

As an aid to flexibility, the first mention of terms found in the glossary is highlighted. Parts II, III, and IV are treated in this respect as though each followed part I. It is expected that this book offers enough material for at least a year's study.

TO THE STUDENT

The theme of this text is that anyone can explore musical creativity through the fascinating sonic resources offered by current electronic music technology. This text is intended to be used in a class context, although nonstudent readers with their own equipment who wish to expand their understanding of electronic music resources may also find it helpful.

"Hands-on" studio work is vital to a better understanding of the material presented here. Since music does involve sound, words remain only words until you realize their meaning in your own terms. Inevitably you will become frustrated that sound doesn't instantly do what you want it to do. By changing one aspect of a sound at a time you can control the gradual development of quite complex sonic material. By following the three phases used in this book, you can create pieces of music out of material that at first seemed quite unlikely to go anywhere. As you gain experience with hardware and software and the musical concepts presented here, you will be better equipped to explore the musical vision that prompted you to begin this study.

ACKNOWLEDGEMENTS

Often as I worked on this book I have thought that I would like to acknowledge the help of this or that person; the list would be long, and I would certainly forget someone. I have learned much from my students (especially Arno Grbac and Gareth Vigus, who have patiently extended the boundaries of my technical understanding, and Ken Volcjak, who turned the sow's ear of many an exercise into the silk purse of beautiful music); their enthusiasm and love for music have energized me. The support and encouragement offered by my wife Marianne is worth more than mere words can say.

PART · ONE

INTRODUCTION

CHAPTER · ONE

BEGINNINGS

Electronic music systems continue an experimental trend that has long been a part of musical tradition. Since electronic music touches many disciplines, it is best approached by dividing the creative work into smaller tasks.

Everyone knows something about music. In the case of those with a formal background in music, this knowledge includes familiarity with music notation and other theoretical concepts as well as some ability to play an instrument or sing. In the absence of such a formal background, one may still be knowledgeable about music, since music must, in the final analysis, be heard to be understood.

It is difficult to escape music, unless one lives the life of a hermit. Television, radio, movies, and shopping malls make liberal use of music to create a mood or sell a product. In the workplace, music may be used to increase productivity. The listener, whether musically trained or not, develops a set of criteria defining "good" music and good performance of that music. It is easy to become compartmentalized in this process. "Classical" music lovers may not like jazz, jazz aficionados may not care for "popular" music, and

3

devotees of popular music may become so attached to one artist or group that other popular artists or types of music may pale in comparison.

GETTING STARTED

Electronic music to some degree crosses over and minimizes such distinctions. At its best, the electronic or **electroacoustic** medium allows for creative sound generation and transmission without regard for stylistic considerations. Of course, we all approach music making, just as any other endeavor, with the various preconceptions, knowledge, and skills we have accrued from prior learning situations, both formal and informal.

The approach taken here combines the intuitive free play of improvisation with the discipline that comes with study. An examination of the workings of familiar musical styles should be complemented by a comparison of these styles with elements of other musical styles that are less familiar. This conscious involvement with musical processes should lead to an increased awareness of the similarities and contrasts among various types of music. It will also give the musician a greater repertoire of creative options.

A BRIEF BACKGROUND

Music has always existed in a state of flux. While some composers and performers refined existing procedures and practices, others were looking for something new. Musical styles and tastes changed—and varied from place to place. Musical instruments were invented, evolved, or fell out of favor. The orchestra, for example, did not evolve into a standard set of instruments until the early nineteenth century, even though the practice of writing for instrumental ensembles had existed for many centuries.

Current musical instruments trace their ancestry back through the ages. The piano developed from the family of plucked-string keyboard instruments. A series of innovations led to today's instrument. The piano keyboard comes from the organ, although early keyboards had fewer keys and were much harder to play. The organ has long been a favorite for innovative tinkering, with the use of multiple keyboards, a wide range of timbres, the swell box that allowed for some control over volume, and the addition of electricity and electronics. In spite of the organ being the oldest keyboard instrument, in many ways it remains the most open to change, and it is certainly a major forerunner to today's electronic keyboards.

As technology and society changed and developed, some musicians sought to exploit the technology in the search for new means of expression. With the development of the telephone and the phonograph in the late nineteenth century came a host of experiments involving electricity and music. Dr. Thaddeus Cahill's "Dynamophone," demonstrated in Holyoke, Massachusetts, in 1906, was envisioned as allowing for electrical creation of music that would be transmitted to listeners over telephone lines. Although his project was not successful financially, his technique of sound generation is still with us in the guise of the Hammond organ.

With the development of the film soundtrack, some work was done around 1930 with drawing waveforms onto film. While quite feasible, this required an accuracy more appropriate to current technology. The tape recorder, first developed by the Germans in World War II as a wire recorder, was used in the creation of **musique concrete**, a type of early electronic music involving the recording and altering of natural sounds.

In the 1950s, the development of the RCA Mark II Synthesizer, now located at the Columbia-Princeton Electronic Music Center, marked a new phase in electronic music. This room-size, expensive machine allowed for the creation of complex music, which was entered on a roll of paper tape. With the development of **transistors** and **integrated circuits**, the way was paved for the development during the 1970s of portable electronic instruments such as the Moog and ARP synthesizers. Such equipment became capable of producing an ever-widening range of musical sounds and effects. As **microprocessors** and computer memory continued to shrink in size and grow in potential, what once took up the space of a room could sit on a desk.

Developments in the 1980s broadened the scope of electroacoustic music, allowing much greater access to procedures such as **sampling** (the digital recording of sound). **MIDI** (Musical Instrument Digital Interface) was developed and became the primary tool in both studio and live electronic music making.

The 1990s is witnessing a rapid expansion of digital technology. Digital recording is becoming more accessible. Software combining MIDI and other digital technologies has been developed, and the borders between sound and sight are narrowing. Synchronization of sound with film and video is easily available, and the potential to combine music with almost anything that can be digitally controlled is being exploited.

This potential has its hazards for musicians. Often the designers of microcomputer hardware and software and synthesizers have an understandable commercial motive. Much of the equipment is either too limited for serious musical work, or is restricted in design to be a mere electronic keyboard, so that the true, exciting nature of synthesized music gets lost in the hundreds of flashy sounds instantly at one's beck and call.

ELECTRONIC MUSIC

All musicians learn to produce sounds in ways that are appropriate for their instrument and the music they will play. A jazz saxophonist may produce a **vibrato**, which gives the instrument a rich character and shimmer appropriate for jazz. The same sound would be out of place in most art music. The opera singer's vibrato, on the other hand, would sound quite pretentious and silly in popular music or jazz.

This differentiation goes beyond mere vibrato or other surface features. Words are pronounced and sung differently in various styles. The absence or presence of a microphone affects how one sings or plays. Jazz may contain "blue" notes that in art music are simply out of tune.

In electronic music, sounds are more likely to be considered "appropriate" or "less appropriate" for a particular context rather than wrong or unmusical. If electroacoustic music may be said to have an idiomatic identity, it is found in the wide range of sounds that the composer can use. Whether composers are paraphrasing or imitating an existing musical style or are composing something original in a particular idiom, they must become familiar with that style or idiom. Their choice and use of sounds must be based on their knowledge of that style, tempered by their own sense of creativity. Close involvement with sound itself allows electronic composers a great deal of freedom.

THE NATURE OF MUSIC

Music is multidimensional. While sound is obviously an important aspect of music, the sounds—and silences—need space and time in which to occur. Musical sound has **duration**, or length. As will be discussed later, attention may be given to the durations of various subdivisions of **tones** (discrete musical sounds), as well as to length and placement of tones themselves in the musical work.

Tones may be grouped together to create **rhythms** and **melodies**. In many musics, the interaction of musical lines and harmonies creates larger, regular pulsations. These give rise to the written **measure**, denoted on the page by a vertical barline (traditionally each measure has the same length), and the concept of regular pulsation, or **meter**. On an even larger scale, musical works may be organized into sections and movements, each needing time to unfold.

Unlike visual art, where the viewer is allowed to structure time in viewing and understanding the object, music has a sequential aspect not controlled by the listener. CD players, tape recorders, record players, and other forms of storage and playback can allow the listener some of the freedom of the art lover, by allowing the listener to play and replay those sections that are particularly pleasing. But in music, the overall sequence of events is often an important aspect of the work, since long-range connections or the cumulative effect of events may be needed to perceive the composer's intent.

The electroacoustic medium is not restricted to the production of tones. Just as there are percussion instruments that produce sonic events with a high noise content or tones that do not fit into the tuning schemes of standard Western music, so also may electroacoustic music freely exploit the whole gamut of possible sounds. Because of this flexibility, electronic music offers composers and other musicians creative possibilities only dreamed of by earlier generations. At the same time, this medium demands that the composer be very involved in all phases of the creative process.

DESCRIBING SOUND

Acoustics deals with the production and transmission of sound. As a branch of physics, acoustics uses terms that have fairly precise means of measurement. Acoustical terms that have musical significance include **frequency, intensity** or loudness, duration, and **waveform**. They allow for the description of the properties of physical systems that produce and transmit sound.

Musical terms tend to be more qualitative than quantitative, based on the perception of the listener. Rather than frequency, the musician speaks of pitch, or of a **note** (the written symbol for the played sound), or of a tone. Intensity is considered in terms of loudness or musical **dynamics** (a set of symbols to indicate relative loudness), while duration is thought about in terms of note length or rhythmic patterns. Waveform, if even considered, is discussed in terms of timbre or choice of musical instrument.

Table 1.1 offers a continuum of descriptive terms that are more appropriate to physics or acoustics on the left, and more appropriate to music on the right. Although the physical terms have separate meanings, they combine in music. A melody consisting of tones with *frequency* and *duration* must be expressive (have different levels of *intensity*) and is often associated with an instrument or voice (*waveform*). Effective harmony may depend on the choice of instruments used to realize it (*waveform*) and have its own rhythm (*duration* groupings), which can be quite important in the ebb and flow music.

In the discussions of these terms in this chapter, an attempt will be made to arrive at working definitions that will be used throughout this book. Rarely in music are all factors equally important. In pieces where rhythmic impulse plays a large role, harmonic activity is often given less attention, and melody may seem to be a byproduct of the rhythm. The purpose here is to aim for the conscious control of the various aspects of musical sound.

FREQUENCY AND PITCH

Imagine a room without sound, aurally as placid as a lake on a summer's morning without a hint of a breeze. Silence is never really silent, of course; the noise of our hearts beating and our circulatory systems working must be there at the least. Into this relative quiet intrudes a brief sonic event: a sound perhaps so fleeting that you doubt it even happened. Again a sound, and then more, each but a fraction of a second. As more sounds occur, it becomes apparent that they can be counted: 5, 6, 7, then 10 per second. Even more sounds happen per second. At around 16 to 20 events per second, you lose the sense of a succession of discrete events and become aware of a low hum. As more events occur, an increasingly higher pitch is heard. Just as the eye is fooled by the succession of frames of film into seeing motion, so the ear may be fooled by the rapid succession of cycles of a waveform. Rather than perceiving faster or slower motion, however, the ear hears higher or lower pitches.

Table 1.1. A continuum of physical and musical terms

PHYSICAL	⟷		MUSICAL
Frequency	Pitch	Tone	Melody and harmony
Intensity	Loudness	Volume	Dynamics (expression)
Duration	Time	Rhythm	Melody, harmonic rhythm, meter
Waveform	Timbre	Tone color (quality)	Instrumentation (orchestration)

The range of audible frequencies stretches from about 16-20 cycles per second on the lower end to about 20,000 on the upper. As one gets older, sensitivity to the upper range particularly declines. Frequencies less than 16 to 20 cycles per second are not perceived as discrete pitches, but actually enter into the realm of rhythm, since the ear is capable of hearing each pulsation as a discrete event.

The term **Hertz**, in honor of German physicist Heinrich Hertz (1857-1894), is usually used in place of "cycles per second." Frequency is measured in Hertz (often abbreviated Hz), while pitch is usually measured in Western music in terms of the note-name system of letters and modifying symbols. With the use of this system, the determination of the frequency of various pitches becomes a matter of convention.

Although the pitch A = 440 Hz is a widely agreed-upon orchestral tuning note in the United States, some orchestras and musical instruments are tuned higher or lower. This diversity was widespread in earlier centuries, and included **temperament** (the relationship among successive notes of a musical scale). The development of equal temperament in the 17th century promoted standardization, so that we can speak of a **half step** (the interval between adjacent notes on a keyboard) as always being 1/12 of an **octave** (an octave—from the Latin root *octo*: eight—refers to the tendency of Western scales to consist of eight tones, such that the top and bottom have the frequency ratio 2:1).

In discussing discrete pitches, the term *tone* is more appropriate than *note*. A note is the written symbol for a tone (in actual practice, both terms tend to be used interchangeably). Tones, when given attributes such as volume, length, and timbre, may be combined to yield melodies and harmonies and ultimately pieces of music.

INTENSITY AND LOUDNESS

Several terms are used almost interchangeably to indicate the loudness of sound: intensity, loudness, dynamics, amplitude, and volume. It is possible to measure the strength of a sound wave produced by a musical instrument in terms of acoustic watts. The units of sound intensity are quite small, but the human ear is quite sensitive.

INTENSITY

The intensity level of a sound can be measured in terms such as "10 to the minus n watts per square meter." To avoid the awkwardness of this means of measuring intensity, the **decibel** is used. A reading of 0 decibels (**dB**) represents the threshold of hearing (very soft), while 120 dB represents the threshold of feeling (the level at which sound produces physiological pain).

LOUDNESS AND DYNAMICS

In music, loudness is measured relatively. Relative loudness is shown by a continuum of basic dynamic markings (shown in table 1.2) based on a set of abbreviations of the Italian words **piano** (soft) and **forte** (loud—pronounced "for-tay") modified by **mezzo** (medium) and occasional suffixes (-issimo: very). This standard set provides for a system of relative volume levels, augmented by other terms such as crescendo and decrescendo, which provide a means to indicate getting louder or softer. Musical dynamics must be relative, since intensity is a function of waveform, frequency, duration, and a host of factors idiosyncratic to each instrument.

Table 1.2. A continuum of dynamic indications

	Soft (piano)			Medium (mezzo)			Loud (forte)	
PPP		PP	P	mP	mF	F	FF	FFF
		pianissimo					fortissimo	
pianississimo			piano			forte		fortississimo

Figure 1.1. ADSR envelope. A common control configuration found on most synthesizers. Attack, Decay, and Release times may be set as well as a Sustain voltage or level. Other levels and stages may also be available.

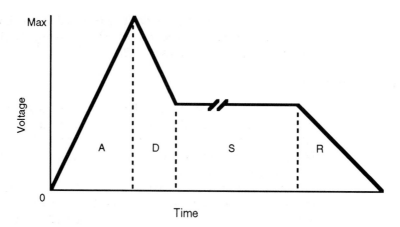

According to John Backus in *The Acoustical Foundations of Music* (New York: W. W. Norton, 1969), **ppp** (pianississimo, or very, very soft) to **fff** (fortississimo, or very, very loud) range from 40 to 100 dB. A forte sound for a flute tends to be softer than a forte sound for a trumpet. In spite of its approximate, somewhat intuitive nature, this relational system works for most Western music.

AMPLITUDE AND VOLUME

The use of **amplitude** will generally be reserved for discussions of waveforms, in which the amplitude of a waveform is its maximum displacement from its average value (see figure 1.3 on page 10). Amplitude may also be used in describing amplifier settings and other details of a specific patch. It is sometimes used as a synonym for volume. They should not be confused. Volume and loudness are used somewhat interchangeably to indicate intensity, which is the physical term for loudness, measured in decibels.

DURATION AND TIME

Duration is the measure in standard units of the length of a tone. A musical tone is often thought of as a monolithic entity: "The piano just played a note that lasted two seconds." This barely scratches the surface. There is an initial attack portion of any tone, which lasts from a few **milliseconds** (thousandths of a second) to as much as 500 milliseconds, according to Robert Erickson in his *Sound Structure in Music* (Berkeley: University of California Press, 1975). This portion is extremely important in the identification of the instrument playing the tone. Various components, or **partials**, of the tone lessen or increase in intensity over the entire duration of the tone. For the same frequency, these partials will act differently at different attack intensities.

In addition to the attack segment, three other phases are often considered useful in electronic and computer music: an initial decay portion, a steady-state portion, and a final decay, or release, portion. These allow for the creation of an amplitude **envelope** (see figure 1.1), useful for controlling various **parameters**, or aspects, of tones, including volume and timbre. This represents a simplification of the richness that characterizes most sounds. Some digital synthesizers allow more complex envelopes.

The musical uses of time, as extensions of duration, are equally complex, but for different reasons. Time may refer to the actual duration of a musical tone or **rest** (one of a set of musical symbols denoting silence for a prescribed period of time), or the **tempo** (speed) of a piece of music, or the meter or any of a number of expressive devices that allow time to be stretched (**ritardando, rubato**) or compressed (**accelerando**). These terms are useful in composition. For the beginning electronic composer, however, the various durational aspects of the single tone first merit more consideration.

When rhythm is discussed, the term *duration* will be used interchangeably with *tone* to signify a component of a rhythmic pattern. If a regularly recurring rhythmic grouping consists of more than 16 or so durations per second, the human ear tends to stop hearing this event as a rhythmic grouping or pattern, and instead hears a pitch with a frequency equal to the number of attacks per second. This allows the electronic musician to explore the terrain between duration and pitch.

WAVEFORM AND TIMBRE

In differentiating between a low clarinet tone and a low flute tone, the former may be called dark and woody, while the latter is breathy, pure, perhaps innocent. These manifestations of timbre, or tone color, are of course subjective and of little quantitative value. Many musicians never get any farther in their study of timbre than the recognition of various instrumental tone colors.

The exploration of timbre is crucial in electronic music. An acoustic musician may spend years developing good tone quality on his or her instrument. It is just as important here, particularly since it is so easy to get sound out of the equipment. Variety from tone to tone, or from musical line to musical line, or within a tone, is useful in developing an expressive product, that ultimately, though electronic, is *music*.

FROM ELECTRICITY TO MUSIC

Music, or at least most Western music, is hierarchical. That is to say, small groups of notes combine to form larger groups that combine to make yet larger groups. An example of this may be found in standard music notation, in which two eighth notes equal one quarter note, two quarter notes equal one half note, and so on.

This concept of hierarchy may be extended to larger levels over an entire piece of music, which often may be found to be subdivided into sections of relatively equal size or importance. Each section, of course, may be further subdivided. This regularity is quite important in both popular music and the art music of the past several centuries.

Hierarchy is not restricted to the "surface" aspects of music. Just as scientists have found increasingly smaller divisions of matter, so have musicians, particularly with the advent of practical electronic music facilities, become more and more concerned with the organization of sound within the musical tone.

THE ACOUSTIC MODEL

Most musical tones, at least on traditional acoustic instruments, exhibit a high degree of regularity or periodicity in their construction. In order to produce sound, the motions of some vibrator is transmitted through the air to the listener's ear. Acoustic instruments use reeds, strings, lips buzzing in a mouthpiece, and other means to produce vibrations.

THE SOUND PATH

On synthesizers a sound generating module replaces the reed, string, or other acoustic vibrator. Rather than air pressure, electrical pressure (**voltage**) or digital information is produced. The electrical pressure is analogous to the waveform produced by acoustic instruments. The digital information is turned into voltage at the audio outputs of a digital synthesizer. The waveform may be processed by other modules and played over speakers, where electricity is transformed into an air pressure wave by the vibrations of the speaker cone, transmitted to our ears, and interpreted as sound (see figure 1.2).

Figure 1.2. Sound path from analog or digital source to the ear

 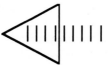

Voltage from wave source   Causes speaker cone to oscillate   Causing pressure wave in air   Received by the ear

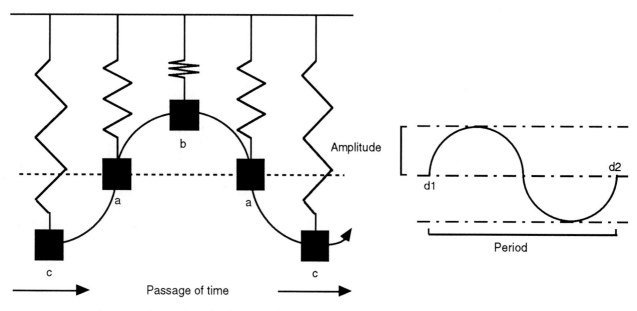

a. *Compression and rarefaction over time*

b. *The waveform*

Figure 1.3. The sine wave:
time versus amplitude

It may be difficult to read the following material about waveforms and have the discussion make sense without trying things out. Those with access to an electronic music system should do so. Many owner's manuals contain a tutorial section designed to give one a chance to get the system going without much explanation of what everything means. If this is the case, follow the recommended procedures, stopping at each step to try out alternate settings of whichever control is being adjusted.

THE SINE WAVE

In many physics books discussions of periodic motion are often begun by looking at the motion of a spring. A weight attached to a spring is at rest at point *a* (see figure 1.3a). When the spring is pulled and then released the weight moves from point *c* through point *a* to point *b*. In a perfect physical system (with no gravity or friction) this motion might continue indefinitely. When charted with reference to the passage of time, this motion may be represented by a **sine wave** (figure 1.3b).

A sine wave can also be thought of as the unfolding of a circle. To demonstrate this, try drawing a circle starting at its left side while someone pulls the paper from the left. It may be necessary to do it with eyes closed, since it is easy to be confused by the moving paper. Essentially the position of the pen or pencil is being plotted against time.

The essence of a musical sound is found in the sine wave. Air is displaced by being alternately compressed or rarefied, in a manner analogous to the motion of the spring. In figure 1.3a, the distance from the point of rest (*a*) to the peak, or maximum pressure (*b*), is the amplitude of the waveform. One period of the waveform occurs when the pressure wave returns to a similar point on the cycle (point *d*1 to point *d*2). Waveforms, such as those shown in figures 1.3b and 1.4, are representations of the pattern of compression and rarefaction created by the vibrating source.

MORE COMPLEX WAVEFORMS

Musical instruments create a variety of waveforms, most of which are more complicated than the sine wave. Rather than a column of air in wind instruments or a string on a piano or violin only vibrating over its entire length, secondary vibrations occur at whole-number divisions (1/2, 1/3, 1/4, 1/5, and so on) . A variety of factors determine the relative strength of these partials. In electronic music, unique waveforms may be created or calculated from scratch, or standard waveforms may be generated and then modified.

Figure 1.4. Time and frequency domains for basic waveforms

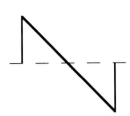

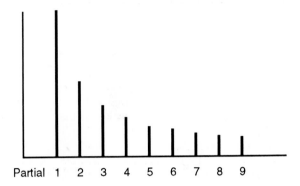

a. Sawtooth wave

$$A = \frac{A}{n}$$

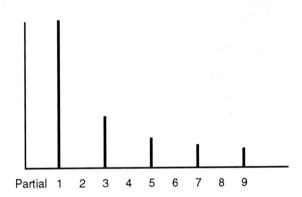

b. Square wave

$$A = \frac{A}{n}$$

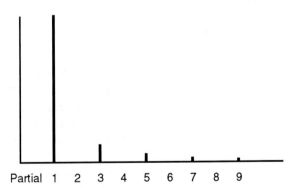

c. Triangle wave

$$A = \frac{A}{n^2}$$

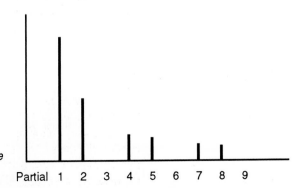

d. Pulse wave with 1:3 duty cycle

$$A = \frac{1}{n} \sin\left(n \, \text{pi} \, \frac{d}{T}\right)$$

BASIC WAVEFORMS

The basic electroacoustic waveforms consist of a **fundamental** frequency (referred to when the frequency of a tone is given) and various **harmonic** partials (*harmonic* refers to the whole-number or integer relationship mentioned previously). Waveforms can be shown on paper in terms of amplitude versus time or frequency versus amplitude (figure 1.4). The former shows one cycle of the sound wave produced by a vibrating body. The latter shows the relative strengths of the harmonic partials of the wave.

SAWTOOTH WAVE

The **sawtooth wave** contains a full set of harmonic partials. If the fundamental, also called the first partial, is 200 Hz, other partials will have frequencies of 400 Hz (200 x 2), 600 Hz (200 x 3), 800 Hz (200 x 4) and so on. At the same time that the frequency of partial n increases n times the fundamental frequency, the amplitude of each partial n is $1/n$ times the amplitude of the fundamental (A).

SQUARE WAVE

Where the sawtooth has its partials formed by all integer multiples of the fundamental, the frequency components of the **square wave** consist of odd number multiples (figure 1.4b). For a 200 Hz fundamental, partials will be found at 600 Hz, 1000 Hz, 1400 Hz, and so on. The amplitude of partial n is again A/n.

TRIANGLE WAVE

The partials of the **triangle wave** are formed by odd multiples of the harmonic series, like the square wave (see figure 1.4c). Unlike the square wave, the amplitude formula of its partials is A/n^2. Where the amplitudes of partials for the square wave are A, $A/3$, $A/5$, $A/7$ . . ., the partials of the triangle wave have amplitudes of A, $A/9$, $A/25$, $A/49$. This gives the triangle a contour similar to the sine wave, although it has an edge to its sound, where the sine wave, consisting only of the fundamental, is purer.

PULSE WAVE

Pulse waves are more complicated. Like the square wave, which is actually a special case of a pulse wave, voltage is either high or low (see figure 1.4d). On most synthesizers the pulse width (the "on" or high voltage portion) may be varied. The ratio of the pulse width to the total period is called the **duty cycle**. Varying the duty cycle alters the **harmonic spectrum** (the set of partials and their relative strength) of the pulse wave.

To determine the amplitude of a given partial of a pulse wave the formula

$$A = 1/n \sin (n \text{ pi } d/T)$$

applies, where A is the amplitude of the partial, n is the harmonic number, d is the duration of the pulse, and T is the period. When the relationship of pulse width to period (d/T) equals $1/a$ where a is an integer, each a'th partial is missing (or, its amplitude is essentially zero). Square waves have a duty cycle of 1:2 and hence lack the 2nd, 4th, 6th . . . partials. In figure 1.4d, the 1:3 duty cycle results in the loss of every third partial.

OVERTONE SERIES

The harmonic partials used to create the sawtooth and other waveforms have long been known by musicians as the **overtone** series. Some confusion may arise when a musician speaks of overtones. Where the first partial (using physical terminology) is the fundamental (using musical terminology) the first overtone (musical) is the second partial (physical). To minimize confusion, the term *overtone* should be avoided. Figure 1.5 shows the first eight partials using music notation.

Figure 1.5. The first eight partials of the harmonic series in music notation, shown here for C2

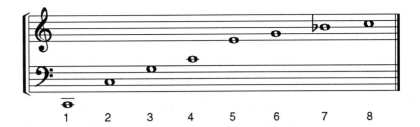

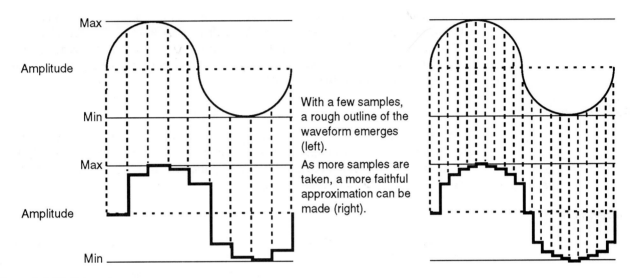

With a few samples, a rough outline of the waveform emerges (left).

As more samples are taken, a more faithful approximation can be made (right).

Figure 1.6. Digital representation of a sine wave

THE DIGITAL APPROACH

Analog synthesis uses electricity to represent sound and digital synthesis uses numbers. In digital synthesis, a waveform may be constructed by computation. The advantage of this approach is that a **wave table**, consisting of numerical values representing one period of a waveform, may be created. Once made, it may easily be sampled many times per second. Several factors, including a higher **sampling rate** (the number of samples per second), will determine how close the waveform comes to its analog counterpart. This may be seen in figure 1.6.

Although this approach works well on minicomputers and mainframes, it has been less successful on microcomputers, due to the relatively slow speed and smaller memory capacity of microcomputers. In a MIDI system, synthesizers and microcomputers may be combined in a hybrid system, with the microcomputer functioning as a recording studio and instrument design facility while digital synthesizers handle the processes of creating sound. With the use of sampling keyboards and specialized computer hardware, recording and editing samples is becoming increasingly commonplace.

SOUND SYNTHESIS

If electronic music consisted solely of the use of the basic waveforms, it would soon cease to be interesting. Most musically useful sounds are more complex. Waveforms may be mixed or added together (**additive synthesis**), filtered (**subtractive synthesis**), and created by various **modulation** processes. In addition, sound may recorded or sampled, and used as the basis for developing useful sounds. Multiple approaches to synthesis are generally not found on any one synthesizer (Yamaha's SY77 is an exception to that rule), although analog synthesizer modules can be used to process digitally-created waveforms and analog waveforms can be sampled and brought into the digital realm, with everything controlled through MIDI.

Figure 1.7. Additive synthesis of a square wave. The positive- and negative-going portions of partials 1 and 3 are added to create a composite waveform. As more partials are added, the resulting waveform more closely resembles the square wave.

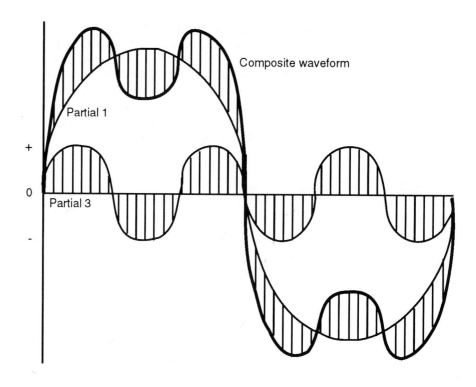

ADDITIVE SYNTHESIS

By applying the work of French mathematician Jean Fourier (1768-1830), it is possible to create a variety of sonorities. He noted that periodic complex waveforms can be produced by adding simple waveforms that have the whole number relationship mentioned in the discussion of harmonic partials. In this process, often called Fourier synthesis, waveforms can be constructed by tuning many sine wave generators to the proper frequencies and amplitude levels to simulate the desired complex waveform. This procedure was used in the early days of electronic music. It can require a great deal of hardware, however.

With the proper programming it can be an excellent tool for computers. On a computer, the addition of waveforms can actually be a fairly simple computation process, involving the addition of numerical values representing waveforms, rather than the physical addition of separate waveforms. The result is a set of numbers representing the desired waveform. Figure 1.7 shows the process of additive synthesis for the first two harmonics of a square wave.

SUBTRACTIVE SYNTHESIS

In this approach, the harmonic spectrum of a basic waveform or of a mixture of waves is modified by various filters to attenuate regions of partials. Any available waveform, as well as bands of noise, may be used as source material. This was the primary approach on analog equipment, and the concept of subtractive synthesis has been carried over to some extent to digital synthesizers.

OTHER APPROACHES

Modulation synthesis allows the generation of more complex signals. The amplitude, frequency, or pulse width of one signal may be modulated by another signal. When both signals are in the audio frequency range, striking effects may be produced. Most analog synthesizers can explore at least some aspects of modulation synthesis. The products of audio range modulation tend to have rich spectra, which may be further modified by subtractive synthesis procedures.

Most digital synthesizers use some sort of modulation process as the primary means of generating and modifying waveforms. The Yamaha DX series, for example, is based on **frequency modulation** techniques. Casio produced a series of synthesizers using a

phase distortion process. Other manufacturers have created their own processes, although the end user often has little involvement with them and is more interested in the sounds that can be created than in the means of their creation. Paradoxically, digital synthesizers often allow less direct involvement with modulation than analog synthesizers.

Modulation synthesis procedures may be simulated by microcomputers. The computer's computational ability may be exploited to allow **waveform synthesis**, in which unique waveforms are created by setting up and manipulating numbers. With the addition of Digital Signal Processing (DSP) boards, microcomputers can store and manipulate recorded sound as well.

FOR FURTHER STUDY

A section like this appears at the end of each chapter, suggesting exercises for studio work, providing a vocabulary list, and offering review questions on the material of the chapter. Most of the exercises can be done in a single three-or-four-hour session. Since more exercises are provided than are likely to be done, please read through the others for information and techniques that may be applicable to other studio work.

Several appendices offer material and suggestions for review and study. Appendix A (page 247) summarizes the information on waveforms and harmonic spectra; appendix E (page 265) provides information on references and suggested reading; the glossary (page 271) provides a broad range of definitions.

EXERCISES

EXERCISE 1.1

Become familiar with the basic waveforms, both in terms of harmonic content and by ear. Work with a colleague at a synthesizer, testing each other on identification of the basic waveforms (one plays a note, the other names the waveform). Is there any difference when pitch is changed? Are the waveforms easier to identify in one portion of the keyboard than in another? It may be necessary to have the instructor set up the synthesizer, since the focus is on simple waveforms, not complete sounds.

EXERCISE 1.2

Use an oscilloscope to look at the waveforms available on the studio synthesizer(s). Notice that the more mellow sounds have fewer jagged edges than the sharper, more buzzy timbres. As long as things are hooked up, and the synthesizer is producing a steady tone (hold a key down or select a drone or gate switch, if one is available), try some of the other controls and see how they alter the waveform. Filter cutoff, frequency ratio on FM synthesizers, and detuning controls can offer some good possibilities — also adding depth and speed (amplitude and frequency) to LFO settings can be interesting.

VOCABULARY

The following terms were used for the first time in this chapter. Make sure that you are familiar with them, since they are used throughout the book. A definition of each term may be found in the glossary.

accelerando	additive synthesis	amplitude
dB	decibel	duration
duty cycle	dynamics	electroacoustic
envelope	fff	forte
frequency	frequency modulation	fundamental
half step	harmonic	harmonic spectrum
Hertz	integrated circuit	intensity
measure	melody	meter
mezzo	microprocessor	MIDI
milliseconds	modulation	modulation synthesis
musique concrete	note	octave
overtone	parameter	partials
piano	phase distortion	ppp
pulse wave	rest	rhythm
ritardando	rubato	sampling
sampling rate	sawtooth wave	sine wave
square wave	subtractive synthesis	temperament
tempo	tone	transistors
triangle wave	vibrato	voltage
waveform	waveform synthesis	wave table

REVIEW QUESTIONS

QUESTION 1.1

Match related terms by writing the letter of the term in the second column in the blank of the term in the first column that most closely relates to it.

Duration	_D_	A.	Cycles per Second
Frequency	_C_	B.	Dynamics
Hertz	_A_	C.	Pitch
Intensity	_B_	D.	Rhythm
Waveform	_E_	E.	Timbre

QUESTION 1.2

Compare and contrast the following terms.

Note — Tone

Written symbol vs. the actual sound

Additive Synthesis — Subtractive Synthesis

Adding wave forms vs. modifying or filtering out sections of a wave form

QUESTION 1.3

Provide the question for the given answer.

ANSWER	QUESTION
2:1 frequency ratio	What is _Partial to Fund. Ratio_ ?
0 dB _Sound we can hear_	What is _the threshold of hearing_ ?
Range of audible frequencies	What is _16 to 20,000_ ?
Ratio of pulse width to total period	What is _____ ?

QUESTION 1.4

Provide frequencies for partials 2 through 8 for each waveform.

WAVEFORM   PARTIALS

	1	2	3	4	5	6	7	8
Sawtooth	200 Hz	400	600	800	1000	1200	1400	1600
Sine	500 Hz	___	___	___	___	___	___	___
Square	300 Hz	___	900	___	1500	___	2100	___
Triangle	150 Hz	___	1350	___	___	___	___	___

QUESTION 1.5

Name the waveform with the given amplitude scheme for its partials.

Sawtooth   A/1, A/2, A/3, A/4, . . . A/n

Square   A/1, A/3, A/5, A/7, . . . A/n

Triangle   A/1, A/9, A/25, A/49, . . . A/n^2

Pulse   A=1/n sin (n pi d/T)

CHAPTER · TWO

THE STUDIO

Just as there are various electronic keyboards and electronic music equipment, each with different features and functions, so are there many types of studios. In keeping with the introductory nature of this book, only basic equipment is discussed here. It is best when getting starting to deliberately restrict your universe, learning how to use a small amount of hardware and software well, rather than many things poorly.

Studios, just like synthesizers, may be primarily analog or digital, or may be a hybrid combination. If a studio has existed for several years it probably has a somewhat eclectic collection of equipment. It is important not to disregard old equipment merely because it is old. On the other hand, it is true that the choice of equipment and sonic material will have an effect on the compositional process. Equipment oriented toward live performance encourages live performance-type activity. The use of a tape recorder and certain tape studio techniques (or MIDI and recording software) encourages the development of more introspective works.

ELECTRONIC MUSIC EQUIPMENT

Electronic music is often associated with synthesizer keyboards or various types of computers. Indeed, even very small studios should include at least one synthesizer and a microcomputer, with appropriate recording facilities. Older analog studios can be retrofitted with MIDI, and new studios will benefit from the acquisition of an old analog synthesizer or two. Other basic equipment includes microphones, mixers, amplifiers and speakers, and the means to patch everything together. Noise reduction equipment, oscilloscopes or other test equipment, more elaborate recording capability, and additional electronic music equipment are among the possibilities for studio growth.

SYNTHESIZERS

With their flexibility and relative ease of operation, synthesizers have become the primary means of generating musical material in the electronic studio. This musical material can be stored on magnetic tape and subjected to various tape editing techniques, or can be stored and processed on microcomputers through the use of MIDI.

In the past, studios tended to contain synthesizers that were modular in concept. That is, the output of any **module** (Voltage-Controlled Oscillator, Voltage-Controlled Filter, Voltage-Controlled Amplifier, and so on) could be patched to the appropriate input of any other module. Most synthesizers on the market today are more performance-oriented, usually with preset patches developed at the factory. Microprocessor technology makes this feasible, since the end user can effortlessly switch from one patch to another.

Monophonic synthesizers—a rarity in today's digital world—produce only a single melodic line. These work well with beginners and as adjuncts to more complex studio equipment. Usually analog, they can be either modular or performance-oriented. **Polyphonic** synthesizers allow multiple melodic lines and other complex **textures**. To be of use in our studies here, it is important, of course, that some patching be possible.

Synthesizers should have a variety of inputs and outputs. As a minimum, there should be an audio out, and either MIDI in and out or control voltage in and out. An audio input will allow the synthesizer to process external signals to some extent (these are an important part of any sampler but rare on other digital equipment). In addition, even the smallest studio should have owner's manuals, as well as a general studio manual to explain studio procedures and the use of the specific equipment at hand.

RECORDING EQUIPMENT

For effective studio composition, the ability to record and play back your work is essential. In earlier electronic studios, the recorded material was often not the final product. After recording electronic or acoustic sources, the composer would rearrange and further manipulate the recorded material to produce the final product. In contemporary studios, recorders may be combined with MIDI to extend the studio, so that one synthesizer may be used several times.

TAPE RECORDERS

Three-head tape recorders are to be preferred over two-head machines, since they have separate heads for erasing, recording, and playing back. Two-head recorders use the same head for recording and playing. This allows three-head machines to use selective synchronization (**sel-sync**) to synchronize previously recorded material with newly recorded sources. As well, the final sound quality may be better on a three-head machine, since each head has one primary function (erase, record, or play).

REEL-TO-REEL VERSUS CASSETTE

Great advances have been made in recent years in the quality of sound from cassette recorders, especially with the advent of **noise reduction** systems. In early studios, reel-to-reel recorders were preferable because they more easily allowed the recorded material to itself be treated as a sound source. Cassettes were not as useful in manipulating sound due to the encased nature of cassette tape, the narrow width of the recording **track**, and the slow speed of cassettes.

Figure 2.1. Common tape formats for 1/4-inch tape. See also the discussion of figure 9.2 on page 161 for more information on stereo formats.

| Full-track mono | Half-track mono | Half-track stereo | Quarter-track stereo | Four-track format |

FORMAT AND SPEED

In general, wider recording tracks and faster recording speeds result in higher quality recorded signals. Professional studios have used speeds of up to 15 or 30 inches per second. Progressively slower speeds (7-1/2, 3-3/4, 1-7/8 inches per second) result in lower quality signals, although noise reduction equipment minimizes the loss of quality. Half-track stereo on 1/4-inch tape has a wider track than quarter-track stereo, thus allowing a higher-quality signal to be recorded and reproduced. The standard quarter-track stereo format has a narrower track than half-track stereo, allowing the tape to be turned over and run in the opposite direction as well (see figure 2.1).

Cassette recorders with four and even more tracks have become common. With built-in noise reduction, they offer a reasonable small-studio environment. Musicians are increasingly turning to video tape, or Digital Audio Tape (DAT) or even direct-to-disk recording as digital technology makes these procedures more accessible.

NOISE REDUCTION

Dolby or dBx noise reduction systems are often available in electronic music studios. These systems act to reduce various background noises, including hum, **print-through**, and high-frequency hiss by compressing the signal when recording and expanding it to its original amplitude upon playback. The various Dolby systems reduce noise by at least 10 dB; dBx provides a larger dynamic range of 30 to 40 dB. On playback, of course, the previously compressed material must be played through the same type of unit for proper expansion. In the absence of a noise reduction system, the best way to ensure a good signal to noise ratio is to use high-quality tape and recording equipment, proper recording levels, and regular cleaning and maintenance procedures. Noise reduction may be added on to an existing studio or may be built into recorders.

MICROPHONES

The primary focus for much of this book is on the synthesizer and microcomputer and their role in the compositional process. Microphones are a useful adjunct, since they allow acoustic sources to be included as resource materials for compositional projects. If one wishes to explore digital sampling, a process that involves recording acoustic material on a computer or sampling keyboard, a good microphone is essential. In addition to being an important element in the recording of sound material, microphones may themselves become a sound source.

Microphones have different field patterns, shown in figure 2.2. Each type has its own advantages. There are both low- and high-impedance microphones. For compositional purposes, the former generally provide a higher-quality signal than the latter. An important element in good recording is a high **signal to noise ratio,** which involves balancing the recording level with the distance from the sound source. Clean equipment and as quiet a recording environment as possible are also important.

Allen Strange, in his *Electronic Music: Systems, Techniques and Controls* (Dubuque: Wm. C. Brown, 1983) notes that the feedback produced by a microphone when it is placed near a speaker can be controlled by moving the microphone within the field of the speaker. The concept that something unwanted (in this case, feedback) may prove to have unforeseen uses should be taken to heart by the electronic, or experimentally-oriented, composer. The intended use of the microphone is as a device to (relatively) accurately

Figure 2.2. Microphone field patterns

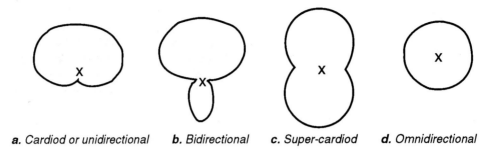

a. Cardiod or unidirectional   *b. Bidirectional*   *c. Super-cardiod*   *d. Omnidirectional*

Figure 2.3. Typical mixer controls

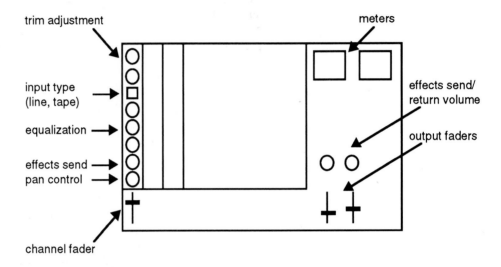

trim adjustment

meters

input type (line, tape)

effects send/ return volume

equalization

output faders

effects send
pan control

channel fader

transform acoustic signals into electrical signals. This should not inhibit you from exploring other uses of the microphone, or tape recorders or any other device at your service.

MIXERS

Often there is a need to mix signals from several sources prior to recording or processing sounds, or during mixdown. Modular synthesizers usually have some mixing capability, primarily intended for use with other synthesizer modules. It may be possible to input some external signal sources directly to this onboard mixer, or indirectly by first routing the signal through a pre-amp module. Some care should be exercised when doing this. Always consult owner's manuals before doing anything drastic.

An external mixer is helpful in recording several sources simultaneously, allowing them to be mixed and recorded on one track of a tape recorder. Be aware that the mixer may well add some noise to the general background noise level. Each input **channel** will normally have its own volume control, either a slider or knob, and some **equalization** (treble/bass attenuation), as well as some means of specifying, in the case of two- and four-channel output mixers, the destination of the signal. There will usually be overall volume controls, an effects send/return capability (for reverb and other effects), perhaps a monitor speaker output, and other controls. A mixer may also help when mixing several tracks of recorded material onto a single track or onto a second tape machine.

In figure 2.3 the trim adjustment controls the strength of the input signal, while the input type selects the source of the input (line or tape). Equalization controls allow adjustment of high, medium, and low frequencies; effects sends route the signal to external effects devices such as reverb or delay. The pan control places the signal in a stereo field or, on some mixers, selects the output channel; the channel fader determines the relative volume of the channel. Other controls can expand this basic set.

EFFECTS DEVICES

Effects devices have become an essential part of the studio. These may be stand-alone or rack-mountable. Most allow a range of effects, from simple reverb or delay through **flanging, chorusing**, and a host of more complex effects. Often digital units will have MIDI input, which allows the selection of an effect to be made remotely.

AMPLIFIERS AND SPEAKERS

It may seem obvious, but without amplifiers and speakers electronic music can not be heard. While it may seem that one can get by with the speakers sometimes supplied with tape recorders, much of the sound is missed. It is important to have a system with as wide a frequency response as possible, preferably along the lines of 20 Hz to 20,000 Hz. A bass guitar amplifier/speaker system is not really appropriate either, since electronic music usually covers a wider frequency range. To restrict the music with inappropriate or inexpensive speakers is to choke it to death.

At one point four-speaker systems (two front, two rear) were popular. While this certainly allows more experimentation with the spatial location of sound, for most beginning uses it is unnecessary. Much can be done with two channels—in fact, a number of tape music techniques only require one channel.

MAKING CONNECTIONS

In all but the smallest studio setting, a spaghetti-like effect is likely to occur when a half-dozen pieces of equipment are interconnected with various patch cords, power cords, and, seemingly, several arms and legs. In situations like this, or in cases where some equipment is used in a standard configuration while other equipment needs to be connected in a more flexible fashion, a knowledge of patch cords and patchbays can be quite useful.

PATCH CORDS AND JACKS

A variety of plugs can be used in connecting studio equipment, including the 1/4-inch phone plug, RCA phono plug, 1/8-inch miniature phone plug, banana plugs, and Cannon XLR-3 connectors (see figure 2.4). In addition to patch cords of various lengths, if the studio requires interconnection of equipment using different plugs, a variety of adapter cables and inline adapter plugs will prove useful. An adapter box with panel-mounted jacks interconnected in various combinations may also be helpful.

Figure 2.4. Standard connectors

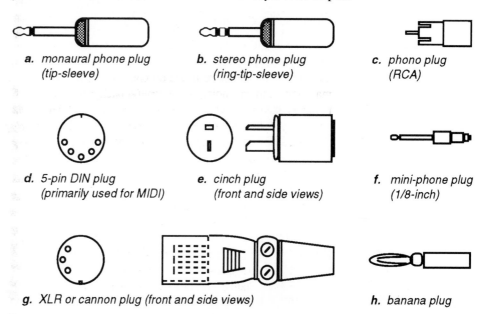

a. monaural phone plug (tip-sleeve)

b. stereo phone plug (ring-tip-sleeve)

c. phono plug (RCA)

d. 5-pin DIN plug (primarily used for MIDI)

e. cinch plug (front and side views)

f. mini-phone plug (1/8-inch)

g. XLR or cannon plug (front and side views)

h. banana plug

The 1/4-inch phone plug is often used in patchbays and as a connector for speakers, synthesizers, and other electronic musical instruments. RCA phono plugs often are used on tape recorders along with 1/4-inch and Cannon connectors, and, particularly on cassette recorders, miniature plugs. RCA plugs are also used on turntables, hi-fi-type amplifiers, and mixers (some offer a choice of input jacks). Miniature and banana plugs are often used for patching on modular synthesizers. DIN plugs are used in MIDI systems.

Patch cords can be a mixed blessing. If mistreated, they may break the electrical connection. Disconnect them by pulling on the plug, not on the wire. Cables, unless shielded, may pick up electrical noise such as power-line hum, fluorescent lights, and so on.

PATCHBAY

Figure 2.5 shows the front panel of a simple patchbay. Although they aren't used very much any more, patchbays offer both convenience and flexibility by gathering equipment connections into one place. With short patch cords, it becomes very simple to connect equipment together. In the figure, the upper row of jacks contains inputs for a mixer, an amplifier, and a two-track recorder. Each jack is wired to the appropriate equipment. Any signal patched to one of these jacks will be present at the specified input.

The lower row contains outputs from the previously mentioned equipment as well as two synthesizers. The signal from one of the synthesizers, for example, may be routed to the mixer, or to the recorder, or directly to the amp. Many contemporary mixers function like a patchbay by allowing for a variety of connections, from low-impedance microphones, line-level sources such as synthesizers, and various effects devices. These may often remain connected, with the active device selected by switch or by using a **normalled** connection.

A normalled connection allows signal flow without the use of a patch cord. One such path would be from the mixer outputs to the recorder inputs to the amplifier inputs. Figure 2.6a shows the electrical connections of the jacks, which can be altered as shown in figure 2.6b so that, in the absence of a plug, a particular electrical circuit is made. The insertion of the plug, illustrated in figure 2.6c, breaks this connection and establishes a different circuit. This procedure was used quite convincingly on the ARP 2600 synthesizer. Various modules were prewired to create a performance-oriented instrument; patch cords allowed the instrument to also be used as a modular instrument.

MIDI networks can easily become complex, even in small studios. Interfaces with multiple ins and outs can function as simple patchbays. More complex boxes can allow filtering and other processing of the MIDI data stream, and can allow the network to change shape without unplugging components (see figure 3.6 on page 42).

MICROCOMPUTERS

As digital technology made its impact on electronic music, analog synthesizers were supplanted by digital synthesizers, digital/analog hybrid systems, and computer-controlled music systems. This trend should be accepted with a grain of salt, however, since analog synthesizers have an immediacy of response and a control over sonic material that is quite different from most microprocessor-controlled systems.

Figure 2.5. A simple patchbay

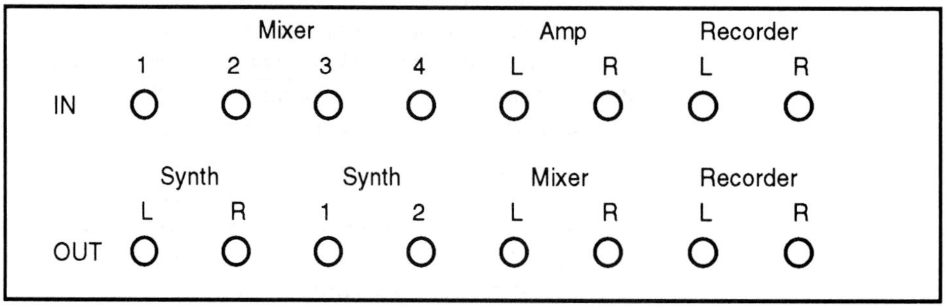

Figure 2.6. A normalled jack

a. Basic configuration (stereo)

b. With the addition of the normalled path

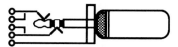

c. Insertion of plug breaks normalled connection

Music on a microcomputer may take several forms. Through programming, the computer may assist in some compositional tasks, may be used to develop waveforms, or may record and modify acoustic material. With the use of MIDI, microcomputers and digital synthesizers can be operated in tandem to create an extended music system.

Most small digital studios will benefit from the use of microcomputers in combination with tape recording facilities. It is often useful to be able to transfer sequenced (a MIDI-related recording) compositions to tape, either for further development through tape-editing procedures or for portability of the final product. By treating the microcomputer as one element of a larger electronic music facility, the scope of limited sonic resources may be greatly enlarged.

When one "logs on" to a timesharing mainframe computer, one enters his or her **directory**. This workspace may vary in size depending on the status of the user and other local criteria. Microcomputers do not generally require passwords, unless the software in use demands it. The computer and monitor are turned on, proper procedures are followed to **boot** or start up the appropriate software, and work begins. The limitation on workspace size depends on the amount of memory present in the microcomputer, less various system and program storage demands.

The concept of the workspace is useful. The microcomputer is located on a table or desk in a (hopefully) well-lighted, secure location, quiet enough to allow one to work. This physical workspace has its analog within the computer. Programs can be brought into the workspace—actually, a range of memory locations—from tape or disk. Programs may be modified or run, and the results stored on floppy or hard disk just as one might file papers in a file cabinet or binder after working with them. Following is a discussion of some of the aspects of this workspace.

GETTING STARTED

Just as with a musical instrument, operating a microcomputer requires regular practice. While those who are familiar with a mainframe may have some initial edge, there are enough differences between large and small computers to force even experienced users to stay light on their feet. One must have good documentation, and the time to read and assimilate it. While each microcomputer has its own quirks, there are some general guidelines to ease the pain of getting acquainted with a new microcomputer.

Read the documentation—a little bit at a time may be best. After reading, sit down at the equipment and try things out. You don't need to be too timid with the computer. Short of physical acts of violence, you are not likely to irreversibly damage anything.

Make a reference card or list of commands and concepts that appear useful. Some documentation comes with reference cards or summary sheets of important commands. Even if one exists, it may be worthwhile to write down those commands, concepts, and procedures that appear to be most useful.

Find the important keys and switches. In addition to those mentioned later in the discussion of the **alphanumeric** keyboard, you might want to find the on-off switch, second in importance only to the wall outlets where the power cords are plugged in. Do remember that if the computer is shut off during use, or power is briefly lost, or a power surge occurs, any program or data stored in **RAM** (random access memory) will be wiped out (**ROM**, or read-only memory, contains permanently stored instructions).

Most microcomputers come with some type of tutorial documentation for new users. Don't be impatient. Do the tutorial. A little more time spent at the beginning may pay off later should the unforeseen occur—and it will.

ALPHANUMERIC KEYBOARD

A microcomputer system can be thought of as a collection of components. Unfortunately for the user, these components are not very interchangeable from system to system, even within the product line of a single manufacturer. Microcomputers such as the Apple II line and the Commodore 64 came with the computer innards encased in the same unit with the alphanumeric keyboard, which has become the standard means of data entry. Others, such as the Apple Macintosh or IBM PC (Personal Computer), have a detached keyboard. Alternate keyboards are available for many microcomputers, if one does not like the keyboard supplied with it.

Although the computer keyboard resembles a typewriter keyboard, there are differences between the two, in large part due to the fact that the keyboard is connected to a computer and not to a typewriter. Almost all microcomputer keyboards will contain a **Control** key (the Macintosh has a Command key). This key functions essentially as a specialized Shift key. When it is held down while a second key is pressed, nonprinting characters are sent to the computer, which interprets them as commands. These commands tend to be mnemonic in nature, to make them easier to remember.

There may be other keys, such as **Escape** or Option, also used in command sequences. Some computers also offer function keys, either factory-defined or user-programmable. These can be assigned various command sequences, and are particularly handy in cutting down on redundant keystrokes. There may be a **Reset** key, which can have drastic effects on one's program if it is pressed inadvertently. It will usually allow a speedy exit from a program, resulting in its immediate termination.

The carriage return, often simply labeled **Return,** or **Enter,** is to some extent a holdover from the days when teletypes were used for data entry. Rather than causing a carriage return as on a mechanical or electric typewriter, the Return key functions to inform the computer that a line of program has been typed, or that asked-for data has been entered. The Return key is usually not used when the line being typed reaches the right edge of the monitor or TV screen, since continued typing will usually cause automatic **wrap-around** of the output to the next line on the screen.

EXPANDING THE MICROCOMPUTER

The microcomputer, like its larger cousins, is a general-purpose machine. While adroit programming will allow the computer to do many things, some functions require additional hardware or circuitry. One way to do this is through the use of internal expansion slots. Expansion cards may be connected to external **peripheral** devices to provide the specialized interface necessary for communication between computer and device. With many commercial products, software is also provided to operate the peripheral devlce.

Not all microcomputers have expansion slots. In this case it may be possible to expand through the use of ROM or RAM cartridges. These plug in to the computer, providing a more accessible means of expansion than internal cards. Some synthesizers also make use of cartridges or PCM cards for instrument storage and retrieval. Some microcomputers may allow both approaches.

Expansion may also be accomplished through the use of input/output ports. Game paddles and similar devices can be connected through a game port. Audio, cassette, and video outputs may be available. Printers and other devices can also be connected.

DISK DRIVES

To do anything more than some extremely rudimentary work it is necessary to have some means of storing programs and data, and of inputting commercial as well as original programs. The most common devices for this are floppy and hard disk drives. Any serious use requires at least two **floppy disk** drives, although musicians increasingly find that hard drives, with their greater storage capacity and speed, are becoming essential.

A disk can be thought of as a flattened-out reel of magnetic recording tape, or as a phonograph record with parallel rather than spiral grooves. These grooves are called tracks. Each track, which may be broken into **sectors**, or blocks, contains the same amount of information. The disk drive unit may contain one or two read/write heads, depending on whether one or both sides of the disk are to be read. These operate somewhat like the tonearm apparatus of a record player, passing over the diskette to read or write the appropriate magnetically encoded information.

MEMORY

Not too long ago, a microcomputer with 16K bytes of memory was state of the art. It is much harder to say how much memory is sufficient now. For musical purposes, there is never enough. An 8-bit microprocessor is generally limited to 64K (and usually has less actually available for program use). It can be programmed to use additional 64K byte banks of memory (it only "sees" the current 64K and is not aware that it is actually handling more) to give the effect of a larger memory capacity. Sixteen-bit and 32-bit microprocessors, now much more common, can handle many more memory locations.

A card or cartridge with extra memory can be a useful peripheral, especially for 8-bit microcomputers. Longer pieces of music may be stored and played. More intricate editing, scoring, or instrument design programs may be used. Various procedures may be sped up by cutting down on the number of times material must be loaded from or saved to disk. Hard disks can be used as **virtual memory**, with portions of a program or dataset being swapped in and out as needed.

PRINTERS

Many microcomputer music systems can do quite well without a printer, although after using one it may be difficult to imagine how life went on without it. Shaped character printers containing a set of preformed characters produce high-quality text output. Dot matrix printers, inkjet printers, and plotters will allow both text and graphics output. Laser printers provide near-publication-quality output. The production of music graphics and notation requires high-resolution graphics on both the microcomputer and the printer.

OTHER PERIPHERAL DEVICES

The keyboard is not the only input device available to microcomputer users. Game paddles and joysticks allow the input of a range of values. The mouse, a device moved by hand on a flat surface, can be used for control or data entry functions. In conjunction with appropriate programming, the mouse provides an alternative to function keys or control sequences. Graphics tablets, light pens, and similar devices allow for easy entry of graphics, which may be stored, manipulated, and printed out.

In addition to their use in graphics and game playing (of course, no one using this book will have time for games . . .) most of the devices just mentioned have potential as music input devices. Since two values, corresponding to the x and y axes on a graph, are input, with proper programming one value can supply pitch information and the other value can represent duration. This could allow real-time performance or could allow an alternative to the alphanumeric keyboard for data entry.

The software supplied with some microcomputer music packages may accept, or even require, these devices for the selection of musical information from displayed menus. In this case, the device allows one to easily move the **cursor** (a flashing character or shape that shows where the next character typed will be placed) around on the screen. When it reaches the item to be selected, a button on the game paddle, joystick, mouse, or pad may pressed to choose that item, or the user can enter data alphanumerically. By the cursor's location on the screen, the computer knows which selection has been made and acts appropriately.

SOFTWARE

Without software a computer is not musically useful. It provides several functions. An operating system is necessary to make things work. Music programs include **sequencers** for recording and editing music, **editors** and **librarians** for handling synthesizer tone data, other programs that function as compositional tools, or handle the tasks of music transcription and notation, or fulfill a variety of specialized studio functions. Computer languages with music-oriented extensions are also valuable.

DISK OPERATING SYSTEMS

In order to use a disk drive it is necessary to have a set of commands and procedures to tell the computer to save and retrieve programs and data files, to keep track of what is stored where on the disk, and to perform a variety of other useful tasks. In keeping with the variety of equipment in the marketplace, there are various **disk operating systems**, each incompatible with the rest.

Some of this incompatibility is simply happenstance: the result of good or bad business decisions, or the result of an industry growing so quickly that standardization has not been possible. Some of the incompatibility comes from the use of different hardware. The 6502 microprocessor has a different internal structure than the 8088 or 68000 family, and thus must be handled differently. Eight-bit microprocessors have different requirements than 16- or 32-bit microprocessors. Even with these differences, there are some similarities between operating systems.

SYSTEM COMMANDS

On most systems, before floppy disks can be used for storing data or files, they must be **initialized**, or **formatted**. This procedure prepares disks so that they may be read by the computer. An image of the disk operating system may be stored on disk, and a directory or catalog may be set up to keep track of the location of disk files, their length, and their file type.

The process of initialization generally requires that the disk operating system first be loaded into the computer from a system master disk or a hard disk (again, depending upon the system, the procedure may vary slightly). A fresh disk is placed in the appropriate disk drive. A command, which may be as simple as Apple's *INIT*, is given. The disk drive goes on, makes a few indignant groans and clanks, and stops in a little while. Since all old data is wiped out, be sure that initialization is required before doing it.

In addition to formatting disks, operating systems load files or programs. These can then be edited or used. If a file has been edited, the new version should be saved to disk, either under the old name (this usually wipes out the previous version on disk) or under a new name (both versions will coexist), before the computer is turned off.

The particular syntax of a command varies from system to system. One system may *LOAD* a file; another may *READ* it. One may *SAVE* or *WRITE* to disk. See the manual with your system for specific details. Even with a fairly comprehensive music system it may be necessary from time to time to back up disks or make use of other DOS **utilities**.

A program can create data files, which can also be stored on disk. An examination of a disk directory or catalog may show a variety of file types. Programs may have special identifiers. There may be various kinds of data files. Special file types unique to a software package may also exist.

UTILITIES

Some operating systems come with a set of utility programs that allow the user greater access to the disk than the basic procedures previously described. A sector map displays a disk's files and the sectors and tracks where they are stored. In those instances where part of a disk "crashes," or has its information scrambled, and there is no backup disk, utility programs can try to reconstruct the damaged sectors, or at least to salvage those that are not irretrievably lost. (An excellent learning experience which quickly converts one to the philosophy "back up early—and often.") Operating systems — or, rather, the screen display — may often be customized to suit the user's needs (in some cases this involves the use of third-party applications).

MIDI SOFTWARE

As MIDI has developed, so has the software related to it. There are a wide range of commercially available programs to exploit MIDI features; if the program doesn't exist, there are programming languages that allow computer programming-oriented musicians to create the appropriate new program. Figure 2.7 presents the primary software areas. The main focus in this book is on sequencing software, along with looks at editors, notation programs, and some compositional programs.

SEQUENCERS

Sequencers generally allow both real-time and **step recording**. In real-time recording, a track may be selected, the start time may be set, and MIDI information is recorded as played. There is often a **metronome** or click or flash available to help fit the music into a particular tempo. If the performer can't play as steadily as desired, there is some sort of procedure that allows attack times, durations, and/or release time to be adjusted.

Step recording avoids some of the timing pitfalls of real-time recording, but loses the spontaneity offered by real-time action. This approach is most effective if the music being entered has already been written down, so that the activity is more one of transcription than composition.

Figure 2.7. MIDI program types and functions

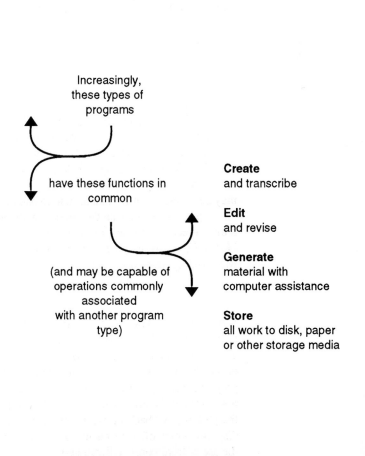

Composition
create and/or generate excerpts and pieces with computer assistance and control of various aspects of the work; transfer material to and from sequencers

Instruction
drill, tutorial, other computer-aided forms of instruction

Multimedia
combine sound with animation, video, film

Notation
notate and transcribe excerpts and complete compositions; transfer work to and from sequencers

Patch Editor/Librarian
store and edit synthesizer patches

Sample Editor/Librarian
store and edit samples; direct-to-disk recording

Sequencing
an aurally-oriented compositional environment in which pieces may be recorded, played back, stored and edited

Utility
various accessory functions

Increasingly, these types of programs

have these functions in common

(and may be capable of operations commonly associated with another program type)

Create
and transcribe

Edit
and revise

Generate
material with computer assistance

Store
all work to disk, paper or other storage media

Sequencers generally allow more than one track may be recorded, although often only one may be laid down at a time. In sequencers with a limited number of tracks it is usually possible to **mix** or **merge** two tracks. Since the information is digital, there is no signal loss, although it may not be possible to unmerge information (be careful when merging, and always make a backup copy before doing any editing procedure).

Although it is often thought that music notation is an essential aspect of composition, it is not necessary in a MIDI sequencer. A track or event list showng information such as note number, timing, velocity, and duration allows for quick and easy editing once its format becomes familiar. Graphic notational schemes including "piano roll" notation offer another approach that is interesting and often quite useful.

Most sequencers allow changes in the attack time, velocity, and duration of any note to be made. There should also be a way to show **program changes** and **controller** activities. On sequencers that are limited in the number of tracks there should be a means of merging material (preferably without changing the MIDI channel of the data) and some means of copying portions of data to other locations (cut/copy and paste).

OTHER SOFTWARE

Patch editors and patch librarians allow computers to store, edit, and create synthesizer information. This information is transmitted and received over a MIDI network. With compositional programs the computer can assist the composer in the creation of musical works either on the notational level or, more often, on the sonic level. It sometimes seems as though the computer becomes a creative partner. Computers may also assist in the process of transcribing music, to the point that more and more composers are publishing their own music with very legible music notation. Computer languages can also have a musically creative aspect when provided with extensions that allow the creation and manipulation of musically useful data.

THE STUDIO ENVIRONMENT

A crucial element in the compositional process is the use of the composer's own critical judgment. In electronic composition this can occur at many points, including during playback of segments of the work in the studio. A poor acoustical environment will make it difficult to judge the effect of the piece when it is moved to a more sympathetic environment. Speakers that are too large or too small for the studio give a false account of the music. Headphones may be useful in monitoring recording, although the sound's interaction with the room may be important for its proper perception. Certainly, **location cues** (left, right, high, low, near, far) are not given properly by headphones, although they may well be preferable to a poor acoustic environment.

The composer should understand the studio's acoustical qualities and learn how to compensate for them. A piece intended for a resonant space needs little echo or reverb. If the planned performance space is very resonant, the composer may need to exercise extra care to create crisp effects, since they will become blurred in their intended setting. A piece to be performed in a carpeted setting, on the other hand, may need attention in the opposite direction.

A particular studio environment may deaden or accentuate some portion of the audio frequency range so that when the work is played in its intended environment the effect is quite different. As a beginning composer, you need not be too concerned with this phenomenon, since the immediate goal is the creation of a reasonably musical outcome. As control of the compositional craft develops, however, you will need to pay more attention to this aspect of sound. Even beginners should strive to develop an awareness of the sounds sought after and created. While serendipity is welcome, it should not be counted on to substitute for good work and attention to detail.

FOR FURTHER STUDY

Appendix D lists major music hardware and software manufacturers; appendix E on page 265 contains suggestions for further reading.

EXERCISES

To be most effective in a creative context, the microcomputer needs to become as "transparent" to the user as possible. It was recommended earlier that any tutorial, either in documentation or in software, be tried. In addition, several exercises are suggested here. These are intended to help you develop a general familiarity with the system.

EXERCISE 2.1

Become familiar with the studio. Find out how equipment is connected (power cords, audio cords, MIDI cables). How is power turned on and off in the studio? What is the signal path from synthesizer to speaker? Draw a diagram of the studio, including all equipment that generates, processes, transmits, or receives audio signals.

EXERCISE 2.2

Become familiar with the system commands of your studio computer (refer to the owner's manual). Catalog or look at the disk directory (commands differ from system to system). Find out how to start and stop programs.

EXERCISE 2.3

Initialize or format your own disk. Make sure that it is blank, since anything stored on the disk will be wiped out by the formatting process. Consult your system's documentation for the precise commands. Once the disk is initialized copy a program from another disk (on some computers this involves running a copy program found on the system master, and following the directions given by the program).

VOCABULARY

The following terms were used for the first time in this chapter. A definition of each term may be found in the glossary.

alphanumeric	boot	channel
chorusing	Control	controller
cursor	directory	disk operating system
editor	Enter	equalization
Escape	flanging	floppy disk
format	initialize	librarian
location cue	merge	metronome
mix	module	monophonic
noise reduction	normalled	peripheral
polyphonic	print-through	program change
RAM	Reset	Return
ROM	sector	sel-sync
sequencer	signal to noise ratio	step recording
texture	track	utility
virtual memory	wrap-around	

REVIEW QUESTIONS

QUESTION 2.1

Match related terms by writing the letter of the term in the second column in the blank of the term in the first column that most closely relates to it.

Analog	____	A.	Chords
Monophonic	____	B.	Duration
Quantization	____	C.	Melody
Patch	____	D.	Preset
Polyphonic	____	E.	Speed
Tempo	____	F.	Voltage Control

QUESTION 2.2

Define "normalled" briefly.

_____

_____

_____

_____

QUESTION 2.3

Compare and contrast the following terms.

Audio Input — MIDI Input

_____

_____

_____

_____

Bit — Byte

_____

_____

_____

_____

Quarter-track Stereo Format — Four-track Recording Format

_____

_____

_____

_____

RAM — ROM

_____

_____

_____

_____

QUESTION 2.4

Identify the given plugs.

A. _____

B. _____

C. _____

D. _____

E. _____

F. _____

G. _____

H. _____

CHAPTER · THREE

A MIDI PRIMER

Imagine describing the process of producing a sound on the piano to someone who's never seen a piano: "You strike a key —" "Which one: my front door key or my car key?" "Neither — a key on a piano keyboard." "What's that?" "Forget that for a moment. After you do that, a hammer strikes a string —" "Wait a minute. Are you putting me on? I pick up a hammer, hit some string, and make music? Are you crazy?"

MIDI —Musical Instrument Digital Interface — is not quite that crazy, but it is almost as mysterious due, in large part, to the complexities produced by its simplicity (not to mention that it was intended to help sell synthesizers and not to become the general-purpose musical tool that it has).

MIDI BASICS

MIDI specification 1.0, first published in 1985, established hardware and software protocols that have allowed digital synthesizers, computers, and other digital equipment to be interconnected. Its role in music has greatly increased in the early 1990s as more equipment and more software has been developed. It can be useful for many music-related tasks, from learning to hear and read music better, to studying composition and orchestration, and as a tool for creative activities in music creation and performance.

BIT BY BIT

Digital computers are set up to operate according to **binary** principles. This involves two states: on and off, or 1 and 0. This principle is at the heart of MIDI. Computation is simple since there are fewer rules than in base 10 mathematics. In the process of addition, for example, there are four rules: $0 + 0 = 0$; $0 + 1 = 1$; $1 + 0 = 1$; $1 + 1 = 10$. The last operation involves carrying the overflow value to the next column in the same fashion as in base ten, where $9 + 1 = 10$. In essence there are only two rules: zero plus a number equals that number, and 1 plus 1 equals 10.

The other arithmetic operations have corresponding ways of functioning. The use of true/false logic (where true = 1 and false = 0) allows logical operations to extend the computer's capabilities. Reducing all alphanumeric characters to binary values allows them to be stored and manipulated in the computer.

The simplicity of binary notation is advantageous from the computer's standpoint, since each place in a binary number can only have two values. This does require a greater number of **bits** (binary digits) to express large values than with decimal notation, where each place may have 10 values (0 through 9).

Going beyond this machine language level (instructions in a form most easily understood by the computer and least accessible to humans), there are various other language levels. Beyond binary notation, **hexadecimal** (base 16) notation makes programming somewhat easier. This system allows the range of values produced by an 8-bit binary

Table 3.1. Numbering systems. Eight-bit binary numbers allow decimal values from 0 to 255; with the use of numbers 0 through 9 and letters A through F, hexadecimal notation expresses these same values with only two integers.

DECIMAL	BINARY	HEXADECIMAL
0	0000	0
1	0001	1
2	0010	2
3	0011	3
4	0100	4
5	0101	5
6	0110	6
7	0111	7
8	1000	8
9	1001	9
10	1010	A
11	1011	B
12	1100	C
13	1101	D
14	1110	E
15	1111	F
16	10000	10
17	10001	11
…	…	…
26	11010	1A
…	…	…
31	11111	1F
32	100000	20
…	…	…
64	1000000	40
…	…	…
128	10000000	80
…	…	…
255	11111111	FF

number (a **byte**) to be represented by only two characters, rather than eight. The decimal numerals 0 through 9 are augmented by the letters A through F where A = decimal 10 and F = decimal 15. In order to distinguish between decimal and hexadecimal notation, the latter will either be proceeded by a dollar sign ("$10") or followed by the letter H ("10H"). Table 3.1 on the preceding page shows the relationship between binary, decimal, and hexadecimal numbering systems.

always "H" no #

The value of a byte can easily be calculated. Each bit will be either 0 or 1. When it is set to 1, a bit represents a decimal value of some power of 2, where the right-hand bit is 2^0 and the left-hand bit (the MSB) is 2^7. Using the values shown in figure 3.1, each bit below the line represents the value given above the line. Adding the values for the bits that are set (128 + 16 + 1) yields the decimal value of 145.

Hexadecimal numbers also relate easily to binary numbers. The right hexadecimal value is the sum of the right four bits (values range from 0 to 15), while the left hexadecimal value is the sum of the left four bits, treated as though they also have the range 0 to 15 (the numbers in parentheses above the values 16, 32, 64, and 128 in figure 3.1).The hexadecimal value in figure 3.1 is 91H.

CHANNEL MESSAGES

At its lowest level, MIDI uses sets of bits organized into bytes to facilitate the transmission and reception of keyboard information. Two MIDI-equipped synthesizers can be connected so that the keyboard of one synthesizer controls both synthesizers. Sounds available on one synthesizer are not transmitted to the other, nor is it possible for special capabilities of one synthesizer to be magically available on the other. With that caveat out of the way, there is much potential in MIDI.

Each MIDI device contains a receiver and/or transmitter. Messages are transmitted **serially** (one bit at a time) at a rate of 31.25 **Kbaud** (thousand bits per second). A five-pin DIN plug (see figure 2.4) has been designated as the standard connector.

To allow any sort of musical complexity it must be possible to send many different messages. Up to 16 channels of information can be sent over a basic MIDI network. With proper software and hardware this number may be increased. Not all channels may be available to a given device. In addition, if a device is asked to do something it cannot do, it will ignore that message.

There are various message types that allow for housekeeping and communication functions. **System real-time** codes start and stop musical excerpts, establish timing, and so on. **System exclusive** codes can be used by each manufacturer to allow transmission of instrument patch data. **System common** information pertains to the whole system, including information about the current measure, choice of piece of music ("song" in MIDI terminology), and the ability to request a synthesizer or other MIDI equipment to go through an internal tuning routine.

Translating the earlier vignette into MIDI, when a key is struck a MIDI **Note On message** is generated (see figure 3.2). This message consists of a **status byte** which says "a key has just been pressed on this MIDI channel" followed by two **data bytes**, one specifying which key was struck, the other how quickly (or hard) it was struck. As soon as the key is released, a Note Off message is generated. It also has three bytes, the first

Figure 3.1. Binary values. Add the values for each bit set to one to find the decimal value for the byte (here 145). The numbers in parentheses are used to find hexadecimal values.

(8) 128	(4) 64	(2) 32	(1) 16	8	4	2	1
1	0	0	1	0	0	0	1

Figure 3.2. Anatomy of a
Note On message

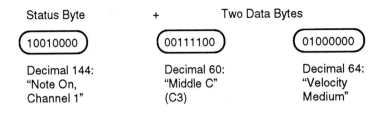

Status Byte   +   Two Data Bytes

(10010000)   (00111100)   (01000000)

Decimal 144:   Decimal 60:   Decimal 64:
"Note On,   "Middle C"   "Velocity
Channel 1"   (C3)   Medium"

Figure 3.3. Varieties of
status bytes

Message Type (8 types may be specified)		MIDI channel (for all but system messages)		
		Binary	Decimal	MIDI Channel
000	Note Off	0000	0	1
001	Note On	0001	1	2
010	Polyphonic Key Pressure/Aftertouch	0010	2	3
011	Control Change/Channel Mode	.	.	.
100	Program Change	.	.	.
101	Channel Pressure/Aftertouch	.	.	.
110	Pitch Bend Change	1111	15	16
111	System Messages			

1   x   x   x   n   n   n   n

saying "a key has been released on this MIDI channel," the other two saying which key
and with what velocity it was released.

Notice that no sound was produced: that is left up to the tone-generating capabilities of the digital synthesizer, tone generator, or other device receiving the message. This
is rather like a pipe organ, in that the organist can choose the tone color of a key from a
set of pipes, rather than each key having only one primary sound, as on a piano.

STATUS BYTES

All MIDI messages have a similar structure. They begin with a status byte which allows
receiving instruments to know that a message is being initiated, as well as the type of
message it is and, where appropriate, the channel affected by the message. Depending on
the type of message, there will be 0, 1, 2, or a variable number of bytes of data following
the status byte

Figure 3.3 shows the makeup of the various status bytes. In addition to Note Off and
Note On messages, a range of other functions may be addressed. Notice that the status
byte is divided into three areas. The MSB is set to 1. The next three bits specify the message type, while the last four specify the MIDI channel for all non-system messages.

The elegance of this system lies in its simplicity: a good amount of information is
packed into a small space, and can be transmitted fairly quickly, even though the **baud
rate** and serial nature of MIDI is not exactly stellar in speed. It allows microcomputers to
play an important role: they can easily record and play music, since they are generating
information about music rather than the music itself. The modular nature of this system

Figure 3.4. The data byte

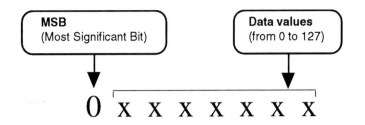

Figure 3.5. Keyboard and velocity data values

0	12	24	36	48	60	72	84	96	108	120	127
		c0	c1	c2	c3	c4	c5	c6	c7		

a. MIDI note values. Notes outside the piano keyboard range (A-1 to C7) may usually be reproduced, even though direct access often requires some form of transposition.

0	1			64				127
off	ppp	pp	p	mp	mf	f	ff	fff

b. Velocity values can be equated to traditional dynamic markings although they allow a much greater degree of subtlety .

allows for expansion, either in tone-generating equipment, in specialized software, or in controllers (although Note messages are thought of in keyboard terms, they may just as well be generated by wind, brass, string, or drum controllers).

In addition to Note On and Note Off messages, other channel messages may be sent. These include **control change** (used when a device other than a key is operated, such as a volume pedal or other specialized device), **program change** (to change the timbre, voice, or instrument — like selecting a different stop on a pipe organ), **aftertouch** (some synthesizers can generate or respond to pressure on a key while it is being pressed down, providing a degree of touch sensitivity like that found on a guitar), and **pitch bend** (like lipping a sound up or down).

DATA BYTES

One or more data bytes generally follow a status byte. They have a decimal value between 0 and 127, giving a range of 128 values. The MSB is cleared, or given a value of 0, as shown in figure 3.4. The range of values can represent whatever the manufacturer would like, although a number of parameters have been determined in the MIDI specification, so that receivers will know what to do with the information they are sent.

For example, keyboard values can be shown as MIDI data (figure 3.5a). It is possible to produce values outside the compass of a keyboard, since keyboards typically range from 61 keys (5 octaves) to 88 keys (a full Grand Piano keyboard) while MIDI allows 128 values. These out-of-range notes may be developed by transposition or remapping MIDI note values, or by creating or modifying values on a keyboard or sequencer. Not all synthesizers will be capable of responding to the entire range, however, even though they may be capable of playing back note values higher or lower than the keyboard itself normally controls (devices other than keyboards may also produce MIDI notes).

Figure 3.5b shows the range of velocity values that are possible. Again, a specific synthesizer may not respond to the entire range, or may not produce the entire range. **Touch sensitivity** (the response to a performer's touch) can sometimes also be adjusted.

Table 3.2 shows typical data uses. Remember that a data byte by itself simply represents a binary or decimal number; in other words, data bytes mean nothing without the

Table 3.2. Data types and values

TYPE OF DATA	RANGE OF DATA	COMMENT OR EXAMPLE
Value range	0 — 127	Control values Pressure/aftertouch Program change
Control change	0 — 120	Defines controllers such as: 1: Modulation wheel 7: Volume 64: Damper (sustain) pedal 67: Soft pedal
MIDI mode	121 — 127	121: Reset all controllers 122: Local control 123: All notes off 124: Omni off 125: Omni on 126: Mono on (poly off) 127: Poly on (mono off)
Velocity	0 — 127	0: off 1: ppp 127: fff

status byte specifying what kind of information is being presented. In addition to giving a range of values showing, for example, how hard a key is pressed as it is being held down (aftertouch), or which sound has been selected on a synthesizer (program change), a data byte may specify a controlling device such as a modulation wheel, a volume pedal, or sustain or soft pedal.

In table 3.2, the third category of data, MIDI mode, is actually an extension of control change data. This allows the MIDI mode of the receiving device to be altered.

MIDI MODES

Receivers may respond monophonically or polyphonically. This may be set on the receiver by means of appropriate switches or often may be determined by a MIDI message. With the appropriate mode, synthesizers may respond simultaneously to data from more than one MIDI channel, with a different timbre on each channel (**multi-timbrally**).

The original MIDI specification described four modes, given in table 3.3. In mode 1 (*Omni On, Poly*), a synthesizer plays as many notes as it can from any and all MIDI channels. In mode 2 (*Omni On, Mono*), the synthesizer still tries to respond to all input but produces only one note at a time. In modes 3 and 4 (*Omni Off, Poly*, and *Omni Off, Mono*) the synthesizer responds to information from only one MIDI channel, either polyphonically (as many notes as possible) or monophonically (one note at a time).

These latter two modes allow a synthesizer to function multi-timbrally, if the manufacturer has so designed the product, since a synthesizer can be set to function as though it were several synthesizers in one case, each responding to a different MIDI channel. On some synthesizers the active channels must be specified, as well as the maximum number of notes that may sound. Increasingly, synthesizers can dynamically allocate voices, so that any channel may be polyphonic at one instant, and silent the next, while the voices just used are reassigned. So far, there is always a maximum number of voices or notes that may be played at one time. If that number is exceeded, synthesizers will have some sort of **algorithm** in place to decide which notes sound and which ones don't.

Table 3.3. MIDI modes

	Poly	Mono	
Omni On	Play (reproduce) as many notes as the synthesizer allows without discriminating input by MIDI channel *1*	Play (reproduce) only one note at a time without discriminating input by MIDI channel *2*	Usually mono-timbral
Omni Off	Play (reproduce) as many notes as the synthesizer allows on/from designated MIDI channel only *3*	Play (reproduce) only one note at a time on/from designated MIDI channel only *4*	May be multi-timbral

SYSTEM MESSAGES

MIDI system messages have no MIDI channel assignment. They allow messages that generally have system-wide significance to be sent. System common and system real-time messages allow for timing and synchronization messages used in linking equipment. They are used in sequencing software.

System exclusive messages allow manufacturers to set up specialized protocols that are unique to a given type of device. They are particularly useful in the design and use of editor/librarian programs, which allow exchange of data between a synthesizer and a computer so that patches may be stored and edited on computer.

MIDI NETWORKS

A MIDI system can take on many configurations. It can be developed and expanded primarily by adding more hardware. Many devices can be included in a MIDI network. These include digital synthesizers (with or without keyboards), samplers, and other controllers such as MIDI guitars, wind controllers, string controllers, drum machines, and even pitch-to-MIDI devices (allowing singers into the MIDI realm).

Various peripherals may be added, including MIDI patchbays, effects devices such as reverb or digital delay, automated mixing devices and even more specialized devices (how about MIDI-controlled lighting?). Synchronizers which convert timing information into a format used by video or recording equipment may also be included.

CHAIN

The standard configuration is the chain (figure 3.6a). One synthesizer is designated the master and is used to send keyboard information to the other devices in the network. The master can send information to a sequencer, where it can be recorded and edited, and can also be used in live performance as a remote keyboard, allowing other synthesizers to be played without the necessity of the performer moving from one synthesizer to another.

Under typical circumstances, particularly where the chain is fairly short, this setup works well. If much data is to be handled due to the complex nature of the music, some

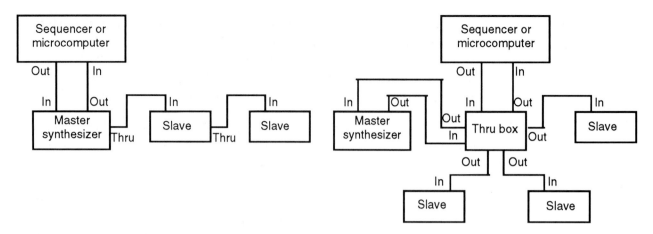

a. Chain network. Information from the master synthesizer may be passed through the sequencer to additional devices. This information may also be recorded by the sequencer.

b. Star network. Data transmission from sequencer to the rest of the network is more direct, allowing quicker, more accurate transmission of both live and sequenced material.

Figure 3.6. MIDI networks

delays may occur. This comes from the serial format of data transmission. A **parallel** interface, allowing more than one bit to be sent at a time, would be faster.

STAR

In the absence of any official parallel protocol, another solution has arisen. It is possible to configure a system in a star network, such as shown in figure 3.6b. This allows the master keyboard or the sequencer to address each member of the network directly. This decreases any potential delay caused by chaining equipment. The MIDI patchbay can be either passive (merely sending data through) or it can be active (allowing different data paths to be selected and modifying or processing MIDI information as it passes through).

In situations where a computer is part of the network, the computer's connection to the network may function as the patchbay. With appropriate software, this can allow the computer to control more than 16 MIDI channels, since each output port on the interface could have its own set of channels. In essence this turns a two-dimensional network like figure 3.6b into a multi-dimensional one, with each port having its own star or chain.

PUTTING MIDI TO WORK

By itself, MIDI allows communication between devices in a network. With the assistance of computer programs like those listed earlier in figure 2.7, a network can be customized and modified for specific situations and musical purposes. In general, a device cannot be made to do something it is not designed to do. An effects device, for example, will not produce musical notes unless it has tone-generating circuitry; a polyphonic synthesizer designed to allow simultaneous sounding of a maximum of eight tones will not normally be able to produce ten or twelve voices.

READING IMPLEMENTATION CHARTS

To avoid making demands that equipment can't handle, an understanding of how MIDI has been implemented on each device in the network is important. This can — and should — be done by reading the owner's manual and any accompanying documentation, as well as by simply experimenting with the equipment. The MIDI Implementation Chart that comes with each piece of MIDI equipment offers a summary of features, giving a good overview of the MIDI capabilities of the device.

Figure 3.7 (on the following page) presents an example of an Implementation Chart. Each chart has header information specifying the synthesizer model and version number. The body of the chart is divided into four columns. The first states each function (these functions are shown on all charts, even if they are not implemented). The second and third columns shows which functions are transmitted and/or recognized (received). The final column contains any remarks that are needed to customize columns two and three.

BASIC CHANNEL

A device may be set to a **default** channel when it is turned on. If it can be set by the user, this may be indicated by "1-16" or "All Channels" in either or both columns. If MIDI channels can be changed by the user during use these are also indicated.

MODE

As with the basic channel, there is often a default MIDI mode on power-up (see table 3.3 on page 41 for a summary of the four modes). If a device can transmit or recognize MIDI mode messages, that information is shown here. Some devices may be set manually to a MIDI mode, even if they don't transmit or recognize a particular mode message.

Devices may also recognize a mode message but alter it to another mode. That will be shown only in the "Recognized" column (the "Transmitted" column will generally have a row of asterisks). Others may alter modes based on the value of the second data byte in the mono mode message. This value, referred to as "M", indicates the number of mono channels the receiver should set up. A device that doesn't implement mono modes could switch to one of the poly modes depending on the value of "M" (this should be indicated on the chart).

NOTE NUMBER

The set of MIDI numbers transmitted by the device is shown in the "Transmitted" column (see also figure 3.5). If the number range is greater than the number of keys or notes normally produced by the unit, there is generally some sort of MIDI transpose feature. In the "Recognized" column, there may be two sets of numbers: the full recognized range (numbers outside this range will be ignored), and the **True Pitch** range (if it is less than recognized range, notes outside the true pitch range will be transposed by octaves into the actual playing range). As with altered modes, true pitch applies only to the "Recognized" column (the "Transmitted" column will generally have a row of asterisks).

VELOCITY

The way that a device transmits or recognizes attack ("Note On") or release ("Note Off") data is shown in columns two and three. The "O" and "X" symbols indicate "Yes" and "No", with the "O" generally indicating affirmation (a key at the bottom of the chart will usually make this clear). A range of velocities may be shown ("v=1-127", for example). If Note Off messages are replaced by Note On messages with a velocity of 0, this will be shown in some fashion (often "9nH v=0" where "9" indicates a Note On message and "n" indicates the MIDI channel).

AFTERTOUCH

This function shows a device's polyphonic or **channel pressure** capability. An indication in the "Keys" row indicates polyphonic pressure capability (the pressure applied to each individual key after it has been pressed and while it is being held down); an indication in

CASIO DIGITAL SYNTHESIZER

Model CZ-101   **MIDI Implementation Chart**

Function		Transmitted	Recognized	Remarks
Basic	Default	1	1	
Channel	Changed	1-16	1-16	
Mode	Default	Mode 3	Mode 3	
	Messages	X	POLY, MONO	OMNI ON/OFF ignored
	Altered	************	Mode1->3, Mode 2->4	
Note		36-84	0-127	0-11,12-23,24-35=36-47
Number	True voice	************	36-96	
Velocity	Note On	O9n v=64	O9n v=1-127->64	
	Note Off	O9n v=0	O9n v=0,8n v=XX	XX=don't care
After	Keys	X	X	
Touch	Channel	X	X	
Pitch Bend		O	O	8 bit resolution, 0-12 semitones
Control	1	O	O	VIBRATO ON/OFF
Change	5	X	O	PORTAMENTO TIME
	6	X	O	MASTER TUNE
	65	O	O	PORTAMENTO ON/OFF
Program		O 0-79	O 0-79	0-15 PRESET
Change	True Number	************	0-15,32-47,64-79	32-47 INTERNAL 64-79 CARTRIDGE
System Exclusive		O	O	TONE DATA
System	Song Position	X	X	
	Song Select	X	X	
Common	Tune Request	X	X	
System	Clock	X	X	
Real Time	Commands	X	X	
Aux	Local On/Off	X	O	
	All Notes Off	X	X	
Messages	Active Sensing	X	X	
	System Reset	X	X	
Notes				

Figure 3.7. MIDI Implementation Chart. All MIDI-equipped devices by a chart such as this one, which shows the MIDI capabilities of the Casio CZ-101 synthesizer. "O" signifies "yes" and "X" signifies "no". The chart shows that the CZ may be set to any MIDI channel; operates in modes 3 and 4; recognizes all note numbers but only produces notes 36-96; is not velocity-sensitive, since only velocities 64 and 0 are sent ("9n v=0" means that a Note On message with a velocity of 0 signifies that a note is turned off), and the synthesizer turns all Note Off velocities greater than 0 into 64; neither sends nor recognizes aftertouch; sends and receives pitch bend; responds to 4 controllers but only transmits 2; sends and recognizes a specified range of program change values; sends and receives system exclusive data; does not handle any other system messages other than recognizing local on/off (see page 46).

Table 3.4. Selected controller numbers. Some of the more commonly available controllers are listed here. A more complete listing is given in Appendix C on page 251.

CONTROL NUMBER		CONTROL FUNCTION
Decimal	Hex	
1	01H	Modulation wheel or lever
2	02H	Breath Controller
4	04H	Foot Controller
5	05H	Portamento time
6	06H	Data entry MSB
7	07H	Main volume
8	08H	Balance
10	0AH	Pan
11	0BH	Expression Controller
32-63	20-3FH	LSB for values 0-31
64	40H	Damper pedal (sustain)
65	41H	Portamento
66	42H	Sostenuto
67	43H	Soft pedal
69	45H	Hold 2
96	60H	Data increment
97	61H	Data decrement
121-127	79-7FH	Reserved for Channel Mode Messages

the "Channel" row shows channel pressure potential (only one pressure value per channel is transmitted or recognized). A device may be able to recognize aftertouch even if it can't transmit it. "OX" or an asterisk usually indicate a function that the user can enable or disable (this information may also be shown in the Remarks or Notes areas).

PITCH BENDER

A device's ability to transmit or recognize pitch bend information is shown in columns two and three, often with qualifying remarks. A remark like "7 bit resolution" indicates that the resolution allows a maximum of 128 steps (14-bit resolution is possible, using a second data byte). The pitch bend range may also be shown.

CONTROL CHANGE

There's a broad range of control functions, ranging from common things like a **modulation wheel** or **volume pedal** to more unusual functions like **breath control** and even **data entry**. Columns two and three indicate which control functions are transmitted or recognized by the device. Some units may be able to transmit functions even if they do not have a specific device that creates or uses that function (internal mapping may allow a modulation wheel, for example, to act as a controller for a range of functions). The way these functions are created will not necessarily be shown, however.

Table 3.4 presents some of the functions defined in the MIDI specification. Notice that control numbers 32 through 63 are actually the second byte (LSB, or **least significant byte**) for control functions 0 to 31 (this allows 14-bit resolution). MIDI also has a number of undefined functions, allowing room for growth, as well as reserving values 121 to 127 for channel mode messages (see also table 3.2).

PROGRAM CHANGE

The range of values shown in columns two and three of the implementation chart (figure 3.7) shows the program change values transmitted or recognized by the device. As with note number, there may be a true range of values that is different from the recognized range of values ("True #").

SYSTEM EXCLUSIVE

System Exclusive or "SysEx" messages have become increasingly important and useful in a MIDI studio. They allow transmission and reception of voice and configuration data through patch editor and librarian programs. While not originally perceived as that important, SysEx features are central to the creation of a flexible network, particularly as networks become more and more complex.

Columns two and three indicate the device's system exclusive capability. Owner's manuals often contain more specific information for users who wish to create their own SysEx programs. Information can also be obtained from manufacturers and through the International MIDI Association.

SYSTEM COMMON

Song Position, Song Select, and **Tune Request** messages are part of MIDI's time-keeping functions (along with **MIDI Time Code** — MTC — messages). The ability to transmit or recognize these messages is shown in columns two and three.

SYSTEM REAL TIME

Clock and **Real-Time messages** (Stop, Start, and Continue) are also part of MIDI's time-keeping activities. A device that transmits these messages can act as a controller in a MIDI network that contains more than one time-dependent device (a drum machine could control a sequencer, for example). Devices that recognize these messages can be synchronized to devices that transmit these messages.

AUX MESSAGES

"Local On/Off" allows a keyboard or other note-number controller to produce MIDI note numbers without controlling any local tone-generating circuitry. "All Notes Off" messages are sent throughout a network telling devices to terminate any active notes. "Active Sense"(-ing) messages are used by some devices every 300 milliseconds when they are idle to affirm that they are still in the network. System "Reset" messages allow everything in the network to be returned to default conditions (and therefore are to be avoided). Columns two and three indicate whether the device transmits or recognizes any of these messages.

NOTES

This final section is reserved for any notes that are not placed in the remarks column. Notes may be either general in nature, or may function more like footnotes, being related by number or symbol to a particular function.

MIDI IN THE ANALOG STUDIO

Prior to MIDI, control voltage and gate and trigger voltages could often be used to link equipment together. MIDI equipment is not quite as standardized as the MIDI specification would lead one to believe; analog synthesizers were even less standardized.

In spite of this, there is a place for analog equipment in the MIDI studio, or for MIDI in the analog studio. A primary ingredient in this mix is a MIDI-to-Control-Voltage converter. With a converter, a MIDI synthesizer can act as the master keyboard, or a computer or hardware sequencer can control both MIDI and analog equipment (see figure 3.8).

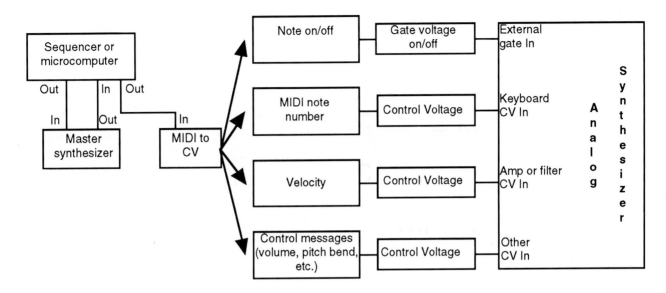

Figure 3.8. MIDI to control voltage. At a minimum, keyboard and gate voltages must be produced by the MIDI-to-CV converter. Velocity and control messages can also produce useful control voltages.

In addition to the converter, it may be possible to retrofit an analog synthesizer so that it responds to MIDI. Alternatively, analog sounds may be sampled (although this loses the flexibility of the analog sound, since it becomes set into a permanent form).

FOR FURTHER STUDY

Appendix C contains more information on the MIDI Specification; appendix E has suggestions for further reading.

EXERCISES

EXERCISE 3.1

If the studio has a program that allows the MIDI data stream to be examined, run it. Press and release a synthesizer key. What happens when a key is pressed? What happens when the key is released? There should be six bytes, unless the synthesizer uses running status, in which case only one status byte need be sent, since Note Off messages may be sent as Note On messages with a velocity of zero. What status byte is used to indicate a Note Off message? What changes when another key is pressed and released? Try different velocity values. Figure 3.9 on the following page shows the screen for *MIDIScope*, a public domain utility for the Macintosh released by Kurzweil..

EXERCISE 3.2

Using a utility program such as the one shown in figure 3.9, examine other messages such as pitch bend and program change. Notice that pitch bend gets a little busy.

EXERCISE 3.3

Do exercise 3.2 using a software sequencer instead of the utility program. Record one note with pitch bend. Thin out the pitch bend information by removing every other bend message. Is there a noticeable difference on playback? Repeat this procedure until the bend becomes too step-like.

Figure 3.9. MIDIScope. In the upper center, a series of messages is shown. The left column gives the byte number, the other three the status and data bytes. The first line shows a Note On message on channel 1 ($90) with the pitch C3 ($3C or decimal 60) and a velocity of 105. This note is then turned off. After another Note On and Off pair, a program change is sent ($C0 is the status byte); pitchbend information is shown, beginning at byte 14. MIDI parameters may be selected or filtered (the checklist on the upper right) and shown (the bottom window). ©1991 Young Chang America/Kurzweil. Printed with permission.

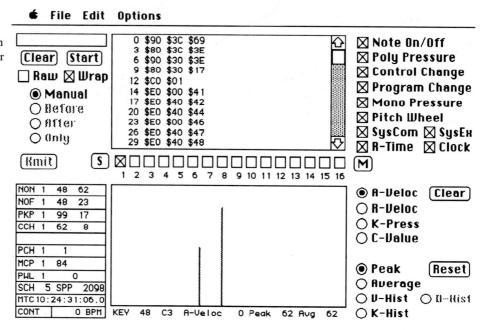

EXERCISE 3.4

Explore the MIDI implementation features of any available synthesizers. What sysex possibilities are there? What MIDI modes are available? How are they selected? Using a sequencer or MIDI utility program, send as many MIDI messages that the synthesizers will recognize as possible (except Note On, Note Off, and sysex).

VOCABULARY

The following terms were used in this chapter, most for the first time. Make sure that you are familiar with them, since they are used later in the book. A definition of each term may be found in the glossary.

aftertouch	algorithm	baud rate
binary	bit	breath control
byte	channel pressure	clock message
control change	data byte	data entry
default	hexadecimal	Kbaud
least significant byte	MIDI Time Code	modulation wheel
multi-timbral	Note On message	parallel
pitch bend	program change	real-time message
serial	song position	song select
status byte	system common	system exclusive
system real time	touch sensitivity	true pitch
tune request	volume pedal	

REVIEW QUESTIONS

QUESTION 3.1

Match related terms by writing the letter of the term from the second column in the blank of the term in the first column that most closely relates to it.

First Column	Answer	Second Column
1 + 1	C	A. 0
10	D	B. 1
Control Change	F	C. 10
False	A	D. A
Program Change	E	E. Preset
True	B	F. Volume Pedal

QUESTION 3.2

Compare and contrast the following terms.

Status Byte — Data Byte

A data byte is a byte that chasa decimal value between 0 and 127 (128 in all) usually one or more follow a status byte, which is a byte that gives the "status" or function (information) of something happening, like a note being pressed. The data byte (0 to 127) tells which one, how fast, etc.

System Common — System Real Time — System Exclusive

Systems exclusive is a message that applies to a certain synth or piece of equipment. Syst. real time is a message that gives real commands (like start, stop, continue) and syst common is a message that applies to all equipment in a network.

QUESTION 3.3

Provide the question for the given answer.

ANSWER	QUESTION
1000 bits per second	What is K baud ?
Basic number of MIDI channels	What is 16 ?
Mode 3	What is Omni off poly ?
Base 16	What is How many channels ?

QUESTION 3.4

Fill in the blanks with the equivalent values of the given number.

Decimal   Binary   Hexadecimal

_8_   1000   _8_

15   _1111_   F

_12_   _1100_ $C

30   _1110_   _1E_

_14_   1110   _E_

_255_   _11111111_ $FF

QUESTION 3.5

Identify the following status bytes by function and channel

BYTE	FUNCTION	CHANNEL
10000010	note off	_____
11000100	_____	_____
10011111	_____	_____
11101101	_____	_____

PART · TWO

INSTRUMENT DESIGN

CHAPTER · FOUR

ANALOG MODULES–
DIGITAL PARAMETERS

A synthesizer is too often thought of as merely an electronic keyboard. Although it can fulfill this role quite well—particularly when designed as a performance instrument—it can be much more. It would be better to consider it to be a collection of potential voices, or instruments, which can be developed or recalled as needed. These instruments all share certain basic design features, regardless of the size or complexity of the host synthesizer.

THE CREATIVE POTENTIAL

A piece of music written for a string quartet sounds quite different performed on a piano. In fact, there are various coloristic effects characteristic of bowed, stringed instruments that can only be hinted at by the piano. Conversely, the piano has its own ways of playing that are difficult to arrange convincingly for strings. As a result, composers tend to write differently for different instruments, and the very characteristics that make an instrument or group of instruments unique may suggest appropriate musical gestures and styles.

This is also true in electroacoustic music. On analog synthesizers one cannot simply perform a piece of music without first creating the sounds that will be used in the piece. On digital synthesizers, while it is possible to use pre-programmed sounds, some studio work is almost always needed to refine the initial patch for the specific piece of music.

In some situations, a **flowchart** or parameter list will help in defining an instrument. In most cases, simple experimentation or "tweaking" of existing sounds will lead to more useful sounds. Just as a composer should have a sonic image of an acoustic instrument to write effectively for it, so should you be familiar with the synthesized instruments at your disposal to use them effectively in both planned and improvisatory music.

VOLTAGE

The output of acoustic instruments can be measured in terms of electrical energy. When a record is played on a phonograph, mechanical energy is transformed into electrical energy, which causes the movement of a magnet attached to a speaker cone, transforming the electrical energy back into mechanical energy (a sound wave). Electrical energy, ultimately transformed into sound waves, is also of primary importance in the synthesizer. Not only are the basic waveforms a product of electricity, but voltage and its effect on frequency, timbre, and amplitude are a vital and unique feature of the analog synthesizer.

PARAMETER

Where voltage is an analog for the acoustic waveform on analog synthesizers, digital bits and bytes organized as parameters present the information that is ultimately heard as sound on digital synthesizers. This makes it easy to store and recall instruments and, paradoxically, often makes it more difficult to develop new sounds, since the visual model presented by the front panel of an analog synthesizer with all its knobs and sliders is often replaced by a small digital readout and a few buttons.

THE THREE-PHASE APPROACH

In traditional composition, most of the technical problems of turning notation into music are left up to the performer(s). Music notation has always had a certain plasticity to it, allowing for adaptation to the musical needs of the time. Conventional understandings have added depth to the meaning of the various symbols and signs used by musicians. The composer has to understand not only the notation and its meanings, but also to some extent how the standard instruments will realize the notation.

Increasingly in the twentieth century composers who wished to write new music found it necessary to create their own musical notation, since the musical gestures or effects they envisioned could not be adequately described using standard notation. Some have explored marginal instrumental sounds, such as **multiphonics** on wind instruments (unusual fingerings that allow more than one tone to be produced simultaneously) or **clusters** on keyboard instruments (groups of adjacent tones struck simultaneously, giving a higher noise content than traditional chords).

Some composers have chosen to expand the role of the percussion section in orchestras and percussion ensembles. In time-honored fashion, some included sound sources not previously considered musical, such as the siren added to the percussion ensemble used by Edgard Varese (1883-1965) in his Ionisation (1931). Still others dreamed of the day when electrically generated music would free them to explore their sonic yearnings in fuller measure.

Other twentieth century composers have stretched the limits of musical sound in a way that is quite in keeping with the spirit of the electroacoustic medium. Rather than adapting current instruments, they have built new instruments, since existing ones could not fulfill their musical needs.

INSTRUMENT DESIGN

The involvement demanded of an electronic composer today, whether he or she works in art or commercial music, is clearly different from that required of more traditionally oriented composers. To better cope with the demands of the medium, the composer may focus on **Instrument Design, Score Construction**, and **Rehearsal/ Performance**.

Instrument design is the process of making choices from the available sonic resources. This goes beyond just choosing one factory sound or another on a digital synthesizer. Two or more sounds may be combined to make a new sonority, as discussed in chapter five. A sound may be modified for a particular purpose. Various modules or components of an electronic music system may be connected or programmed to create usable sounds.

In order to create useful synthesizer instruments, it is important to become familiar with the various synthesizer modules and their typical functions. Some synthesizers, as well as **samplers** and sample players, use approaches to sound generation that vary a bit from the concept of modules used here. Even in such cases, the same principle applies.

It is possible to take a "cookbook" approach to electronic music, using only preset or factory-supplied instrumental configurations without understanding much about the nature of sound. However, even the best of presets may require some refinement to fit a specific need, or the possibilities inherent in one patch (a term left over from the early days of electronic music, when much interconnection of modules with patch cords was necessary; it is used here synonymously with *instrument*) may lead to the creation of yet more complex and interesting sounds. Each synthesizer, no matter how apparently simple, may offer its own options for the creation of new, unique instruments.

SCORE CONSTRUCTION

In addition to designing instruments (a process that is often more conceptual than physical) the composer needs to place sounds in time and space. This may involve some sort of notation on paper or the creation of sequencer files (many sequencers offer some sort of notation option). Score notation ranges from traditional music notes to unique graphic representations of sonic events to MIDI files. In an improvisatory approach, the score may be a few cryptic notes designed to help the composer recreate an effect or instrument or may simply be the event list of a sequence.

Much can be done with synthesizers and computers with little understanding of standard music notation. This notation can, in fact, sometimes intrude on the creative process, since it suggests rather traditional ways to use the equipment. Nonetheless, it is difficult to do much beyond free-form improvisations without planning out potential musical ideas and their relationships before and during studio work or practice sessions.

The five-line staff need not be used, but it is useful to develop some type of systematic notation. Information such as the passage of time, the character of the musical event or idea (loud, soft, fast, slow, high, low, thin, thick, long, short), and its spatial location (channel 1 or 2, or left or right speaker) should be noted. Technical data should include the event's storage location on tape or disk and the settings and values used to create the event. Most sequencers handle such information, either through the use of comments, or indications on a graphic representation of a sequence, or through a good implementation of MIDI, allowing much of this information to be built into the piece itself.

Figure 4.1 gives an example of a score using a highly graphic notation. Time is shown horizontally and pitch vertically. Some imagination is needed to interpret events. Do dark lines suggest bands of noise, or loud sounds, or both? Should each different activity have its own timbre? Although at first they may appear forbidding, graphic scores have their own charm and offer the performer/composer a fascinating challenge.

The same material may be presented in a computer data file. An important difference between a graphic score and a computer file is that the former suggests actions which can

Figure 4.1. A simple
graphic score

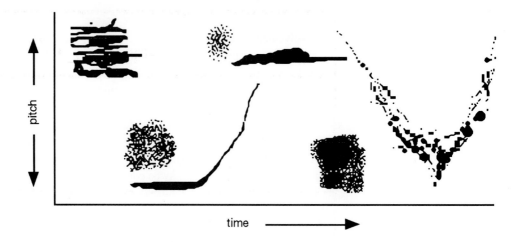

pitch

time

be interpreted and realized by a performer, while the latter is often an actual realization. To the extent that the program allows the performer to participate in making choices (when does an event happen, or does it happen?) it becomes creative, rather than merely re-creative.

The individual composer may be more or less formal in score construction and documentation, depending on his or her method of working as well as on the needs of the situation. If the composer is also the performer, the score may be much more sketch-like than when performance instructions must be communicated to a second party. With the exercises given in later chapters will come the opportunity to read and realize scores, as well as to construct scores representing original work.

REHEARSAL/PERFORMANCE

As instruments are being designed and ideas about the organization of the piece of music are being developed, sections of the music can be listened to, or rehearsed. Unlike a traditional rehearsal, where the music has to be previously composed and clearly notated, the music and the sounds producing the music can be constantly modified.

Rehearsal/Performance includes compositional activities and hands-on experimentation to develop new sounds (the "playpen" phase) and refine previously designed sounds. If the material is being produced by automated procedures, critical listening and appropriate adjusting of the procedures take the place of physical performance. Included in this phase is the performance, recording, and editing of sonic material.

Improvisation is an important means of becoming familiar with the various media of electroacoustic music. As skill is gained, it becomes possible to create more extended pieces. In the studio, it is necessary to rehearse the material, listening critically to its effect. Use of a music keyboard may require development of physical coordination and timing. Recording levels may require adjustment, or an instrument may need to be revised to fit its actual use in a musical passage for which it was not originally designed.

In general, synthesists and computer musicians more than most musicians act as both composer and performer, since there is no sheet music market for electronic music, nor much standardization among synthesizers or computers (in spite of MIDI). Synthesizers may be treated in a traditional fashion as keyboard-like solo or ensemble instruments, or they may be exploited in the studio to function as the composer's notebook as well as a many-colored palette for the final production phases of complete musical works.

BOX · 4.1

EDITOR/LIBRARIANS

MIDI has been designed to allow for communication between digital musical instruments. It is flexible enough to also be an effective tool in designing instruments. The use of the system-exclusive protocol comes into play in this procedure.

With the aid of MIDI, the microcomputer becomes a development and storage facility. Individual instruments and sets of instruments can be designed on a computer, stored to disk, or transferred to the synthesizer for use. Parameter values and amplitude envelopes may be shown on the computer screen, which gives a clearer overview of an instrumental patch than the display on the digital synthesizer allows. With proper programming, the screen display can also be used interactively in the instrument design process. Instruments originally created on the synthesizer can also be transferred to the computer for further editing or storage.

GENERAL OPERATION

Manufacturers who take advantage of system exclusive codes can devise digital data that may be transmitted to other digital synthesizers of the same type or to a MIDI-equipped microcomputer. The computer must of course run a program that receives instrument patch data. This may be a commercial patch librarian designed to handle data from a particular synthesizer, or a portion of a larger "universal" editor program, or may be a home-grown program.

Each manufacturer can (and most do) structure tone data in a unique way. This may be due to a wish for proprietary secrecy as well as to the fact that each synthesizer has different types of modules with different sets of parameters.

BASIC MODULES AND PARAMETERS

When a digital synthesizer is turned on a default set of instruments, or presets, is generally available. The musician often develops his or her own default set or selects from other sets supplied by the manufacturer or other sources.

One of the best ways to become familiar with a digital synthesizer is to modify a preset instrument. Waveforms can be changed, parameters can be modified, envelopes can be altered, and modules can be added or taken out of the patch. On digital synthesizers a buffer (a designated portion of RAM) is generally provided for instrument development.

Once any parameter of an existing instrument is modified, the now-altered copy of this instrument is automatically placed into an edit **buffer** for further development. The original, unmodified version still resides in memory. Once an instrument is developed, it should be saved, either to synthesizer memory or to an add-on cartridge or to disk. If this is not done, the instrument may be lost, since any parameter change of another instrument will place that revised instrument into the buffer, causing any parameter settings already in the buffer to be lost. Since digital synthesizers have a battery to sustain information in RAM when power is off, parameter settings in the edit buffer should not be lost when power is off.

Analog synthesizers are different, in that presets often do not exist. This requires more involvement with synthesizer modules to develop useful patches. The primary focus in this chapter is on a basic set of analog modules in order to strengthen that involvement and understand better what happens with digital versions of these modules.

This set, typical of many small analog synthesizers, includes two Voltage-Controlled Oscillators, a noise generator, a low-pass Voltage-Controlled Filter, a Voltage-Controlled Amplifier, two envelope generators and a Low Frequency Oscillator, and a keyboard. The ability to have some control over the way these modules are interconnected, either through patch cords, manual switches, or other programming capability is, of course, quite important.

These modules may be given different names on various digital systems. For the most part, their function from the musical perspective is quite similar. There will be some means of generating an audio waveform, some filtering or waveform modification procedure, some means of shaping the amplitude of the signal, and some means of creating timbre modification or amplitude contours and controlling pitch.

Additional features may exist on many synthesizers, including Ring modulators, Sample-and-Hold modules, sequencers, and effects devices. Since these features are not as standardized their exploration is primarily left up to the individual, although from time to time suggestions for their use will be made. The owner's manual may be helpful.

THE SIGNAL PATH

An acoustic event involves several phases. There is the moment of generation of the sound, the transmission of that sound by means of pressure waves in the air, and the realization of that signal by the listener. In the transmission phase, the original signal may be modified as it becomes weaker over distance, or as echoes are created or portions of the signal are devoured by carpets and drapes, or emphasized according to the acoustical characteristics of the environment. A similar path is found on most synthesizers, whether analog or digital.

Most modules may be considered to either generate or modify signals. Generation modules produce periodic waveforms or, in the case of the noise generator, various types of **random noise** spectra. In table 4.1 the basic signal path modules are classified by function. Other sources of generation include natural sounds, pre-recorded material (including CDs), and complex patches, which themselves contain both generation and modification phases. Generation modules, including audio-range VCOs and noise generators,

Table 4.1. Classification of basic modules

TYPE	GENERATION	MODIFICATION
AUDIO	Oscillator (VCO)	Filter (VCF)
	FM Operator	Various Effects
	Noise Generator (NG)	Amplifier (VCA)
	Acoustic Sources	Mixer
	Sampled Sounds	
CONTROL	Low Frequency Oscillator (LFO)	
	Envelope Generator (AR, ADSR, other)	
	MIDI Controllers	
	MIDI features such as aftertouch	
	Music Keyboard, other MIDI note producers	

may also have control uses, although this is more true in the analog realm. Control sources may affect both generation and modification modules or functions.

Many digital synthesizers are modelled loosely on the analog path. A waveform is generated and then modified by some procedure. It is usually possible to follow an initialization procedure to establish a neutral sound in the instrument buffer of a digital synthesizer. From this point, a waveform can be selected and other parameters can be varied to arrive at the desired product.

With the aid of digital sampling equipment, it becomes possible to develop waveforms derived from acoustic or analog sources. Some synthesizers which themselves do not sample offer a set of samples as basic waveforms. Systems using wavetables may provide for the development of unique waveforms by allowing the composer to create his or her own wavetables.

In the following sections discussions of analog and digital modules and parameters are combined. Just as a studio is richer for the presence of several synthesizers, the understanding of either analog or digital should be deepened by the presence of the other.

GENERATING WAVES AND TONES

The sound wave produced by an analog VCO is itself an electrical pressure wave, in the form of a periodic **alternating current** (AC). When one volt of **direct current** (DC) is added to this voltage within the VCO the frequency of the waveform is doubled. The frequency, or pitch, of the VCO output may be controlled manually or by **control voltage** sources. Controlling modules include the keyboard and other signal-generating modules. Some VCOs also produce low-frequency waveforms, used to control various characteristics of the output of other modules.

Analog equipment relies on a combination of filtering and various types of modulation to produce interesting sonorities. While some digital synthesizers follow this same approach, others often include modulation processes as an integral part of the waveform generation module.

Yamaha's FM synthesis is an example of this. At the heart of an instrument patch is the **algorithm**, which structures the relationship of a set of **operators**. These operators may be mixed like oscillators or may modify one another in various ways (see chapter five). Each operator may have its own envelope (see the section on envelope generators beginning on page 64). An operator therefore has characteristics of both an oscillator and a signal path.

Other synthesis procedures can have their own wrinkles. The end result is to create musically useful sound. The challenge is to discover how to make and mold interesting sonic material.

TYPICAL GENERATION CONTROLS

Table 4.2 lists common generation controls and parameters. Analog and digital synthesizers have similar features, although with the flourishing of MIDI the range of control options has greatly increased. Frequency may be adjusted manually on analog synthesizers by a **coarse tune** (or octave or range) switch or **potentiometer** and a fine tune potentiometer. Potentiometers, or "pots," are devices—usually rotary or sliding—that can be used to alter voltage levels. They may control a DC **offset voltage** used to determine various settings on VCOs and other modules. Waveforms may be selected by rotary switch or individual switches, **pulse width** (PW) may be selected or adjusted, and the amplitude of incoming control signals controlled. If waveforms are selected by individual switches, it may be possible to output two or more simultaneously.

A "keyboard on-off" switch determines how the keyboard controls the frequency of a VCO. If the off position is selected, the keyboard will still affect the operation of other

Table 4.2. Summary of
oscillator/generator
functions

FUNCTION	ANALOG CONTROLS	DIGITAL PARAMETERS
Set initial frequency	Coarse and fine tune potentiometers	Detune or transpose functions; default setting of A3=440 Hz is common
Respond to keyboard	Keyboard control voltage (often hardwired)	Internal connection; may respond to external MIDI
Select tone color	Selection of basic waveforms; pulse width control	Variety of timbres depends upon synthesis approach
External frequency modulation	Control voltage inputs, often dedicated (modulation wheel, LFO, keyboard)	LFO, often with broad range of waveforms; list of MIDI controllers; pitch envelope
Other external controls	Pulse width mod, keyboard control voltage input; pitch bend	MIDI controllers (depends on MIDI implementation); pitch bend
Audio output	Monophonic or polyphonic; mono-timbral	Generally polyphonic; may be multi-timbral as well

modules, while not changing the frequency of the selected VCO. A **sync** switch forces one oscillator to lock on to the frequency of the nearest partial of another oscillator's output and to keep this relationship when the leading oscillator changes pitch. A "low-audio range" switch can be combined with the keyboard on-off switch, allowing keyboard control of the VCO only when it is in the audio range.

On digital synthesizers, a combination of front panel controls and a digital readout window allow access to the parameters that control functions similar to those on analog synthesizers. There will be a choice of waveforms, a way to determine frequency (sometimes in conjunction with a pitch envelope), and often specialized parameters needed for the particular type of waveform generation process.

OTHER GENERATION SOURCES

Various types of noise are produced by analog noise generators. **White noise** has constant power per bandwidth, while **pink noise** has constant power per octave. Since an octave represents the distance from frequency f to frequency $2f$, an octave low in the audio range will be smaller in terms of Hertz than an octave higher in the audio range (for example, 100-200 Hz yields 100 Hz, while 1,000-2,000 Hz yields 1,000 Hz). Pink noise will distribute its energy over the octave regardless of its size in Hz, while white noise will have the same power per constant number of Hz. White noise thus sounds stronger in the higher frequencies than pink noise, which is distributed exponentially and consequently is heard as being more evenly distributed (see figure 4.2).

Noise generators tend to be simpler in terms of front panel controls than VCOs. They may function as both an audio source and as a source signal for modules such as the Sample-and-Hold. This module outputs more or less random control voltages obtained by sampling an input signal at an interval determined by a clock or oscillator. Due to this use, the noise generator may be built into the Sample-and-Hold module, at least as

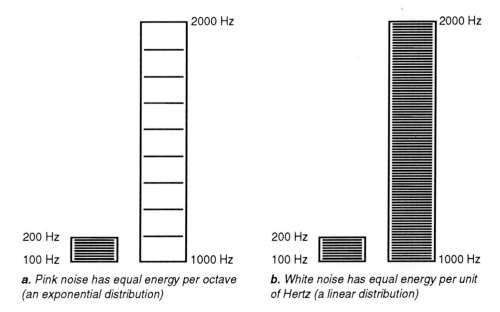

Figure 4.2. Energy distribution of pink and white noise

a. Pink noise has equal energy per octave (an exponential distribution)

b. White noise has equal energy per unit of Hertz (a linear distribution)

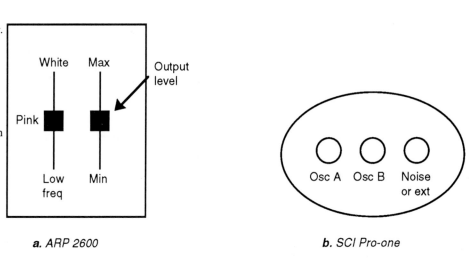

Figure 4.3. The noise generator. While the ARP 2600 allows internal filtering and control over signal amplitude, Sequential Circuit's Pro-One places its noise generator in a mixer unit, where it also controls the level of an external audio input (when an external source is input, the generator is bypassed).

a. ARP 2600

b. SCI Pro-one

far as the view from the front panel suggests. Figure 4.3 shows front panel controls for two noise generators.

Digital synthesizers rely less on noise sources than do analog synthesizers. Some, like the Casio CZ series, have a noise modulation process for those times when a less strongly pitched event is needed. In cases where choices are made from a palette of waveforms, there may be noise-like waves to choose from. Samplers and sample players, of course, can use a wide range of acoustic and electronic sounds.

There is in general less focus on digital synthesizers on the raw material of sound and more on a multiplicity of finished product. Rather than using a noise source to create a snare drum sound, one would look for a preset snare drum sound.

WAVEFORM MODIFICATION

On analog synthesizers filters are the primary means for processing audio signals. This filter is most often a low-pass filter, which attenuates those portions of the audio signal whose frequency is higher than the **cutoff frequency** (Fc) of the filter. As in the VCO, analog control voltage affects the Fc at the rate of one volt per octave. DC voltages may be supplied by a potentiometer or control voltage sources. Both DC and AC voltages (low or audio frequency) can be input via control voltage inputs. Ideally any frequency higher

Figure 4.4. Low-pass filter
attenuation

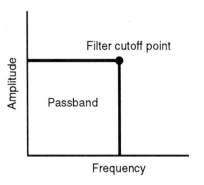

*a. The ideal cutoff with a
sharply defined passband*

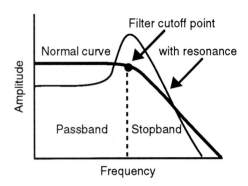

*b. Typical low-pass filter slope (dark
curve); with resonance, energy is
concentrated at the filter cutoff point
(light curve)*

than the cutoff point would be completely attenuated (figure 4.4a). In practice, the slope is more gradual, ranging from 6 dB per octave (a one-pole filter) to 24 dB per octave (a four-pole filter).

The range of possible raw waveforms is generally greater on digital synthesizers than on analog. As more waveforms are available, there is less need for filtering. In the case of synthesizers using modulation processes, the role of waveform modification is tied to the process of waveform generation.

On synthesizers with filters, the Fc can be controlled manually, by control voltages produced by the keyboard and other signal-generating modules (analog), or by various MIDI controllers. Most filters have variable Q (**resonance** at the cutoff frequency), which is usually controllable as well. This effect, also called **corner peaking**, tends to concentrate energy at the cutoff frequency. As a result a steeper curve is produced at frequencies above the cutoff point, and some attenuation of lower frequencies occurs as well (the lighter curve in figure 4.4b). If enough energy is concentrated at the cutoff frequency, the filter itself may start to oscillate.

The cutoff frequency is technically known as the **half-power point**. This is the point at which the filter reduces the amplitude of the input signal to about 70 percent of its maximum amplitude, causing an attenuation of 3 dB. In more (musically) practical terms, this distinction will be implicit, rather than stated. It is easier to think in terms of the cutoff frequency being that point at which one becomes aware of attenuation. The portion of the signal that is not attenuated is known as the **passband**; the attenuated portion is referred to as the **stopband**.

Table 4.3 shows the controls and parameters on a typical **low-pass filter**. The cutoff frequency may have one or more controls. The amount of resonance may be controlled (Q). There may be controls for envelope and keyboard strength as well as means of controlling the relative strengths of control and audio inputs.

Other types of filters include **high-pass**, **band-pass**, and **band-reject**. Figure 4.5 shows the contours of these filters. By placing a low-pass and a high-pass filter in series, setting the low-pass filter to a higher -3db point (Fc) and the high-pass filter to a lower Fc, a band-pass filter may be simulated. By doing the reverse, a band-reject or notch filter may be simulated. This procedure is more likely to occur on modular analog synthesizers or computer sound generation programs than on most digital synthesizers.

SHAPING THE SOUND

There will generally be an output section that allows final dynamic control over the amplitude shape of the sound. This contour is essential in developing successful sounds. On

Table 4.3. Waveform modification

FUNCTION	ANALOG CONTROLS	DIGITAL PARAMETERS
Set cutoff frequency	Coarse and fine tune potentiometers	Cutoff frequency function
Type of filter	Usually low-pass; more options on modular synthesizers	Usually low-pass if present at all; wider range of timbres or synthesis approach may make filtering unneccessary
Respond to keyboard	Keyboard amount pot or full/half/off switch	Internal connection; may be sensitivity control or response to MIDI note number
Resonance	Continuous control potentiometer	Often a result of timbre selection, not filtering
External sources of modulation	Control voltage inputs, often dedicated (modulation wheel, LFO, AR or ADSR envelopes)	LFO, often with broad range of waveforms; list of MIDI controllers; filter envelope
Audio input	Raw waveform or mix of waveforms; sometimes more complex patches or external sources	Raw waveform; sampled waveform or sound; more complex source (depending upon synthesis approach)
Audio output	Shaped waveform; timbre may be time-variant through use of envelope or other modulator	Similar to analog output; shape may be modified by MIDI controller

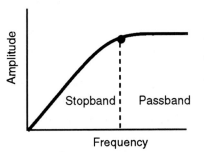

a. High-pass filter attenuates lower frequencies

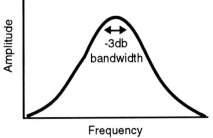

b. Band-pass filter attenuates frequencies on either side of the desired band.

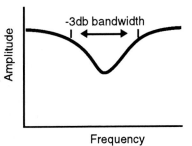

c. Band-reject filter attenuates frequencies in a selected band.

Figure 4.5. High-pass, band-pass, and band-reject filter slopes

an analog synthesizer amplitude shaping involves at least an amplifier and an envelope generator. On digital synthesizers there will be at least an amplitude envelope. There may also be an onboard effects section, allowing delays and other effects.

On analog synthesizers, a VCA follows the VCF in the signal path. It allows control of the amplitude of the filtered signal. The **gain**, or initial amplitude setting, can often be set manually and then controlled by voltage, usually by an envelope generator. On some systems, the envelope generator may appear to be built into the VCA on the front panel, so that the sustain pot, in conjunction with a gate or drone switch, sets the initial gain (see table 4.4).

Some VCAs have both **linear** and **exponential** control voltage inputs. The effect of one control volt via an exponential input is to alter the gain by 10 dB. Small synthesizers may not have any VCA control voltage capability beyond an envelope generator.

ENVELOPES AND LFOS

Modification and shaping processes may be made more dynamic through the use of modules that provide contour information that varies over time. Envelope generators produce a one-time contour that can modify pitch, filter and amplifier settings. **Low Frequency Oscillators** produce a regularly recurring contour often used for effects like vibrato.

ENVELOPE GENERATORS

In response to keyboard and timing information, envelope generators produce control curves. Although analog and digital envelopes are most often used to modify amplitude and timbre through control of filter and amplifier settings they may be used in other contexts, including pitch modification (see figure 4.6).

Each of the primary modules on a digital synthesizer may have its own envelope generator. This includes waveform generation modules, modification modules and amplitude shaping modules. This allows a level of complexity not easily obtainable on analog synthesizers.

The control curve includes several segments. On the standard analog ADSR (**attack, decay, sustain, release**) format, a rising attack outputs a voltage that generally goes from

Table 4.4. Amplitude control

FUNCTION	ANALOG CONTROLS	DIGITAL PARAMETERS
Set gain	Initial gain or sustain level on hard-wired ADSR	Sustain level on amplitude envelope
Respond to keyboard	Generally controlled by ADSR which is triggered by keyboard trigger and gate voltage	Also controlled by amplitude envelope, which is triggered by the keyboard
External sources of modulation	AR or ADSR envelopes; control voltage inputs are rare (mod wheel, LFO, etc.)	LFO, MIDI controllers in more flexible synthesizers
Audio input	Final stage for processed sound waveforms	Final stage for processed sound, unless onboard effects are still to be added)
Audio output	Waveform with both timbre and amplitude time-variant shapes	Waveform with both timbre and amplitude time-variant shapes

Figure 4.6. Amplitude control. Digital envelopes may have more flexible configurations, although both analog and digital envelopes modify pitch, timbre, or amplitude.

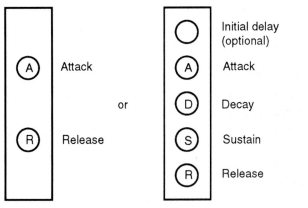

a. Analog envelopes tend to be configured as AR (ASR) or ADSR. They are usually triggered by the keyboard and often control more than one module at a time, since they tend to be few in number.

b. Digital envelopes have more flexibility and are usually more plentiful than analog envelopes. They are also triggered by the keyboard and often control only one module at a time.

zero to full voltage, with the time determined by potentiometer setting. An initial decay segment allows a move from full voltage to the sustain voltage level, with the time again determined by potentiometer setting. A sustain voltage level is set by potentiometer, with the length of the sustain period determined by how long the gate voltage continues after the attack and decay segments. A final release segment returns the voltage curve to zero following the end of the gate voltage.

Envelope generators come in different configurations, including AR (attack-release) and ADSR. Figure 4.7 (on page 66) shows several curves and their relationship to **gate** and **trigger** voltages. Notice that if the gate is shorter than the sum of attack plus decay times, the release begins at the current level, rather than at the sustain level.

A second trigger during the course of most analog ADSR envelopes causes a repeat of the ADS portion. This retriggering capability can often be enabled or disabled by a front panel or keyboard module switch. Some analog synthesizers will also allow the user to determine whether voltage slopes will be linear or exponential.

Many digital envelopes use the same ADSR format, although it is usually possible to set intermediate levels in addition to the sustain. Some, like the Casio CZ series, allow for more complex envelopes. On the CZ-101, for example, it is possible to have a complex attack phase consisting of several attacks and decays (figure 4.7d) or to have a release that seemingly lets the sound take on a life of its own after the note is released (figure 4.7e). An envelope modifying the generation phase allows oscillator functions to be tuned (common on the Yamaha FM synthesizers) or allows pitch to be treated dynamically.

LFOs

Low Frequency Oscillators, or LFOs, are dedicated to providing control information. They produce AC voltages or periodic contours that can be used to modify the frequency or pulse width of a VCO or other generator, the cutoff point of a filter, and the gain of an amplifier. In such control situations, the output frequency is increased or decreased, or modulated, according to the amplitude and frequency of the controlling waveform. Figure 4.8 shows a low-frequency sine wave modulating an audio frequency sine wave. A change in the amplitude of the modulating signal causes a corresponding frequency change in the modulated wave, while a change in frequency of the modulating signal (not shown) causes the frequency change of the modulated wave to occur more or less rapidly.

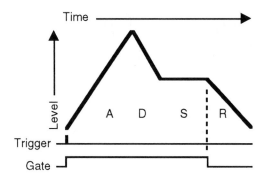

a. *The ADSR standard. Altering attack (A), decay (D), and release (R) times modifies slopes. On analog envelopes only the sustain (S) level is adjustable.*

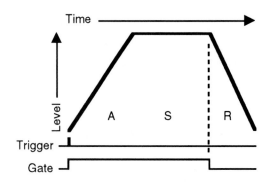

b. *AR or ASR format. Sustain level is set at maximum. Attack and release slopes may be altered.*

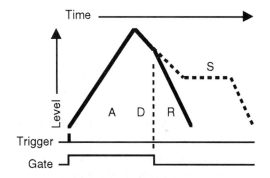

c. *Key release prior to reaching sustain level. Sustain setting is ignored, and release slope is begun. Some modules may operate differently.*

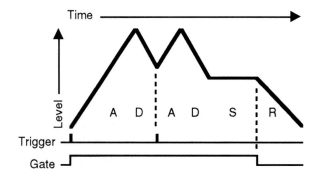

d. *Retriggering an envelope. With analog envelopes the attack usually begins from the current voltage level. Digital envelopes may allow such contours without retriggering.*

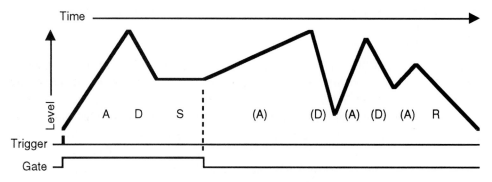

e. *Complex releases. With flexible location of the sustain phase, digital envelopes may allow complex release contours, which take place after the gate ceases.*

Figure 4.7. Envelope contours. Gate and/or trigger voltages (analog) and gate information (digital) initiate various envelopes, which move through attack, decay, and sustain phases. When the gate stops the release phase begins. Analog envelopes set a standard often copied by digital envelopes (*a* through *c*). The latter usually provide more flexibility in setting levels and may allow greater complexity by providing additional stages (*d* and *e*), although analog envelopes can be more complex through retriggering (*d*).

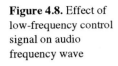

Figure 4.8. Effect of low-frequency control signal on audio frequency wave

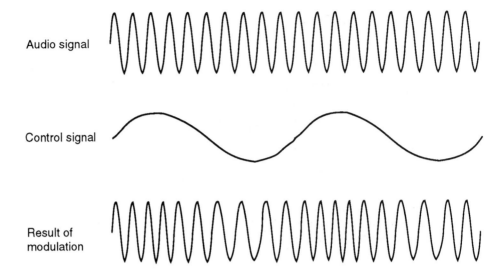

Audio signal

Control signal

Result of modulation

CONTROLLERS AND KEYBOARDS

The music keyboard has long been considered to be the standard means of controlling pitch. This is less true of digital synthesizers, however. MIDI has allowed the development of other controllers to a degree greater than in the earlier analog world. Guitar controllers, wind controllers, and devices that even allow voice to be a controller by converting pitch information to MIDI have been developed.

Along with choice of controller, however, comes the responsibility to pick sounds that work convincingly with that controller. Patches may need some modification to respond properly to the different attack characteristics of a controller. Some controllers may work well with slower music, but may not allow clean conversion of information to MIDI data at faster rates of play.

Tuning is relative, rather than absolute, on most synthesizers. This means that a key does not have to produce only one specified pitch. MIDI works against this, to some extent, since it is assumed that key number 60 (called either C3 or C4, depending upon the preference of the manufacturer) will sound middle c. On analog synthesizers, equal-tempered DC control voltages can be used for various control functions of VCOs, VCFs, and other modules, which do not depend on the keyboard for their initial tuning.

KEYBOARD CONTROL INFORMATION

Analog and digital keyboards produce no audio signal, in spite of appearances to the contrary. In fact, it is possible to create effects that do not use the keyboard at all, or that use the keyboard as a switching device, rather than as an originator of discrete tonal events.

Analog keyboards produce voltage which controls functions on other modules. In figure 4.9, assume that the key marked C2 outputs 2 volts DC. Key C1 is one octave lower, with an output of 1 volt DC. Likewise key C3, one octave to the right, outputs 3 volts DC. Each key (whether short or long) outputs 1/12 of a volt more than its leftmost neighbor. Key A2, for example, outputs 2-9/12 volts DC. If a VCO produces a tone with the frequency of 440 Hz when key A2 is pressed, pressing key A1 will produce 220 Hz, while A3 will allow 880 Hz to be output.

The user doesn't need to be as concerned with the electrical output of a digital keyboard. In a MIDI system, the MIDI note number is of primary importance. Figure 4.9 shows the MIDI note numbers for C1 (36), C2 (48), and C3 (60). To find intervening numbers, simply count up or down from the nearest C. For example, A2 is number 57.

Figure 4.9. Voltage, frequency, and MIDI note numbers

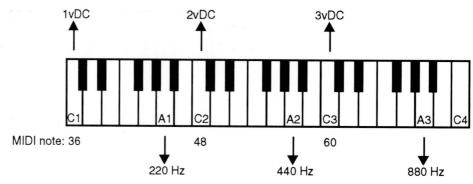

TRIGGER AND GATE VOLTAGE

In addition to the one volt per octave output of the analog keyboard, there are also trigger and gate voltages produced when a key is pressed. Some systems use the gate voltage to also fulfill the function of the trigger voltage. Briefly, some modules need to be triggered at the moment the key is pressed. This function is taken care of by a short pulse, which is often in the range of 5 to 15 volts. This varies widely from system to system, and is one of the problems that had to be overcome to mate different synthesizers before MIDI.

The gate voltage remains on as long as a key is held down. The continued functioning of some modules depends on this information. Figure 4.7 on page 66 shows the effect of gate and trigger voltages on the ADSR curve produced by an envelope generator. The length of the sustain phase depends directly on the length of time the key is pressed.

Digital keyboards also provide trigger and gate information where needed. From the user's point of view, the digital keyboard operates much like its analog cousin.

PROGRAMMING PITFALLS

It is easy when developing or modifying a patch to turn a knob or alter a parameter value without actually changing the sound. Sometimes nothing changes because the parameter or module affected is not in the signal path. Other times, it is in the signal path, but the change is not detected because something later in the path is masking the effect.

For example, it is possible to have a patch with an envelope on the filter as well as on the amplifier. If the envelope on the amplifier closes down very quickly it creates a fairly short tone. If the envelope on the filter has a longer setting, it will have no effect on the sound after the amplifier envelope has finished. To hear the entire effect of the filter envelope, make sure that the amplifier envelope is at least as long.

On digital synthesizers there's another problem. Some functions may be activated or deactivated from a different menu than the one where levels are set. For example, it may be possible to control the placement of the signal in a stereo field: left, right, or somewhere in between. The Pan on/off control may be located on a different menu than the pan level setting.

Two general guidelines may be stated: when working on the local level, look ahead in the signal path to see if the setting will be heard; if the first guideline has been followed and nothing happens, see if there is some other parameter or switch that needs setting elsewhere. One could always look in the owner's manual (assuming that it has been reasonably well written...).

FLOWCHART NOTATION

Since synthesizer brands differ from one another, and analog synthesizers are different than digital, flowchart notation provides a flexible and simple tool in discussing and comparing functions. All audio- and low-frequency signal generating modules are denoted by

Table 4.5. Flowchart notation

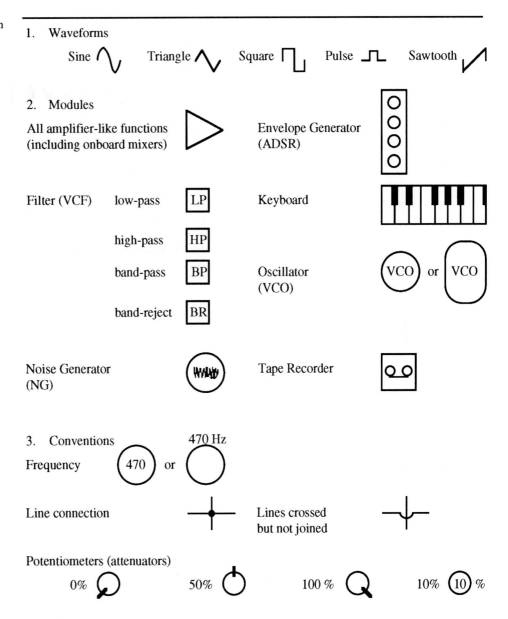

Signal inputs on left, modulation/control inputs on top and/or bottom, outputs on right

circular or oval symbols. Amplifier-like signal processors are shown by triangles, and filters and other formant modification processors are symbolized by squares. Rectangular shapes specify devices such as envelope generators, sequencers, tape recorders, effects, and keyboards. These symbols often incorporate a pictorial quality in their characterization, particularly the symbol for the keyboard. Table 4.5 presents a list of useful symbols.

The audio signal path is always shown horizontally, from left to right. Controlling modules are connected to the appropriate audio generator or processor with vertical lines, either from above or below the controlled module (the choice is the composer's). There are various ways of showing waveform, amplitude, filter settings, and other data. Figure 4.10 shows the basic signal path in flowchart notation. In this figure, a generation module produces a sawtooth wave, which is sent to a low-pass filter for modification and on to an amplifier for amplitude shaping (each of these two stages is subject to envelope generator control) before being sent on to some output device.

Figure 4.10. A basic
synthesizer instrument patch

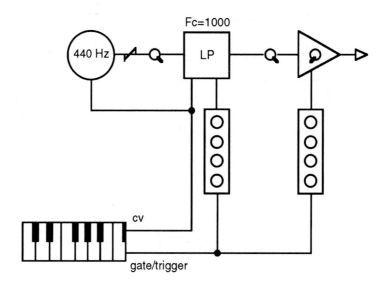

Any generation, modification, processing, or alteration of the signal must be shown, since a feature considered standard on one synthesizer may not be standard on another. Flowcharts should not only speak to the immediate situation, but should provide a record and a means of communication with other composers and performers and ultimately be part of a growing repertory of patches and ideas upon which one may build.

TWO SCORES FOR BASIC INSTRUMENTS

The process of designing an instrument can, in some cases, actually be the score for a piece. Figure 4.11 presents a rather rudimentary score for an analog instrument that actually changes its design in the process of realizing the score. Since the keyboard is not used to control the VCO, conventional music notation seems inappropriate. Instead, pitch is designated in terms of approximate placement on a field ranging from low to high.

Other parameters are also treated unconventionally. Time is designated in seconds rather than measures. Dynamics are shown with the usual musical symbols for **crescendo** (gradually increase the volume) and **decrescendo** (decrease the volume), combined with an arbitrary volume range of 0 (inaudible) to 10 (full volume). Timbre is designated only roughly (it is constantly changing) and duration and **articulation** are basically not shown, since the piece consists, essentially, of but one continuous tone.

Figure 4.11 would be more difficult on a digital synthesizer, since there aren't as many parameters available for real-time alteration. It's not impossible, but it is less in the spirit of digital synthesizers, which allow more contrast between different instrumental sounds than within a single instrument. Figure 4.12, on the other hand, can work easily with either type of synthesizer. It requires two performers, one playing the keyboard and the other altering various front panel settings or parameters. Since the keyboard is used by one of the performers, there is some advantage to using traditional notation, although it functions in a somewhat nontraditional fashion.

The box notation allows the performer to choose any event in any order he or she wishes. The double vertical bar lines separate events. The diverging beams of the second event suggest a speeding up. **AFAP** means "as fast as possible." Notice that the events accompanying this direction have no noteheads: the speed and rough contour is more important than specific pitches.

The score for the second performer consists of written directions, rather than notes. This performer must be able to interact with the first performer: in some ways, this is more difficult, requiring a critical ear to keep things interesting and changing. Settings

---

BOX · 4.2

WHY USE FLOWCHART NOTATION?

There is a strong tendency in the electronic musical instrument industry to design unique instruments, even though MIDI offers standardization in interfacing digital instruments. Some, like the Yamaha FM series, produce fascinating sounds but require a somewhat different programming approach. It is often tempting to use only factory presets rather than to take the time to develop original sounds.

The use of flowchart notation will not solve the problem, but it does offer a tool for better understanding patches. As a composer works with a synthesizer, a front panel facsimile or parameter chart can aid in remembering the details of patch modifications. Flowchart notation can also assist here. It can provide a means of comparing sounds designed on different synthesizers, and aid in moving a patch from one synthesizer to another.

It is short-sighted to say "Why should I worry about a generic approach when I'm only using one synthesizer and have no plans to purchase or use another?" A flowchart gives insight into the design of a patch. It may suggest convenient points for developing variants, and it will more easily show similarities between patches designed on different synthesizers than instrument-specific notation will do.

One purpose of this book is to promote a general understanding of procedures and concepts of both electronic music and music composition. That you can become familiar with both the specific synthesizer at hand and also expand your general knowledge of synthesizers is a plus. Given the rapid evolution of electronic instruments, it is quite likely that you will be exposed to many synthesizers. Flowchart notation is a useful tool in programming and using synthesizers more effectively.

Figure 4.11. Score one

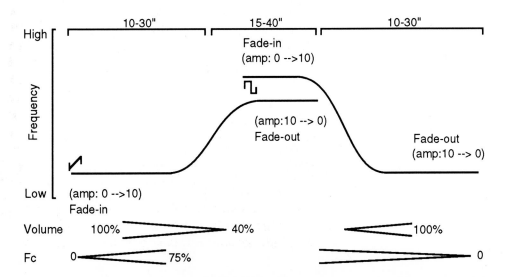

Performer I
Randomly select events, moving from longer to shorter pauses between events, occasionally stringing together several events without any pause.

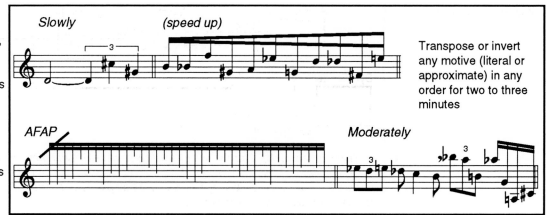

Transpose or invert any motive (literal or approximate) in any order for two to three minutes

Performer II
Randomly change any of the following parameters:

Attack and/or decay	Waveform or timbre (when performer I is not playing)
Master tune/detune (VCO tuning)	Output amplitude
Filter settings	Any other major parameter

Start your operations slowly and gradually increase the rate of change.

In general, move from long to short attacks,
                              soft to loud,
                              simple timbres to complex
but follow the principle of two steps forward and one backward (if you can confuse your partner, so much the better!)

Figure 4.12. Score two   *a. Score for two performers*

may be changed on the same synthesizer that the first performer is playing, or the control voltage or MIDI information may be sent to a second synthesizer where the changes may occur. In a MIDI environment, it may be possible for the second performer to make changes with the help of an editor/librarian, or perhaps several dozen sounds may be developed ahead of time, and then selected during the performance.

One additional element, not discussed in this chapter, is the tape echo. It provides for a richer texture, since old sounds continue for a while as new ones emerge. A digital delay will, of course, also suffice. Tape echoes are discussed in chapter eight. Rather than echo, of course, one could patch in the digital effects box and experiment with different delay times.

FOR FURTHER STUDY

Appendix E suggests ideas for further reading on page 265.

EXERCISES

The exercises given here will suggest additional ways of becoming more familiar with analog and digital instruments. As an instrument is explored, various refinements may suggest themselves. It is not expected that all of the exercises will be done, although it is important to read them, since they do continue the discussions in the text. Some modifications may be necessary to fit specific resources.

Figure 4.12–*Continued*

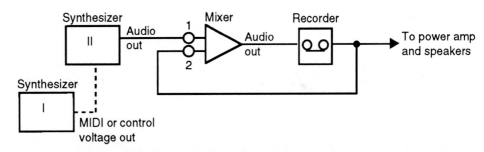

b. *Patch for tape echo. Keep echo volume (mixer input 2) lower than the source (mixer input 1) to avoid distortion and feedback. Rather than performing on the same synthesizer, performer I may use a second synthesizer, providing note or control voltage information for the synthesizer controlled by performer II.*

The importance of documentation in this process is hard to overstate. This includes flowchart information with explanatory notes. A descriptive title of the patch with a narrative description of the result and its intended use can be helpful. As excerpts and projects are recorded on tape or disk, a recording log should be kept, so that material may be found without the necessity of searching through reels of tape or disk catalogs for that one special effect that has "gotta be here somewhere." Any particularly interesting variants resulting from these exercises should be noted.

Exercises 4.1 to 4.3 are intended for use on analog instruments; exercises 4.4 to 4.6 are more appropriate on digital synthesizers; exercises 4.7 and 4.8 may be made to work on any synthesizer. Since patches on digital synthesizers generally come fully assembled, it's often better to start at the output end and work backwards, towards the generating modules, rather than forward, as on analog synthesizers.

EXERCISE 4. 1

Experiment with the effect of the keyboard on VCO and VCF. If envelope generators are patched to the VCF and VCA, either take them out of the patch or use ADSR settings of 0-0-100-0 (100 is maximum).

First set the Fc and the initial gain at maximum and try the keyboard (if the VCF or VCA have "keyboard amount" pots, set them for 1 volt per octave). The tones have a fairly bland shape at this point, since the VCF and VCA are simply passing the audio signal relatively unchanged.

Try various Fc settings in conjunction with playing the keyboard. If the keyboard or front panel has a **glide** or **portamento** pot, explore its operation.

EXERCISE 4.2

If possible, disable the keyboard control voltage to an oscillator and patch that oscillator to the VCF. Use a low Fc setting and play the keyboard. The VCO frequency should not change, but the Fc setting should. As higher keys are pressed, the tone color of the audio signal becomes brighter.

If possible, reverse this procedure, so that the keyboard controls the VCO frequency, but not the filter Fc. With an appropriately low Fc setting, high keys should produce a weaker signal than low keys.

EXERCISE 4.3

Explore the effects of the envelope generators on the VCF and VCA. This is best done by setting one module at maximum and experimenting with the other.

First set the Fc at maximum and the filter ADSR at 0-0-100-0. Set the VCA initial gain at minimum, then try different attack settings on the ADSR controlling the VCA: a gradual attack that abruptly cuts off; a fairly short attack followed by a long decay to nothing; short bursts of sound (little more than clicks); a long attack followed by a short decay to a medium sustain level, with a long release.

Then reset the initial gain to minimum and the VCA ADSR at 0-0-100-0. Explore different Fc and filter ADSR settings, following the pattern used with the VCA. What needs to be done to the VCA ADSR in order to hear the release on the VCF ADSR?

EXERCISE 4.4

Pick an interesting brass or keyboard patch. Find the front panel controls or menu selections dealing with the global or amplitude envelope. Experiment with different attack rates, then different attack levels. Work through the other segments in similar fashion.

If additional envelope segments are available, add them into the amplitude envelope, either prolonging the attack/decay portion, or creating an extended release portion.

EXERCISE 4.5

Explore the use of the envelope on the filtering or waveform modification portion of the signal path as was done for the amplitude in exercise 4.4. Also explore the effect of an envelope on pitch.

It may be necessary to modify the amplitude envelope a bit to do these operations, because if the amplitude envelope cuts off before an earlier envelope, the effect of the earlier envelope will not be felt.

EXERCISE 4.6

If two different types of synthesizer are available, try to reproduce an electric piano sound found on one synthesizer on the other. It will be necessary to write down all settings, either using a parameter chart (supplied with the owner's manual) or a flowchart.

EXERCISE 4.7

Construct and perform a score, using figure 4.11 or 4.12 as a model. Make the piece abstract, rather than telling a story. Explore, for example, changing tone colors, or the movement from thick to thin texture, or from a few random events to many rapid events. If two synthesizers are available, write for both instruments. Avoid using extra modules, such as sample and hold or sequencers, at this point.

EXERCISE 4.8

With a partner, explore the possibilities of figure 4.12. It may be necessary to look ahead to chapter eight for more information on tape echoes. The improvisational character of this score also offers the possibility of multi-synthesizer performance, or of synthesizer with acoustic instruments. It is also possible, of course, to design original melodic cells, rather than using those given in the figure.

VOCABULARY

Many of the following terms were used for the first time in this chapter. Several may have a different use than earlier in the book. Make sure that you are familiar with them, since they are used throughout the book. A definition of each term may be found in the glossary.

AFAP	algorithm	alternating current
articulation	attack	band-pass
band-reject	buffer	clusters
coarse tune	control voltage	corner peaking
crescendo	cutoff frequency	decay
decrescendo	direct current	exponential
flowchart	gain	gate
glide	half-power point	high-pass
Instrument Design	linear	Low Frequency Oscillator
low-pass filter	multiphonics	offset voltage
operator	passband	pink noise
portamento	potentiometer	pulse width
random noise	Rehearsal/Performance	release
resonance	sampler	Score Construction
stopband	sustain	sync
trigger	white noise	

REVIEW QUESTIONS

QUESTION 4.1

Match related terms by writing the letter of the term in the second column in the blank of the term in the first column that most closely relates to it.

Attenuation	F	A.	Corner Peaking
Envelope	E	B.	Filter
LFO	C	C.	Modulation
Parameter	F	D.	Offset Voltage
Potentiometer	D	E.	Shape
Resonance	A	F.	Value

QUESTION 4.2

Compare and contrast the following terms.

Linear — Exponential

Both are ways to describe the control of Volume

Voltage — Parameter

Voltage is one of the variables of a Parameter.

QUESTION 4.3

Define briefly.

Buffer

An area where info. can be stored and manipulated.

Instrument Design

The processes of making choices from various sonic resources.

QUESTION 4.4

Provide the question for the given answer.

ANSWER	QUESTION
MIDI key number 60	What is *the key the always sounds mid.C* ?
A generation module (any)	What is *a way to produce a sound* ?
A modification module (any)	What is *any type of filter* ?
Four stages of the basic envelope	What is *Attack Decay Sustain Release* ?
The half-power point	What is *Cutoff Freq.* ?

QUESTION 4.5

Identify the given flowchart symbols.

Triangle WF	∿	Keyboard	🎹
Amplifier-like functions	▷	Sawtooth WF	⌇
Oscillator	(VCO)	Env. Gen.	⊡
Square	⊓	Sine wave	∿
Low Pass	LP	Tape Rec.	⊡
High Pass	HP	Freq. or Osc.	○
Attenuators	Q	Pulse	⊓
Band-Reject	BR	Noise Gen.	(∿)
line Connection	+	Lines Cross but not joined	⊥
0% Pot	Q	50% Pot	○
Band Pass	BP	10% Pot	(10) %

CHAPTER · FIVE

INSTRUMENT DESIGN PROCEDURES

The major weakness of electronically generated sound is that it tends to be too regular, too . . . electronic. Electronic organ manufacturers, for example, have devoted much time and expense to make their product seem "real." Pipe organs ("real" organs) necessarily involve a human element in their construction and tuning that lends a certain uniqueness to each instrument. Also, tones are produced by the passage of air through pipes; in spite of advances in the technology of air pressure regulation, a slight wavering of pitch is often produced. The reproduction of certain sounds, such as the "chiff" of a baroque pipe organ flute stop, is desired by consumers. While the chiff (a short, high-pitched sound that occurs at the onset of a tone) is a simple byproduct of the pipe's construction, it is not so easy to duplicate electronically.

Without such attention to detail, electronic organ sound quickly becomes uninteresting. To make up for this lack of interest, some manufacturers of home organs supply rhythm boxes, sequencers, and even some limited user-programmable synthesizer capability. It is not usually necessary to go as far as electronic organ manufacturers have gone in their attempt to reproduce both the glories and the imperfections of the pipe organ in silicon. It is worthwhile, however, to design instruments that have flexibility and their own characteristic identity.

79

CONTROL PROCEDURES

The concept of modifying or controlling aspects of one module by another is central to synthesizers. It allows for the development of patches that avoid the steady-state aspect of electronic sound. When one or more characteristics of a signal (frequency, timbre, or amplitude) are varied according to the characteristics of another signal, a more dynamic instrument may be created.

Even without patching, control procedures are used. When the frequency of a waveform, the filter cutoff point, or an amplitude level is adjusted, an analog DC offset voltage level or digital parameter value is established. This is then used in the module to set the appropriate frequency or amplitude level, and may be combined with any external control information.

FREQUENCY

In music the term **modulation** is often used differently than is intended here. One speaks of modulating from one key to another. This involves altering musical relationships so that the music changes its focus from one home chord to another. Modulation in electroacoustic music also involves the element of change, but usually occurs periodically, depending upon the nature of the modulating signal.

The three aspects of a signal subject to electronic modulation are frequency, timbre, and amplitude. **Frequency modulation** (FM) occurs on VCOs and other generation modules. Timbre, or formant, modulation occurs on VCFs and other filter-like modules or on generation modules through **pulse width modulation** (PWM). **Amplitude modulation** (AM) takes place on VCAs and other amplifier modules.

Frequency modulation involves the control of generation modules by the keyboard, LFOs, envelope generators, and/or other sources. Often more than one control source will be used. In addition to low-frequency sources, audio range signals may be input. Some analog synthesizers have separate front panel modulation sections where control voltage attenuators and switches to route control voltages are found. Other makes will have the control inputs and modulation potentiometers on the VCO portion of the front panel. Digital synthesizers are often responsive to a range of MIDI controllers, both internal and external.

Many effects are possible. **Vibrato**, siren effects, trills, and simulation of chords are among the simple manifestations of FM involving a periodic increase and decrease of the audio frequency. Envelope generators produce one-time changes in frequency. Sequences and **microtones** (involving musical systems with more than 12 tones per octave) are included under this category as well.

VIBRATO

Two controls are of prime importance in vibrato and other LFO effects: the frequency control for the LFO, and the LFO or vibrato amplitude amount. These controls are found either on the control input of the audio generation module or in the vibrato or LFO module. Vibrato speed is determined by the LFO frequency. Vibrato depth depends on the amplitude of the incoming signal.

Vibrato is an effect often used by acoustic musicians to impart a slight shimmer to the output signal. To produce it select a sine or triangle wave on the LFO (the waveform of the modulated generator is unimportant). Its frequency should be set around 6 to 8 Hz, or fairly slow. Since vibrato is usually a somewhat subtle form of expression, care should be taken to keep the amplitude of the modulating signal (the LFO) fairly low.

A typical instrumental patch used to create vibrato is shown in figure 5.1a. The keyboard provides the standard 12 tones per octave. The LFO, with a frequency of 6 to 10

Figure 5.1. LFO frequency modulation patches

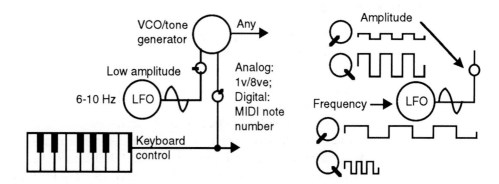

a. *Vibrato is produced by the use of a low amplitude sine wave. A triangle wave is also effective.*

b. *A trill is produced by a square wave. Its amplitude determines the pitch distance between the trilled tones; its frequency determines the speed of the trill.*

Hz, is producing a sine wave (a triangle will also work well). An attenuator to control the depth, or amplitude, of the modulating wave is shown with a low setting. Many variants of vibrato can be created by changing the LFO frequency, its waveform, and/or the amplitude of the LFO's signal.

SIREN

A somewhat different effect can be achieved by setting a low frequency on the LFO and a high amplitude on the control input of the audio generation module or LFO amplitude amount. This will cause the modulated signal to have a wide variation in pitch, following the contour of the controlling waveform. By appropriate adjustment of the control input amplitude, the extremes of this effect can be tuned.

TRILL

This effect involves the rapid alternation between two different pitches. In art music this term is most often thought of as involving adjacent or near-adjacent tones (a half or a whole step). The synthesizer allows a much greater range as well as speed that surpasses human performance capabilities. Rather than setting up a patch that involves the performer playing the two pitches, one creates a patch that makes the synthesizer do the actual trilling, while the performer presses a single key.

Select a square wave on an LFO which is patched to control the frequency of a VCO or other generation module. The LFO frequency controls the speed of the trill, while the control input of the audio generation module or LFO amplitude amount tunes the trill by determining the amplitude of the controlling square wave (see figure 5.1b). As the attenuator is opened from its minimum setting, the output signal should noticeably begin to alternate between two pitches. Further opening increases the distance between the two pitches, while increasing the LFO frequency increases the rate of alternation.

CHORDS WITH TWO VCOs

Small, monophonic analog synthesizers may not have three VCOs available for those times when three- or four-tone chords are desired. Chords can be created with only two VCOs, although they function differently than piano or polyphonic synthesizer chords. Melodies can be created with these chords. Since this effect is rather mechanical, it should be used with care.

Figure 5.2. Trilled chords
in music notation

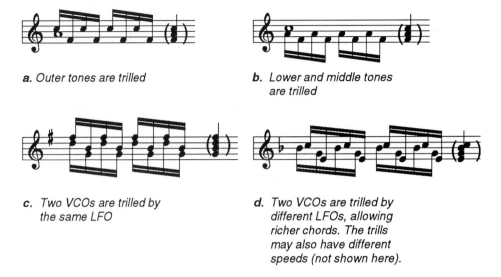

a. Outer tones are trilled

*b. Lower and middle tones
are trilled*

*c. Two VCOs are trilled by
the same LFO*

*d. Two VCOs are trilled by
different LFOs, allowing
richer chords. The trills
may also have different
speeds (not shown here).*

Chord formations can be simulated by modulating one VCO so that it produces a medium-fast trill between two tones of the chord, while the second VCO plays the third tone. A different feeling is created depending upon which note of the chord is not in the trill. In figure 5.2a, a major triad is shown, with the outer tones trilled and the second VCO playing the middle tone. In figure 5.2b, the second VCO is used on an outer note, and the other two are trilled. Both VCOs can be modulated by the same LFO to simulate four-note chords, as shown in figure 5.2c and d. With two LFOs, each trill may have a different frequency, creating a cross-rhythmic effect, in addition to the chord simulation.

MIXING WAVEFORMS

If the LFO allows simultaneous output of more than one waveform, or if there is more than one LFO available, mixing different waveforms will give a more complex control contour. Figure 5.3 shows the results of mixing triangle, square, and sawtooth waves in various combinations. Further refinements may be obtained if the LFO itself may be controlled by another module, producing a periodic change in the LFO frequency, which causes the audible modulation effect to increase and decrease accordingly.

ENVELOPE GENERATOR

The envelope generator is most often thought of as a control module for filters and amplifiers. It can also be used as a voltage source for modulating the frequency of generation modules. The tone generator or oscillator output frequency will vary with the level/time curve created by ADSR or other envelopes.

With an envelope, if the sustain level is set at 0, the oscillator frequency will rise and fall according to the attack and decay settings. If the sustain level is greater than 0, the oscillator output frequency follows the curve as before, but stops at the frequency determined by the sustain level, while a key is pressed down. When the key is released, the release time takes over. Assuming that the release time of the envelope controlling the amplifier is at least equal in length to the release time of the envelope controlling the oscillator frequency, a drop in pitch will be heard following the release of the key.

ANALOG SEQUENCES

Random noise sources and **sample-and-hold** modules offer interesting possibilities for generation of random sequences of frequency, just as sequencers offer the possibility of

Figure 5.3. Combining waveforms. When added, one waveform appears to modify or displace portions of another.

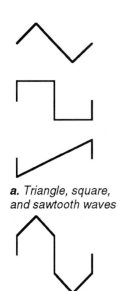

a. Triangle, square, and sawtooth waves

b. Triangle + square

c. Square + sawtooth

d. Triangle + sawtooth

e. All three

creating controlled sequences that can be played while the composer is doing something else. These modules provide control voltages for analog frequency modulation that are not dependent on real-time keyboard performance technique for the creation of melodic material (a blessing for those whose keyboard skills are somewhat rusty). Composers who prefer to specify the overall, or global, parameters for some portion of a composition with less concern for determining the specific order of tones in a piece will find random generation devices to be of great utility, while others who wish to specify details but lack the performing ability or lack the requisite number of hands (often three or four at once) can use a sequencer to achieve the precision they desire.

Two kinds of information are necessary to create analog sequences: pitch information in the form of control voltage, and duration. Control voltage values can be entered by setting a series of potentiometers to the desired values or by pressing the appropriate keys on the keyboard if the sequencer can be set to record this information. Duration can be determined quite simply by a clock, which may be an LFO producing a square wave. Each pulse advances the sequence one step. Upon reaching the final step, the sequencer returns to the first step and continues cycling through the sequence.

On some sequencers, duration values are also recorded. Usually one can adjust the clock speed so that the sequence can be entered slowly and played back in a faster tempo. It should be possible to correct individual control voltage and duration values. Sequencers are either monophonic or polyphonic, allowing in the latter case more than one key value to be recorded at a time. MIDI-equipped microcomputers, most current hardware sequencers, and a number of synthesizers and samplers have this type of sequencer. It functions somewhat like a tape recorder, allowing sequences to be saved to disk for later playback (see chapters ten and eleven for more discussion of MIDI sequencers).

Another option on potentiometer-based sequencers is that there may be more than one bank of pots that can be cycled through in parallel. This allows two or more different sets of voltages to be produced at the same time, each controlling a different module. While this type of sequencer requires more setup time to achieve correct voltage settings, it has an advantage over keyboard-based sequencers in that it is not limited to the equal-tempered pitch system. This is also its weakness: one must have a good ear—or use some tuning device—to establish precise intonation.

Once a sequence is created, it may be used to provide pitch and timing information in place of the keyboard. The sequence itself contains no timbral information, so it must modulate a generation module to produce an audible product. Some analog sequencers may cycle fast enough, either with the built-in clock or through provision for an external clock, to produce an audio waveform. In this case the sequencer output may itself be treated as an audio signal, with changes in the voltage settings of individual steps producing changes in timbre.

TIMBRE

The potential for diversity of timbre is an aspect of electronic music that can be explored on even the smallest analog and digital synthesizers. With but a single low-pass filter and several control sources, a synthesizer may produce a rich palette of sonic effects. In FM the amplitude of the modulator is used to modify the frequency of the tone generator. In **formant modulation**, control amplitude acts upon the cutoff point of a voltage-controlled filter or digital counterpart. In pulse width modulation, the duty cycle of a pulse wave can be controlled. This product can be further modified in the filter.

FORMANTS

A formant may be thought of as a frequency or range of frequencies that is emphasized. Most rooms and musical instruments will have one or more formant areas. Formants are particularly noticeable in the shower or in an empty stairwell. On a filter the formant created by the Fc can be brought out by using the filter resonance control. As resonance increases, the filter increasingly emphasizes the cutoff frequency. At a certain point, some analog filters break into oscillation and can be used to some extent as generation modules, particularly for microtones.

This effect can be exploited to tune the filter. With a high resonance setting, the filter can be manually swept through its range. As the Fc equals the frequencies of the various harmonic components of the audio signal it emphasizes them. When the desired frequency is reached, the resonance control may be turned down to make the resonance more subtle, or left where it is, depending upon the sound quality one is after.

TYPICAL PROCEDURES

One approach to instrument design involves developing a consistent timbre throughout the range of an instrument. An LFO controlling a filter allows for some variety within this consistency. With a low input amplitude, and the LFO set at 6 to 10 Hz, a nice shimmery effect is produced.

As the amplitude of the control source is increased, the Fc is swept over a wider frequency range. Silence, or a very low amplitude, is produced when the Fc is pushed low. If this is not desired, the Fc may be adjusted upward to offset the lower end of the sweep. This will of course increase the maximum reached by the filter. Should this maximum then be too high, the amplitude of the modulating signal may be reduced to compensate.

While this type of formant modulation is interesting, it becomes predictable, due to the periodic nature of the LFO. An interesting effect can be obtained if the synthesizer has an LFO whose own frequency can be controlled by the keyboard. As an ascending scale is played, for example, the keyboard output increases in voltage or MIDI note number, producing a corresponding increase in the LFO frequency.

As in frequency and amplitude modulation, when the frequency of the LFO passes the threshold of hearing a more complex waveform is created. In this case the ear perceives both the audio signal and the oscillation of the Fc as well. This results in the production of **sidebands**.

Envelopes are useful in simulating acoustic instruments. The initial attack, with the subsequent decay to a steady-state level, is evocative of the effect produced by acoustic instrumental envelopes. The effect of an electronic envelope is generally much simpler than its acoustic counterpart. With different envelope settings for filter and amplifier, one can hint at the complexity of most acoustic instruments.

OTHER CONTROL SOURCES

Virtually any analog module that produces voltage has control possibilities for formant modulation; digital synthesizers are often more limited, depending on the nature of the waveform generation process. In addition to the previously-mentioned modules several others are useful. Keep in mind that the focus here is on the small synthesizer. Larger instruments offer more control possibilities, as well as other filter configurations.

Analog sequencers may prove useful, functioning as a substitute for the keyboard by providing voltage and duration information. This information is usually used to control VCO frequency and filter Fc through control voltage inputs and to provide trigger and gate voltages for envelope generators. On synthesizers with sufficient flexibility, a sequencer may be dedicated to providing control information for the filter independent of any real-time keyboard activity. This can add an element of unpredictability to an instrument. Some sequencers may have more than one output channel, allowing one voltage pattern to be sent to the VCO and another pattern to the VCF.

Figure 5.4. Sample-and-hold gating

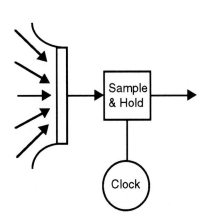

b. A sawtooth may be turned into stairs. . .

a. Input is sampled at the rate set by the clock and output until the next sample is taken.

c. Or may produce a less regular succession by being sampled at a rate that does not coincide with its period.

MIDI sequencers can actually have an analogous effect on a melodic line. They may be able to send system exclusive information allowing parameter changes to a patch on the fly. Alternatively, several versions of a patch may be created ahead of time and the sequencer can send patch change information to give the effect of changes in timbre, even though they are not really dynamic in the same sense as on their analog counterpart.

Audio VCOs and other analog sources such as noise generators provide the opportunity for the creation of more complex signals. Random noise, as opposed to white noise, may be available as a control source. It can provide subtle changes in Fc to avoid the all-too-steady state of most electronic sounds. A low LFO amplitude, done subtly, can also serve this function.

Another analog source of random voltages is the Sample-and-Hold module (see figure 5.4). Often used in conjunction with a noise generator, this module outputs voltages selected at regular intervals from the voltage input. With a noise source as the input voltage, the sampled voltages will tend to be fairly random. These voltages may be used for modulating frequency, timbre, or amplitude.

The keyboard may also have a control function beyond its standard role. Route an audio signal that is not dependent on the keyboard for pitch determination through a low-pass filter whose cutoff frequency can be modified by pressing various keys. The higher keys brighten the tone color, while lower keys produce a darker tone.

PULSE WIDTH

Interesting timbral effects can be obtained through dynamic modulation of the duty cycle of the pulse wave. Rather than affecting the amplitude of a region of frequencies, as on a filter, the change of duty cycle causes a rich spectrum shift. Modulating with a low-frequency sine or triangle wave allows a gradual sweeping of the range of possible pulse wave settings. For this procedure, choose a medium pulse width value: should the sweep be too large, the output returns a DC voltage on some analog synthesizers (not terribly useful in an audio signal). The use of other low-frequency waveforms results in pulse width behavior characteristic of the controlling waveform's shape.

As the sweep takes place, the harmonic spectrum constantly changes, producing a rich, always-evolving waveform. As the LFO frequency is increased, the periodic nature of the sweep becomes quite apparent. The amplitude of the PWM should be controllable, whether on the LFO itself, or on the synthesizer's modulation section, or on the generation module's control input section. As with formant modulation, almost any source can be used for PWM. Envelope control of PWM is often useful. It may be possible to use the same envelope to control the filter and the pulse width, adding brilliance and warmth not found without PWM.

AMPLITUDE

An amplifier functions as a gate. When it is closed, no signal should be heard, even if the input signal has a high intensity level. At its maximum, the amplifier allows unity gain. On analog synthesizers, the VCA's initial gain setting can be controlled manually by establishing an offset voltage level. When used in conjunction with an envelope, the initial gain is usually set at minimum. This avoids any signal leakage from the VCF, which usually precedes it in the signal path, since the filter's Fc may not necessarily be set at minimum. Some small synthesizers may not have a specific initial gain pot; instead, the sustain pot of an ADSR, in conjunction with a gate enable/disable switch, may serve this function. When the gate is enabled, the sustain pot may be manually adjusted to control the amplitude of the audio signal; when the gate is disabled, the initial gain is internally set at minimum, and the sustain pot has its usual function.

Some analog VCAs have both normal and inverting inputs. In the latter, the polarity of the input voltage is reversed, so that a rising slope becomes a descending slope (figure 5.5a). This is useful for the development of more complex instruments, such as the panning instrument shown in figure 5.5b. The effect of this patch, using an LFO and an inverting VCA as pan source, is to make the sound appear to move from one speaker to the other at the rate determined by the frequency of the LFO. Other control voltages and values may also be pan sources, making amplitude a function of pitch, velocity, envelope shape, and a range of MIDI options including aftertouch.

VCAs often have a switch to allow operation in either linear or exponential modes. There may also be linear and exponential control inputs. If the owner's manual does not say much about this, the VCA is probably exponential, since this is in keeping with the way we perceive sound. Digital amplifiers are generally simpler, providing primarily the ability to shape the amplitude of the audio signal with the assistance of an envelope.

TYPICAL PROCEDURES

The procedure for using control sources in amplitude modulation is the same as previously discussed for other types of modulation. Some synthesizers don't allow the LFO to control the VCA, however. An amplifier with a low input amplitude, modulated by an LFO outputting a sine or triangle wave at 6-10 Hz, produces a tremulo. You may need to advance the VCA gain slightly (increase the offset level) when it is being modulated, since otherwise the audio signal may periodically become inaudible as control values reach their minimum amplitude. The composer can create a variety of effects with different low-frequency control waveforms, different frequencies, and different input amplitudes. As the LFO frequency approaches 16 to 20 Hz, sidebands are produced.

The final stage in most synthesizer instruments is a VCA or other amplifier whose gain may be controlled by an envelope. As mentioned previously, with the amplifier initial gain set at minimum and no gate, no sound gets through. As a key on the keyboard is pressed, or some other controller is played appropriately, gate and trigger voltages or messages are sent to the envelope, which then opens and closes the amplifier according to its settings.

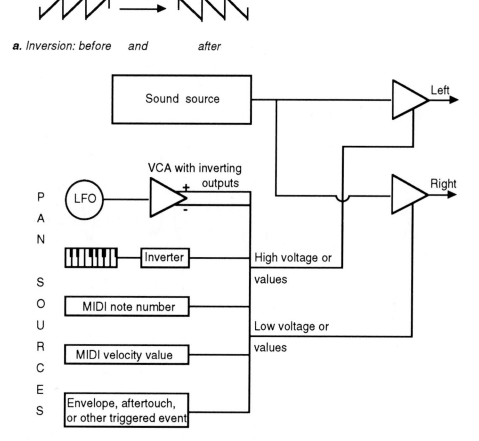

Figure 5.5. Wave inversion and panning

a. Inversion: before and after

b. A panning patch with a variety of possible pan sources. Panning can be periodic (controlled by an LFO), dynamically responsive (pitch, velocity, or other values), and shaped (envelope, aftertouch, other events).

OTHER CONTROL SOURCES

On many small synthesizers, there are few amplitude modulation possibilities. More flexible synthesizers may allow indirect sequencer or Sample-and-Hold control (through gate/trigger control of an envelope), audio generation module or random noise control, MIDI control, and even keyboard control. The latter procedure is similar to the keyboard control of the filter mentioned earlier: as the keyboard control voltage or MIDI note number rises, the amplifier gain rises, providing that the keyboard control output is patched into an amplifier control input or the keyboard control is enabled. This effect can be simulated on the filter if there is a means of enabling the keyboard control of the filter (on some synthesizers this may be called "keyboard follow").

SOUND GENERATION AND MODIFICATION

The use of audio-range waveforms for modulation purposes was, for most commercial synthesizer use, a bit of a dead end in the days of analog synthesis. For others, however, it was a rich source of sonic material that led, eventually, to some of the current digital synthesis procedures. Before looking at Yamaha's FM synthesis, audio-range procedures often used on analog synthesizers are presented.

AUDIO-RANGE MODULATION

The advantage of working with a limited set of synthesizer modules is found in working with, against, and through, those limitations. The sonic possibilities of this set have not

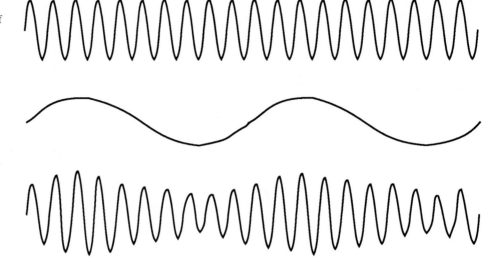

Figure 5.6. Amplitude modulation. The amplitude of one signal may be varied according to the amplitude and frequency of a second, controlling signal.

yet been fully explored in this chapter. Richer, more complex sounds can be created by audio-range modulation of the audio signal. If this is possible on your synthesizer, you have by now undoubtedly already tried it, whether on purpose or by accident. Modulation of amplitude, frequency, and timbre may be possible.

AM WITH SINE WAVES

Many small synthesizers do not have the flexibility to allow much exploration of amplitude modulation. Even so, it is the best point of departure for a study of audio-range modulation. In low-frequency modulation, one often "hears" the contour of the modulating wave as it modifies some parameter of the audio wave. Figure 5.6 shows the effect of amplitude modulation on a sine wave. As the modulating wave approaches the audio range, the fluctuations caused by the modulating wave shape increase. As the 16-20 Hz threshold is reached, sidebands are produced.

If both modulating and modulated signals are sine waves, audio-frequency AM will produce at least three signals. In addition to the modulated signal, or **carrier**, upper and lower sidebands representing the sum of and difference between the modulating signal, or **program**, and the carrier will be present. These sidebands are softer than the carrier signal and tend to be nonharmonic overtones and subtones, thus allowing the construction of more complex timbres than are produced by VCOs. If, for example, a 500 Hz sine wave were amplitude modulated by a 100 Hz sine wave, the spectrum of the resulting signal would the 500 Hz carrier plus sidebands at 400 Hz and 600 Hz (figure 5.7a).

AM WITH MORE COMPLEX SIGNALS

Program and carrier signals may contain more than one frequency component. The signal may be a waveform with a high harmonic content such as a sawtooth or a rich pulse wave, or may be the result of mixing two or more signals to create a more complex signal. Two sidebands will be produced for every component of a program or carrier.

Figure 5.7b shows the effect of the first three partials of a 100 Hz triangle wave modulating a 500 Hz sine wave. The first partial (100 Hz) creates sidebands at 400 and 600 Hz, the second (300 Hz) gives sidebands at 200 and 800 Hz, and the third (500 Hz) adds a sideband at 1000 Hz. Since the amplitude of the partials of a triangle wave decreases by $1/n^2$, the sidebands will diminish greatly in amplitude the farther they are from the carrier frequency.

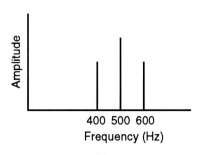

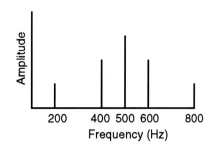

Figure 5.7. Amplitude
modulation spectra

a. *500z sine modulated
by 100 Hz sine*

b. *500 Hz sine modulated
by 100 Hz triangle*

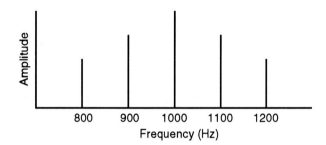

Figure 5.8. Frequency
modulation spectrum. A 1000
Hz sine is modulated by a 100
Hz sine with a modulation
index of 2.

FREQUENCY MODULATION

In both AM and FM, program signal frequency and amplitude are important in determining the resulting wave shape. In AM, the program frequency determines the rate of carrier amplitude change and the program amplitude determines the amount of change. As the program frequency increases, this amplitude change becomes audible in the form of sidebands. FM also depends upon these two parameters of the program signal, but with different, often richer, results.

As with amplitude modulation, frequency modulation in the audio range produces sidebands. Unlike AM more than one sideband may be produced on either side of the carrier. The interval between sidebands again is dependant upon the frequency of the program signal, with the number of sidebands being determined by a **modulation index**.

For example, assume that a 1000 Hz sine wave (the carrier) is modulated by a 100 Hz sine wave (the program). If the amplitude of the program signal is set to cause the carrier frequency to modulate up to 1200 Hz and down to 800 Hz, a **peak frequency deviation** of 200 Hz occurs. Dividing the peak frequency deviation (here 200 Hz) by the program frequency (here 100 Hz) yields a modulation index of 2. This means that the number of significant sidebands on each side of the carrier in this example is 2, for a total of 4 (see figure 5.8). Any sidebands existing beyond the peak frequency deviation will be quite weak. For practical purposes, they can be ignored.

As the number of sidebands increases, the amplitude of the carrier decreases. If one wishes, it is possible to have the total amplitude of the carrier signal distributed over the frequency spectrum of the modulated signal. This will weaken the pitch definition of the modulated signal. Experimentation with various modulation indexes will soon show the wide range of percussive and clangorous sounds that can be produced with FM.

It is, of course, possible to frequency modulate with program and carrier signals other than sine waves. The results will often be complex. A modulation index must be calculated for each frequency component of the program signal. If the components of the program signal have a harmonic relationship, the upper partials may actually reinforce existing sidebands.

Table 5.1. Frequency
modulation

PARTIAL 1 (50 Hz)	PARTIAL 3 (150 Hz)	PARTIAL 5 (250 Hz)
700	700	
750		750
800		
850	850	
900		
950		
	(1000 Hz carrier)	
1050		
1100		
1150	1150	
1200		
1250		1250
1300	1300	

Figure 5.9. Formant
modulation patches

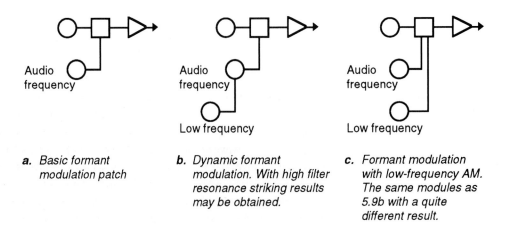

a. *Basic formant*
modulation patch

b. *Dynamic formant*
modulation. With high filter
resonance striking results
may be obtained.

c. *Formant modulation*
with low-frequency AM.
The same modules as
5.9b with a quite
different result.

Table 5.1 offers such an example. A 1000 Hz sinewave is modulated by a 50 Hz
square wave with an amplitude that causes a 300 Hz peak frequency deviation. For the
first three partials, modulation indexes of 6, 2, and 1 are produced, giving the frequencies
shown in the table. The use of nonharmonic spectra in FM will produce even thicker
spectra, although the availability of such spectra varies from synthesizer to synthesizer.

TIMBRE MODULATION

Both pulse width and formant modulation fall under the heading of **timbre modulation**.
In pulse width modulation the duty cycle is modulated, causing a rapid shift in the spectrum of the pulse wave. In formant modulation the filter Fc setting is modulated.

In the absence of audio-frequency AM, formant modulation (figure 5.9a) offers a
useful substitute. It can also be done dynamically, as in figure 5.9b, which causes the
modulating signal to itself be frequency-modulated over time.

Another AM-like patch is shown in figure 5.9c. In this patch low- and audio-
frequency control contours are mixed. The result is that the audio-frequency formant
modulated output varies in amplitude according to the frequency and amplitude of the
low-frequency input. In addition to periodic contours, control sources may include envelopes and, in MIDI systems, information from various MIDI controllers.

Figure 5.10. Flowchart of
basic operator functions

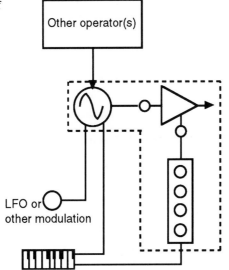

Table 5.2 Ratio tuning
frequencies

RATIO VALUE	FREQUENCY IF PARTIAL 1=440 Hz
.5	220
1	440
.	.
.	.
2	880
.	.
4	1760
.	.
.	.
.	.

FM SYNTHESIS

Yamaha developed commercial procedures based on the FM principle discussed earlier in this chapter: an audio-frequency carrier may be modulated by an audio-frequency program or **modulator.** The heart of this approach is the **operator,** a digital function which combines the procedures of sine wave generation with sound amplification. The sine wave frequency may be controlled by a keyboard or other MIDI controller, LFO, pitch envelope, and other operators. The amplifier may be controlled by an ADSR envelope with selectable levels and rates. An operator may function as either a carrier or a modulator. Figure 5.10 shows the operator in flowchart notation.

Operators are combined into various **algorithms**, or configurations. The number of possible algorithms depends on the number of operators available on the synthesizer. The DX 21 has four operators, which may be combined to produce eight different algorithms. The DX 7, long the flagship of the DX line, has six operators which may be combined to produce 32 different algorithms.

BASIC OPERATION

There are two ways to tune the sine wave in an operator: fixed frequency, and ratio. In the former, a specific frequency is selected and maintained, regardless of note number (this corresponds to turning off the keyboard control voltage or not patching the keyboard into a VCO on an analog synthesizer). In the latter, a frequency range is selected by picking a ratio number, with "1" indicating standard pitch (A3=440 Hz), "2" iindicating an octave higher, "4" yet another octave higher, and so on. Table 5.2 shows selected ratio values and their frequencies when the initial frequency is 440 Hz. The ratio number becomes important when operators are combined in algorithms.

The best way to understand an algorithm is to consider the simple pairing of two operators. If they are both carriers, their output is mixed, much as the output of two VCOs is mixed (see figure 5.11a). By setting parallel carriers to appropriate frequency ratios, simple additive synthesis may be carried out. Additional features found on some FM synthesizers allow level scaling of operators, so that keyboard splits may be created, with some operators responding to low notes while others respond to high notes.

Operators may also be coupled so that the output of one modulates the other (figure 5.11b). The result of this is to produce sidebands, much like the earlier-discussed FM. Since the primary parameters in each operator that vary are amplitude and frequency,

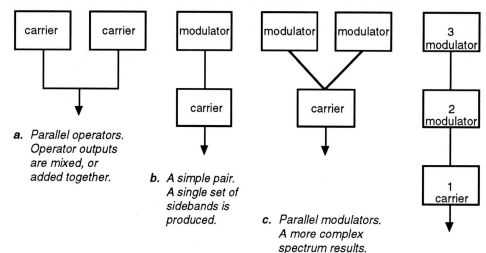

Figure 5.11. Various algorithms

a. Parallel operators. Operator outputs are mixed, or added together.

b. A simple pair. A single set of sidebands is produced.

c. Parallel modulators. A more complex spectrum results.

d. Stacked modulators. A simple sideband set is produced by operators 2 and 3; each of these sidebands modulates operator 1.

Figure 5.12. From algorithm to flowchart. Modulator and carrier frequency and amplitude have functions that relate closely to the three phases of the analog signal path.

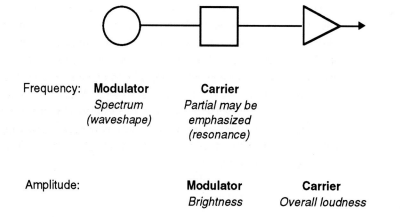

Frequency: **Modulator**   **Carrier**
             Spectrum   *Partial may be*
             (waveshape)   *emphasized*
                               (resonance)

Amplitude: **Modulator**   **Carrier**
                               Brightness   *Overall loudness*

each parameter has a different effect on the output. Varying the modulator frequency affects the harmonic spectrum (the distance of sidebands from the carrier is determined by adding and subtracting the frequency of the modulator from the carrier). Varying the modulator amplitude affects the brightness of the sound (higher amplitudes put more energy into the sidebands and less into the carrier frequency). Varying the carrier frequency alters the partial that is emphasized (much like resonance), while varying the carrier amplitude affects the overall loudness of the sound.

This is summarized in flowchart notation in figure 5.12. The figure shows a correspondence between the three main modules in the analog synthesizer sound path and the four parameters in the carrier/modulator pair.

RATIOS AND TIMBRES

In general, the more complex the ratio of carrier to modulator, the more complex the resulting timbre. To some extent, whether the ratio is simple or more complex, it is possible to determine the sideband content of the resulting waveform. Since the modulation index is not available on FM synthesizers (at least as of the early 1990s), the actual number of pairs of sidebands present in any sound is somewhat dependent on one's ear.

Table 5.3. Ratio rules

MODULATOR RATIO	RESULT	TIMBRE
1	Fundamental always present	All harmonics. Ratio 1/1 yields sawtooth-like wave
2	Odd harmonics	Like square wave
3	Every third partial missing	Like pulse with duty cycle 1:3
Even	Odd harmonics	Hollow
≥5	...if carrier is also integer:	Some combination of harmonically-related partials; may include fundamental
Non-integer	Non-harmonic partials	Often distorted, metallic, or bell-like

Steve De Furia, in *The Secrets of Analog and Digital Synthesis*, presents a number of rules about ratios and the timbres they produce. These are summarized in table 5.3. To find the set of possible sidebands in any carrier/modulator pair, add and subtract the modulator value from the carrier, then add and subtract the modulator value from those two values, and so on. Figure 5.13a shows this procedure for a 5/1 ratio, and also demonstrates the rule that the resulting spectrum is sawtooth-like (figure 5.13b shows the spectrum in standard harmonic order). Negative sideband numbers are out of phase.

Modulator and carrier values need not be integers. A non-integer value in either one will cause non-harmonic partials in the resulting spectrum. These can produce rather interesting and colorful results.

ALGORITHMS

Algorithms can be either simple or complex. Simple algorithms use one or more sets of carrier/modulator pairs. Complex algorithms contain either parallel modulators (two modulators act on a single carrier) or at least one modulator stack (figure 5.11c). Stacked modulators produce complex non-harmonic partials. This happens because the first pair produces a harmonic spectrum, which then modulates a third operator, producing a harmonic spectrum for each member of the previous harmonic spectrum (figure 5.11d).

DYNAMIC MODULATION

It is normal to have tone-generating modules respond consistently to DC control voltages or MIDI note messages, particularly for tuning and use with a keyboard. In order to achieve more interesting and complex musical material it is important that they also respond to other forms of control. A fascinating range of effects can be obtained by patching the output of an oscillator (LFO or VCO) or other module to a control input of a module in the basic signal path. The result may range from very subtle, in the case of a low-amplitude control signal from an LFO, to quite blatant, in the case of a high-amplitude audio-range control signal from a VCO.

Periodic waveforms, whether low or audio frequency, one-time envelopes from various envelope generators, and any other voltages that may be available on a particular synthesizer can contribute to the creation of a more dynamic instrument. Such an instrument

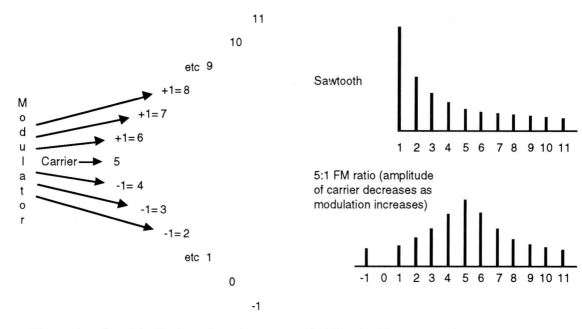

a. The number of partial pairs depends on the modulator amplitude (stronger yields more sideband pairs); the value of the pairs depends on the sum and difference of modulator and carrier.

b. This algorithm contains the same partial series as a sawtooth wave, but will sound somewhat different since the amplitude of partials decreases from partial 5, not partial 1; also partial -1 will be out of phase, lending a shimmer not usually found on a normal sawtooth.

Figure 5.13. Spectrum for 5:1 carrier/modulator ratio

need not resemble a traditional acoustic instrument in its sonic characteristics, although it should exhibit some characteristics analogous to the life found in sounds of traditional acoustic origin, where the relationships among the various parameters of sound are constantly changing.

If the *amplitude* of an FM program or modulator is varied over time, the peak frequency deviation will vary over time causing a dynamic shifting of the spectrum of the modulated signal. In similar fashion, varying the *frequency* of the program signal will also cause changes in the modulation index. Small synthesizers may not allow control of the program amplitude, but in many cases will allow control of the program frequency.

Since many analog synthesizers use exclusively exponential VCOs, it is important to be aware that with an increase in the FM program signal amplitude, there will be an upward shift in carrier and sideband frequencies. Although this shift may not be noticeable for low program signal amplitudes, it can become quite prominent at larger amplitudes. This phenomenon can have some effect on dynamic frequency modulation, but in the absence of linear VCOs any irregularities should just be considered to be part of the effect.

BEYOND THE DIGITAL WINDOW

In the "good old days" of electronic music, a patch could be as complicated as allowed by the available modules, since it was just a matter of patching modules together and controlling them from a keyboard or other controller. As patching became more of an internal function, what synthesizers gained in the ability to switch quickly from one stored sound to another they lost in flexibility of patching. This loss doesn't bother everyone, since many musicians like having a variety of sounds at their fingertips. With MIDI, however, there is the potential to return to the earlier days of modularity.

USING SYNTHESIZERS AS MODULES

A patch can consist of two or more instruments triggered by one MIDI controller. They can be on the same or different synthesizers. Sounds can be coupled at the same pitch level for chorusing effects or, with appropriate envelopes, for a crossfade effect from one sound to the other. Sounds can be coupled at different pitch levels to create a kind of fused sonority (this borrows from the concept of additive synthesis). Some envelope modification may be necessary to allow sounds to blend together properly.

With software like *Megalomania* or *Max*, discussed in chapter eleven, or with control over sensitivity to velocity or MIDI note number, a second patch could sound only when a minimum velocity or note number is reached or exceeded. This feature is also available on some synthesizers.

The important concept here is that one need not be limited by the physical constraints of one synthesizer. Cool FM sounds may be warmed up by doubling them with an analog synthesizer under MIDI control, for example (a MIDI-to-CV converter is useful). A xylophone patch may add an attack to a string patch. A brass ensemble may crossfade into a woodwind choir with appropriately designed envelopes.

SCALAR MATERIALS

Western music offers the musician a range of scales based on the division of the octave into 12 tones. The **major** and **minor** scales, consisting of patterns of half and whole steps, have developed from the Ionian and Aeolian modes, respectively. These and other modes were part of a theoretical system of music, known as Gregorian chant, that was available to medieval church musicians. Using only the white, or letter-name keys of the piano keyboard, Ionian starts on C, Dorian on D, Phrygian on E, Lydian on F, Mixolydian on G, Aeolian on A, and Locrian on B (figure 5.14a). Although they have been around for a while, modes offer a way to inject a feeling of newness into otherwise standard musical material.

Since synthesizers or microcomputer-based music systems are both more and less than traditional musical instruments, they should have their own idiom. Part of their idiomatic character should be based on the openness of the performer or composer to the exploration of scalar materials. In addition to modes, whole-tone scales, pentatonic scales, other scalar patterns such as those organized by French composer Olivier Messiaen into "modes of limited transposition," and original scales should be explored (figure 5.14b).

Since the Western world became aware of Eastern cultures, Western musicians have been fascinated and stimulated by the Eastern musics. The relationship between scale and a piece of music often seems more integral. Equal temperament represents a compromise between natural tuning and the musician's desire to play in all keys. Other musics have not necessarily accepted this compromise. Although a study of Indian raga or Javanese gamelan is not possible here, such an investigation may offer new insights into musical relationships, scales, and certainly tone color.

MICROTONES

One way to develop richer tonal relationships (or, if not richer, then at least new and unusual to our ears) is to explore microtonal divisions of the octave. These could allow the creation of scales that still use the standard seven primary tones like the major/minor system, but with the dividend of slightly different-sized **intervals**. They also allow the creation of even more unique scales leading to the development of more exotic melodies and chords. Combined with studies of timbre, this could lead to the development of a unique and idiomatic approach to the use of electroacoustic instruments.

Composer Easley Blackwood has written a series of 12 microtonal etudes exploring scales with 13 to 24 tones to the octave. In an article in *Keyboard Magazine* he discussed

Figure 5.14. Scales and modes

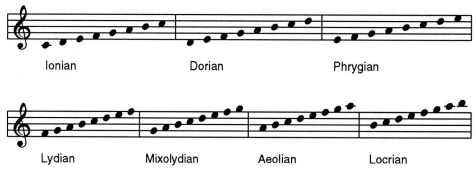

a. Church modes

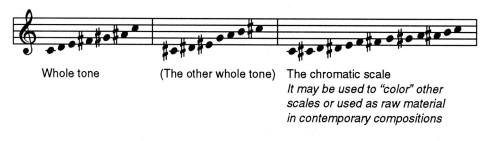

b. Other useful scales

his work and microtones. He found that the 24-tone scale (the quarter-tone scale) is probably the least interesting, primarily because the standard 12-tone scale is an easily accessible subset. To create this scale on analog synthesizers the keyboard control voltage should be attenuated so that it takes two octaves of the keyboard to double the frequency.

For **serial** music (a contemporary art music in which tones, considered to be of equal significance, are arbitrarily fashioned into a series that is then subjected to various operations, thus generating a piece of music) the 13- and 23-tone scales were considered good, since they are quite different from the 12-tone scale. The 19-tone scale Blackwood suggests is the easiest to learn after 12, although it is hard to imagine how the scale will sound (and those with perfect pitch will find themselves at somewhat of a loss).

Blackwood explored each scale, trying to develop melodic and harmonic usages that were appropriate. For those composers who find harmonic progression to be an important element, microtonal scales allow one to develop chords that will be somewhat out of tune, but analogous to familiar ones. On monophonic synthesizers it may be best to explore the melodic aspects of microtones, since chord progressions require the use of tape recorders for either **multitrack** or **sound-on-sound** operations.

MICROTONAL INSTRUMENTS

In *A Theory of Evolving Tonality* (New York: DaCapo Press, 1975), Joseph Yasser suggested that music may be moving toward a microtonal scale. Just as the **pentatonic** scale, represented by the five raised keys on the music keyboard, was once standard, and we

BOX · 5.1

TEMPERAMENT

When two tones are sounded together, they form an interval. When the ratio of their frequencies forms a simple numeric ratio, the interval is most in tune. An octave (a distance of eight scale degrees, or steps—for example, C D E F G A B C in the case of an ascending C major scale) has the ratio 2:1. When the strings of a harpsichord are tuned using the ratio 3:2 (a perfect fifth, from C to G using the previous example) certain intervals end up not being quite in tune (C to G is tuned, then G to D, then D to A, then A to E). This procedure, called just intonation, requires some tempering of intervals to avoid this problem.

Various temperaments are feasible, but the one that has gained widest acceptance in Western music is equal temperament. This is predicated on an equal division of the octave. In so doing, the tempering process actually creates a compromise intonation that is out of tune in terms of some of the intervals of just intonation, but that avoids some of the extreme problems of the latter.

Since most musicians have been raised on equal temperament, they don't know any better. Equal temperament is a simple system, particularly well suited for electronics. It has allowed composers greater freedom with musical pitches, particularly in the area of harmony. The 12-tone-per-octave, equal-tempered system also provides a standardization that allows many different instruments to play together. Although most electronic music systems rely exclusively on 12-tone-per-octave equal temperament, some allow exploration of systems with more than 12 tones per octave—a fascinating musical arena that has long been underdeveloped.

have moved to seven-tone scales and beyond to 12-tone scales, so may we eventually see the 19-tone scale in a more respectable light, according to Yasser. A number of twentieth-century composers have explored various scales, with some going so far as to develop their own instruments to allow a fuller expression of their creative vision.

In the 1970s Motorola developed the Scalatron, a fascinating electronic instrument that allowed each key to be tuned. This allowed not only the exploration of microtones, but also the exploration of tuning systems other than **equal temperament**. Unfortunately, this instrument didn't catch on, and as of the early 1990s microtones are still considered to be esoteric. There has also been a revival of acoustic instruments capable of various historical temperaments. Perhaps electronic manufacturers will decide to pursue this and develop instruments that will allow consumers to explore this area, as well as microtones.

Microtones are accessible on some analog synthesizers by patching the keyboard control voltage into an attenuator-controlled VCO control voltage input. This makes it possible to attenuate the control voltage so that it takes more than one volt from the keyboard to double the frequency of the audio signal, producing more than 12 notes per

Table 5.4. Microtuning

CHROMATIC SCALE TONE	MAJOR SCALE DEGREE	DISTANCE FROM TONE 1 IN CENTS		DETUNING NEEDED IN CENTS	CZ DETUNE SETTING
		Equal Temperament	*Just Intonation*		
1	1	0.00	0.00	0.00	0
2		100.00	111.73	11.73	+7
3	2	200.00	203.91	3.91	+2
4		300.00	315.64	15.64	+9
5	3	400.00	386.31	-13.69	-8
6	4	500.00	498.04	-1.96	-1
7		600.00	590.22	-9.78	-6
8	5	700.00	701.96	1.96	+1
9		800.00	813.69	13.69	+8
10	6	900.00	884.36	-15.64	-9
11		1000.00	996.09	-3.91	-2
12	7	1100.00	1088.27	-11.73	-7
13	8	1200.00	1200.00	0.00	0

heard octave. Of course, this makes it more awkward to play standard scales and chords, since they require different, and often larger, keyboard spans to be covered.

Most small analog synthesizers will not allow exploration of this area without modification. One option that may be available involves using the VCF as an oscillator. If resonance can be set so that the filter oscillates, and if a potentiometer on the VCF controls the amplitude of the keyboard control voltage, one can at least try out microtones. In this case, the Fc pot functions to tune the filter.

On digital synthesizers, microtones may not be readily available, since MIDI is based on the 12-tone-per-octave scheme. Some synthesizers store a set of alternate temperaments in memory. These generally create irregular spacings between adjacent tones, based on historically useful schemes.

Two procedures offer access on digital synthesizers. The first involves instrument design, just as was the case with analog synthesizers. Multiple versions of an instrument may be created and stored, each tuned (or detuned) to a different pitch in the scale. Table 5.4 shows the tuning for **just intonation**, which allows certain intervals to be tuned more purely than is possible with equal temperament. In equal temperament there are 100 **cents** between each tone, or 1200 cents in an octave. In the table, the amount each tone is "off" from equal temperament is given in cents.

To tune a synthesizer patch, find out the number of steps available for fine tuning or detuning. On the CZ 101, for example, there are 60 steps, so a detuning of 50 cents will be done by setting the synthesizer detuning to 30. In the table, detuning amounts for a CZ 101 are given. On the CZ this involves using two sound paths, setting the amplifier of the first to a level of 0 and only using the second. Once a set of detuned patches is created, MIDI program change messages are used to select the right patch for each pitch.Other synthesizers may require similar work-arounds; experimentation may be needed to make this procedure work properly.

Another alternative, most effective with the help of a sequencer, is to send pitch bend information for each tone. If the bend range can be adjusted, set it for a **half step** (or one semitone, or step). Most pitch bend wheels have a center value of 64; increasing raises pitch, while decreasing lowers pitch. As with the CZ tuning mentioned earlier, this gives fewer than 100 values, so some calculation is needed to produce the closest value. Both approaches work well in mono- or multi-timbral modes, with one note per MIDI channel.

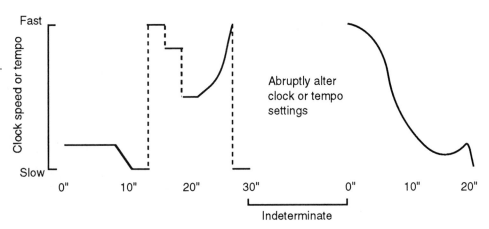

Figure 5.15. Score for exercise 5.3. Variety and interest is created by varying clock speed or tempo settings.

FOR FURTHER STUDY

Owner's manuals are an important aid in instrument design. Chapters eight and ten look at recording and sequencing basics, and may well be looked at in conjunction with further study in this area. Appendix E suggests ideas for further reading on page 265.

EXERCISES

As studio work is being done, be on the alert for unusual sounds or sequences of sonic events that develop. Devote a reel or a cassette tape to their storage (and RAM and disk space in the case of digital sounds and sequences), and also keep notes about each sound: where it may be found, the patch used to get that sound, how the keyboard was played, and so on. Each tape event should be "cushioned" by silence so that it can later be spliced out or re-recorded without disturbing neighboring events. This sonic library will prove to be a useful tool in later work, particularly if it is well documented so that finding a specific event is easy.

EXERCISE 5. 1

Explore the vibrato, siren, trill, and triad FM effects discussed in this chapter. Record short excerpts of particularly interesting versions.

EXERCISE 5.2

If the synthesizer allows, set up an amplitude modulation patch with an LFO. Tremulo may be obtained with an LFO frequency of 6-10 Hz and a low input amplitude. Try various settings.

EXERCISE 5.3

Perform the score given in figure 5.15. Program a 10- to 20-tone analog sequence or patch a sample and hold module or loop a MIDI sequence. With the synthesizer output patched to a tape echo (see figure 8.4) or delay device, "play" a piece by manipulating the clock speed to vary the speed of the sequence.

EXERCISE 5. 4

Set up a patch allowing microtonal scales on an analog synthesizer (figure 5.16a or b). If the keyboard amount on the VCF can only be set at full-half-off, then it may be possible to set up a 24-tone scale with the amount set at half. If the keys indicated in figure 5.16c are tuned an octave apart, a 19-tone scale will be produced. In using microtunings, it may

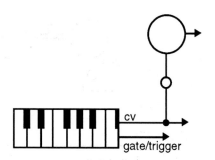

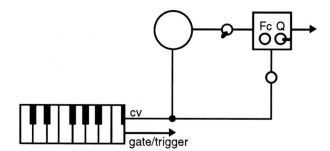

*a. Patch keyboard control voltage
   through attenuator to VCO*

*b. No audio signal enters VCF. With high resonance,
   vary keyboard amount controlling Fc to tune the filter.*

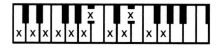

*c. Tune the marked keys one octave
   apart for 19-tone scale*

*d. An 11-tone subset, based on a simple pattern.
   Many interesting subsets may be found*

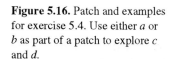

Figure 5.16. Patch and examples for exercise 5.4. Use either *a* or *b* as part of a patch to explore *c* and *d*.

be useful to develop a smaller subset, in the same way that major and minor scales are a subset of the 12-tone chromatic scale. An 11-tone subset is shown in figure 5.16d. Note that 12 tones are marked; the last is one octave higher than the first.

If the patch of figure 5.16b is used, it will take some care to get a pleasing sound. A medium-high register setting of the Fc along with short-to-medium VCA attack and decay settings may give a bell-like effect. The addition of a slight amount of LFO formant modulation may be nice, particularly if the amount of modulation can be controlled in performance by a modulation wheel.

Using the subset shown, or developing another, create and record a melody. Just as chromatic tones may enrich a diatonic melody, so may tones not in the subset be used occasionally, either by substituting for an adjacent subset member, or by embellishing a subset member.

EXERCISE 5.5

Modify the analog microtonal patch of figure 5.16b so that there is also sound from a VCO (see figure 5.17a). The filter resonance may produce a microtonal scale while the VCO produces a 12-tone scale. Explore this effect. Also try the variation of figure 5.17b, in which the audio VCO is pulse width modulated by an audio wave. The results of this patch can be a bit unpredictable, and rather delightful. Play a rising scale such as figure 5.16d and explore various settings of the two VCOs.

EXERCISE 5.6

Create a set of patches on a digital synthesizer exploring the discussion of microtones and table 5.4. Since methods of tuning or detuning presets vary from synthesizer to synthesizer, the owner's manual will be helpful. It may be necessary to set a pitch envelope (not likely to give the small increments necessary). The solution may not be immediately obvious. On the CZ 101, for example, detuning works best by setting the amplitude of one

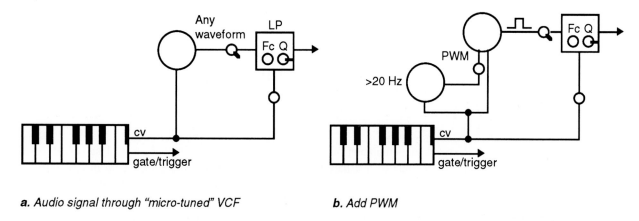

a. *Audio signal through "micro-tuned" VCF*   **b.** *Add PWM*

Figure 5.17. Patches for exercise 5.5

audio signal path to zero, and detuning the second path, so that only the detuned path sounds (this has a somewhat drastic effect on some patches!).

EXERCISE 5.7

Some exotic scale effects can be developed through microtones. With the aid of a multi-track tape recorder, an interesting multilayered piece can be built up by successive recording of sequences, each somewhat different from the others. MIDI systems can use a hardware or software sequencer, and apply pitch bend to each note as needed (refer to the discussion of table 5.4).

Channel one should contain the original sequence with medium to fast durations (end at the three-minute mark). Channel two enters after channel one has started with the same sequence altered to be higher in pitch and faster (end at about two and a half minutes). Channel three presents yet a further alteration of the sequence in a different register with different envelope settings, perhaps using figure 5.17a or b for the basic signal, slower than track one (end at three and a half minutes). Channel four enters at about the one-minute mark with a free improvisation on the original sequence, with mixed durations, occasional pauses, and periodic repetition of some melodic idea (end with or after track three).

EXERCISE 5.8

Explore LFO control of the filter frequency cutoff point. Experiment with changes in LFO waveform frequency and amplitude, filter Fc, and oscillator waveform. If the keyboard can control the frequency of the LFO, develop a short improvisation that takes advantage of this effect. Record the improvisation and construct a score (include patching information) that would allow someone else to perform the improvisation. If possible, have someone perform the score and compare the results.

EXERCISE 5.9

On an FM synthesizer, explore variations of an existing preset, focusing on changing modulator output levels and ratios. Develop several useful alternatives, exploring their use on different regions of the keyboard.

EXERCISE 5.10

Transfer a preset from one synthesizer to another, first making a parameter chart, then developing a flowchart and otherwise exploring how the preset functions. Reproduce the sound as best possible on the second synthesizer (this exercise requires synthesizers using different synthesis procedures, and works well with both digital and analog synthesizers).

EXERCISE 5.11

Explore the simulation of several acoustic sources, whether musical or not. Record the source sounds so that they are readily available for comparison with the developing instrument. Make appropriate documentation and record samples of the finished instruments. If a commercial version of the instrumental patch exists (in digital memory, patch books, or other documentation) compare your patch with it, noting the differences. Are they substantial or more cosmetic? Whose patch is better?

EXERCISE 5.12

Explore the various audio-range modulation procedures on synthesizers that allow them. Set up an audio-range AM patch (an oscillator should be patched to a control input on the amplifier). The only difference between this and low-frequency modulation is that an audio frequency wave is used to modulate the amplitude. Experiment with the modulating frequency and amplitude. What is the difference between controlling both the audio and the modulating oscillators by the keyboard as opposed to disabling the keyboard control of the modulator?

Create a patch allowing audio-range pulse width modulation. Explore its possibilities. What is the effect of different modulating waveforms?

Also explore audio-range formant modulation. Use a variety of program amplitudes and frequencies. If possible, compare the resulting signal with audio-frequency AM.

EXERCISE 5.13

Create an audio-range FM patch (quite simple on an FM synthesizer). Experiment with the modulating frequency and amplitude. With a given modulating frequency, try a wide range of modulating amplitudes. What happens to the signal? At several different modulating amplitudes, try a variety of modulating frequencies. Again, how is the signal affected? Keep a record of the more promising results (write down the various potentiometer or parameter settings). Also explore audio-frequency FM using waveforms other than sine or triangle. Keeping the carrier signal the same, vary the program signal waveform. Reverse the procedure by trying different carrier waveforms.

EXERCISE 5.14

Explore dynamic frequency modulation using a patch which varies the amplitude of the program signal over time. In the absence of the capability to modulate the amplitude of a control signal, the effect can be approximated by manually varying the amplitude pot for the program signal. Also try varying the frequency of the program signal over time.

While exploring dynamic FM, try different filter Fc settings. Also explore the effect of audio-range FM where the program, or modulator, is not under keyboard control. What is the effect caused by the absence of keyboard pitch information? Play a sequence or melody with the program signal controlled by keyboard pitch and then not controlled.

EXERCISE 5.15

Develop a freeform sonic fantasy on the theme of tuning the electronic orchestra (based on the marvelous cacophony that occurs when a symphony orchestra tunes). Use as many of the instruments developed in this chapter as possible. This is a good project to do with one or two colleagues, since it will give a larger pool of instruments and musical ideas. Record or sequence the piece.

In planning the fantasy, develop short melodic/rhythmic ideas appropriate to each instrument (part of orchestral tune-up often involves each musician getting some last-minute practice on some difficult passage or simply warming up on a favorite riff, as well as tuning the instrument to the orchestral A = 440 Hz). Make a rough score before recording, to plan where each instrument plays (they should not all play at once, since such a thick texture would not allow individual ideas to be heard). There should be much overlapping. Aim for a total length of two to four minutes.

VOCABULARY

Most of the following terms were used for the first time in this chapter. Some may be used differently than they were used earlier in the book. A definition of each term may be found in the glossary.

algorithm	amplitude modulation	carrier
cents	equal temperament	formant modulation
frequency modulation	half step	interval
just intonation	major	microtone
minor	modulation	modulation index
modulator	multitrack	operator
peak frequency deviation	pentatonic	program
pulse width modulation	sample-and-hold	serial
sideband	sound-on-sound	timbre modulation
vibrato		

REVIEW QUESTIONS

QUESTION 5.1

Match related terms by writing the letter of the term in the second column in the blank of the term in the first column that most closely relates to it.

Algorithm	_____	A.	LFO
Formant	_____	B.	Operator
Frequency	_____	C.	Pitch bend
Microtones	_____	D.	Program
Modulator	_____	E.	Ratio
Vibrato	_____	F.	Resonance

QUESTION 5.2

Compare and contrast the following terms.

Vibrato— Tremulo

_____

_____

_____

_____

Amplitude Modulation— Frequency Modulation

_____

_____

_____

_____

QUESTION 5.3

Define briefly.

Cent

_____

_____

_____

_____

Temperament

_____

_____

_____

_____

QUESTION 5.4

Provide the question for the given answer.

ANSWER	QUESTION
In AM with sine waves, the sidebands produced by a 1000 Hz carrier and a 200 Hz program.	What is _____ and _____ ?
A determining factor in the number of sidebands in FM with sine waves.	What is _____ ?
The determining factor in the distance between sidebands in FM.	What is _____ ?

CHAPTER · SIX

SAMPLERS

An important element in any sound is its waveform. As discussed in the previous two chapters, the waveform may be modified or combined with other waveforms and then given an amplitude envelope.

Rather than selecting from available waveforms or digitally synthesizing waveforms, it is possible to select a waveform from the entire world of sound through the use of a sampler. This involves several phases. A sound is recorded and stored on a sampler; it may be altered by various editing procedures either on the sampler or on a computer; the finished product is stored internally or on some external storage device (often some form of floppy disk) and recalled for use as needed.

SAMPLING ANALOG INPUT

To begin with, sound must be gotten into the sampler. A microphone is plugged into the microphone input, or a line-level signal is fed into the line input. There may be several steps to be followed on the sampler before actual sampling takes place:
- selecting a sample number or name or storage location;
- selecting a **sample rate** or bandwidth;
- selecting a reference pitch;
- monitoring the recording level;
- setting a minimum threshold or sensitivity level.

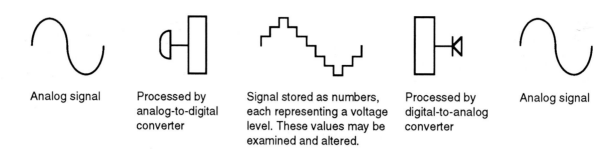

| Analog signal | Processed by analog-to-digital converter | Signal stored as numbers, each representing a voltage level. These values may be examined and altered. | Processed by digital-to-analog converter | Analog signal |

Figure 6.1. Converting signals: From analog to digital to analog

Once these steps have been taken, it is usually a fairly straightforward procedure to sample: start recording, and start the sample. As soon as the sample is recorded, it should be saved to disk or other storage medium before it gets lost or is modified.

WHAT IS RECORDED

A microphone converts sound into voltage. As voltage from a microphone or a line-level source enters the sampler, an **analog-to-digital converter** (ADC) converts the waveform to a succession of digital values, each representing the voltage level at a given instant (see figure 6.1). Each of these values is a **sample** (with the size of the sample typically ranging from 8 to 16 bits).

In order to accurately reproduce a waveform, at least two samples must be taken of each cycle. To record sound near the upper limit of human hearing a sample rate of at least 40,000 Hz (twice 20,000 Hz) is needed — actually, for technical reasons the rate needs to be somewhat higher (the standard Compact Disk rate is 44.1 KHz).

Samples use one of two general storage approaches: fixed or dynamic. In the former, memory is allocated statically, with a specific number of sample locations. In the latter, each successive sample follows the previous; shorter samples take less space, thus allowing more samples to be recorded.

Sequencers may also be available on a sampler. If memory is allocated dynamically, the musician may have to choose between the number of samples available and the length of a sequence.

QUALITY VERSUS QUANTITY

With either fixed or dynamic storage, the ability to adjust the sample rate affects the length of a sample for a given number of samples. For example, if 32,000 bytes are available, and each sample is one byte long, a half-second sound may be recorded with a sample rate of 32K. If the rate is reduced to 16K, a one-second sound will fit into the same space, while a rate of 8K will allow a two-second sound.

There is a penalty to be paid for the lower rate: a narrower band of frequencies may be recorded. For low-frequency sounds (including speech) this will make little difference. For many sounds, however, the result will be a dulling of the sound since sounds past one-half the sample rate will not be sampled properly

THE NYQUIST FREQUENCY

To accurately reproduce a waveform, the sample rate must be at least twice the frequency of the highest desired frequency (the **Nyquist theorem**). Passing this limitation causes **aliasing**, or **foldover**. The Nyquist frequency, half the sample rate, acts as a mirror, reflecting or folding over any frequency above it (see figure 6.2).

Phoney e
Not the Same

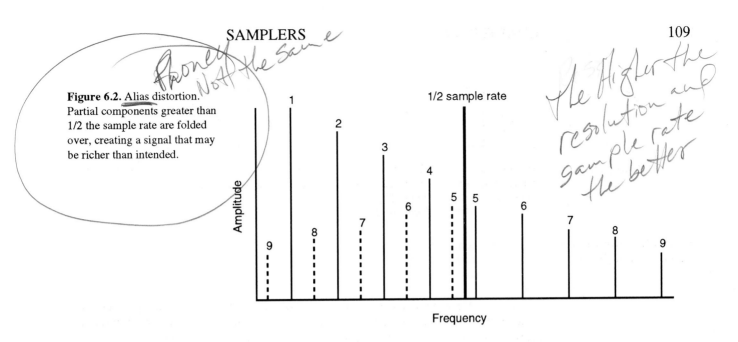

Figure 6.2. Alias distortion. Partial components greater than 1/2 the sample rate are folded over, creating a signal that may be richer than intended.

The Higher the resolution and sample rate the better

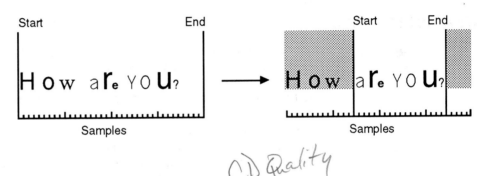

Figure 6.3. Truncating a sample: "How are you?" to "are you?" Moving start and endpoints normally does not change the sampled material; rather, it changes the portion we hear.

QUANTIZATION

CD Quality

Another element of the quality of a sample is the level of **resolution**, or **quantization**, of a sampler. An 8-bit sampler has 256 levels of amplitude (2^8) while a 12-bit sampler has 4096 levels (2^{12}) and 16 bits offer 65,536 levels (2^{16}). The greater the number of levels, the more accurate a single sample can be.

In general, therefore, a high sample rate and a high quantization will yield a high-quality sample. Of course, whatever is input is sampled, so every effort must be made to obtain a strong signal with little background noise.

Some sampler manufacturers have compensated for quantization levels by concentrating on better input and output filtering. Input filtering attenuates or filters unneeded high frequencies (to avoid the aliasing shown in figure 6.2) while output filtering helps smooth out the sound as it is converted from its digital version with a Digital-to-Analog converter, or DAC (to weaken the stair-step effect of quantization).

EDITING SAMPLES

In the early days of sampling, it was enough to get a recognizable recording of a sound. Once the sample is recorded, however, it may need to be modified for a specific use, or mixed with other samples. There are a number of basic editing procedures that should be accessible through the front panel of any sampler. In addition, there are more involved procedures that may be either onboard or available through sample editing programs on microcomputers. In the latter case, samples may usually be transferred between sampler and computer over MIDI cables, relying upon system exclusive programming.

BASIC MODIFICATIONS

If the threshold has been set properly, when a sample is played back, or triggered, it will start precisely when desired. There may be times, however, when the initial or ending portion of a sample is not wanted, either due to the presence of unwanted noise or due to

Figure 6.4. Basic loop types

Forward Loop *Particularly good for music excerpts, speech, and other events that need to be accurately reproduced*

a ꞓ. ʏ o ᴜ a ꞓ. ʏ o ᴜ a ꞓ. ʏ o ᴜ a ꞓ. ʏ o ᴜ

Alternating (Reversing) Loop *For steady tones, this type may smooth out any amplitude mismatch between start and end points*

a ꞓ. ʏ o ᴜ ᴜ o ʏ. ꞓ a a ꞓ. ʏ o ᴜ ᴜ o ʏ. ꞓ a

Crossfade Loop *Start and end regions have overlapping material to make a smoother loop*

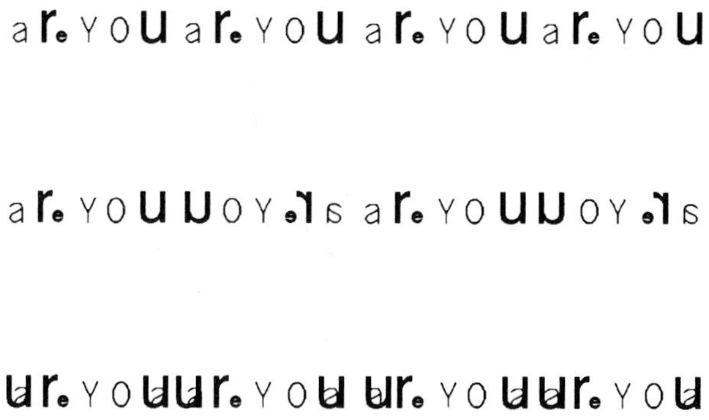

ᴜꞓ. ʏ o ᴜᴜꞓ. ʏ o ᴜ ᴜꞓ. ʏ o ᴜᴜꞓ. ʏ o ᴜ

Table 6.1. Summary of basic editing functions

PROCEDURE	FUNCTION
Create, Edit Loop	*Sustain loop*: Allow sample to continue while key is held *Release loop*: Allow sample to continue after key is released
Create, Edit Splice	Join two samples end-to-end to create a new sample *Butt*: Move abruptly from one to the other *Crossfade*: Move smoothly from one to the other through a transitional area containing elements of both samples
Edit Start Point	Remove unwanted sound or silence before desired sound
Edit End Point	Remove unwanted sound or silence after desired sound
Envelope	Shape amplitude, add release
Filter	Shape tone color, usually applying a low-pass filter to alter brightness and remove unwanted highs
Merge, Mix	Overlay all or parts of two samples to create a new sample
Modulate Sample	*LFO*: Add vibrato and other effects *Pitchbend* Other modulation options depend on specifications, and may include velocity or aftertouch control of filter and envelope levels

an interest in hearing only a portion of the sample. As shown in figure 6.3, it should be a fairly simple procedure to alter the starting or ending point of the sample on the sampler. This procedure is usually non-destructive (as with any procedure involving digital data, make backup copies before trying any modifications).

There are usually various modes of scanning the sample data. It should be easy to play a sample either forward or in reverse. One may be able to gate the sample so that a brief touch of a key causes the entire sound to occur (drum trigger) or, on the contrary, the touch of the key determines the length of the sample (one shot).

In this latter mode, looping becomes important if a sample needs to last longer than the original event. There are often different types of loops, such as forward loops, alternating loops, and crossfade loops, as shown in figure 6.4.

Figure 6.5. Loop with start and end points

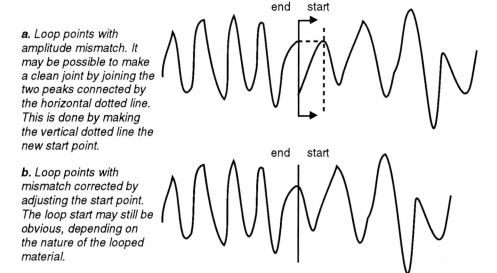

a. Loop points with amplitude mismatch. It may be possible to make a clean joint by joining the two peaks connected by the horizontal dotted line. This is done by making the vertical dotted line the new start point.

b. Loop points with mismatch corrected by adjusting the start point. The loop start may still be obvious, depending on the nature of the looped material.

Samplers usually allow some of the modification procedures found on synthesizers. These include an LFO for vibrato, some sort of filtering capability, some control over amplitude envelopes, tuning or transposing options (including the ability to have a sample play back at a constant pitch regardless of the key that is pressed), and the ability to configure (split and layer) the keyboard. Additional modulation capabilities through the use of MIDI controllers, various ways of layering and combining samples, and onboard effects add to the modification possibilities.

EDITING PROCEDURES

It is often worth the effort, even with full-featured samplers, to do editing on a computer, since the monitor displays the sample in more detail than samplers can. Editing programs often have more flexibility and more features, and may even offer the bonus of being able to take a sample from one sampler and change it into the format recognized by another sampler. With the development of a MIDI-based sample dump standard, this may become less important. Table 6.1 summarizes basic editing functions, which may take place either on the sampler or on the computer.

Generally useful tools include the ability to **cut, copy,** and **paste**. Cutting removes a selected portion of a sample and stores it in a buffer. This allows material to be moved from one region to another, or to simply be discarded. The edit buffer does not provide permanent storage, so material in the buffer will be lost if a new cut or copy procedure is initiated.

In copying, a selected region is again placed in the buffer, but this time without removing material from the sample. Material that has been cut or copied can be pasted into a desired location (either inserting the material, causing the old material after the insertion point to be shifted later in time, or overwriting old material).

LOOPS

As a sample is played back, it must be transposed as higher or lower pitches are desired. To do this, the sampler "plays" the data faster or slower. If the sample needs to be longer than originally recorded, it must be possible to loop the sample.

This procedure varies from sampler to sampler. It will often be possible to manually set loop points — a procedure that can be frustrating, since the end of the loop should flow smoothly into the start.

In figure 6.5 the end and start points of a loop are shown. Figure 6.5a shows an amplitude mismatch, which will cause a click each time the loop cycles. The dotted lines and arrows show that a smoother joint may be made by displacing the start point a little bit, at the next peak. The result of this operation is shown in figure 6.5b.

Table 6.2. Typical utility
functions

PROCEDURE	FUNCTION
Gain Change	Adjust the amplitude of some portion of a sample
Normalize	Set the amplitude of the loudest portion to 100% and scale the rest accordingly
Reverse	Reverse direction of some portion of a sample
Scaling	Adjust the display of the sample on either axis
Zero	Set the amplitude of some portion of a sample to zero
Zoom	Adjust the display to "zoom" in or out, concentrating on a small area or on an overall display

To create a loop, locate a fairly stable portion of the sample (remember that this portion will repeat, allowing a sustain function as a note is held or a release function as an envelope causes the sound to fade out). If possible, find repeating patterns in the displayed waveform and set the start point at some recognizable place on the pattern (a zero crossing or a peak, for example). Repeat this procedure at the endpoint, so that the the material at the end of the loop runs right into the material at the start of the loop.

Ideally this is all that needs to be done. If small clicks exist, it may be necessary to further fine-tune the start or end points. Many samplers will have automated procedures for determining loops that help relieve some of the drudgery associated with this procedure. If there are still clicks, it may be necessary to use another loop type, or to choose another loop location, or perhaps to begin anew with a fresh sample. Before going that far, if the material allows, try creating a **crossfade** loop.

In crossfade looping, material from the area around the end of the loop is mixed with material from the area at the start of the loop. It may not smooth out areas with violent amplitude disagreements, so crossfade looping still benefits from a stable loop area.

Since crossfade looping relies on procedures found on the sampler or in the editing program, it is difficult to generalize about features. It may be possible to select different types of crossfades, or to adjust the length of the crossfade. This procedure may also involve crossfading with material before and after the loop area.

SPLICES

A sample may also be lengthened or modified by splicing. Material may be shifted or copied from one portion of a sample to another, or from another sample. A **butt splice** simply places the start of the material being added at the insertion point, butting up against the end of the previous material. This causes an abrupt shift from one the one area to the next. As in looping, various crossfades may be available, to allow a smoother transition than the butt splice.

UTILITY FUNCTIONS

When cutting and pasting procedures are used, it is often possible to cause clicks at the edit points. These are the result of differences in amplitude between the various sample sections. There may be a smoothing function which reduces these clicks by creating crossfade at the edit points. This function may need to be selected before editing. Other functions that facilitate the editing process are summarized in table 6.2.

Figure 6.6. Velocity control of layering. Options vary from sampler to sampler.

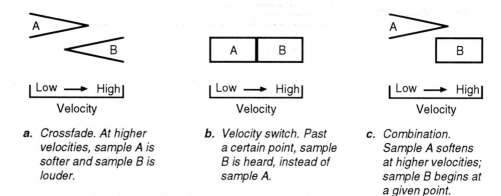

a. *Crossfade. At higher velocities, sample A is softer and sample B is louder.*

b. *Velocity switch. Past a certain point, sample B is heard, instead of sample A.*

c. *Combination. Sample A softens at higher velocities; sample B begins at a given point.*

MULTISAMPLES

Multisampling addresses a different problem than looping, splicing or smoothing. As a sample is transposed, as it must be to be played by a keyboard or other MIDI controller, some of its characteristics become less recognizable. For example, a piano sample may become more out-of-tune with itself or may become more artificial as it gets farther away from its reference pitch. The solution to this problem is to record a number of samples, each covering a different pitch region. Using the key range or configuration options, each sample is assigned to its portion of the keyboard. Often these programs or performance settings can be saved for easy recall. Naturally, the complexity of a multisample is dependent upon the number of samples that can be stored in sampler memory.

DESIGNING FOR PERFORMANCE

Several functions deal both with individual samples (as an aspect of instrument design) and with sets of samples (allowing samples to be combined, as in multisampling). These typically are front-panel performance options which can be stored either with a specific sample (in the case of key range and velocity sensitivity) or as part of a performance memory (in the case of keyboard configurations and MIDI setups).

There must be a way to determine the key range of a sample, usually by setting a low and high key or MIDI note number. This is called a **keyboard split** on some synthesizers. Key ranges may overlap for crossfade-type effects or may be duplicated for **layering**. The drawback of either of these is that the total number of notes playable at one time decreases, as one note is tying up two voices. If the layering isn't dynamic (modified by velocity, MIDI note number, or some modulation process) it may be better to mix the layered samples, creating a new sample and avoiding the voice duplication.

When layering is dynamically controlled by velocity, as velocity passes a certain point one sound gets weaker and another gets stronger (figure 6.6a). Rather than causing a fading in or out, velocity may cause a sample to switch on at a certain point (this could be thought of as a performance variant of a butt splice) or may cause a combination of crossfade and switching on (figures 6.6b and c).

A sampler may be multi-timbral in several different ways. A performance configuration (keyboard split) allows different sounds to be active on different regions of a keyboard or other controller. Samples may be assigned to different MIDI channels, so that a sequencer or remote controller may address them. Different configurations may be assigned to different channels. All of these procedures are subject to the limitation of the maximum number of voices playable at any one time.

SIGNAL PROCESSING FUNCTIONS

Since samples are merely chains of numbers, any procedure that involves arithmetic functions may be used. This includes mixing and equalization. Compression, pitch shifting, and other procedures may also be available.

Table 6.3. Filter configurations

FILTER	SHAPE	FUNCTION	PARAMETERS
Peak	⌃	Boost selected band	Fc, Bandwidth, Amount
Notch	⌄	Reduce selected band	Fc, Bandwidth, Amount
High-Pass	＼	Attenuate band below cutoff frequency	Fc, Slope
Low-Pass	／	Attenuate band above cutoff frequency	Fc, Slope
Shelf	／‾	Boost or reduce selected region	Fc, Boost/cut Amount

MIXING AND MERGING

In **mixing**, two samples are basically added together, one sample at a time. The result will be the creation of a new sample (assuming that the old samples were previously saved, there are now three samples). It is usually possible to set the percentage of the mix, so that one sample may be stronger than the other. It may be possible to offset one sample in time to create interesting effects.

In **merging**, mixing also takes place, but in combination with a crossfade. In this procedure, two samples are actually spliced together, so that one begins and then shifts into the other. Typical parameters to be set include marking the location of the splice, determining which is the "from" and which is the "to" sample, the length of the merge area itself, and possibly the crossfade shape. As with mixing, this creates a third sample.

EQUALIZATION

It should be possible to modify a sample by applying various filter types to its amplitude. These include a peak or notch filter, high- and low-pass filters and high and low shelving. In editing software, it should be possible to preview the effect of the filtering operation. While this type of **equalization** lacks the dynamic aspect of real-time filtering, it allows samples to be edited in an extremely detailed fashion. Figure 6.7 shows the results of these various filtering configurations.

ADDITIVE SYNTHESIS

An important approach to creating musical tones in the early days of electronic music involved adding sine waves of appropriate frequency and amplitude to create more complex timbres. This approach involved a good number of sine wave generators. Since these tended not to be as stable as one would like for musical purposes, and since it took many generators to develop a harmonically rich waveform, it was not commercially viable.

With the development of subtractive synthesis and the modular synthesizer, usable waveforms could be made more easily by using filters to shape the initial source material, in a simplified form of the equalization discussed in the previous section. The computer allows a return to additive synthesis in a more practical fashion, since the additive process may be computational, just as mixing and equalization are. When the computer is used in combination with a sampler, the results can be quite striking.

CREATING SAMPLE DATA

Material from the sampler can be created by calculating a waveform and sending the results to the sampler. This requires some use of system exclusive programming, and some knowledge of the form in which the data should be so that the sampler can use it. Short of developing an original program (not terribly difficult given the range of programming environments with MIDI utilities) one could use commercial programs for the creation of samples, such as Digidesign's *Softsynth* or *TurboSynth*, both for the Macintosh.

When sine waves are added, using the harmonic series and the standard amplitude formulas, more complex waveforms may be created. The results of such addition may be seen in figure 1.7 on page 14, where the beginning stages of creating a square wave are shown. The screen image is the result of plotting a series of numbers; a sound from a sampler is merely a plot in sound over time.

By combining such calculations (which, of course, do not need to be restricted to the harmonic series or to standard amplitude schemes) with equalization and other signal processing algorithms, a wide range of sounds can be created on computer and played back on a sampler, even though they were not first sampled.

SIMULATING SYNTHESIS

The role of the computer in creating samples need not be restricted to additive synthesis. **Object-oriented programs** like *TurboSynth* allow one to simulate the operation of an analog synthesizer or synthesis processes not available on the synthesizers at hand. Modules may be connected using simulated patch cords, parameter values supplied and modified, and interesting results saved and sent to the sampler. This is basically an applied version of flowchart notation. Naturally, many of the dynamic features that make synthesizer patches so effective may not be available once the patch is sent to the sampler, since one is restricted to the features of the sampler. Nonetheless, the combination of computer and sampler extends the creative range of both pieces of equipment.

FOR FURTHER STUDY

Chapter one and appendix A contain information on basic harmonic spectra and the amplitude of partials. Chapter eight presents a discussion of recording basics which may help in recording new samples. Appendix E on page 265 offers ideas for further reading.

EXERCISES

Sampling and editing features vary greatly on both hardware and software. In addition to doing the exercises that follow, become familiar with specific controls and capabilities of the available resources. Looking at and modifying existing sample settings and configurations is worthwhile, as is the procedure of developing a project which requires the use of the hardware and software in new ways so that two things are accomplished at the same time: completing an interesting project, and learning more about the equipment used to complete the project.

EXERCISE 6.1

Sample someone speaking the phrase "My name is _____ ," trying different sample rates. After deciding which rate works best (defined here as the rate at which the sample reproduces authentically but takes the least amount of memory—a concern for those with dynamic use of memory) experiment with other factors: microphone placement, loudness of the source, recording location (how important is location as the microphone distance decreases?). Store the best results for possible future use.

EXERCISE 6.2

Sample different acoustic sources, keeping track of the major recording parameters such as microphone placement (also microphone choice, if different types are available), sample rate, source loudness, and any other important variable.

EXERCISE 6.3

Develop a multisample of an acoustic musical instrument. Start by sampling one tone per octave or register — consult the performer for help on this topic. Each tone should be in the middle of the region. Set the key range of each sample so that the set allows the entire compass of the instrument to be played. Do the edges of the sample regions match? Before recording new tones midway between the previous ones (and adjusting key ranges accordingly), consider whether the source loudness or other recording parameters need adjusting. Interpolate new tones as necessary.

EXERCISE 6.4

Loop a speech sample so that one or two words repeat while a key is held down. What happens when release is added to the amplitude envelope?

Also try turning a speech sample into an instrument-like sound. With very short loops, a buzz can be produced. Try different length loops. Also try different areas of the keyboard or other controller, since the results can be quite different in different regions.

EXERCISE 6.5

Loop several acoustic musical instrument samples. Explore both manual and automatic setting of loop points, if possible. Editing software can be a marvelous tool in this process, since the visual display allows much better precision. If smoothing can be turned on and off, try both ways. Explore standard and crossfade loops, using the same loop points. Which works best? If more than one type of crossfade is available, compare and contrast them with the same material.

EXERCISE 6.6

Explore the mixing and merging features of the available system. Select two samples that contrast in character and mix them (how about pouring water and a violin tremulo?). Try different amplitude ratios. Then begin again with the same two samples and merge them, experimenting with any variable settings allowed by the system.

EXERCISE 6.7

Explore the available options for equalization or filtering of a sample. At the least, there will be some form of front-panel control of a (low-pass) filter and amplitude envelope. Often there will be more options, either through the sampler or through studio software.

Make a sample that has a glitch in it, such as a cough or a hand-clap while a steady tone is being sampled. Using a notch filter configuration and any other appropriate resources, get rid of the offending glitch.

Take a sample that has a portion with a low amplitude and increase the amplitude of that portion. Do the reverse with another portion of the same sample.

VOCABULARY

Most of the following terms were used for the first time in this chapter. Make sure that you are familiar with them, since they may be used later in the book. A definition of each term may be found in the glossary.

aliasing	analog-to-digital converter	butt splice
copy	crossfade	cut
equalization	foldover	keyboard split
layering	merging	mixing
multisampling	Nyquist theorem	object-oriented program
paste	quantization	resolution
sample	sample rate	

REVIEW QUESTIONS

QUESTION 6.1

Match related terms by writing the letter of the term in the second column in the blank of the term in the first column that most closely relates to it.

Bandwidth	____	A.	ADC
Duration	____	B.	Aliasing
Foldover	____	C.	DAC
Input	____	D.	Nyquist Frequency
Output	____	E.	Nyquist Theorem
Resolution	____	F.	Quantization
Sample Rate	____	G.	Sustain Loop

QUESTION 6.2

Compare and contrast the following terms.

Input Filtering—Output Filtering

_____

_____

_____

_____

CHAPTER SIX

Mixing—Merging

_____

_____

_____

_____

QUESTION 6.3

Define briefly.

Multisampling

_____

_____

_____

_____

Sample Rate

_____

_____

_____

_____

QUESTION 6.4

Provide the question for the given answer.

ANSWER	QUESTION
Minimum samples needed per cycle	What is _____ ?
About one-half the sample rate	What is _____ ?
A smooth splice or loop point	What is _____ ?
44.1 kHz, for example	What is _____ ?

PART · THREE

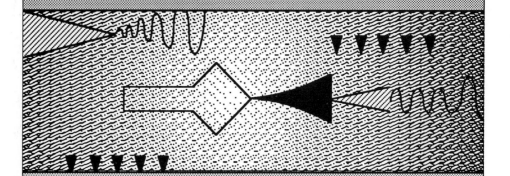

SCORE CONSTRUCTION

CHAPTER · SEVEN

NOTATION

Documentation is a necessary part of electronic composition, whether in the form of a musical **score** or technical notes. The wide-ranging nature of the sonic output requires a corresponding flexibility in notation, particularly if information about a piece is to be conveyed to other performers.

The function of a musical score is to provide information. The composer/performer needs to keep track of and organize his or her studio work. Performers need to be able to coordinate their musical tasks with the electronic elements of a piece (tape, computer, or live electronics). Some listeners may wish to better understand the music they hear.

A variety of score materials is needed by the electronic composer. These include flowcharts and other technical notes to document instrument patches. Computer printouts and programs often accompany computer-related composition. Various sketches of intended musical effects can be used in planning compositions in any medium.

In traditional composition, this type of precompositional documentation would be summarized and refined in a finished score. In electronic music the final score is often a master tape or set of computer files. Since the composer is often the primary performer, it is worthwhile to extend the concept of the score to include the extensive recordkeeping needed to most effectively use the studio, whether analog or digital.

The task of communicating the composer's wishes to other performers falls within the traditional definition of a score. Given that electronic sounds may not easily be described with traditional notation, other forms of notating sonic events may be needed. These range from extensions of traditional notational practice to graphic representations evocative of the material to be performed. These types of notation may either describe the sonic output or may be used to tell the performers what or how they should play, without attempting to accurately define the sounds that will be produced.

RECORDKEEPING

To some extent there is a close relationship between how an instrument is played and the notation used to inform the performer what to play. For example, the piano is notated on two **staves**, often in the form of the **grand staff**, which allows the multiple-note display necessary for piano music. Pipe organ music includes an additional staff for the pedal part, while some percussion parts are notated on a single line, since the pitch differentiation provided by the five-line staff is irrelevant to many percussion instruments.

A composer must keep records. As synthesizer instruments are developed, patches should be notated in a flowchart or on a replica of the front panel of the synthesizer. For digital instruments, an appropriate chart should be developed to record parametric values. To rely solely on digital storage devices is to court trouble. If material is being stored on disk or tape, a list of contents should be kept—preferably annotated, since titles that now appear clear may in a month become cryptic.

How a piece of music is developed varies from composer to composer and piece to piece. Often, the process of designing instruments and becoming better acquainted with equipment and/or software will suggest musical ideas. At some point in this process, it is usually a good idea to step back and examine the material being created. It may be necessary to put tasks in succession and to plan other events needed to complete the piece. While descriptive phrases may suffice to describe the needed material, the use of notational tools will often enhance this phase of composition.

TRADITIONAL NOTATION

Perhaps one of the most amazing things about music notation is that it works. It implies more—and actually says less—than it apparently states. Music notation has always been a weak link in the chain of creation-to-reproduction of musical works—and, of course, is not an essential element in all musics. Folk musics have thrived in the absence of a strong notational tradition. Jazz is primarily aural, with **lead sheets** and **charts** giving but the most general of frameworks.

The lack of notation has its hardships. Music must be "handed down," and in the process is altered. If a tradition is not carried on, it may die. Pop music groups that develop "head arrangements" may spend endless hours painstakingly creating their music. The interpretational practices of earlier generations of musicians may be lost, and their music incorrectly performed by early music enthusiasts who can only play what's written down.

PITCH

Most Western music is currently based on an equal-tempered set of 12 **pitch classes,** consisting of the letter names A through G, some of which may be modified by **sharp** or **flat** signs to round out the 12-tone set. Fretted instruments and keyboard instruments like the

Figure 7.1. Measuring time

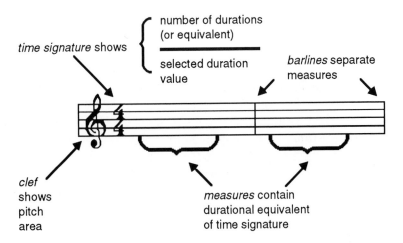

piano produce primarily the equal-tempered tones. Instruments like the violin, however, or the voice, are under no such constraint. Nonetheless, they often tend to be used to produce equal-tempered music.

MIDI note names use traditional labels plus a **register** indicator. Middle C on the music keyboard (MIDI note number 60) is called either C3 or C4, depending upon the manufacturer, with each higher C starting a new register and each B in descending starting the next lower register.

DURATION

Rhythm is the organization of durations into larger groupings. In traditional notation, the basic rhythmic symbols tend to be divisible by two: a quarter note equals two eighth notes, a whole note equals two half notes. A number of extensions allow triplets, quintuplets, and a variety of more complex relationships. Rhythmic material is usually grouped into **measures**.

MEASURE

A fairly simple system for marking the passage of time has been developed in traditional notation. A **time signature** indicates the size of the units to be measured (figure 7.1), and vertical **barlines** measure off the appropriate temporal space. Although it is common for measures to keep the same size throughout a piece or significant section of a piece, they may change in size as needed. To do so, a new time signature is placed at the beginning of the changed measure.

MIDI makes use of *measure, beat,* and fractions of a beat (**PPQN**—pulses per quarter note—or **ticks** or some other descriptive term). A quarter note, for example, may be assigned a value of 480 ticks by simply defining the quarter note as that duration which moves at the tempo (defined in beats per minute) set on the **metronome** of the MIDI sequencer. In this scheme, an eighth note has a clock value of 240, an eighth-note triplet has a value of 160, and so on. Beats may be grouped into measures. This allows for ease in editing and synchronization.

The measure will not always be the best means of marking time in electronic music. Implicit in the current use of *measure* is the definition of the first beat as the strongest, thus receiving a regular stress. If a piece is not based on the regularity of pulsation implied by the use of measures, it may not be possible—or even necessary—to think of measuring material in this way.

It may be easier to simply mark the passage of time in seconds. Recording tape can easily be measured, since tape speed is defined in terms of inches per second. Sketches or score material may use graph paper, where each horizontal unit marks some fraction of a

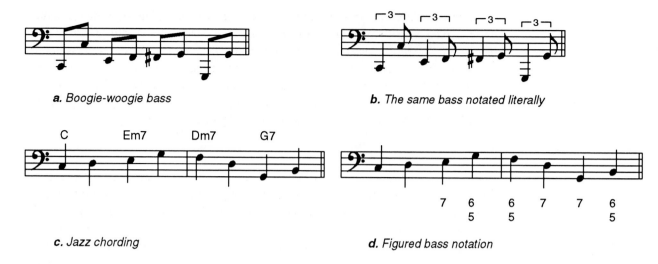

a. *Boogie-woogie bass*   b. *The same bass notated literally*

c. *Jazz chording*   d. *Figured bass notation*

Figure 7.2. Performance-
oriented notation

second. Sketches may also be made on blank paper, with time marked in seconds across the page. Sequencers often offer several different ways of measuring time.

VOLUME

Loudness, intensity, amplitude, and **volume** (and the lack thereof) are quite important in music. Traditional volume notation is somewhat inexact and relative. Various accent marks and descriptive phrases augment the pp-p-mp-mf-f-ff continuum.

Instrumentation, or choosing which instrument plays what, is almost as crucial as the selection of dynamic markings. A *forte* tone played in the low register of one instrument may be softer than the same tone played *forte* on another instrument playing in a higher register. In this process, tone color and other instrumental characteristics—in short, the acoustic analog of the electronic instrument design process— are important in determining amplitude.

Volume is used here with a more global meaning than amplitude. One might speak of an amplitude setting on a VCA, yet, in considering the overall musical activity, speak of volume or musical dynamics. In general, amplitude may be more precisely measured, while volume is relative and qualitative.

EXTENDING TRADITIONAL NOTATION

Music notation has constantly evolved to meet the needs and changing technical demands of performing musicians and composers. Its great strength comes from the use of a limited number of symbols, which have conventionally accepted meanings that are capable of being modified or interpreted by stylistic or personal considerations.

Although traditional notation is considered to be fairly precise, it is the application of stylistic rules and common practice assumptions that make the notation most meaningful. Figure 7.2a, part of a boogie-woogie bass pattern, would be played literally by many a conservatory-trained musician, who might not know how to "swing" it (sounding like figure 7.2b).

Both twentieth-century jazz/popular music and Baroque period music have "shorthand" notations, advising the musician of important harmonic aspects of the music (figure 7.2c and d). The first tells the performer what chord to play, and the second implies chords by giving the distance above the bass of some of the sounding notes. There are many possible ways to realize chords within each genre. In all cases, a knowledge of style and a feeling for what is appropriate is essential.

Due to its broad acceptance and use in an extensive body of musical literature, the basic features of traditional musical notation are not likely to be altered greatly in the near future. Instead, a notational pluralism, in which the composer invents new symbols or uses symbols others have developed to augment this basic notation, is more likely to continue. Perhaps due to the eclectic nature of the new symbols as well as the overwhelming presence and use of traditional notation, new symbols and usages remain little known and relatively unused by most of the musically literate public.

PITCH AND DURATION

The synthesizer, like the violin, need not be limited to equal-tempered music. The use of the piano/organ music keyboard does suggest that equal temperament is the norm. An expanded notation may allow more freedom for exploring the pitch domain. For example, if a musical effect is desired, but the pitch content of the effect is less important than the general impression created by the effect, it is more useful to indicate in general terms the desired gesture, leaving the choice of specific events up to the performer or, in the case of a computer, to a random number generator. Pitch notation in electronic music may range from the traditional notation of pitches through generally notated gestures to, at the other extreme, totally indeterminate notation (which may even offer the performer the option of not playing).

As with pitch, rhythm notation can be represented along a continuum from total precision to total freedom or randomness. Durations can be much longer in electronic music than in most acoustically performed music, since breathing is not a factor in determining note length (orchestral string sections may of course play quite long notes, since changes in bow direction may be staggered). At the other end of the spectrum, notes may be so short as to be virtually nonexistent.

INDICATIVE AND POSITIONAL NOTATION

With traditional notation and the use of an appropriate number of five-line staves, a wide variety of textures can be notated. In traditional usage, the concept of musical line generally implies that the line is a succession of single, discrete events, or pitches. This need not be so in electronic music, where bands of noise and other complex signals allow for a much wider definition of the single event.

If a keyboard is being used in the performance of such a broad-band event, one could simply notate the keys to be pressed with traditional notation, much as one would write a musical line and at the beginning of the score specify which instruments would play it. This is an example of **indicative notation**, in which the actual outcome is not described. In combination with technical information (patch panels, flowcharts, or digital parameter data lists) the correct sound(s) can be produced.

In traditional notation pitch is shown by the vertical placement of a duration symbol on the five-line staff. Higher notes go toward the top of the paper, lower notes toward the bottom. Since there are only four spaces and five lines, and many more possible pitches, a system of clefs modify the staff to allow it to show various ranges of pitches.

The key to notation for electronic music is the principle that the very position of the symbol or graphic image on the page tells something, apart from any other significance. In a nontraditional score, position can be used to show the location of a sound in a sonic field, the amplitude of an event, or the mixture of two waveforms. In short, position can be used to define any parameter in terms of its location in a continuum of values.

This extension of **positional notation** can be especially useful and liberating to a composer. Notational systems may be designed to fit the musical material, rather than the musical ideas being adapted to fit the demands of the notation.

Figure 7.3. Extending
traditional notation

a. *Proportional notation.*
Relative pitch length
is shown.

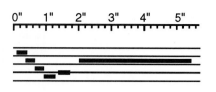

b. *Timing. Accurate measurements*
of time may be made.

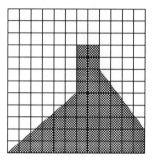

c. *Amplitude (vertical)*
mapped over time.

Krzysztof
Penderecki   Alois Haba

♪	or	‰	= 3/4-tone ♯
♪	or	♩	= 1/4-tone ♯
♭	or	♩	= 1/4-tone ♭
♩	or	♭	= 3/4-tone ♭

d. *Pitch. Quarter-tones and other*
microtones may be shown by
modifying traditional accidentals.
Shown here are Penderecki's and
Haba's quarter-tone modifiers.

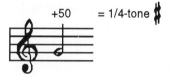

+50   = 1/4-tone ♯

e. *Pitch. The offset to*
standard pitch may be
shown in cents.

FRAMES

During the 20th century two contradictory, and yet complementary, attitudes towards composition have been explored. In the first, more control over all aspects of musical sound has been sought by the composer. More attention has been paid to **articulation** (the envelope) of each individual tone, levels of volume, the exploration and specification of tone color (instrumental fingerings, choice of drumsticks, mutes), and the other secondary parameters. Other composers have been less concerned with specific local events. They choose to deal more with the overall design of a piece, allowing chance, or random procedures, or the performer, to decide which sections or notes are played.

If a composer seeks absolute control in a piece by many, rapid changes in the various musical parameters, the effect often approaches the more random effect sought by less-demanding colleagues. In the quest for control, one can choose to modify traditional notation, using it in a more precise fashion. Duration may be shown proportionally (figure 7.3a). Pitch may be indicated more precisely (figure 7.3d and e). The passage of time may be marked in seconds (figure 7.3b) or specified on graph paper in place of or in combination with the five-line staff (figure 7.3c).

Frame notation allows the composer to specify in general what happens in a piece, while leaving more choice to the performer. This sets up an environment for guided or limited improvisation. For the composer more interested in expressing musical concepts (either prescriptive— before performance—or descriptive—after performance) the frame can be quite useful.

Figure 7.4. Frame notation

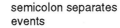

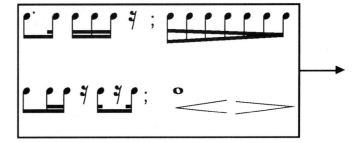

semicolon separates   slanted beam suggests a
events   rhythm that slows down

a. Bracket. Material is
repeated until the end
of the dark line. Usually
pitch order is varied.

b. Box. Select one or more
rhythms (or other events).
Perform as specified by
the composer.

Figure 7.5. A graphic score

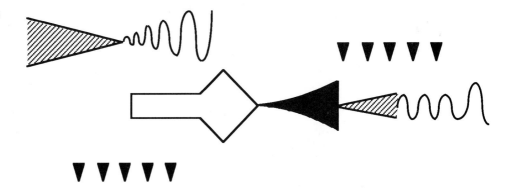

The box, or frame, or brackets, shown in figure 7.4a and b, contains the material to be performed. It can be extended by a solid line or arrow to cover a specific amount of time. This can be a good vehicle for notating looped sequences or complex textures. Rather than specifying each detail, the general effect or intent is noted. Once in the studio, the box can be realized more fully and easily.

GRAPHIC REPRESENTATION

There is a tendency to think of music notation as being "graphic." Traditional music notation does have graphic aspects, but is symbolic in its use of a set of symbols to indicate pitch and duration. Just as letters can be combined to form many different words, so can music symbols be combined to create many different melodies and harmonies.

Music symbols tend to be indicative: a certain symbol placed on a staff indicates a fingering, or a particular key on a keyboard. A symbol may sound different on different instruments. Crescendo and decrescendo markings have a graphic character. They portray the outcome of an action, leaving the production of the gesture up to the performer.

Graphic notation shows or suggests the sonic result of musical activity. This notational approach is ideal for describing on paper what will be heard on tape. The performer who waits for a sonic cue before playing can follow the progress of the taped material more easily. He or she does not need to know *how* material was created; it is enough to know *what* was created.

A wide range of visual images can be used as the impetus for a piece of music. The composer can examine the object and develop sonic analogs following guidelines such as those given in this chapter. No two musicians are likely to interpret a visual image in the

Table 7.1. Guidelines for
graphic notation

PARAMETER	CHARACTERISTICS
Pitch	Positional (high/low)
Rhythm	Proportional (long/short)
Intensity	Size and/or darkness (darker = louder)
Texture	Thicker = fuller
Articulation	Related to timbre. Sharp, short sounds use sharp symbols; rounder sounds are less angular.
Timbre	Generally quite free. Noise is often shown by cross-hatching (▨). A combination of articulation, texture, and intensity are usually interrelated with timbre.
Dynamic events	◁ (growing) and ▷ (dying) may be combined with the above. Becoming darker, thicker, sharper may indicate growth in one or more parameters.

same way. For that very reason, some composers have chosen to create graphic scores. In so doing, they affect the sonic output in very broad ways, while leaving much of the actual musical detail to the discretion of the performer.

The score given in figure 7.5 presents an example of graphic notation. Talent as a visual artist may be helpful in constructing such scores. Their realization requires a good imagination and a certain lack of musical inhibition.

A graphic score may be presented for performance without comment, or the composer can provide some help in its interpretation. A range of values can be implied by different sizes or shadings of a symbol. Pitch can be a function of a symbol's position on the paper. Articulation characteristics, density, and texture can be suggested by the relative length of symbols or contrasts in shading and size of symbols.

Most symbols tend to be evocative of the effect to be produced. In effect, this is a timbre notation, and since timbre is difficult to describe, the notation remains somewhat loose. Symbols could also be used to suggest some action (a human hand plucking strings inside a piano, for example). Some general guidelines are suggested in table 7.1. See also table 9.2 on page159 for timbre notation appropriate for tape music.

Purely graphic scores may be less useful to the beginning electronic composer than a combination of graphic and traditional notation. Annotation in the form of written detail and technical support (patches, flowcharts, printouts) is helpful. Such documentation is useful in developing clarity of detail and precision in working out musical ideas—and is essential to planning and managing studio time.

Rather than work with a two-dimensional representation of a piece, one can transform three or more dimensions into two to show simultaneous activity of parameters, as in figure 7.6. This is helpful in trying to understand the relationships among the various parameters and can be used as a tool in top-down design activities.

In figure 7.6a events can be plotted against three axes, showing dynamics, pitch, and time all at once. These axes could be unfolded slightly, as in figure 7.6b. Each pitch event above the time line has a corresponding dynamic envelope below the line. Pitch can be given different shapes and colors to show different types of activity. Dynamics can have a corresponding richness. Even more dimensions can be brought into play, as in figure

Figure 7.6. Scoring parameters

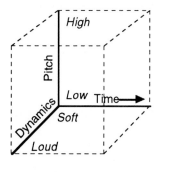

a. Three dimensions. . .

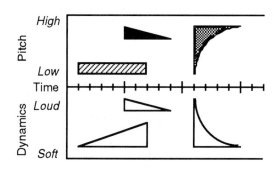

b. Unfolded

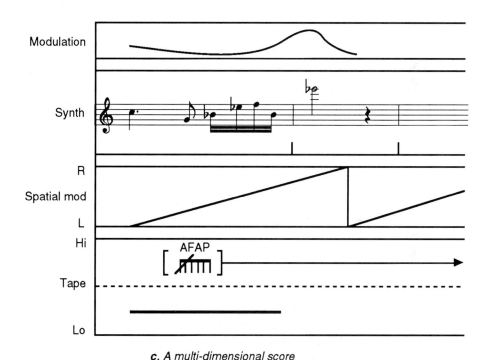

c. A multi-dimensional score

7.6c. Synthesizer activity is shown in traditional notation in parallel with other dimensions showing a modulation contour, spatial modulation (the output is being panned from left to right), and graphic representations of accompanying prerecorded material.

TWO SHORT EXAMPLES

In figure 7.7 on the following page an introductory excerpt is presented. So that it might be realized with whatever resources are available, timbral suggestions have been left general. Pitch and amplitude are mapped against time. Frame notation is used to show the continuation of the sustained low tone and to show a simple indeterminate sequence. The tones of the sequence are roughly indicated, depending upon the length of the stems. A third, percussive element is shown, beginning about 20 seconds into the excerpt. This could be filtered noise, some sort of clangorous timbre, or even a chord or cluster of nearby pitches. Also notice the **quantized** stair step or **glissando** effect near the end.

Amplitude is shown in two ways. Words and symbols are used above the dotted line to indicate volume level. Below the dotted line, amplitude is shown in profile. Karlheinz

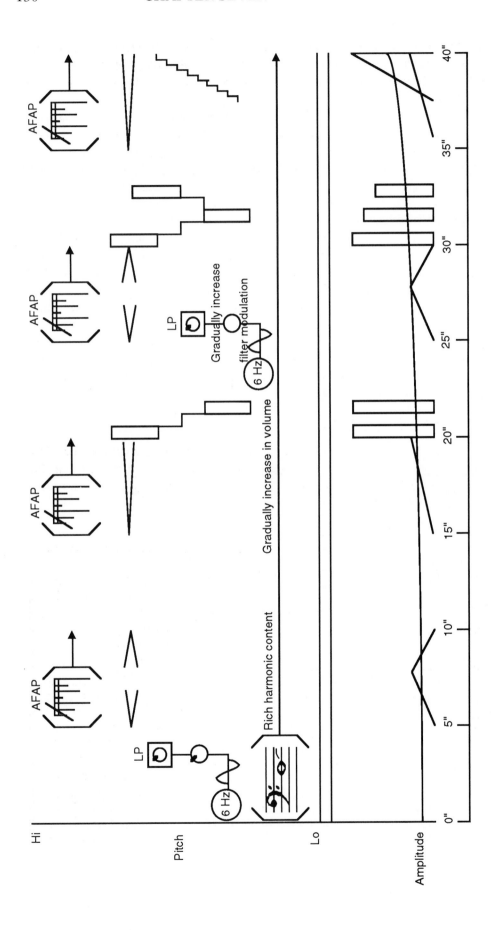

Figure 7.7. An introductory excerpt

Stockhausen made use of this technique in his *Studie II* (1956). It gives amplitude a more visual aspect, and gives the composer a tool for better manipulating amplitude. A decibel scale could be used to quantify amplitude, or a somewhat more intuitive or relative approach could be taken, as is done here.

Notice the level of activity. The piece is relatively slow-moving, with a gradually growing **pedal point** (on the organ, a pedal tone can be held with more active material above gradually cycling through a chord succession), and a few brief counterpoints that become somewhat more active through the excerpt. Even though the sequence is marked "AFAP" (as fast as possible), or rather, because of that marking, the sequence will be heard more as a solid entity rather than as a fast passage. There are implications here that a large piece is in the making, with this being but the first phase.

Figure 7.5 (page 127) also consisted of a small number of elements. Due to a lack of accompanying documentation or directions, the realization of this score is wide open. The first event appears to be a fairly high-pitched band of noise that diminishes in contour (amplitude envelope, possibly filter width), changing into a rapidly oscillating wave that opens in contour. Underneath this are two events: a set of sharp, repeated attacks, and a larger structure of points connected by lines. This leads to a shape evocative of a trumpet bell, out of which issues material derived from the first event, against which the repeated punctuations occur, now in a higher register. But does one go through the score from left to right? Can things repeat? Is there an overall character, or does the character change? And how long should it be, anyway?

NOTATION AND TRANSCRIPTION SOFTWARE

The concept of the computer as a device to avoid repetitive tasks makes the use of the computer as a tool for printing music irresistible to a musician. Composing is fun. The cleanup—legible copying of score and parts—is boring and takes some of the element of play out of music.

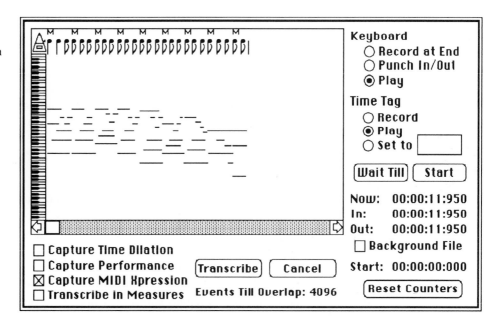

Figure 7.8. *Finale*'s transcription window in action. Used by permission of Coda Music Software.

Figure 7.9. *Finale's* tool palette. Used by permission of Coda Music Software.

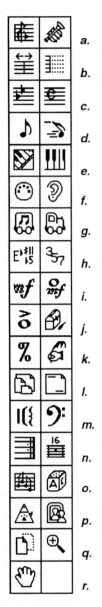

Music notation has a complex set of rules, and copying music is an art. The choice of stem direction alone has a variety of guidelines. Downward stems go on the left side of a notehead, upward stems on the right. Notes below the middle line of the staff take upward stems, those above have downward stems, those on the middle line depend on the context. With chords, a certain amount of averaging comes into play. When two instruments are notated on one staff, one uses upward stems, the other uses downward.

When mixed durations are added in, one must decide when to use flags or beams with eighth notes, whether to "dot" a note or tie one note to another. With the use of a good editor, most of these problems can be dealt with. As yet, no satisfactory serious solution has presented itself, without the knowledgeable involvement of the musician.

Programs like Coda Software's *MusicProse* and *Finale* (for IBM and Macintosh families) have several means of note entry. Like Mark of the Unicorn's *Professional Composer* (for the Macintosh) they allow note entry from a music keyboard and from a MIDI keyboard. Unlike most programs, *Finale* offers possibilities of real-time transcription (see figure 7.8, showing *Finale's* transcription window in action). While still with its problems, this offers a glimpse of the dream of composers to simply sit down, play, and get printed music in return.

There's still much room in the music notation process for composer involvement. Any useful program should offer a range of options like *Finale* (figure 7.9 shows the **icon** palette presenting *Finale's* main program options). In *Finale*, clicking on an icon with the mouse allows access to a group of related procedures. These include (a) creating and deleting staves and determining their general characteristics; (b) creating and deleting measures and determining their general characteristics; (c) creating and changing key and time signatures; (d and e) entering music through various procedures, ranging from single note to real-time entry and transcription; (f) controlling and playing back MIDI data; (g) editing a wide range of data; (h, i, j) creating and deleting chords, triplets and other multiple-note combinations, adding various expression marks and phrases, and controlling beaming, stems, and other aspects of notes. Other options allow precise control over page layout, lyric entry, measure number regions, and just about every facet of the printed page. Since MIDI input and output is available, written scores can be played back, although some effort must be exerted so that the result is not unmusical.

The tradeoff with having a powerful program is that it does require a good bit of computer memory, it may in fact offer too many features for a specific task, and yet may not be strong enough in some areas. Some musicians may find it better to use one program for sequencing and preparing music data, another for preparing music notation, and even a third for page layout chores. As music notation software has become more powerful, such work-arounds have become less necessary.

RESOLUTION

An important limiting factor is found in **resolution** of both monitor screen and printout device. The former is important, since it determines both how much music can be fit on the screen and how legible it is. In general, not much information is contained on screen; it should be possible to treat the screen as a window, moving the window up or down, or side to side, to view the rest of the score.

The resolution of the printout device is crucial. Currently laser printers offer the best alternatives for music printing, with a resolution of 300 dots per inch. Dot matrix printers will suffice in many cases, although the higher the number of dots per inch, the higher the quality of the printout.

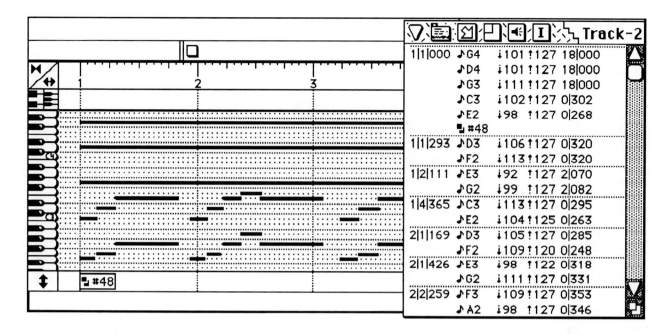

Figure 7.10. Listing MIDI note data. On the left: piano-roll graphic notation; on the right: an event list. From Mark of the Unicorn's *Performer*. Used by permission

GRAPHIC EXTENSIONS

Sequencing software has taken several approaches in providing a look at the information it captures. Event lists (figure 7.10, right) provide a time-ordered listing of MIDI information. Graphic representations — a variant of piano-roll notation — may either supplement or be the primary display (figure 7.10, left). Both approaches show the temporal location of a note: the event list starts by showing *measure|beat|fraction of a beat* to indicate the start time, and concludes each line with the note's duration in *beats|fractions of a beat*; the graphic display shows time horizontally, with longer notes having longer duration (there will usually be a simple means of getting a listing of note information for each note as well). Pitch is shown in the event list by letter name and register, while many graphic displays relate notes to a keyboard display. *On* and *off* velocities complete most event listings (shown in figure 7.10 with down- or up-arrows); graphic displays can use different shadings of notes to show relative *on* velocities, or may have a separate graphic display area (in *Performer* this area is below the note display).

Some sequencers can also display data using music notation, although, given the complexities of notation, the display tends to fall short of the offerings of notation programs. Some may offer the means of getting an overview of the work, as in *Performer's* Chunks window (figure 7.11 on the next page).

Still other programs offer linkage between the visual and the audible. Intelligent Music's *Ovaltunes* offers a musical response to changing screen images. Several computer animation programs include some means of sending MIDI commands. Although this area is somewhat rudimentary as of 1990, it offers opportunities for interdisciplinary exploration for adventurous musicians.

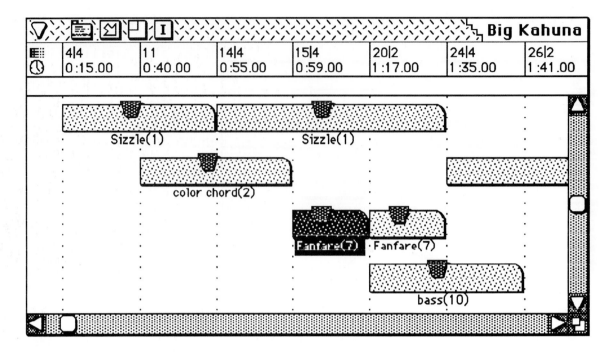

Figure 7.11. Putting graphics to work. *Performer's* Chunks window allows blocks of music to be treated compositionally. Used by permission.

FOR FURTHER STUDY

Chapters eight and nine explore the use of tape recorders and related equipment; chapters eleven and twelve discuss composition and creative approaches to sequencing; appendix E on page 265 offers ideas for further reading.

EXERCISES

Since this chapter has dealt with scores and score notation, the exercises focus on constructing and realizing scores. Constructing can take place either before a work is realized in sound, in which case it is part of the compositional process, or after realization, in which case it is part of the process of description and analysis. This latter process may be important in conveying information about the piece to other performers who will be performing with the electronic material, or it may be important so that one better understands the composition.

EXERCISE 7.1

Notate, using appropriate symbols and graphic procedures, at least 10 short recorded events. The material can be taken from work done in previous chapters.

EXERCISE 7.2

Realize figure 7.5 or construct and realize a similar original score. What guidelines must be developed before doing this exercise?

EXERCISE 7.3

Realize figure 7.7. Since this excerpt represents a building up of tension and energy, compose (both score and realization) a successor event that might logically be the goal of this excerpt.

EXERCISE 7.4

Construct a descriptive score to a piece composed by someone else. The piece can be recorded or be a live improvisation. If possible, compare notes with the composer. Does the representation meet the expectations of the composer?

EXERCISE 7.5

Make a score for a short piece for live performer and recorded or live electronics. Try to get an interesting dialogue going between the performer and the electronics. Write a score that allows the performer to know when to play and when to rest. Have the piece performed. How does the performer feel about the score?

EXERCISE 7.6

Write a score for a work you have composed and recorded previously. Using the score, examine the work critically and decide if it has a good balance of repetition, contrast, and variation. Decide what needs to be done to strengthen any weak spots and devise a plan to rework and expand the piece, giving as much detail as possible.

VOCABULARY

Some of the following terms were used for the first time in this chapter. Several may have a different use than earlier in the book. A definition of each term may be found in the glossary.

amplitude	articulation	barline
chart	flat	frame notation
glissando	grand staff	graphic notation
icon	indicative notation	instrumentation
intensity	lead sheet	loudness
measure	metronome	pedal point
pitch class	positional notation	PPQN
quantized	register	resolution
rhythm	scoretick	sharp
staves	tick	volume

REVIEW QUESTIONS

QUESTION 7.1

Match related terms by writing the letter of the term in the second column in the blank of the term in the first column that most closely relates to it.

Articulation	____	A.	C1, C2, C3
Measure	____	B.	Division of beat
Pitch Class	____	C.	Dynamics
PPQN	____	D.	Envelope
Volume	____	E.	Temporal Space

QUESTION 7.2

Compare and contrast the following terms.

Symbolic — Graphic

_____

_____

_____

_____

Positional — Indicative

_____

_____

_____

_____

QUESTION 7.3

Provide the question for the given answer.

ANSWER	QUESTION
An octave above E2	What is _____?
The pitch below C5	What is _____?
The MIDI value for C4	What is _____?

QUESTION 7.4

Create the graphic representation of a series of high, percussive chords followed by a texture of three slow-moving rising lines periodically interrupted by short chords like those of the beginning that gradually move lower in pitch.

CHAPTER · EIGHT

RECORDING BASICS

Traditionally-trained musicians work for years to learn to control their instrument and to produce beautiful tone. Along the way they may produce all manner of squeaks and squawks that they are told are unmusical. If they play the work of some contemporary composers they may have to relearn some of these noises that they were previously taught to avoid.

Noise can have, and should have, a fairly broad, plastic definition. Terence Dwyer in his *Composing with Tape Recorders* (London: Oxford University Press, 1971) defines noise as unwanted sound. Therefore music is "wanted" sound, subjected to organizing principles by a composer. This definition may be too broad for some, who may concede with reluctance that certain musics are music at the same time that they find the nearness of these musics annoying, or noise ("unwanted sound").

OPERATING A TAPE RECORDER

Electronic music does require a broader definition of both music and musical material. Indeed, virtually any sound becomes a candidate for inclusion in a musical work. This has been possible in the past through the use of the magnetic tape recorder. With the continuing development of digital sampling capability, computers may be used in this fascinating exploration of musical resources.

137

The tape recorder can be an important tool for organizing sounds. Even in a digital studio it is often important to be able to store compositions on tape for portability and easy dissemination. In addition to allowing recording and playback of material being worked on, the recorder, by storing sound on magnetic tape, allows sound to almost be treated as a physical body, since the tape may be cut and the recorded events thereby placed in different relationships.

IMPORTANT FEATURES

Most recorders operate in a similar fashion. Although the various controls and meters may be arranged in different configurations, an understanding of basic features should allow you to operate most equipment (customized installations may not be as accessible). Major controls and functions are discussed here.

POWER AND MOTION

The power on-off switch is primarily useful when the power cord is plugged in. While this statement may seem absurd, it is often the simple, obvious details that get overlooked. In addition to the power switch, the motion controls, which determine the direction and speed of the tape, are essential. They include reverse (rewind), stop, forward (play), and fast forward. On many machines it is a good idea to stop the tape before changing its direction to avoid damaging the motor. On newer, electronically-controlled machines this is no longer necessary, although it is always wise to avoid sudden changes of direction, in order to minimize the risk of tape breakage.

PAUSE CONTROL

This lever or button is used to temporarily stop the tape when it is in play or record modes. The tape usually remains in contact with the tape heads rather than dropping away, as it would in stop mode. This can be quite useful for tape editing.

RECORD CONTROL(S)

On many machines, recording begins only when both play and record controls are simultaneously engaged. On three-head machines, there usually are separate record controls for each channel. Machines with **sel-sync** capability may also have a record-play-sync switch that must be set before the record/play controls will have any effect.

MONITOR SWITCH

The user may select "source" (to hear the incoming signal) or "tape" (to hear the recorded signal via the playback head). To listen to previously recorded material or to play back material that has just been recorded, switch this to "tape." When preparing to record, use the "source" setting to obtain a signal amplitude level reading on the level meters of the recorder. The loudest signal should rarely surpass the "0" setting toward the right end of the meter. Meters are generally calibrated to allow some further movement into the red portion without causing distortion.

LINE AND MICROPHONE LEVEL ATTENUATORS

These allow control over the volume of incoming signals. To see the effect of these controls, place the monitor switch on "source," input a signal, and use the level meters as an aid to achieve the proper volume level.

TAPE SPEED

Most machines offer two or three speeds, ranging from 1-7/8 inches per second, or **ips** (the standard for cassette recorders), to 30 ips (a professional standard). Though more tape is used at higher speeds, a higher-quality audio product can be produced. 7-1/2 ips is the standard for 1/4-inch reel-to-reel recorders. Some cassette recorders offer 3-3/4 ips as a high-quality option.

OTHER USEFUL CONTROLS

Bias and equalization controls allow the equipment to be adjusted for special characteristics of the tape or of the room. Output volume may be controlled, normal or metal oxide tapes may be designated, and **noise reduction** may be built-in. Most of these may be preset in a studio situation, depending upon studio procedures, and should not need to be altered under normal operating conditions.

GETTING STARTED

Using a cassette recorder basically requires putting a cassette in the machine, adjusting recording levels, and recording. Some cassettes have a mixing board attached, so it may be necessary to set controls to route the signal (mixers are discussed in chapter nine).

Reel-to-reel, or open-reel, recorders require a bit more work. Tape must be threaded from left to right across the tape heads to the take-up reel, as shown in figure 8.1. Include in this threading the appropriate tension take-up levers. If the tape is stored **tails-out** to minimize print-through, thread from right to left. To play pre-recorded material, set the monitor switch on "tape," the output volume at an appropriate level, any output amplifier controls at appropriate levels, and play the tape.

On both types of machines source material patched in via microphone or line inputs can be heard by setting the monitor switch to "source," adjusting line or microphone level input attenuators, setting relevant output controls, and starting the source. Watch the level meters to avoid pinning the indicator needle. If a microphone is in use, it may be a good idea to avoid using speakers at the same time, unless feedback is desired.

To record the source signal, use the "record" and "play" controls simultaneously. Unwanted noise may be introduced on the tape. This can be reduced by setting the input level control at minimum, starting the record mode, and then moving the input volume to the proper recording level. Alternatively, one can record "silence" for several seconds before and after the source material, and later edit out unwanted silence and noise .

Consider the recording environment very carefully: does it enhance, or at least not intrude upon, the source? If recording must occur in a room near a busy corridor or road intersection, attempt to record at night or at some other less busy time. If reverberation is needed, in the absence of a reverb unit try recording in a live corridor, bathroom, or stairwell. When recording, try a variety of microphone volume settings and be very critical of the results. Any unwanted sound present now will be magnified later.

Tape should be stored away from stray magnetic fields. Reel-to-reel tape should be stored tails out (it must first be rewound before it can be played) so that the effects of

Figure 8.1. Reel-to-reel threading pattern. Tension levers should be put under tension; the tape must pass between the capstan and the capstan roller; the tape must make contact with the heads during playback and recording. The path is similar for cassettes, although much simpler from the user's point of view.

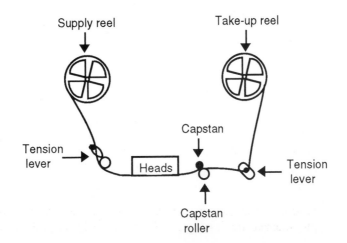

print-through are minimized. If a strong signal leaks through to the adjacent tape, the "shadow" it creates will follow the original signal and will either be hidden by the stronger signal or will be perceived as a weak echo. Used tape should be **degaussed**, or cleaned, by a bulk eraser before being recycled, to avoid any extraneous noise.

In addition to the studio being kept clean and smoke-free, the recorder itself should be cleaned periodically. Tape heads and other parts that come in contact with the tape should be cleaned often with approved cleaning fluids. Tape heads also need periodic demagnetizing, to minimize the recorded noise level, using a head demagnetizer. The owner's manual may suggest other procedures.

BASIC TAPE EDITING

Editing of recorded tapes was one of the mainstays of early tape music composition. It is still important in studio work in spite of recent technological advances. There are two main tape-editing procedures: **stop-start editing**, and cutting and splicing. In the former, events are ordered on tape by simply recording them in their desired sequence; in the latter, the order of events may be changed. In addition, tape editing allows unwanted noise between events or unwanted musical material to be deleted.

STOP-START EDITING

Before an event can be edited or modified, it must be recorded. Actually, microphone placement and recording volume already begin the modification process. Soft events record best if the microphone is close to the event (often less than 12 inches). The intent is to have a clean recording of the event with as little background noise as possible. Louder events can be farther from the microphone. As distance increases, however, the volume control may have to be turned higher, so that more environmental noise is picked up along with the signal.

In stop-start editing the order of events must be planned before recording. First one event is recorded, then the next. It is possible to order musical material by re-recording onto a second machine, although this increases background noise. It is difficult with this procedure to obtain precise timing of the interval between events. One must also exercise extreme care not to record any extraneous sounds or noises, since with stop-start editing, there is no means of removing them.

TAPE SPLICING

If one is using a stop-start approach to editing, splicing may help to get rid of extraneous room and recording noises that often get recorded before and after the desired musical

Figure 8.2. Splicing materials

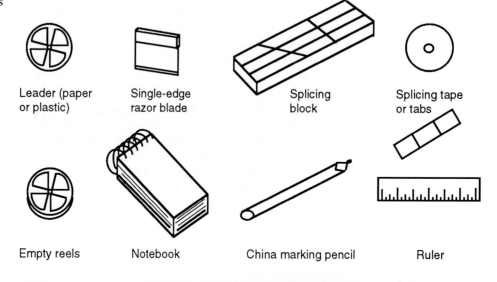

Leader (paper or plastic)　　Single-edge razor blade　　Splicing block　　Splicing tape or tabs

Empty reels　　Notebook　　China marking pencil　　Ruler

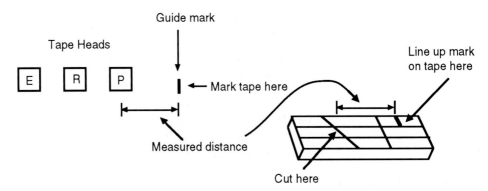

Figure 8.3. Measuring for the splice

material. If one wishes to create or rearrange sonic sequences, or modify already recorded material, splicing is a necessity. Material may be modified by truncating it or reversing its direction relative to other recorded material. Unusual juxtapositions of sonic material may be made, creating strange and interesting effects.

Equipment needed for splicing includes a splicing block, single-edge razor blades, splicing tape or tabs, paper or plastic leader tape (paper is less expensive and less likely to create static electricity), a china marking pencil, and empty reels to store tape segments on during the editing process (see figure 8.2). Other splicing materials that combine the splicing block and razor blade into a single unit are available. Although they suffice for lightweight work, they are often not precise enough for the editing discussed here.

To prepare for splicing, first play the tape until it reaches the point where material is to be inserted or deleted. Keeping the tape in contact with the playback head (with the help of the "pause" or "edit" control), turn the reels by hand to determine the exact point to cut. Due to the slow tape speed this causes, sounds are quite low in pitch and amplitude: often the output volume must be turned up quite high for the recorded material to be heard. The tape may have to be rocked back and forth (one hand on each reel to maintain tension across the heads) to determine the precise beginning or ending of the event. Mark the spot for the cut with the marking pencil, preferably at a measured distance from the playback head rather than on the playback head itself (see figure 8.3).

Place the tape, marked side up, in the channel of the splicing block. The mark on the tape should be placed opposite a corresponding mark on the splicing block, so that the beginning or ending of the sound will be centered on the angled cutting guide on the block. Draw the razor across and down the angled cutting guide.

Tape is spliced by placing two cut ends in the channel of the splicing block so that they touch without overlapping. A splicing tab or short piece of splicing tape (1/2 to 3/4 inches long) is centered over the ends lengthwise and gently pressed down, then rubbed to ensure a good splice.

This procedure can be repeated as necessary. In the case where several segments are first cut and then spliced, it may be useful to attach a piece of paper leader and label each segment. These segments can then be temporarily stored on a take-up reel before being added to the master tape.

Check all splices visually. No splicing tape should show through on the recording side of the tape. There should be no click when the splice passes over the playback head. It is good practice to place splices directly before a sonic event: if a splice is well placed, any noise created by the splice will be covered by the ensuing attack.

Paper leader may be used when silence must be spliced in, although the absence of background noise may prove distracting. Silence usually isn't silent. For a more natural effect use blank recording tape or even recorded "silence," keeping the same noise floor as is present during the rest of the tape play.

MULTITRACK RECORDING

It is best to begin to develop recording skills with monophonic projects. These allow the exploration of useful tape-editing techniques, along with the creation of simple, yet interesting compositions. Tape music, in general, tends to avoid the multilayered complexity of much acoustic music. This may be due to the complexity provided by the manipulation and juxtaposition of the striking timbral resources at the disposal of the electronic composer (horizontal rather than vertical detail). Still, there are times when layering or spatial location is an important part of a composition.

SOUND-WITH-SOUND

Sound-with-sound refers to the recording of different musical material on two or more channels. Material can be recorded on one channel. While it is played back, new material is recorded on a second (or third, or fourth . . .) channel.

A synchronization (sel-sync) switch is needed for this procedure. It allows the record head to function as a temporary playback head (of much lower quality than the playback head) for one channel while acting as a record head for another channel. Without the sel-sync switch, previously recorded material will normally be heard via the playback head, located on the recorder following the record head. At the same time, new material will be recorded on the record head. Since the playback head is located after the record head, the old and new material will always be out of sync.

SOUND-ON-SOUND

Sound-on-sound differs from sound-with-sound in that the old material is placed on the second channel along with the new material, rather than just recording the new material on a separate channel. The old material is recorded from the playback head to ensure the best quality signal at the same time that new material is added. Channel one contains the first signal, while channel two contains the composite signal.

It is now possible to re-record this material back onto channel one with yet a third musical idea. The original material is of course erased by the erase head, although it still exists in the composite signal from channel two. A word of warning: each re-recording adds noise. Rarely should one go beyond the third generation of a signal if it is important to maintain a reasonable **signal to noise ratio**.

TAPE ECHO

It is possible to take advantage of the distance between the record and playback heads to create a tape echo. The time delay can be determined by dividing the distance between the heads by the tape speed (either inches and inches per second or centimeters and centimeters per second). In the patch shown in figure 8.4a the source is heard both directly and via the tape delay, producing a single echo. The monitor switch must be set on "tape" or "playback" to take advantage of the distance between heads, and the source must be patched as shown in the figure.

A multiple-echo patch is shown in figure 8.4b. Since the recorded signal is constantly being mixed with the source signal, some care must be exercised with the recording level of each signal. If the volume level of the "echo" signal approaches or surpasses that of the "source" signal, a feedback situation may result. Under some circumstances, this effect may prove useful.

Multiple echoes can be created on a four-track machine as well. With the use of the intervening tracks it is possible to create a longer delay (figure 8.4c). With a speaker on each channel, the echo can be made to move around the room (adding the dotted lines in figure 8.4c). Different tape speeds will affect the length of the delay; a variable-speed recorder or **flanging** (gently applying pressure to the supply reel to vary tape speed) allows for interesting effects. Room resonance can be added by using a microphone to record the echo (figure 8.4d).

Although initially interesting, tape echo may become rather predictable. As one of a broad repertoire of synthesizer-tape techniques it is worth exploring.

FOR FURTHER STUDY

Appendix E contains suggestions for further reading on page 265 .

EXERCISES

Exercises 8.1 through 8.6 explore different aspects of stop-start editing and splicing through a series of short, compositionally-oriented projects. Exercise 8.4 uses cutting and splicing techniques to combine the first three exercises. In exercises 8.7 through 8.10 sound-with-sound, tape echo, and sound-on-sound are explored, while 8.11 and 8.12 require more precompositional score planning to develop an electronic "ensemble" and an acoustic-electronic live performance piece.

EXERCISE 8.1

Patch the synthesizer output to the line input of a tape recorder (or mixer attached to a recorder) and the output of the recorder either to headphones or to an appropriate amplifier and speaker. With the monitor switch on "source" establish a good recording level (the loudest playing should only dip slightly into the red zone on the recorder's level meter).

Create a short (20- to 30-second) monophonic or simple multivoice excerpt using one instrumental patch. It should involve a general increase in activity from slow to fast notes and should end abruptly rather than sound finished. Record this excerpt.

Make an appropriate score of the excerpt, including any relevant patch information. Also start a log of the contents of the recording tape.

Figure 8.4. Tape echo patches. Monitoring the tape while in record mode exploits the distance between the record and play heads.

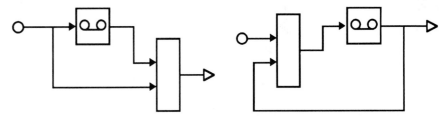

a. Single-echo patch   *b. Multiple-echo patch*

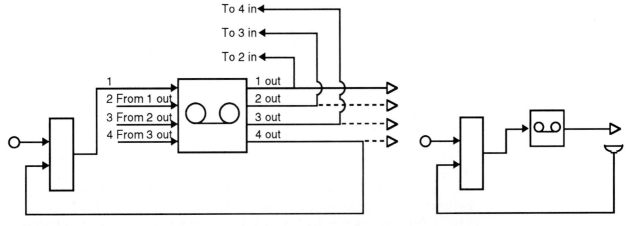

c. A longer delay is created by processing the signal through more tracks before mixing the echo and the source signal. Adding speakers to each track (dotted lines) allows each stage of the echo to be heard.

*d. This modification of **b** introduces room resonance (and noise) through the use of a microphone in the loop.*

EXERCISE 8.2

Using the same procedure as exercise 8.1, develop and record another segment. It should have a different tone color than exercise 8.1 and should have a contrasting character. Pitched material is to be presented in short, irregular bursts of rapid notes, which over the course of the excerpt should slow down.

Make an appropriate score of the excerpt, including any relevant patch information. Don't forget to log the contents of the recording tape.

EXERCISE 8.3

Using the same procedure as exercise 8.1 and 8.2, create and record a final segment, which quotes from the first two and acts to summarize and complete the action. As in exercises 8.1 and 8.2, make an appropriate score of the excerpt, including any relevant patch information. Log the contents of the recording tape.

EXERCISE 8.4

Using tape splicing techniques, cut and splice the end of exercise 8.1 and the beginning of exercise 8.2 so that the second immediately follows the first. Do the same with exercises 8.2 and 8.3. Evaluate the quality of the splices. If they are too noticeable, redo them. It's generally best to hide a splice by following it immediately with a loud passage (it distracts the ear from any click the splice might make). Different background noise levels will also cause one to notice a splice.

EXERCISE 8.5

Using stop-start editing procedures, create a monophonic excerpt of at least 60 seconds in length, consisting of a succession of short musical events. Each event should have 1 to 10 tones of randomly varying duration and pitch. Each of the first five events should have its own unique timbre (vary filter, resonance, and waveform settings between events on analog synthesizers). All succeeding events should reuse one of the earlier tone colors, with no two neighboring events using the same timbre (in order to retrieve or reproduce a patch on an analog synthesizer, it is necessary to keep a record of patches).

In addition to patch information, make a score showing the number of tones in each event (1 to 10), its timbre (use the letters A to E or descriptive labels), and its rough length in seconds. Listen critically to the finished work. Is stop-start editing satisfactory? Was the recording done cleanly, with a minimum of noise? Is the recorded material as random as you thought, or do patterns, either planned or unplanned, develop?

EXERCISE 8.6

Using stop-start editing, create a sequence of at least 12 tones, each different in timbre, envelope, and duration from the others. Cut and splice this sequence to create an interesting succession of tones. Tones need not remain in their recorded order (but don't splice one in backwards . . . yet).

EXERCISE 8.7

On one channel, record a repetitive, rhythmic bass line for 30 to 60 seconds. This patch should suggest a plucked, stringed instrument. If an analog synthesizer is available, try setting a short attack and medium decay, experimenting with different release times on the envelope generator patched to the VCA. Whether analog or digital, play the patch with short keystrokes. Using sel-sync, set the recorded channel to sync and record a more lyrical but still rhythmic counterpoint on the other channel.

EXERCISE 8.8

Using figure 8.4a, create a tape echo. This patch does not record the echo: a second machine or a different patch is needed for that purpose. The echo interval will be longer for slower speeds. To use the echo, thread a reel of tape on the recorder, set up the patch (monitor switch on "tape"), select a synthesizer instrument, press the record and play controls, and experiment. Try playing various synthesizer instruments through this echo patch, also exploring with different tape speeds.

EXERCISE 8.9

Set up the multiple-tape echo patch of figure 8.4b. After experimenting with the patch, write or improvise and record an excerpt that suggests the beginning, development, and ending of a brief spring rainstorm. On an analog synthesizer, short ADSR settings in conjunction with some experimentation with VCO and VCF settings will be necessary (some discrete lightning might also be appropriate; what role can a noise generator play?). On a digital synthesizer, adapt presets or create new patches for this exercise. Sometimes playing a sound in a register other than its intended register, or one or two parameters is all that is necessary.

EXERCISE 8.10

Realize a four-voice Bach chorale or other musical excerpt using sound-on-sound, recording one musical line, or voice, at a time. Each line should have a distinctive timbre.

On analog synthesizers it may help to use a tuning fork or a tuned acoustical instrument to tune the VCOs. Alternatively, record a reference tone and tune the VCOs to that tone. If there is a "sync" switch on one of the VCOs, explore its use on a patch or two (the synced VCO can be tuned to emphasize different harmonic partials of the VCO to which it is synchronized, or it can be tuned in unison to give a fatter sound to the signal). If the synthesizer does not have the sync feature, it can be simulated by mixing the output of two VCOs, tuning them in unison or setting one to some harmonic of the other.

On digital synthesizers, try layering sounds or using a dual voice function for a fatter sound. Since the synthesizer will be recorded four times, there's no need to save voices, so experiment with unique sounds that normally would use up too many voices.

Figure 8.5. Patches for exercise 8.10

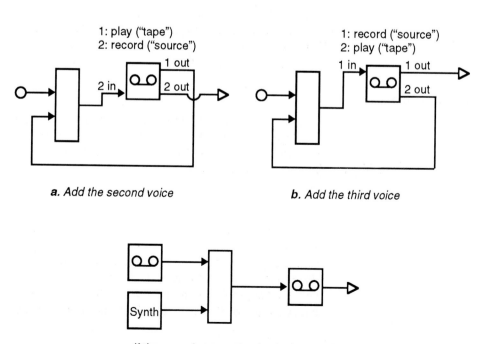

a. Add the second voice

b. Add the third voice

c. If the recorder cannot selectively record a designated track, two recorders will be needed.

Following the recording of one line, create a patch for the second line, rehearse its performance against the first line, and (using the appropriate patch in figure 8.5) record both lines on the second tape channel. Determine the patch for the third voice, rehearse it with the other two, and record all three back on the first channel (figure 8.5b or c). The fourth voice may either be recorded alone on the second channel (using sound-with-sound technique) or recorded with the other voices on channel two. In either case, the end result is to be played monaurally through one speaker.

EXERCISE 8.11

Using figure 8.6 as a model for constructing an original score, create and realize a work for a four-instrument "percussion" ensemble and record it using sound-with-sound or sound-on-sound. Each patch should relate rather loosely to some acoustic percussion instrument and should have some characteristic rhythmic patterns or modes of playing. Since the piece will be recorded one instrument at a time, plan the overall effect before recording. There should be at least one rhythmic pattern (of your own choosing) almost constantly present in at least one instrument or another.

EXERCISE 8.12

Develop a score for a synthesizer ensemble or a mixed synthesizer and acoustic percussion ensemble in any familiar style. Figure 8.6 may serve as a model, if desired. Rehearse and perform the piece. How can tuning problems be avoided? How are the different parts (electronic versus live) coordinated? Is there a leader? Does everybody do whatever he or she wants, or is there a choice of events or even a specific succession?

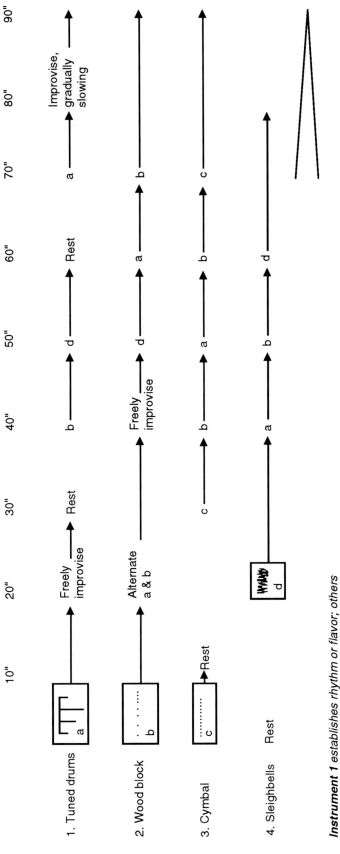

Instrument 1 *establishes rhythm or flavor; others should fit in against it. Short amounts of silence are appropriate at any time.*

Figure 8.6 Sample score for exercise 8.11

VOCABULARY

Most of the following terms were used for the first time in this chapter. Several may have a different use than earlier in the book. A definition of each term may be found in the glossary.

bias	degauss	flanging
ips	noise reduction	print-through
sel-sync	signal to noise ratio	sound-on-sound
sound-with-sound	stop-start editing	tails-out

REVIEW QUESTIONS

QUESTION 8.1

Match related terms by writing the letter of the term in the second column in the blank of the term in the first column that most closely relates to it.

Bulk Eraser	_____	A.	Degaussing
Input	_____	B.	Sound-with-sound
Playback	_____	C.	Source
Print-through	_____	D.	Tails-out
Sel-sync	_____	E.	Tape

QUESTION 8.2

Compare and contrast the following terms.

Sound-on-sound— Sound-with-sound

_____

_____

_____

_____

Stop-start editing— Tape splicing

_____

_____

_____

_____

QUESTION 8.3

Define briefly.

Equalization

_____

_____

_____

_____

Print-through

_____

_____

_____

_____

QUESTION 8.4

Provide the question for the given answer.

ANSWER	QUESTION
Compensation for distortion	What is _____ ?
Standard cassette speed	What is _____ ?
Unwanted sound	What is _____ ?
Gap between playback and record head in conjunction with controlled feedback loop	What is _____ ?

CHAPTER · NINE

SOUND EXTENSIONS

Peripheral Equipment
  Mixers
  Effects Devices
  Compressor/Limiter
  Noise Reduction
Using Space
  Placing the Sound
  Panning and Spatial Modulation
Planning for Performance
  Recorded Material
  Live Electronics
  Live and Recorded
Classic Tape Studio Techniques
  Classifying Sounds
  Modifying Sounds
For Further Study

In previous chapters, the focus of the compositional approach was on the synthesizer and the microcomputer, particularly on their use in instrument design. In this chapter, we will look at some extensions of these forces in recording, spatial placement, and performance.

Once instruments are designed, they must be recorded, sequenced, or played in some fashion. Peripheral equipment can both strengthen reproduction of sound and extend the process of instrument design into the recording itself. The use of space should also be a design consideration, as should the ensemble (electronic or electronic/live) in which an instrument is to be used.

Prior to the development of the synthesizer, the recording tape itself was extremely important in the development of complex pieces of music. The use of tape techniques tends to be somewhat time-consuming, and requires more precompositional planning to avoid the creation of a mountain of small pieces of recording tape. The dividend of unusual sonorities and sound successions not available by other means awaits composers who are patient enough to become proficient in this area.

PERIPHERAL EQUIPMENT

An important sonic extension comes from the addition of equipment originally intended to enhance the quality of sound. Current technology allows mixers, effects devices, **compressors, limiters, noise reduction** systems, and other devices, to shape and vary signals with a range of procedures.

MIXERS

Sound is dealt with in several important ways in a mixer. The most obvious is that sound from different sources is mixed together. **Faders** allow relative loudness of each signal, which typically is either a line-level signal (from a synthesizer, for example), a high- or low-**impedance** signal from a microphone, or an input from one channel of a recorder. There will also be some means of attenuating the input signal with a trim pot or attenuating pad so it doesn't overload the system.

A mixer can also shape the sound through **equalization** (EQ) controls. These can range from simple treble and bass controls to three-band equalization on each input channel to multi-band equalization on the output stage. EQ allows emphasis or attenuation on each band, and is useful in both playback situations (cleaning up and enhancing the recorded signal) and recording situations (accentuating the highs so that, on playback, there is a stronger signal-to-noise ratio).

A third use of the mixer is to route signals and mixes of signals to various locations. Mixing for recording or playback, routing signals to effects devices, or preparing a headphone mix for use by performers in recording are among its functions. It is often possible to solo a channel, muting all the others, with the push of a button. The mixer also receives the results of an effects send, and has the capability of mixing the effects return in with the other signals present in the board. Figure 2.3 on page 22 shows a portion of a typical mixer front panel.

EFFECTS DEVICES

In earlier times, a musician was proud to possess a spring **reverb**, which added a certain, if somewhat metallic, echo to the sound. Tape echo boxes were also available. These basically contained a loop of tape and allowed the distance between record and play heads to be varied, giving some control over the length of the echo. Hammond organ players long enjoyed the Leslie speaker which imparted a rotating effect to the sound by either using a rotating speaker or digital circuitry to simulate the rotation.

All these and many more are currently available, often in one box. Sometimes, several effects can be produced at once. **Digital delay** allows the repetition of the input signal at specified times and amounts. **Flanging** is a digital form of an earlier technique of making a sound go out-of-tune with itself by lightly pressing on the flange of the reel of a tape recorder. **Chorus**, reverb, and a host of other effects can extend any input signal. Multi-effects boxes often include various types of filters and equalization schemes which can be put into various series, so that a signal may be processed by several effects in a row. Table 9.1 offers a list of the most common effects along with brief definitions. While some effects are part of the design of a sound, others have their main use in processing signals for recording and playback.

Most current digital effects devices have MIDI input, so that the choice of an effect can be controlled from another MIDI device. With the help of a software or hardware MIDI mapping device, a program change message sent to a synthesizer can be remapped (changed to another value) and sent to an effects device, so that sound and effect both change simultaneously.

As wonderful as these effects are, a certain restraint is needed, since many are rather obvious. Certainly a bit of delay or other effect to give the sensation of being in a large

Table 9.1. Various effects and signal processing procedures

PROCEDURE	FUNCTION
Chorus	Signal is played with a copy of itself set at a fixed delay interval
Companding	Combines *compression* and *expansion* so that both dynamic range and background noise are reduced (compresses signal before recording, expands signal at playback)
Compression	Reduces the dynamic range of a signal (reduces high-level signals, boosts low-level signals)
Delay	The time between the direct sound and each early reflection; the time before the onset of *reverberation* (a range of delays is offered by a digital delay device)
Echo	An identifiable repetition of a signal (often divided into **early reflections** and **echo clusters**)
Equalization	Alters the frequency response of a signal (**preemphasis**: raise low and/or high frequencies above noise levels before recording; **postemphasis**: restore frequencies to normal levels at playback)
Expanding	Increases the dynamic range of a signal (reduces low-level signals, boosts high-level signals)
Feedback	Regeneration or emphasis of some portion of a signal caused by the combination of that signal with itself in a feedback loop
Flanging	Signal is played with a copy of itself at a variable delay interval, reinforcing or cancelling various frequencies as the interval changes (the term refers to applying pressure to the flange of the supply reel of a tape recorder, causing the recorder speed to vary from the speed of a second machine with the same signal)
Limiting	Limits a signal to a specified maximum amplitude (compression of 10:1 or greater cause sharp attenuation at the desired level)
Noise gate	Sharply reduces any signal below its threshold setting (a form of *expansion*, used to minimize background noise)
Noise reduction	The application of various combinations of *compression, expansion, limiting, equalization,* and/or filtering to reduce noise and increase the signal to noise ratio
Panning	Moving a signal from one speaker to another by varying the amount of signal present at each speaker
Phase shift	A somewhat subtle electronic version of tape *flanging*, in which the copy of the signal is made to be out of phase through application of a short *delay*
Pitch shift	Signal is played with a copy of itself that has had its partials shifted by the same frequency, generally creating a mix with non-harmonic components
Resonance	A concentration of energy at a filter cutoff frequency
Reverberation	Persistent echoes so closely spaced that they are not individually identifiable
Ring Modulation	Amplitude modulation usually resulting in the sum and difference frequencies of all partials of two input signals

room is worthwhile. Often this can be simulated by modifying release values on the synthesizer voices or instruments used in a piece.

COMPRESSOR/LIMITER

During recording, or, for that matter, any time microphones are used, an input signal may suddenly become too strong for the system, causing a rather unpleasant distortion. A compressor is intended to prevent this kind of distortion by flattening peaks and compressing the dynamic range of the signal. It increases the strength of low-level signals and lowers the strength of high-level signals. This can create a "breathing" effect if the input signal fluctuates around the threshold setting.

It is generally possible to set attack and release times, input and output levels, compression ratio, and threshold level. Some devices will also have **expander** capabilities, which are opposite in effect to the compressor: low-level signals are attenuated, and high-level signals are boosted. Compression is also used by limiters (compressors with a high compression ratio). They tend to have a very limited or virtually fixed dynamic range, and are used to set an absolute maximum level, rather than providing the more gradual approach offered by standard compressors.

These types of devices can be great assets in the studio. Strong signals can be compressed or limited to avoid distortion, and the dynamic range can be adjusted to attenuate background noise. In addition to providing clearer, more natural sounds, the compressor/limiter can be used to give a sound more punch, or to deliberately give a sound a somewhat unnatural quality.

NOISE REDUCTION

One reason for the increase in quality of cassette recorders over the last decade, and indeed of tape recorders in general over the past several decades, has been the development of effective noise reduction systems. While the compressor/limiter discussed previously could be used for noise reduction, it doesn't go far enough for practical use.

The first **Dolby** system was introduced in 1966. There are currently a number of different Dolby systems. Dolby A works on portions of the audio signal, compressing or expanding segments during recording and reversing the procedure during playback. Dolby B and C types, designed to reduce hiss, are simpler and are commonly built in to many cassette recorders. Some cassettes will also have **HX Pro**, which effectively works to reduce distortion, rather than noise, as in the other types. Where B and C are active in both record and playback modes, HX Pro is only active in recording.

The other commonly used noise reduction system is **dbx**. Prior to compression, there is a boost of high-frequency signals, to make them louder than the hiss. Unlike Dolby, compression is applied to the entire dynamic range. Like Dolby, dbx is used in both recording and playback.

USING SPACE

With the present ease of producing sounds on the synthesizer, the wealth of sonic possibilities available through the use of recording equipment is often overlooked. With two-track capability, sound-on-sound makes it possible to overlay musical events, producing vertical complexity. The **classic studio** techniques discussed here encourage horizontal complexity to a great extent. With tape techniques it is easy to juxtapose and sequence unrelated events. With four-track capability, yet another world is opened.

Multitrack recording (four or more tracks) offers the opportunity to create yet further vertical complexity and diversity or to position sound with greater ease throughout the listening environment. As more tracks are laid down, however, it becomes possible for a

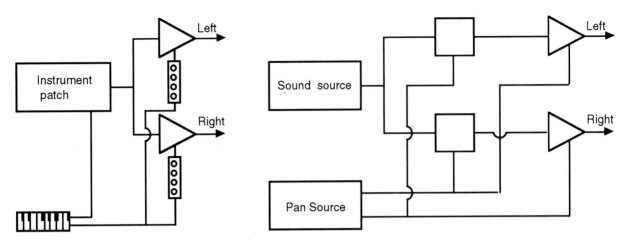

a. Delay as an extension of
an instrument patch

b. Panning (a variant of figure 5.5b). This
patch allows more control over signal
quality as it is panned. The extremes
may be softened and the center accentuated.

Figure 9.1. Delay and panning
patches

piece to lose cohesion or precision. Often, as an aid to recording, a **click track** will be
made on one track as a guide for recording on the other tracks. The click track serves as a
metronome: short pulsations that indicate the regular passage of time. The click track will
usually not be a part of the final product, except possibly as an inaudible (to the audience)
guide for the performer, when tape music and live performance are combined.

PLACING THE SOUND

The standard output format for recorded material involves two channels. Although it is
assumed that the output is stereophonic, this does not necessarily have to be the case. In
producing a two-channel recording format, there are several options for the placement of
the recorded material. The output can be monophonic, with the sound placed exclusively
on one channel. The output can be **binaural**, with one pattern of events occurring on one
channel, and a separate pattern taking place on the other. This is often called stereo, even
though it really is not, since the two signals are isolated.

Stereophonic output can take different guises. It ranges from the presentation of a
single pattern equally strongly on each channel, so that the sound is centered between the
two speakers, to the presentation of two patterns, each strongly presented on one channel
but mixed at lower amplitude on the other channel, to the presentation of many patterns
whose position in space depends on the event's relative strength on each channel.

Although a stereo effect can be made by using a panpot on a mixer to determine the
location of a signal, there is actually more to it than that. If a sound is located "near" a
speaker, the portion of that sound heard on the second speaker should arrive slightly later,
to simulate the effect distance has on sound.

This can be simulated by running the signal through a module designed to delay it.
On analog synthesizers, route the signal through an envelope-controlled VCF or VCA
with an attack setting that is slower than the attack of the signal. The envelope can either
be triggered as part of the original patch (figure 9.1a) or triggered by the musician.

PANNING AND SPATIAL MODULATION

Spatial modulation gives the effect that a sonic image moves from one point to another. The signal may appear to move from one speaker to the other or from far to near. An effect worth exploring is the frequency shift (the Doppler effect) that occurs in the train whistle when a train passes the point of observation.

AUTOMATED PANNING

Large analog synthesizers may have voltage controlled **panning** devices (VCAs, mixers, panpots) to facilitate spatial modulation procedures. Lacking these, a panning patch can be constructed, such as shown in figure 5.5b on page 87. This may require modules not always available in small studios.

Digital synthesizers may also have panning control, at least by LFO. Often other control sources, including a range of MIDI controllers, may be used. For example, a signal may be panned according to location on a keyboard, or according to velocity, or according a modulation wheel or volume pedal.

In figure5.5b, a low-frequency sine wave is available in normal and inverted forms (this happens in an inverter module or as the output of the VCO). One form controls each VCA, so that one is open while the other is closed. The output of each VCA is sent to a power amplifier and speaker, or to left and right tape recorder channels. By adjusting VCA initial gain and control voltage inputs, the sound can be made to move from speaker to speaker at the rate determined by the LFO frequency.

The danger in this procedure, in addition to its obvious periodic character, is that the signal may appear to be stronger at the endpoints than in the middle. This may be avoided by adding in the VCFs shown in figure 9.1b. They actually work against their respective VCAs, since the Fc of one channel is controlled by the same signal that is controlling the VCA of the other channel. With proper setting, the VCFs soften the signal as the VCAs increase it, strengthening the signal as it crosses between speakers.

MANUAL PANNING

With a stereo mixer, panning can be done manually. The synthesizer is patched to the mixer, and each output channel is patched to one channel of the recorder. If the event also requires operation of the synthesizer, manual panning will require two people, one to play the synthesizer, the other to handle the panning. If the material is first recorded without panning, it can be panned during re-recording. The material is played back on a second machine and panned manually as the signal is sent to the recording machine.

In either case, set the appropriate volume controls, start recording, and pan the signal with the panpot on the input channel of the mixer. Without a panpot (or a mixer), things get difficult. It is possible to simulate panning by the expedient of recording an event on one channel while fading it out. After rewinding, the same event can be recorded on the second channel with a fade-in. Moving patterns are very difficult to coordinate in this fashion, unless they are more-or-less random collections of very fast notes, where the lack of coordination may be hidden by the random effect of the pattern.

MIDI sequencers work well for this sort of panning, since editing can be quite precise. The track to be panned is recorded and copied to a second track. Velocity is edited to create appropriate fadeouts and fade-ins (editing is discussed in chapter ten). The tracks are put on separate MIDI channels and sent to different synthesizers or different portions of the same synthesizer. In multitrack tape recording, the same synthesizer may be used in successive passes, with one track of the recorder providing a synchronizing code to keep everything coordinated (also discussed in chapter ten).

PLANNING FOR PERFORMANCE

Performance of electronic music takes place in three primary ways. Often, the results of studio work will be a tape-recorded composition, performed in a standard concert hall over loudspeakers. Sometimes recorded material is performed in conjunction with live performance forces. As well, electronic equipment can be treated as real-time performance instruments, without substantial addition and intervention of recorded material.

RECORDED MATERIAL

Many listeners and composers find the standard concert hall setting unsatisfactory for the performance of recorded material. It does not fit the idea of a normal concert for people to sit and watch an empty stage (and applaud the tape recorder when the music is done).

Alternative performance situations, including museums, churches, and other resonant areas are worth considering. They often encourage ambulatory rather than stationary listening, allowing the audience to sample the music from different locations. Light shows or other multimedia events allow electronic music to function as one element of a larger creative experience.

Equally as important as considering the room the music will be heard in is considering the speakers that will be used. In studio situations monitor speakers should give a fairly flat response, along the lines of "what-you-hear-is-what-you-recorded." Other speakers may accentuate the bass, for example. Speakers in an automobile or in portable tape players may not effectively handle as wide a bandwidth as in the studio. It may prove useful, therefore, to make several different mixes or versions of the work, each intended for a specific combination of speaker and acoustical setting.

LIVE ELECTRONICS

This involves both the possibility of the synthesizer as a real-time performing instrument and as a modifier of material performed on an acoustic instrument during the act of performance. **Phase shifters, ring modulators**, various voltage-controlled filters, and digital effects devices offer the possibility of interesting timbral results. A composer who has been particularly effective in this area is Morton Subotnik, who has some specially designed equipment, including recording capability to make what he calls a "ghost tape," containing control signals that affect the operation of various black boxes to provide wonderful, unexpected effects during performance.

REAL-TIME SOUND PROCESSING

A synthesizer equipped with an audio input or a pre-amp input can function as an audio processor. An acoustic instrument can be miked and the signal sent to the synthesizer. It can be run through the filter, subjected to **resonance** and voltage control, and sent back out to be combined with the acoustic signal itself. A ring modulator or digital effects device can process the signal, if available.

Sounds can also be sent to a tape recorder set up to produce a tape **echo**. Sounds that are normally hard to hear, such as some of the effects produced by playing on the strings inside the piano, or many of the sounds made by human vocal cords, can be processed by a synthesizer before being amplified by the output amplifier and heard by the audience. In this way acoustic and electronic forces combine to create unique ensembles.

LIVE AND RECORDED

Recorded or sequenced material may accompany, or be the soloist, or be an equal partner with the performer(s). There are problems of coordination between performers and tape, but with some planning this option can be quite attractive. It may be necessary to have someone control the operation of the tape machine. Clocks or timers help performers keep their place. Well-constructed scores with cues indicated for the performers are useful. The tape or sequence itself may contain a click track to aid in synchronization of acoustic and recorded events.

COORDINATION

Recorded music goes inexorably onward, with none of the flexibility expected from a live performer. Some composers surmount this problem by having one performer operate the tape machine or sequencer, stopping it from time to time to allow the other performers to provide the expressivity lacking in the recording. Some composers provide recorded space as best they can for performers to be flexible, or they will not insist on total coordination between musical forces. A notated score is generally quite important for the performers; this should give as much useful information about the tape portion as possible. Sometimes a click track or other recorded cues, which the performers hear via earphones, may be needed. If these problems of coordination are not enough to make one give up, there still remains the problem of timbre (and a close relation: intonation).

TIMBRE, PITCH, AND INTONATION

Electronic sounds tend to have a steady-state quality about them, with little of the warmth provided by the vagaries of acoustic instruments. This makes it important to strive for the development of richer, often time-variant, timbres and amplitude envelopes. In combining acoustic and electronic forces, one should strive for a feeling of warmth and expression in the sonic output. Some consideration should be given to the timbral makeup of the intended acoustic partners, so that the electronic material blends or contrasts effectively.

If predominantly pitched material is being used, it is important that the tuning of the electronic material be consistent and in agreement with the tuning of the acoustic forces. As an aid to intonation, a tuning tone may be recorded on tape. If multiphonics or other unconventional instrumental uses are being featured, intonation may be of less concern. Several of the composition projects at the end of the chapter concentrate on these problems, and suggest some solutions. Although there may be some reinvention of the wheel, composers often seem to find unique solutions for each situation, rather than developing a single approach to the electronic/acoustic combination.

SPEAKER PLACEMENT

Consideration should be given to the location of all sounding material. If the acoustic forces are seated conventionally on a stage, should the speakers be placed among the acoustic forces, or at a distance? With ambulatory performers, the effect of moving the acoustic performers may be explored. Since four speakers can be placed at corners of the hall, might not each speaker have a complement of musicians? If only two speakers are in use, a similar effect might be obtained by dividing the ensemble into two groups.

A problem of the contrast between electronic and acoustic timbres can arise. This can be minimized by some "enhancement," or subtle miking, of acoustic sounds or by devising an arrangement of speakers that simulates the omnidirectional spray of sound common to acoustic instruments, rather than the simple point location of a speaker system.

CLASSIC TAPE STUDIO TECHNIQUES

Before the development of the synthesizer as a readily available package of modules, electronic composers made use of a broad range of sounds, including virtually any acoustic event, in constructing their works. **Musique concrete**, or music based on real, rather

Table 9.2. Graphics symbols for tape music

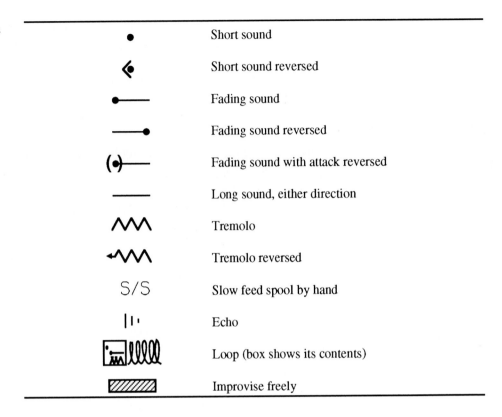

●	Short sound
◀●	Short sound reversed
●——	Fading sound
——●	Fading sound reversed
(●)——	Fading sound with attack reversed
——	Long sound, either direction
⋀⋀	Tremolo
◀⋀⋀	Tremolo reversed
S/S	Slow feed spool by hand
❘ ⋅	Echo
▨▨▨	Loop (box shows its contents)
▨▨▨	Improvise freely

than electronic or synthetic, sounds developed and flourished for a period of time. Tape editing was the primary means of arranging and juxtaposing events into a coherent and meaningful order.

CLASSIFYING SOUNDS

It is helpful to have some means of classifying and organizing sonic material. Terence Dwyer, in his *Composing with Tape Recorders* (Oxford University Press, 1971), proposed a simple system to describe the essential features of pitch, duration, timbre, and volume. He described pitch as high, medium, or low, and stated that the volume of a sound source is of little importance, since it can be augmented or diminished in the recording process. He recommends that graph paper be used to make a score, with timing represented horizontally and pitch represented vertically, and also suggests some symbols that the composer can use to represent various durations and devices (see table 9.2).

Sounds can be classified into four duration groups. *Short sounds* are little more than a click or a tap. *Long sounds* must have at least a half-second duration at the same volume level. *Fading sounds* start with a clear attack and die away. *Tremolos* are a class of rapidly reiterated sounds such as drum rolls or crumpling paper.

Most sounds of the first three duration groups can be converted into tremolos by repeating them. In this case it is difficult (and unnecessary) to tell which group the single sound would have belonged to. Tremolos may appear to the casual ear to be continuous sounds, but they are in fact more interesting and exciting than the flatness of long sounds.

Timbre is often difficult to describe precisely. The composer should listen critically to the sounds he or she is creating. Although it is good to have unity, one should also seek diversity of timbre and duration type. The application of speed change or the reversal of tape direction may contribute to variety by changing the character of an event.

The process of classification makes a good starting point for the exploration of acoustic sound sources. As they are modified, either by the techniques discussed later or by the use of effects devices or synthesizer modules, their classification becomes more difficult. Some sources defy easy categorization. The human voice is a good example, due to the wide range of sounds it may produce. Extended vocal techniques, in fact, have become an important area of vocal specialization in twentieth-century music. The voice offers itself as an interesting and readily available source of sonic material.

MODIFYING SOUNDS

Standard techniques were developed for modifying basic sound sources, which often allowed the creation of strange and wonderful sounds quite different from their point of origin. A piece of musique concrete could be based on a combination of almost any sound sources, from crackling leaves to street noises to traditional instruments—the only limit was the composer's imagination and need. Even the acoustical feedback caused when a microphone is placed too close to a speaker could be useful. Another term for musique concrete is **tape music**, since much of the modification and storage of sonic events takes place on the tape recorder.

SPEED CHANGE

This technique, in combination with cutting and splicing (discussed in chapter eight), can produce fascinating results when everyday sounds are removed from their normal contexts and modified. If the tape speed of a recorded excerpt is doubled, its pitch rises an octave (frequency is doubled) and it takes place in half the time. Likewise, halving its speed lowers the event an octave and slows it down. This is a useful, if somewhat tricky modification technique. If a singing voice is played back at twice the speed, its vibrato also doubles speed and sounds consequently somewhat unusual.

Some recorders have pitch controls that allow for some control of tape speed during recording and playback. They often allow a pitch change of up to plus or minus one-third of an octave. In addition, there are commercial devices that may control a recorder's speed and allow tape to be synchronized to a sequencer or video recorder.

BACKWARD SOUND

A recorded sound played backwards sounds like . . . a recorded sound played backwards. Nonetheless, this technique can produce interesting effects. Again, this technique is of greatest utility used in combination with other techniques. For example, rather than merely playing a passage backwards, the composer can combine forward and backward events in a single passage through tape editing and multitrack recording procedures.

Not all tape recorders lend themselves easily to backwards play, nor is this procedure necessarily useful for all tape formats. In full track monaural mode merely exchange the positions of the two reels, thread the tape normally, and play back the recorded material. This reverses tape direction, so that the end of the sound is heard before the beginning. Record this on a second machine and insert the excerpt into the master tape.

Alternatively, splice out the events to be reversed and reinsert them, reversing their direction. Do be sure to keep the same surface toward the tape heads. This avoids the extra noise caused by re-recording but, of course, alters the source tape.

For half-track monaural recording, proceed as just described. Be aware, however, that the signal will appear to have switched channels (figure 9.2a and b), since the tape has been turned upside down, even though the same surface is presented to the tape heads. If this material is to be spliced into a work in progress, plan ahead by recording the original on the opposite channel, so that reversal moves it to the proper channel.

With recording in half-track stereo, reversal again causes the signal to switch channels. Backward sound is most often done in the context of monaural recording, or in the

Figure 9.2. Half- and quarter-track stereo tape formats

a. Half-track
(forward)   *b.* Half-track
(reversed)   *c.* Quarter-track
(forward)   *d.* Quarter-track
(reversed)

Figure 9.3. Normal and reversed tape threading

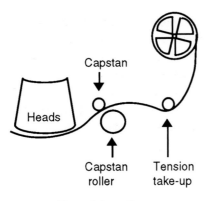 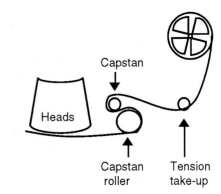

a. Normal threading   *b. Reversed threading*

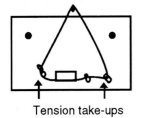

Tension take-ups

Figure 9.4. Tape loop threading

preparation of a musical line before it is mixed with other material. If both channels are recorded on, and a small section is taken out and reversed, not only will the material on both channels be backwards but the signals will have crossed to the opposite speaker.

In quarter-track stereo, tape reversal also moves the signal. Unlike the half-track format, however, the signal can't be heard when it is reversed. Figure 9.2c and d show the forward and reversed placement of the recorded signals. Regardless of the numbering of the channels (one to four), the record and playback heads are set to act upon material placed in positions one and three: the reversed signals become invisible to the tape heads. Neither splicing nor reversing supply and take-up reels will create backward sound. It may be possible to thread the tape backwards around the capstan, causing a reversal of tape play direction (figure 9.3b). This procedure may result in broken tape or damage to the tape machine, so its use is not advised.

Backward sound, and indeed most musique concrete techniques are little used with four or more tracks, since the entire tape is affected. As mentioned earlier, these techniques are best used in monaural formats, with the result perhaps being one element of a more complex multitrack project.

TAPE LOOP

A length of recorded tape can be spliced into a loop and placed on a tape machine for playback. Avoid twisting the tape when making a loop. Supply and take-up reels may not be necessary, although something is needed to take up the tension at the top of the loop (see figure 9.4). A microphone stand, or a weighted glass jar, or other smooth, rounded surface may be used. During playback the loop can be re-recorded on a second machine, mixed with other events, or patched through synthesizer modules or signal processing devices and modified before re-recording.

TAPE MANIPULATION

During recording or playback, the sound may be altered by applying a little pressure with the hand to the edge, or flange, of the supply reel. Flanging done during recording slows the tape causing the sound to appear higher at that spot on playback. Flanging done during playback slows the tape and lowers the pitch of the material playing back.

It is also possible to move the tape by hand rather than by motor. Both hands are needed, one on each reel, to keep the proper tension (most machines will stop recording or playing back if the tension drops too much). This gives a somewhat irregular effect to the resulting signal. During recording, material will be recorded only when the tape is moving, Since the material is being recorded at quite a slow rate, during normal playback events will appear to be quite high-pitched, as well as irregular. During re-recording, manipulation of the playback machine will produce irregular alteration and changes of pitch that may be recorded on a second machine.

OTHER PROCEDURES

Musique concrete also makes use of tape echo, sound-with-sound, and sound-on-sound, discussed in chapter eight. The combination of recorded acoustic events with electronically produced events offers the chance to expand sonic resources. Spatial modulation, discussed earlier, can make a sound appear to migrate from one location to another.

The tape techniques discussed in this chapter can be replaced, to some extent, by procedures available through sampling (especially in combination with a flexible sample editing program) — but only to a point. Digital effects also offer sound extensions only dreamed of by earlier composers. Musique concrete should not be dismissed, however, as being too old-fashioned. They can certainly be modernized by being used in conjunction with contemporary resources.

Interesting effects can be created and then sampled. In turn, samples can be put on tape, manipulated, and then resampled. As recording to disk becomes more feasible and widespread, those interested in musique concrete can take fuller advantage of digital technology to create innovate sounds and effects. Certainly, the spirit of experimentation, combined with the attitude that any sound (or portion of a sound) can have musical significance, is worth adopting and cherishing.

FOR FURTHER STUDY

EXERCISES

Exercises 9.1 to 9.9 are intended to develop familiarity with various tape techniques. A number may be done just as effectively using a sampler and sequencing software (several also appear in chapter six); the focus here is on achieving familiarity with tape equipment and peripherals. Exercises 9.10 to 9.12 deal with realizing scores, using techniques explored in the earlier exercises. Exercises 9.13 to 9.15 are somewhat more extended, requiring either more advanced planning or more attention to compositional detail. In some of the exercises mention is made of an appropriate peripheral. Use of other resources when appropriate is encouraged.

EXERCISE 9.1

Record a variety of different acoustic events. Each sound should be recorded in as many of the duration groups (short, long, fading, tremolo) as are appropriate. Keep appropriate notes so that these events may be retrieved for use in other exercises.

Run the events through a digital effects device and find several useful modifications of each sound.

EXERCISE 9.2

Record a human voice producing several examples of each duration category. Experiment with different pitch areas and different vocal effects. For example, a tremolo may be made by gargling, by rapid lip movement (p-p-p-p-p), by trilling an r with the tongue, or by very slow motion of the vocal cords (the initial component of the sound ah).

If a sampler is available, record the same events and compare them. Which sounds better? What needs to be done to get a better signal?

EXERCISE 9.3

Juxtapose 8 to 10 of the events recorded in exercises 9.1 and 9.2 to create an interesting abstract sequence. Re-record events in their planned order to avoid destroying the source tape. Use tape-editing techniques where needed for a clean final product. This sequence should be monophonic. Some events should follow immediately from the previous event, while others may occur after a short pause (in other words, be creative: do not just mechanically move from event to event).

EXERCISE 9.4

Record the start of the Gettysburg Address. Using tape-splicing techniques, create a sentence ordering your favorite kind of pizza.

EXERCISE 9.5

Change the speed on the recorder to produce at least four altered versions of a low-pitched acoustic event. This exercise requires two recorders. Each speed change will raise the pitch one octave. Notice that the initial event should be long, since each generation will have half the duration of the previous one.

Also modify a high-pitched acoustic event by speed change in a similar manner. Each generation will be lower and longer.

Try this exercise both with and without a compressor/limiter or similar device. How much better is the signal with its use?

EXERCISE 9.6

Create a short excerpt exploring speed change and backward sound. Choosing a single event as a basis for this exercise, create eight variants involving either or both techniques and splice the variants together into an interesting succession.

EXERCISE 9. 7

Experiment with tape manipulation while you are recording. Provide a repetitive source (either a tape loop or a sequence) and apply pressure to the supply reel while recording the source.

Additionally, place the tape machine in record mode with the pause lever on. Experiment with recording while you move the reels by hand.

EXERCISE 9.8

Explore the spatial location modulation possibilities of the available studio equipment. Try different types of one-time spatial movement of a sonority. Alter various parameters in conjunction with the move (create your own version of the Doppler frequency shift or add some sort of timbral modification) .

Using the patch in figure 9.1b, experiment with automated panning. Modify the patch as needed.

Figure 9.5. Score for a tape loop

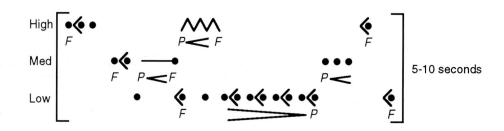

EXERCISE 9.9

Explore live/electronic modification possibilities with the available equipment. If possible, modify the live performance of an acoustic instrument or voice, using a microphone to input the sound to a synthesizer or effects device.

EXERCISE 9.10

Create a tape loop that realizes the short score given in figure 9.5. See table 9.2 for an explanation of the nontraditional symbols.

EXERCISE 9. 11

Realize the score given in figure 9.6 using primarily acoustic sound sources. Some source material may be developed on the synthesizer, and any material can be processed by the synthesizer. Two tape machines and sound-with-sound capability on one machine are needed.

EXERCISE 9.12

Record an acoustic event. Modify the recorded event with recording and/or synthesizer techniques (don't overlook the addition of effects) to produce a chain of events that progress from the original event to steadily less recognizable versions of the event. The piece can also be designed to do the reverse: move from the most distorted to steadily simpler versions, ending with the actual acoustic event. Extraneous recording noises should be edited out. If there is to be space between events, allow for it in the recording phase or splice in leader tape of the appropriate length.

EXERCISE 9.13

Develop a piece based on the structural use of texture. One possible plan is to move from thin to thick, keeping in mind that progress is not always in a straight line. The structure may be arbitrary.

Try using a telephone number as source material. Each successive section in the piece derives its textural density from the next digit of the number. How could this be done? Should textural density be relative? Should each number indicate the number of active musical lines, or the number of events per unit of time?

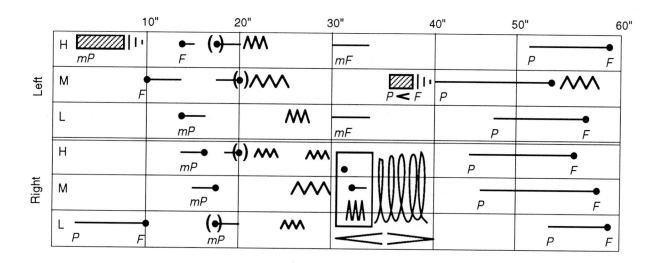

Figure 9.6. Score for exercise 9.11

VOCABULARY

Many of the following terms were used for the first time in this chapter. A definition of each term may be found in the glossary.

binaural	chorus effect	classic studio
click track	compressor	dbx
digital delay	Dolby	early reflection
echo	echo cluster	equalization
expander	fader	flanging
HX Pro	impedance	limiter
musique concrete	noise reduction	panning
phase shifter	postemphasis	preemphasis
resonance	reverb	ring modulator
spatial modulation	tape music	

REVIEW QUESTIONS

QUESTION 9.1

Match related terms by writing the letter of the term in the second column in the blank of the term in the first column that most closely relates to it.

Compression	____	A.	Amplitude
Fader	____	B.	Distortion
Pan	____	C.	Mixer
Panpot	____	D.	Preset
Program Change	____	E.	Spatial Modulation

QUESTION 9.2

Compare and contrast the following terms.

Dolby — dbx

_____

_____

_____

_____

Compression — Expansion

_____

_____

_____

_____

QUESTION 9.3

Provide the question for the given answer.

ANSWER	QUESTION
When tape speed doubles	What is _____?
Music based on the use of real sounds	What is _____?
Another term for the previous question	What is _____?
Common built-in noise reduction	What is _____?
Dwyer's four duration groups	What are _____ ,

_____ , _____ , and _____?

QUESTION 9.4

Define briefly.

Click track

_____

_____

_____

_____

Limiter

_____

_____

_____

_____

PART · FOUR

ELECTRONIC COMPOSITION

CHAPTER · TEN

SEQUENCING BASICS

A digital recording program that has some capability for overdubbing and editing can be quite useful as a compositional tool. Unlike magnetic recording, no additional noise is added during recording, since numerical values or data, rather than voltage, are recorded. This makes it possible to record material and work it over until it comes out right. With the rapid access made possible by disk drives, it is easy to store alternate versions on disk and quickly recall a previous version for comparison.

As of the early 1990s, magnetic tape recording is much more prevalent than digital recording, either to Digital Audio Tape (DAT) or direct-to-disk recording using computers with Digital Signal Processing (DSP) boards. A third approach, one that has links to magnetic tape on the one hand (through various synchronization time codes) and to direct digital recording on the other (since they both involve digital manipulation of data), is offered by MIDI sequencing software and hardware.

TO RECORD OR TO SEQUENCE?

The answer to this depends on the nature of the material to be recorded. Traditional acoustic musical instruments, voices, and other similar events must be recorded—either by a tape recorder, a sampler, or some other digital process. Digital synthesizers and related devices can also be recorded like other sound sources. Additionally, however, they can be sequenced using sequencing software and a computer or a hardware sequencer.

171

Recording and sequencing have many similar features. Different material may be recorded on different tracks (sequencers often allow a virtually unlimited number of tracks, however). Sound-on-sound and sound-with-sound capabilities exist. Both approaches typically offer the same sort of motion controls (play, record, fast forward, rewind).

One outstanding difference is that once material is recorded on tape, it is basically done (although skilled use of equalization and various effects during mixdown can do much to modify the character of the material). Material that has been sequenced is still very much open for modification. Virtually every aspect of sequenced material may be edited: when it starts, when it ends, its duration, its loudness, its timbre ("let's see if trumpet sounds better than sax"), its texture, its pitch (either by punching in, as would be done with magnetic tape, or by altering single pitches as needed), and a range of associated parameters. In one sense, then, sequencing is more flexible than recording—although sequenced material must either be digital in origin, or under digital control (this distinction blurs with direct digital recording, however, since digitized sound may be subject to many of the manipulations common to MIDI sequencing).

RECORDING AND PLAYBACK

The easiest use of a sequencer is to simply record whatever is played by the MIDI synthesizer or controller. To do this, the synthesizer is connected to a sequencer or the computer interface (see figure 10.1). This involves connecting the synthesizer "MIDI out" to the computer or sequencer "MIDI in," and the synthesizer "MIDI in" to the computer or sequencer "MIDI out."

After booting or starting the recording software there may be pre-recording setup procedures that must be carried out. It may be necessary to select an instrument or voice, to specify recording **parameters** such as the tempo of the built-in metronome and the number of beats that will be counted off before recording begins, and to place the desired track into record mode. Once the sequencer is ready, the recording may be made.

As indicated in chapter three, at its simplest MIDI records what keys are pressed and for how long. When a key is pressed, a **Note On** message is transmitted. The information sent includes MIDI channel information, which key was pressed, and keyboard velocity information for systems with velocity sensitivity.

When a key is released, a **Note Off** message is sent. It contains similar information. If recording is stopped while a key is still pressed, Note Off information is not recorded. On playback, the tone produced by that key will keep sounding, since it has not been told to stop. To end such an errant event, select a different instrument, or press the offending key if the synthesizer or controller is a keyboard or press the panic button (there's usually a procedure for sending a whole host of Note Off messages for just such occasions). If all else fails, shut the system down (and be more careful next time).

If a multitrack recording is to be made, it is often wise to make a backup copy (that is, save the file to disk) of the first track before recording new material. This guards against the unlikely event of material accidentally being erased or of some unforeseen

Figure 10.1. MIDI ins and outs. See also figure 3.6 on page 42 showing basic MIDI networks

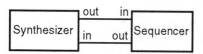

a. Sequencer may be dedicated hardware, communicating with one or more synthesizers.

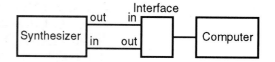

b. Sequencer may be computer software, communicating with one or more synthesizers through an interface box connected to a serial port or plugged into a computer slot or built into the computer to begin with.

Table 10.1. Functions of typical sequencer windows. The name "Chunks" is found only on *Performer*. Its overview function is found on many sequencers.

WINDOW	FUNCTION
Chunks	Allows flexible ordering of sequences (sets of tracks) and songs (sets of sequences)
Controls	Play, record, punch-in and -out, and related activities
Counter	Time display in measures and beats, SMPTE time code, or real time
Marker	Set markers to specific locations in a sequence
Memory	Keep track of memory space in the computer
Metronome	Set and alter tempo
MIDI monitor	Show when MIDI activity occurs on each channel
Remote controls	List, create and modify alphanumeric keystrokes that can control most of the sequencer functions
Sliders	Create fader sets for MIDI controller information
Tracks	Create, delete and access, tracks in a sequence

software malfunction. It is an easy matter to select a second track for recording, allowing the first track to play back while new material is recorded on the second.

THE VIEW FROM THE TOP

Software sequencers may offer a great deal of flexibility in their presentation of controls as well as the sequenced material itself. One may select functions from a list, or menu, and be directed to a submenu where a new selection is made. This mode-oriented approach (play mode, record mode, edit mode, and so on) is being largely supplanted by the more modeless approach offered by graphical user interfaces, first made commercially viable by Apple's Macintosh computers.

In this latter approach, functions and data may be approached either by menus or through on-screen windows, which can often be moved around on the screen, allowing the screen to be customized. Version 3.3 of Mark of the Unicorn's *Performer* sequencer contained windows for controls, counter, marker, metronome, memory, chunks, tracks, remote controls, sliders, and MIDI monitor. In the rapidly changing world of software development it's difficult to state precisely what a minimum set should contain, but these windows, described in table 10.1, offer a good set with a broad range of options.

Once data is recorded, it may be viewed in various ways. The easiest is simply as a list of events, containing **start time**, type of event, note number, on- and off-velocity, and duration. Some type of graphic display, often in the form of piano-roll notation may be used instead, or as an additional option. Both of these ways of viewing data may be seen in figure 7.10 on page 133. Notice that the **event list** and the **graphic notation** are displaying the same data.

Many developers and customers insist on seeing data in standard music notation, in spite of its cumbersome nature (and the fact that many sequencer users are not doing music that easily reproduces in standard notation—nor are they usually performing from a notated score, nor, for that matter, are they even comfortable with standard notation!). This type of display is available on some sequencers, thus narrowing the gap between sequencers and notation programs, which are increasingly adding sequencing features to their bag of tricks.

Start time may be shown in real time, in terms of a time code (see the discussion of time code later in this chapter) or in terms of measure, beat, and subdivisions of a beat. In early sequencers a beat was often divided into 24 ticks or pulses per quarter note (**ppqn**).

Sequencers now often divide the beat into as many as 480 or more ppqn. The advantage of the larger number lies in the greater precision in reproducing exactly what was played when; the disadvantage is that it also allows human inaccuracies to be displayed with great precision.

BASIC FUNCTIONS

In addition to the familiar recording and playback controls of tape recorders, sequencers offer additional features. There may be a setting for **overdubbing** (recording material onto a previously recorded track). It may be possible to set various memory features, such as recording or playback start and end times. In addition it should be possible to set the length of a count-off (clicking or flashing of a metronome) before the piece begins— a great tool for those pieces where more than one track must begin at the same time.

Table 10.2 summarizes many of the basic functions used in recording and playing back sequences. The following several sections present and discuss those functions which are in frequent use.

MIDI INTERFACE

On some sequencers it may be necessary to specify information about the MIDI interface at the beginning of each session, although the trend has been to make this information part of the default values that only need to be established once, and are then remembered by the program. Among the needed information is the choice of **port** and the speed of the interface (the standard speed is 1MHz). On systems using the **MPU401** standard (IBM PCs and compatibles) there can be a choice between the interface operating in smart or dumb (**UART**) mode. Interfaces with more than one set of MIDI outputs may require additional information to direct the output to the correct cable or output device.

PATCH THROUGH

A sequencer can be hooked into a MIDI network even when it is not recording or playing. In some networks the sequencer will be located between the master controller and the other members of the network (refer back to figure 3.5a). While some interfaces will automatically pass on or **echo** incoming MIDI data, others may offer control over this feature. The simplest would be a direct echo: what comes in is sent directly back out. A more complex but quite useful option would be some form of **mapping** data, so that material comes in on one channel, but is echoed out on a different channel. This may be done by only echoing on the channel of the track currently in record mode; alternatively, there may be more elaborate means of mapping through a list or table.

While mapping might seem pointless, it can be quite valuable. Kurzweil's K1000 synthesizer, for example, echoes incoming data. If it is hooked up to a sequencer that is also echoing, it is quite likely to overload the system, creating a MIDI lockup. The echo must be disabled on one device, or channeled so that feedback is avoided. By mapping data away from the master channel and by setting the synthesizer's **local control** to "off" (so that the keyboard produces MIDI information but does not produce sound), the keyboard information may be directed to any of the other 15 channels, playing whatever sound is selected on that channel.

A simpler use of mapping is to send program change information to one device, which then sends it to a second, so that both devices change in response to the one message. Although channel mapping may be helpful in this case, the ability to map a program change from one number to another is even more useful, since effects can be matched to sounds (this kind of mapping is usually not directly available on sequencers, although with editing any kind of message may be created or modified).

Table 10.2. Basic sequencer functions

FUNCTION	PURPOSE
All notes off	Sends a variety of MIDI messages intended to turn off any stuck notes.
Click/Flash	Once tempo is set with the metronome a click or flash may be used to state the tempo. The click may often be played over an internal speaker or over MIDI (it may be necessary to select MIDI notes and velocities for the MIDI click).
Editing	Ideally a sequencer should allow any aspect of any entry to be modified: note number, duration, start time, velocity. Continuous controller data (pitch bend, modulation wheel, and so on) should be included.
Input filter	Allows selection of MIDI data to be recorded, as well as specification of channel from which to record.
Looping	Procedures vary, from automatically looping tracks to the ability to specify start and endpoints, number of repetitions, and triggering events. Some sequencers allow loops to be nested.
MIDI configuration	Allows specification of port, clock speed, type of interface device, cable and channel routings on more complex setups.
Patch through	Echoes incoming data back out. Data may be sent over the same MIDI channel, or may be mapped or rechannelized.
Regions	Regional editing should be possible, either by selecting a whole measure or group of measures, or by selecting any region of notes. Procedures include changing duration or velocity, deflamming (aligning chords), quantizing (lining notes up with beats and fracitons of a beat), transposing, selecting groups of notes (high or low notes, specific pitches or durations), creating or modifying controller data (pitch bend, modulation, and so on), shifting portions of a track forward or backward in time, and reordering notes (inverting, reversing order, modifying the time scale).
Sequences	A set of tracks. Some sequencers allow sequences to be treated with all the procedures available to tracks and combined into multilevel structures.
Step record	Allows note-by-note entry of data. Select start time, duration, and pitch of note, advance to next start time (usually directly following end of previous duration) and enter next duration and pitch or indicate a rest for a given duration.
Synchronization	May send or receive timing information. Sending is often automatic; to receive select type of sync, speed, and other details specific to each type, set sequencer into sync mode, put it in play or record, and begin external device (which must send the type of sync the sequencer expects).
System reset	Resets all MIDI devices to their startup state; use sparingly if at all.
Tracks	Add, delete, select, name, and edit are among basic functions. It may be possible to set start time (on some sequencers this is done on the sequence level) and loop all or part of the track.

RECEIVE AND TRANSMIT SYNC (SLAVE TO EXTERNAL SYNC)

These functions are used when the sequencer and some external device must have their timing synchronized. One may specify the type of sync and provide specialized information about the nature of the timing (some knowledge of both devices is needed, or else the willingness to try options until a satisfactory result is obtained). The "slave to external sync" function must be selected if the sequencer is to wait for timing information from another device (audio or video recorder, sequencer, drum machine, or other device).

METRONOME CLICK AND FLASH

In real-time recording, if the performer wishes the information to fit into a measure/beat scheme, timing information is needed from the sequencer either during the recording or afterward. By selecting a click or a flash, the performer may be given an audible or visual cue. One can set the speed of the click, can often determine the value of the click (quarter note, eighth note, and so on), and may be able to direct the click to an internal or external speaker or to MIDI. In the latter case, it is usually possible to select MIDI channel and provide note and velocity information for the click. In most sequencers, it should be possible to select the meter (the number of beats per measure). On some, it is possible to set up a meter map ahead of time, for those pieces that have metric changes (on these sequencers tempo is often mappable as well).

STEP RECORD

For those times when the creativity and complexity of real-time recording is not needed, or when great precision is the order of the day (or one is not up to speed on keyboard or some other controller), **step recording** offers itself as a useful tool. Generally, a track is selected and prepared for recording, and step record is selected or step mode is entered. A duration value is selected, a MIDI note played (this usually can be a chord just as easily as a single note), and the counter advanced to the next step. The advance may be manual, or may occur automatically as Note Off information is received. Unlike real-time recording, other tracks usually do not play back at the same time (if this is desired, record in real time at a slow tempo).

It should be possible to select **tuplet** values (triplets, quintuplets, and so on) as well as standard notational values. There may also be provision to simply type in a numerical value for a note, or to hold a note for more than one step.

EDITING

Anything recorded on a sequencer can be edited. This goes beyond the addition of equalization or effects, or setting mix levels, or punching in and out, and all the other tricks of the tape recording trade. To a much greater extent, a sequence is raw material, like paint awaiting the artist's brush. This is as true for bare-bones software as for the latest full-featured mega-system.

BASIC FUNCTIONS

Table 10.3 lists and describes the various basic editing functions that most sequencers will offer. These allow material to be copied or cut from one area and discarded or added into another. These operations will generally be available regardless of the means of showing data (event list, graphics, or music notation) although some sequencers still edit on a measure level rather than the beat and sub-beat levels necessary for serious editing.

Most of these procedures involve selecting an event or series of events. The actual data in this area that is to be edited may be further defined by an edit filter, so that when material is placed in a buffer, or storage, area, it is possible that only some of the material

Table 10.3. Edit functions

FUNCTION	PURPOSE
Copy	Places a copy of data from the selected region in a buffer without altering the original region.
Cut	Removes data from the selected region, leaving blank space in that region. The data is placed in a buffer and may be used elsewhere in the piece (generally, any material already in the buffer is overwritten).
Edit filter	Specifies type of data to be edited.
Erase	Removes data from the selected region, leaving a blank space in that region. Unlike *Cut*, the information is not placed in the edit buffer.
Insert	*See* paste and splice.
Merge	Combines contents of the edit buffer with the existing material on a track, beginning at a selected start point.
Paste	Inserts contents of the edit buffer into a track, beginning at a selected start point. Existing data is replaced. *See also* merge.
Repeat	Copies data from the selected region, then *pastes*, *splices*, or *merges* it directly following the selected region the number of required times.
Select All	Selects all items in the specified window or edit area.
Shift	Moves the selected region forward or backward in time.
Snip	Removes data from the selected region, then closes up the time gap, moving events at the end of the region to the beginning. The data is placed in a buffer and may be used elsewhere in the piece (generally, any material already in the buffer is overwritten). *See also* cut.
Splice	Inserts contents of the edit buffer into a track, beginning at a selected start point. Existing data is moved later in time to make room for the new data. *See also* paste.
Undo/Redo	Undoes the last edit command. *Redo* undoes the *undo*. Not all commands are undoable.

performer only [handwritten margin note]

is copied or cut. Once material is in the buffer, it may be copied to another time region in the track, moved to another track or another sequence, or perhaps merely discarded. Placing new material in the buffer usually causes the previous material in the buffer to be replaced with the new material.

There are different types of cutting and pasting. The normal cut removes the selected material and leaves a time gap. Snip performs a cut and then closes the gap, moving material at the end of the cut to the start of the cut. Erase performs a cut but, unlike cut or snip, does not place the material in the edit buffer.

The normal paste places the contents of the edit buffer into a track, beginning at the selected start point, replacing any previously recorded material. Splice performs a paste, but shifts previously recorded material, making room for the insert. Merge performs a paste, but in this case combining previously recorded material with the newly placed material. In the absence of a merge option, paste the material into a new track set to the same MIDI channel (most sequencers offer enough tracks so that there should be little risk of running out of new tracks).

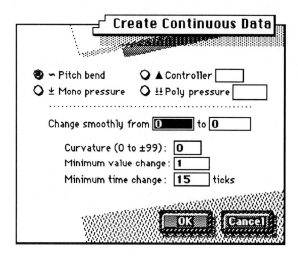

Figure 10.2. Continuous data creation window in *Performer*. Used by permission of Mark of the Unicorn.

The actual names of these procedures may vary from sequencer to sequencer. Note the distinction between the destructive and non-destructive approaches to copying and pasting, and be clear which approach is most appropriate. Not all procedures may be reversed (undone) so always make backup copies before doing anything.

REGIONAL REVISION

In addition to the modification procedures described in the following sections, it is possible to create data, either over a designated time span, or on a point-by-point basis. Regional data creation is particularly useful when developing data for devices like MIDI controller #7 (volume). This allows expressive control to be added after the original recording, and can be done either through the use of hardware or software faders, functioning much like a mixing console, or by creating data curves for the region. Information can either be stored in a track with note information, or, better, stored on a separate track set to the same MIDI channel as the note information it is modifying.

Figure 10.2 shows one of four windows *Performer* uses for continuous data. The type of data may be selected, and, in this case, a curve may be constructed with different slopes (initially steep to fairly even to steep ending). Minimum value and time changes allow specification of the density of the continuous data, which will depend on the synthesizer, the type of data, and the effect desired.

Information can also be inserted point by point. Table 10.4 provides a list of typical insertion items. Since a device may not recognize a MIDI message, it is important to know how MIDI is implemented on each piece of equipment in the network. Several of the items have more of a bookkeeping or notational function: key change (notational), markers (mark sections within the sequence to make it easier to find material), meter change (allows the display to agree with the music), tempo change (allows the display and the music to coincide, but also can be extremely useful fitting music into a specified time span). Once items are entered, they may be modified on a regional basis along with previously recorded material.

CHANGE VELOCITY OR DURATION

Often some aspect of velocity or duration needs modification. Certain notes may be too loud, or an entire track was played too softly, or the notes below C2 need boosting—or maybe all notes with a duration of 2 beats or more need to be softer. Perhaps a line was step recorded; the timing might be perfect, but the notes need a crisper articulation. Figure 10.3a and b show some of the common velocity and duration modifications that can be done in *Performer*.

Table 10.4. Typical insertion items

EVENT	PARAMETERS
Aftertouch	*See* mono key pressure, poly key pressure
Controller	Start time, controller number (continuous: 0 to 63; switch: 64 to 93), value (continuous: 0 to 127; switch: On or Off)
Key change	Start time, key name
Loop	Start time, end time, number of repetitions
Markers	Start time, marker (depends on sequencer)
Meter change	Start time, time signature, click value (usually in terms of standard notational values; eg ♩, ♪, etc)
Mode change	Start time, mode name (Omni on/off, Mono mode, Poly mode, Local control on/off, All notes off)
Mono key pressure	Start time, value (0 to 127)
Note	Start time, pitch, on/off velocites (0 to 127), duration
Patch change	Start time, patch number (0 to 127, or 1 to 128)
Pitch bend	Start time, value (-8192 to 8191)
Poly key pressure	Start time, pitch, value (0 to 127)
Program change	*See* patch change
Song change	Start time, song number (0 to 127)
System exclusive	$F0, manufacturer ID, appropriate number of data bytes
Tempo change	Start time, duration value (♩, ♪, etc), tempo value (beats per minute)
Tune request	Used to tune analog synthesizers (no values)

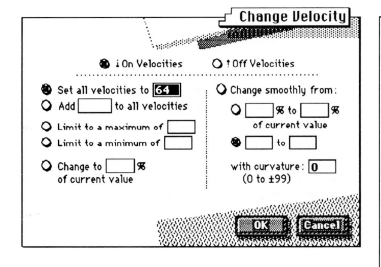

a. Velocity

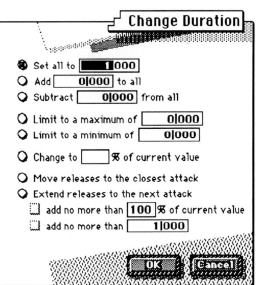

b. Duration

Figure 10.3. Velocity and duration modification windows in *Performer*. Used by permission of Mark of the Unicorn.

Figure 10.4. Melodic
operations

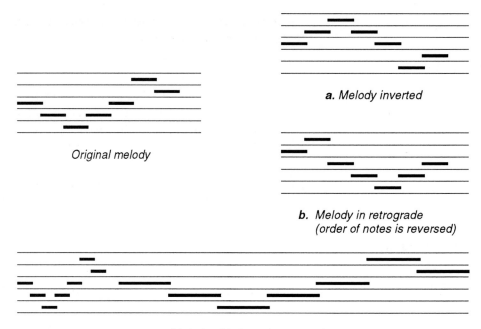

Original melody

a. Melody inverted

*b. Melody in retrograde
(order of notes is reversed)*

*c. Melody with time compressed
(left) and expanded (right)*

DEFLAM

Try as we might, we humans rarely play a chord such that all notes are struck at the same moment. With MIDI, we can't even hear notes at the same instant, since MIDI is a serial protocol, and sends notes one-at-a-time. Happily, our ears are not too discriminating, and the system works well for most situations. For those cases when there is too much roll in a chord, or when it's desirable to make the note display show the chords, rather than a succession of events, the **deflam** feature is useful.

To use it, select the offending region, set the width of the deflam, and let it happen. On *Performer*, which has a resolution of 480 ticks, the default setting of the deflam feature is 20 ticks. Covering a wider area may create a noticeable difference.

TRANSPOSE AND OTHER OPERATIONS

The **transpose** function is usually simple to use. Select a region to be transposed, and select the amount of the transposition. It may be an interval, it may be a matter of setting values in an expression like "from ___ to ___," or there may be more complex options. Notation programs often allow a choice of transposing everything (**diatonic** transposition), or of staying in the same key (**modal** transposition).

It may be possible to **invert** a melody around a chosen center point (figure 10.4a), or to reverse (**retrograde**) a melody (figure 10.4b). Sometimes time may be compressed or expanded (figure 10.4c). Compositionally-oriented procedures like altering note order or generating new material may also be available.

SPLIT NOTES

It is useful at times to be able to split a track into two tracks, particularly if a variety of split criteria is available. One may be able to select the top or bottom notes of a chord, or a range of pitches, or a range of durations, or even a range of velocities. With procedures such as these, material originally recorded on one MIDI channel can be given different timbres: the top note in a chord could be copied and doubled with a second tone color; the bottom note could be moved to its own track and turned into a more effective bass line. A piano part could be prepared by splitting a track into left- and right-hand parts (perhaps for eventual transcription).

SHIFT

Invariably the need arises to shift a track or a portion of a track earlier or later in time. Sometimes this can be accomplished by changing the start time of a track, if this feature is available. Alternatively, there will usually be a procedure for delaying a selected range (making it happen later) or advancing a selected range (moving it closer to the beginning). Remember that music starts with measure 1, beat 1; if material that starts in measure 3, beat 2, is to be advanced to the beginning, shift it by 2 measures and 1 beat, not 3 measures and 2 beats (if the sequencer asks instead for a starting time rather than a shift amount so much the better).

QUANTIZATION

Figure 10.5. Quantization

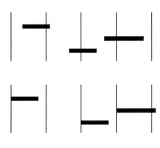

a. Original (upper) and quantized attacks

b. Attacks and releases both quantized

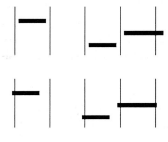

c. Positive (upper) and negative grid offset

100%   50%

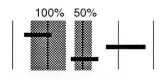

d. Sensitivity regions. The second note would not be quantized at 50%.

Human beings have a certain tolerance for error. A musical passage may appear to be played accurately, on the beat, and yet be a little ahead or behind the beat. For many situations, this is desirable, since music must have a give and take to be living rather than mechanical. It does make the development of works through multitrack recording difficult. The ability to correct timing errors has become standard in most digital sequencers.

Error correction, or **quantization**, may affect several aspects of a note. The attack point may be moved without altering the duration of a note (thus also moving the note's release). The release point may be moved (either causing the attack point to move if duration is left unchanged or causing the duration to change if the attack point doesn't shift or is shifted by a different amount). The duration itself may be the focus of alteration, generally by shifting the release point.

In general, a quantization value is selected. The value may be given in terms of traditional notation or in terms of fractions of a beat. This creates a grid, with each node spaced according to the value selected (often the shortest desired duration). This grid would normally coincide with the measure/beat scheme, but may often be **offset**. It may be possible to set a **sensitivity level**, so that events more than a certain distance away from a node are not moved. In addition, it may be possible to determine the **strength** of the quantization.

Basically, if a region needs quantizing, a quantization value is selected and the area is quantized. Figure 10.5a shows a short excerpt before and after quantization of attacks. Notice that all notes have the same duration but have been moved to the closest node. This means that notes closer to the following node are shifted later, while notes closer to the preceding node are shifted earlier. If releases are also quantized, durations change as release points are also moved to the nearest node (figure 10.5b).

Putting everything on the beat may result in a rather wooden, or mechanical, performance. Offset, sensitivity, and strength offer ways of achieving more precision without loosing the flexibility and swing of freely played material. The use of an offset value is also shown in figure 10.5. The grid of figure 10.5a has been offset with both positive and negative values, causing the musical material to play behind or ahead of the beat (figure 10.5c). This can help contribute to a sense of reflection or urgency, depending upon the situation (as well as the amount of offset).

Sensitivity and strength both offer valuable modifications of quantization. The former determines how far from the node the quantization effect will reach. At a value of 100% the effect reaches from one node halfway to the preceding and following nodes. At a value of 50% only half of this region is covered (25% back, 25% forward), allowing attacks or releases outside this region to remain as they are (figure 10.5d) .

Strength determines whether the material will be pulled all the way to the node or only some lesser percentage. With a strength of 50%, material will be pulled only half the distance, for example. This allows material to be tightened up but to retain some of the human feel that we like in our music. Offset may be combined with sensitivity and strength to allow for some fairly sophisticated quantization options.

It is often possible to toggle between quantized and unquantized versions. One should always back up work before quantizing or doing any editing, just in case things don't go as planned.

STUDIO PROCEDURES

Always keep backup copies of work in progress. When making copies use similar names for a piece and any related files. In spite of publicity to the contrary, paperwork does not decrease with a computer. It is particularly important to keep a record of which instruments are used (and where they are located in synthesizer memory or on disk).

If it is possible to store sets of instruments on disk or tape, store a set with a name that relates to the piece in which it is used. Some microcomputer systems may have several files devoted to a piece. Develop a system for file handling that makes it easy to assemble all necessary files. It is easy to lose much time and temper hunting through disks for a misplaced or misnamed file—do not be tempted to take shortcuts.

Keep lists of disk catalogs or directories, lists of disks, even lists of lists if necessary. Store related items on the same disk. Learn proper techniques for caring for electronic storage media. Make backup copies of all your work.

MAKING TRACKS

It is possible to record more than merely what keys are pressed when and for how long. Through MIDI, it is possible to change active instruments and record these changes so that they are reproduced during playback. Take advantage of this feature and include program change information in all sequences. This makes setup much easier, since patches will be selected when the sequence starts. This also allows sequences of instruments to be developed, creating multiple timbral effects either vertically (through poly mode playback) or horizontally (through successive instrument changes).

This can be done while a line is being played, or it can be done later. In the latter case, a separate **control track** may be created. No musical material is recorded. Instead, as material is played back, instrument changes may be recorded on a free track (much as a conductor might cue in different instruments in an orchestra). After the control track is laid down, it may be kept separate or mixed with the musical material it is modifying.

Control tracks are also useful for pitch bend, volume data, and any other MIDI controller data. Pitch bend, for example, produces so much data, that it is difficult to see the musical line in an event list. By keeping control data separate, it is easy to see what is being edited. This consideration is less critical—and, in fact, may be counterproductive—in graphical editing systems that allow parallel displays of data, since it won't be possible to see the parallel activity. In this case, it still may be useful to record data separately (especially if data is being created in the computer rather than being generated by a MIDI device) and then mix tracks to take advantage of the graphical display.

SYNCHRONIZATION

As long as sound is only being produced and modified by MIDI devices, and all activity is being recorded and played back by a MIDI sequencer, there is likely to be no problem synchronizing parallel activity, since it can be recorded on different tracks in a fashion similar to a multitrack tape recorder. If acoustic sources, non-MIDI electronics, or video images enter the mix, synchronization can become more of a problem.

Table 10.5. Synchronization time codes

CODE	FULL NAME	SYNCHRONIZATION BY	PROS AND CONS
FSK	Frequency Shifted Keying	Generation of high and low pulses in the range of 1000 to 3000 Hz (there are various standards). Uses line-level inputs and outputs, FSK generator	Tempo must be determined before recording; generally must begin at the beginning for effective synchronization; inexpensive
Smart FSK	Smart FSK; SPP FSK; Poor Person's SMPTE	Generation of time code producing MIDI Song Position Pointer messages along with FSK pulses	Compromise between absolute tempo of FSK and absolute location of SMPTE code; inexpensive
SMPTE	Society of Motion Picture and Television Engineers Time Code	Digital generation of information about the absolute time in hours, minutes, seconds, and frames (several standards; 30 is most common for music)	Tempo provided by software, not time code; very accurate (to about .4 milli-second); can keep track of location in music or video; somewhat expensive if all units are locked up
MTC	MIDI Time Code	A MIDI translation of SMPTE time code	Allows MIDI synchronization in absolute time, rather than the tempo-oriented messages of standard MIDI; for those with the right software, an inexpensive add-on

If there is only one non-MIDI instrument, it could be added when all the sequenced material is played back for recording to tape or for use in a performance. Of course, with more performers present, more non-MIDI material can be played, creating a mixed ensemble that could take advantage of the precision of studio preparation with the spontaneity and life of live performance. If the intent of combining forces is to produce a recording or to produce a video soundtrack, some means of synchronizing the sequencer with tape and/or video is needed. With appropriate click tracks, time codes and synchronization devices, a tape or video recorder may function as an element of a MIDI network. Conversely, the MIDI network may function as an extension of a multitrack recorder, enhancing and augmenting the studio session.

CLICK TRACKS

Synchronization protocols tend to fall into two basic types: **click tracks** and **time codes** (table 10.5 provides an overview of this material). In tape recording, a regular click may be recorded on one track, providing a tempo reference for all other tracks. In the early days of MIDI this audio click could be generated by the sequencer interface, recorded on its own tape track, and then used to control the sequencing software, thus allowing acoustic and digital material to be set to the same tempo. Some sequencers could be set so that they would not begin until they received a pre-recorded start code from the tape recorder. In addition to the two procedures that are discussed here, various proprietary sync codes have been developed from time to time. These work well, as long as one is content to stay with the equipment of a single manufacturer.

FSK

FSK (Frequency Shifted Keying) is essentially a click track. It is an audio signal consisting of two pitches: a carrier and a higher pitched modulation. Different systems operate with a different number of ppqn, most with some multiple of 24 (24, 48, 96, and so on). The advantage of FSK is that it is a relatively simple system, and is relatively inexpensive. Disadvantages include the establishment of a fixed tempo once the click is recorded to tape, and the lack of determining location during a piece. Like earlier click tracks, it's great as long as the piece is always rewound and playback or recording always starts from the beginning.

As with basic audio click tracks, FSK may be recorded to tape. When played back through a converter, it may control any device for which the converter is capable of generating appropriate information. Some devices need no external converter, since they may have a "tape sync" input that handles FSK. Before recording the timing pulses, FSK generates a pilot tone that should be recorded for several seconds. The tone functions as a reference level for the tape recorder and prepares sync devices for the pulses to come. It is always a good idea, when recording FSK or other click information, to record more sync information than will probably be needed, to allow for late flashes of inspiration that seem to make things longer than planned.

MIDI CLOCKS

The basic timing procedure in MIDI uses **MIDI Clocks**, which are essentially a click sent at a rate of 24 clocks per beat, with the beat defined as equal to a quarter note (composers who use timebases other than a quarter note can best ignore this discrepancy between paper and internal beat). The tempo of the quarter note is set by the sequencer or other master device; regardless of the quarter note's speed, 24 clocks will be sent. This click, like FSK and other audio clicks, does not contain location information.

The basic MIDI specification provides for several messages which take MIDI clocks beyond the realm of the click track. From the user's point of view these messages are generally transparent. That is to say, the software should know how and when to send or receive the message.

When a MIDI sequencer is not playing or recording, location information may be sent by using MIDI **Song Position Pointer** (SPP) messages. These tell the number of sixteenth notes or equivalent musical time that have passed since the beginning of the piece. At 24 ppqn, each sixteenth marks the passage of six pulses. A second MIDI clock-based device may stay synchronized with the first if, after stopping in the middle of a piece, the first resumes by using a **continue** command (the equivalent to taking a recorder out of pause mode) rather than a start command.

Be aware that the music may not always sound quite right when it continues. Any notes that started before the continuation point will not sound; any patches changed during the pause will continue in force, rather than be replaced by the "correct" patches initiated before the pause, since the sequencer doesn't know what was happening before the pause. Some sequencers offer the option of **event chasing**, which, when selected, allows the sequencer to look back through the stored sequence to see if program changes, notes, or other selected information, should be in force when the music continues. This may cause a slight delay when the sequence continues, but allows it to continue intact.

MIDI also augments the clock procedure with the **song select** message, which some devices, notably drum machines, can use to select the next song (sequence, excerpt, piece) that it will play.

TIME CODES

Click tracks have a basic simplicity which is rather elegant. Tempo is aligned with the click, the music always is started from the beginning, and the sequencer is controlled by the incoming click. For short or fairly simple pieces, or for low-budget operations, this procedure is hard to beat. It does have the drawback, however, of not allowing any determination of location during the playback or recording, since that information is not provided by the click. Several time codes have been devised to remedy this situation.

SMART FSK

Smart FSK is a variant of FSK. In addition to the establishment of tempo also caused with ordinary FSK it generates information which may be turned into MIDI SPP messages which a sequencer can use to determine location. This means that a tape encoded with smart FSK could begin in the middle of a piece and a sequencer that has been slaved to external sync would jump to the correct location, continuing in sync with the recorder. As with other FSK systems, it is simple and inexpensive.

SMPTE TIME CODE

The Society of Motion Picture and Television Engineers has developed a time code that is used in video: **SMPTE Time Code**. Rather than providing tempo information, it provides rather accurate timing information, including hours, minutes, seconds, and frames per second (frames may range from 24 to 30 per second).

SMPTE Time Code comes in two flavors: **LTC** and **VITC**. The former is generally recorded on an audio track on video tape (*Linear Time Code*), while the latter is recorded on the space between frames (*Vertical Interval Time Code*). LTC requires 80 bits per frame and VITC 90 bits per frame to provide full information about location. In addition to timing information, both versions can provide information about color, video fields, and user-generated identification.

VITC can be read even when video recorders are operating at slow speeds, while LTC will sometimes be unreadable if the playback speed changes, since it requires a fairly consistent frequency for recognizability. LTC, on the other hand, is fairly easy to use and can fit on the audio track of any VCR, where VITC requires more expensive equipment to work.

Most time code generators will have a feature called **jam sync**. This is basically a re-generation of incoming SMPTE time code. Some devices can freewheel over occasional code dropouts; jam sync is also an element of video editing, allowing new code to be recorded on the edit master along with the edited video (this is essential for VITC, which cannot be pre-recorded in the same way as LTC).

SMPTE time code is more expensive than click track codes. There must be a time code generator to create time code in the first place. Since MIDI doesn't read SMPTE code, some device (usually the generator) must translate the code into a MIDI format. Some video recorders and tape recorders can respond to synchronizing information, but usually need an external synchronizer to process the SMPTE code and turn it into the appropriate motion commands the recorders expect.

MIDI TIME CODE

A MIDI version of SMPTE time code is available in the form of **MIDI Time Code** (MTC). MIDI timing is usually tempo-oriented, using clock information as indicated previously. With MTC, MIDI can also function in absolute time. Although MTC can be used in straight MIDI setups, it is especially useful in the process of synchronizing MIDI equipment with devices producing or synchronized to SMPTE Time Code.

An important part of MTC which operates behind the scenes is the MTC **Quarter Frame message**. There are actually eight different such messages, each consisting of two bytes. The first is the status byte, and the second is one-eighth of the information needed to establish the location. Since it takes a total of two frames, this procedure only works during play or recording. There is also a 10-byte-long **Full message** which can be used at those times when the quarter frame approach is impractical, including during fast-forwarding or rewinding, when too many messages would be generated.

The main advantage of MTC is that it is tempo-independent. At a frame rate of 30, location is updated 15 times per second. When two devices that can handle this information are synchronized, a great degree of accuracy is possible. In addition, Song Position Pointer and Song Select messages can also be used with MTC, allowing another means of updating location when devices are not involved in timing operations.

ONE-WAY SYNC

One use of synchronization has already been mentioned: an audio tape recorder may function as an extension of the MIDI network, providing a means of synchronizing acoustic and digital events. In most situations, the MIDI sequencer is put under the control of the sync track coming from the recorder. To do the reverse would be to invest in a SMPTE-controlled synchronizer. In essence, then, the MIDI network is an extension of the audio recorder, providing as many virtual tracks as memory and equipment allow.

A second use of synchronization is to allow the MIDI network to operate in tandem with video, providing coordination between sound and sight. The sync code (usually a form of SMPTE time code) is played from the video recorder and received by the sequencer or by a converter placed in the data stream between recorder and sequencer, which then responds to the information. This system doesn't allow very easily for acoustic sound sources, other than those which may be sampled and thus put under direct MIDI control.

An example of this one-way use of sync is shown in figure 10.6. The audio or video recorder acts as master, sending timing information through the time code generator to the sequencer (either hardware or software), thus driving the MIDI stack. This approach is common in the film industry, with music and sound effects added after the image. While appropriate in a medium where sound acts to enhance the visual, a more creative approach might allow for two-way communication.

TWO-WAY SYNC

Figure 10.7 shows the upper left portion of figure 10.6, adding in a synchronizer. If the video and/or audio recorders are equipped to handle the output of a synchronizer, any of the three main players (audio or video recorder or sequencer) may be in charge. One advantage of this system should be quite clear. Rather than having to find the musical event that matches an image, the composer can find the image that matches a particular musical event. In other words, one can work on the music and have the image follow along, rather than having to find the music by guessing what the video action is at the time. The same holds true if acoustic and digital sounds are being synchronized: the focus can shift from the acoustic to the digital event, rather than the digital event always responding to the acoustic event.

Figure 10.6. One-way sync

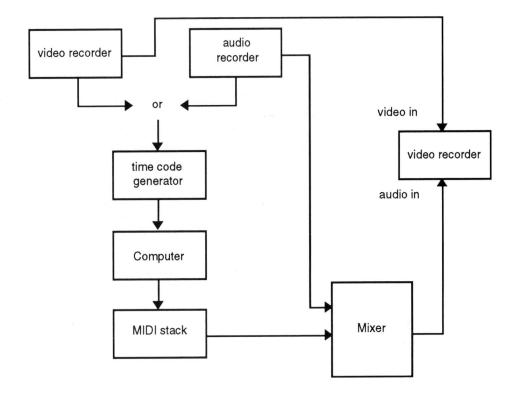

Figure 10.7. Two-way sync

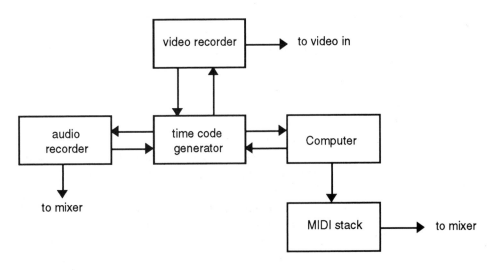

The other primary advantage is that acoustic events can be tightly synchronized to video, whether the acoustic event is sound effect-like ("Foley effects") or more musical in nature. As mentioned previously, the creative control may come from any aspect of the work, rather than from only one direction.

MIDI FILES

Each piece of software saves data in its own proprietary format. This makes it difficult to send material from one sequencer or computer to another, short of hooking up the MIDI inputs and outputs of two computers and sending a MIDI sequence in real time. This process can be a little slow, particularly if the receiving sequencer can't handle multitrack real-time recording.

The **MIDI file format** offers a way around this difficulty. It establishes standard formats for saving MIDI data. As it was being developed, various intermediate forms were created. With up-to-date software, sequencers will save data in one of three formats. A Format 0 file contains a single multi-channel track; a Format 1 file contains one or more simultaneously-occurring tracks or MIDI outputs of a sequence; a Format 2 file contains one or more sequentially independent single-track patterns.

When saving data to a MIDI file, there are generally various options to select to determine the type of MIDI file to be created. If you're not sure what format the receiving program will prefer, save the data several times, using the various options that are offered. In loading a MIDI file, the same approach may need to be taken. If you're not sure of the format of the file, try the offered options until a satisfactory result is obtained.

MIDI files can be read by different types of computer, since the MIDI file formats tell how information is stored. Some conversion is still necessary, since the material needs to be in a form readable by the computer.

FOR FURTHER STUDY

Chapter three presents an overview of MIDI, and chapters eight and nine discuss various aspects of audio recording. Appendix E suggests ideas for further reading on page 265.

EXERCISES

The exercises offered in this chapter are intended to lead to chapter twelve, which consists of 65 exercises that explore many facets of sequencing. Become familiar with the nature of the basic features of sequencers through the exercises given below before moving on to chapters eleven and twelve.

In some cases, several exercises are intended to be worked on as sets. The material of exercise 10.2 is used again in exercise 10.9, and the material of exercise 10.3 is used in 10.4, 10.5, and 10.6, and is referred to in other exercises as well. Always save material to an appropriate storage medium immediately after recording.

EXERCISE 10.1

Send MIDI data through the sequencer, experimenting with the various patch through options. How can data be sent in on one channel and echoed or mapped out to another?

EXERCISE 10.2

Record a simple melody in real time, synchronizing first to click, and then, on another track, to a flashing click, if available. When recording the second track, mute the first track. Compare the two event lists or view the graphical display and see which is more accurate. Try again with another melody, but do the flash first this time. Is one type of click easier than the other?

Before leaving this exercise, create a MIDI click, if the sequencer allows. It should be possible to specify MIDI channel, and pitch and velocity of the click (and possibly one pitch for the first beat of the measure and a different pitch for the other beats). Also find out how to set different meters and tempos (In a metronome window? In a utility menu? In a special pull-down menu?).

EXERCISE 10.3

Step record a short two-voice piece. First use two separate tracks, one for each musical line. Then see if it is possible to to input the same two lines, but using only one track and entering the two lines at the same time. This may involve holding down one note while changing the other line. Can this be done on your sequencer? Is there any advantage?

EXERCISE 10.4

Listen to either version of exercise 10.3. Does the step recording sound good? After saving your work, try editing durations, changing them all to 90% of their original value. Try other percentages as well.

EXERCISE 10.5

Listen to the velocity of the step recording of exercise 10.3. Does it work well? Edit velocities so that all are set to 64. If this sounds too bland, try creating velocity curves, getting louder or softer over the course of the excerpt. With two voices, of course, one could get softer while the other gets louder.

EXERCISE 10.6

Again working with the material of exercise 10.3, try random velocity and duration changes, so that by the end, each note has had some parameter altered.

EXERCISE 10.7

Play and record a series of chords. If you're not a keyboard player, just grab a set of notes (it doesn't need to be pretty). Examine the track display and analyze your chord-playing technique.

Record the same series of chords again, trying to manually solve some of the problems you noted (maybe one finger is weak, or the thumbs always play before the other fingers, or one hand plays before the other). If chords still show some flamming (as is likely unless the sequencer has some quantization built into the recording process), explore deflamming options. Try different deflamming widths. Where is the chord placed: at the time of the earliest event, at the time of the latest event, or at an average time?

EXERCISE 10.8

Transpose any material recorded in previous exercises, exploring the range of transposition options offered by the sequencer.

Try copying the material to be transposed to a second track, then transposing it an octave or so up or down, and playing the two tracks back together. If the sequencer allows operations such as inversion or retrograde, experiment with the transposed track, comparing it with the untouched original (it may be interesting to play the original and the altered version together as well).

EXERCISE 10.9

Using the melody of exercise 10.2 or creating new material, try out the various quantization features of the sequencer. Explore different quantization values, and try quantizing different aspects (attacks, releases, durations).

EXERCISE 10.10

Using the material of exercise 10.3 or something similar, try quantizing one voice to an offset grid, moving the material ahead of the beat. Also make multiple copies of one track and quantize each to a different offset. This can create a kind of delay (with synthesizers operating in mono mode, each track should address a different MIDI channel; this also allows each delay to have a different timbre).

EXERCISE 10.11

Investigate the studio options for synchronizing to external devices. If feasible, synchronize the sequencer to an audio tape recorder. This may require striping time code on one track of the recorder, then setting the sequencer so that it waits for the external sync code. Rather than recording new material, use any sequence created previously.

VOCABULARY

Most of the following terms were used for the first time in this chapter. Several may have a different use than earlier in the book. A definition of each term may be found in the glossary.

click track	continue	control track
deflam	diatonic	echo (MIDI)
event chasing	event list	FSK
Full message	graphic notation	invert
jam sync	local control	LTC
mapping	MIDI Clock	MIDI file format
MIDI Time Code	modal	MPU401
Note Off	Note On	offset
overdub	parameter	port
ppqn	quantization	Quarter Frame message
retrograde	sensitivity level	Smart FSK
SMPTE Time Code	Song Position Pointer	song select
step recording	start time	strength (quantization)
time code	transpose	tuplet
UART	VITC	

REVIEW QUESTIONS

QUESTION 10.1

Compare and contrast the following terms.

Event List— Graphic Display

An event list shows things such as start time, type of event, on-off velocity and duration. Graphic Display, such as piano roll notation may be used instead. may be used in addition to, also

Click Track — Time Code

synchronization protocols: Click track is a recorded click used to aid in synchronization material, to be recorded.(not heard in actual recording) The time code provides accurate timing info such as hours, minutes, seconds and frames per second.

LTC — VITC

LTC the stripe. VITC

Both are simple time codes. Linear time code is recorded on an audio track on video tape. Vertical Interval time code is recorded on the space between frames. (embedded right into the track.

QUESTION 10.2

Provide the question for the given answer.

ANSWER	QUESTION
Standard speed of MIDI	What is _____ ?
24 per quarter note	What is _____ ?
One multi-channel track	What is _____ ?
One or more simultaneously occurring tracks	What is _____ ?

Transmits across cable at 32k B.P.S

1 M.H.

24 (pulses) ppqn pulses

C c t i c s.

QUESTION 10.3

Define briefly.

Deflam

The ability to take out unwanted notes (~~similar to a grace note~~) if the mistake was played immediately before the correct note. (like a grace note is played)

Quantization

Error correction
the ability to retime in metronomic perfection

FSK

Frequency Shifted keying
Clock based, Tells the computer to speed up or slow down.

PPQN

Pulses per quarter note
How many separate divisions of a quarter note. I.E. 96 PPQN = 96 separate divisions.

SPP

Song Position Pointer
(measures) Tells you where you are in a piece, this is needed in sequencers for editing

CHAPTER · ELEVEN

ASPECTS OF COMPOSITION

Every musician and composer deals differently with music. The basic strategies presented here offer a means of developing more conscious control over compositional activities, either directly or with computer assistance. Previous chapters have touched on aspects of composition as well. Chapters four through six dealt with developing sounds. Chapters seven through nine looked at notating and recording sound. Chapter ten looked at the basic use of sequencers, which will be followed up in chapter twelve.

The exercises in those chapters generally involved an immediate response to sound or some set of musical conditions. Creating a piece of music involves more than picking up an instrument, or selecting patches, and playing. There must be some prior planning, and certainly some feeling for music, whether intuitive or the product of formal training. As part of the compositional process, you need to become more aware of what holds a piece of music together.

Different musical styles make different use of musical material. In spite of this, there is enough commonality to make a discussion of musical parameters and procedures fruitful. Regardless of style, if there is a focus on one or two main parameters, such as pitch or duration, there will often be a corresponding decrease in attention to other parameters.

A slow rate of harmonic change will often be compensated for by a richer melodic life, while simpler melodies may have a relatively quick rate of harmonic change (compare the linear and harmonic activity of a blues piece with that of a four-part hymn).

PRELIMINARY CONSIDERATIONS

Some meditative music—whether New Age or Gregorian chant—seems to simply exist without much sense of direction or suggestion of motion. More often there will be elements of change, or contrast, or progression, no matter how subtle, in a piece of music. This sense of direction comes from the interaction of musical parametersr.

MUSICAL PARAMETERS

In traditional art music, and much of jazz and the popular musics, the primary musical elements are pitch and duration. These allow the creation of tones, rhythms, intervals, chords, melodies, and ultimately pieces of music. In addition, timbre, texture, dynamics, and tempo add depth and further meaning to the musical experience.

A piece of music unfolds in a manner that almost appears to be inevitable. Upon examining the work, networks of relationships are often found that create tension or provide contrast, and give a background of continuity against which change and contrast take place. A composer must balance a work between too much variety and too little contrast.

Both change and an increase in the rate of change can contribute to tension, or an increase in the sense of direction or movement in a piece. Too much complexity can be perceived as tending towards randomness and may result in a loss of direction, as the listener becomes overwhelmed with detail. In general, the reverse leads to a release or relaxation of tension. Table 11.1 summarizes the primary and secondary parameters and their effect on the musical flow.

Table 11.1. Basic parameters and tension-producing activity

	PARAMETER	TYPE OF CHANGE	COMMENT
P **r** **i** **m**	DURATION	To shorter events To more rapid events To less regularity	Gives shape to pitch
a **r** **y**	PITCH	Rises Wider jumps and skips More chromaticism	A primary parameter: gives a sense of direction, provides tension and release
	TIMBRE	Richer More dynamic Harsher More variety	A function of instrument design, combined with registral placement, texture, and dynamics
S **e** **c** **o**	DYNAMICS	To louder events More, rapid changes in dynamic levels	Adds expression, color, contrast, and drama
n **d** **a**	TEMPO	Faster More erratic	Somewhat elusive: a measure of the pacing of a piece
r **y**	TEXTURE	More sound sources More activity More independence of musical lines	Primarily a measure of vertical complexity

DURATION

While musical parameters rarely act in isolation, aspects of their use can be consciously controlled to deliberately determine the musical effect. The duration of a tone or other event may be determined by a music keyboard or other gating device or by the parameter values or envelope settings of an instrument patch itself. In the case of sequencing or tape editing, splicing procedures may allow duration to be edited.

A note may have a written, or notated, duration. It may also have a performed duration that is different (usually shorter). This performance duration, or **articulation**, is part of the expressive interpretation of a piece. Anyone who has quantized an excerpt on a sequencer is aware that repetition of a note is unclear if the first note ends at the same time that the second is begun. Articulation helps in grouping notes together, strengthening rhythmic patterning.

PITCH

The other primary parameter, pitch, must have duration. Most durations, of course, will also have a sense of pitch, unless they are very brief or have a high noise content. The interaction of pitch and duration according to some coherent set of musical guidelines is called melody.

The distance between successive pitches is called an interval. Conjunct melodies, where the melodic motion is primarily from scale degree or tone to adjacent scale degree, using the Western major/minor scale system, tend to exhibit less energy, or tension, than disjunct melodies. A high degree of chromaticism, involving motion from harmonic area to harmonic area in some disregard for major/minor scale patterns, may also create tension, perhaps because a type of thick linear texture may be created.

Another aspect of pitch that should be considered and controlled in constructing a piece of music is **register.** Shifting from register to register may create tension, particularly if durations become shorter or more frequent. Some instruments may be mellow in one register and more strident in another (a registral aspect of timbre). The use of higher registers may create more tension than lower, though the spectral content and activity of lower tones may counter this to some extent.

TIMBRE

In traditional music theory this parameter often gets overlooked. All sound has timbre. In this sense, then, timbre is a primary parameter. It rarely is the focus of compositional activity to the same extent as pitch and duration, and thus usually is considered to be of secondary importance. It can be used structurally, and can provide as much interest, contrast, and sense of direction as pitch and rhythm. While good use of timbre may be little noted, poor use will weaken even the most brilliant exposition of pitch and durational expertise.

OTHER PARAMETERS

In addition to timbre, the other secondary parameters (dynamics, texture, and tempo) all offer creative options. Louder sounds, moves from softer to louder, or more and quicker fluctuations in loudness may all create tension and provide a sense of direction. The roles of timbre and texture have already been recognized. More harshness or variety of spectrum, or a registral placement that emphasizes portions of the spectrum, give timbre an increased importance. Likewise, textural changes such as an increase in the number of sound sources, or increasingly rapid shifts in texture will increase tension. Faster tempi, or increasingly erratic tempi may also contribute to tension.

The common quality is an increase in the rate of change. A reverse of the previous observations may lead to a decrease in tension, which one might want at the end of a piece or to some extent at points of relative repose, or **closure,** during a piece. It is possible to relax the tension-producing effect of some parameters and yet cause an increase in tension by increasing the effect of other parameters.

MOTIVES IN MUSIC

In essence, then, without some type of change or contrast there cannot be music. Lost in the simplicity of this statement is any suggestion for the beginning composer of how to accomplish musical change. Some ideas were given in the discussion of the parameters of musical tones. Although simple, they are actually quite important and useful.

Many Western musics rely on the concept of the musical **motive** in constructing musical works. The motive is the smallest recognizable unit in a piece of music (see the main motive from Beethoven's *Fifth Symphony*, given in figure 11.1a, example a1). It may be recognized as a coherent series of pitched durations. In order to qualify as a motive, it ought to be used more than once in a piece of music, with its recurrences being substantially similar but not literally identical to its first presentation. Different musical styles make different use of motives.

A motive can be altered by changing one or more of its basic parameters. It may be put in another register. One or two pitches may be altered, thus modifying the interval succession. Figure 11.1a offers some examples of this. Examples a2 and a3 have only one pitch altered; the first preserves the general direction of the motive, while the second rises, rather than falling. In example a4, all but one pitch have been changed. The strength of the rhythmic pattern maintains the family relationship.

Dynamics may be modified, or a motive may appear with a different timbral treatment. It may be played faster or slower, or some of its durations may be altered. Example a5 of figure 11.1a applies these options. A rich variety of dynamics is specified; the motive is performed by three instruments, each presenting one of the first three notes, then all three combining for the last note; durations have been lengthened, although the proportions remain the same (each eighth note is now three quarter notes long), and articulation has been stated more precisely than in the original.

While the secondary parameters can be altered without too much regard for losing the sense of the motive, more care needs to be exercised with the primary parameters, particularly duration. One may change pitches, timbre, and dynamics, and yet have a chance to sense the continuity of a statement with earlier versions of the motive if the duration succession (the rhythmic pattern) is essentially the same.

Melodies may be made out of a single motive by combining a motive with some of its variants, as is done in figure 11.2. A motive can be developed throughout the course of a piece, or can be used as the opening unit of a melody that continues in different ways upon each repetition. A motive can also be present in different voices of a **polyphonic** texture, creating the effect known as imitation.

A motive need not be solely melodic. A succession of harmonies or **simultaneities** (a term for chord-like structures that do not necessarily fit the major/minor scale system) may be motivic. With the sonic possibilities of electronic and tape facilities, a motive could consist of a sequence of high-noise-content events, or recorded and altered acoustic events, or the dynamic output of instrument patches that defy easy transcription into conventional music notation.

A succession of timbres, combined with an interesting succession of durations, could be treated motivically, with little concern for the pitch of the elements in the succession. The same might also be done for texture, or registral placement. In such a case, the effect may be rather subtle, providing more of an underlying sense of unity within contrast, since there is a tendency for listeners to focus on the rhythm/pitch aspect of music.

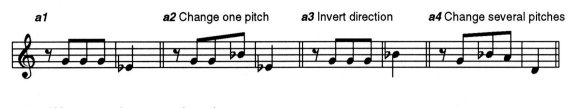

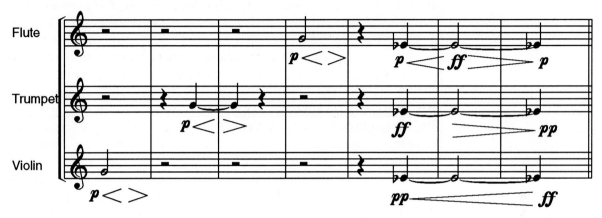

a. In music notation

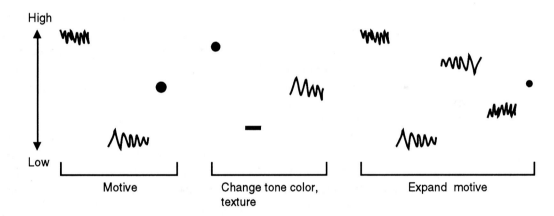

b. In graphic notation

Figure 11.1. Motivic alteration

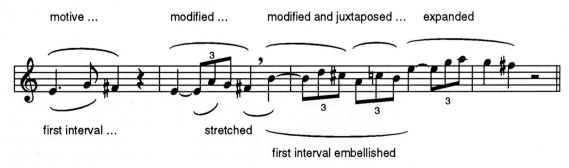

Figure 11.2. Melody based on
a motive and its variants

BOX · 11.1

THE SCOPE OF MUSICAL RESOURCES

ACOUSTIC RESOURCES	SONIC ORGANIZATION	ELECTRONIC RESOURCES
Standard musical instruments	Equal temperament, discrete tones	Analog and digital synthesizers; most computer music systems
Non-Western instruments and ensembles (such as Gamelon); replicas of older instruments; eclectic instruments (such as Harry Partch's)	Other temperaments and microtones with primarily discrete tones	Synthesizers with ribbon controllers or other means of modifying keyboard control voltage; digital synthesizers and computers
Various percussion instruments; woodwind multiphonics; other nonstandard means of playing standard instruments	Noise bands and complex sounds with indefinite pitch or chord-like pitch complexes	Synthesizer modules including noise generator and ring modulator; digital modulation processes; computer "unit generators" analogous to modules; tape music
Theater pieces combining movement and music; various philosophical approaches to music and its meaning	Environmental sounds and other nonmusical noises	Tape music ("musique concrete"); digital sampling devices; sound processing equipment used in the studio or on stage

Western acoustic music tends to focus on the interaction of discrete tones, primarily in the realm of equal temperament. Electroacoustic music gains in strength with the exploration of sounds moving beyond standard Western notes and tone colors.

   Just as acoustic music has a wealth of instruments, timbres, styles, and approaches to playing, so should—and does—electronic music. Rather than only using the latest in electronic gadgetry, we should appreciate each generation of electronic instruments for its strengths and special characteristics.

There must necessarily be a certain amount of "talking around" the concept of motive. Music does not lend itself well to verbal description. The best way to understand the idea of motive is to experiment. Begin with pitch and rhythm. Record a small motivic unit and develop variants. When you are comfortable with this, extend the concept to the secondary parameters. In doing this, some compensation will be necessary: if the focus is to be on a timbral motive, simplify the melodic material, perhaps even to the point of making the initial motive on a single tone.

MUSICAL FORM

Anyone using this book already has an internal model of what a piece of music is. One could do worse than use this model, which includes stylistic information as well formal criteria. What holds that model together? How important is rhythm, or melody, or harmony? Is tone color important, and if so, what kind of tone color? Some conscious examination of the ways musical parameters are used is essential to the development of musical style. The questions given in table 11.2 can help in that examination.

In addition to looking at the use of musical parameters, consider the overall shape, or form, of the pieces you create. Do sections repeat, or reappear after intervening material? Are pieces tightly constructed, or freeform or improvisatory in character? Are there texts or lyrics, and if so, how does the music express the texts? Could one develop a sectional map of texture or of other secondary parameters? Are some instruments or tone colors used in one part of the piece, but not in others? Does each instrument have a clearly differentiated role (bass line, rhythm, chords, melody), or are these roles traded?

The more conscious analytical information you have, the better you will be at constructing the score, whether on paper or on tape. The questions asked here are intended to be as style-free as possible. Within the academic context of most electronic studios, such questions have validity, if only to encourage you to examine yourself and to expand your boundaries.

Table 11.2. Summary of analytical questions	FORM	What is the overall structure? If the piece divides into sections, what elements contribute to the sectional division? Is the piece improvisatory or tightly constructed?
	PARAMETERS	Are timbre, texture, dynamics, or tempo important? How are these secondary parameters important? Can a sectional "map" or a formal structure be defined in terms of one or more secondary parameters? Does this map agree with the overall structure? What happens at points of disagreement?
	STYLE	What holds things together? How are the various parameters used? What is the role of tone color? What kind of tone color is used?
	TEXT/LYRICS	Is there a text? How does it contribute to the definition of structure?
	TEXTURE	Does each instrument have a unique function? Do instruments produce discrete tones, or are some indeterminate in pitch? Does the piece rely on horizontal or vertical complexity?

Motivic and formal structures may depend upon instrument design. The ramifications and implications of an instrument and the material it produces can be explored without concern for fitting it immediately into a piece of music. When appropriate, material may be organized, modified, or discarded.

Whether a piece develops from this studio work, or the studio session is molded to fit a previously developed compositional plan, it is important to listen critically, early, and often. Paradoxically, perhaps, it is not good to be too critical. Other listeners may like material which the composer feels does not quite reach the goal. It is difficult to be objective about one's own creations.

BASIC STRATEGIES

The electronic studio has been called the composer's "playpen." Where else can one so easily experiment with sound? Some musicians prefer to go into the studio without much preparation and basically just see what develops. In doing this, they are relying on their critical faculties to help them decide when they have developed a good piece of music. In addition to this bottom-up approach, music may be designed from the top down, developing structures before music, or a piece may be based on already existing pieces or types of pieces.

BOTTOM-UP DESIGN

Faced with so many fascinating sonic possibilities, a musician often doesn't know how to begin or to continue, or when to stop. For the beginner, improvisatory experimentation is a good way to become familiar with the equipment. Promising sonorities and musical events can be recorded on tape or disk. The reliance on instinct and spontaneity will sometimes lead to the creation of some interesting music.

START AT THE BOTTOM

Well-structured pieces can be created by starting at the bottom, with short segments and basic musical materials, and building upward. Musical material can be developed in the process of becoming familiar with interesting sounds. Short ideas can be recorded.

ANALYZE, DEVELOP, AND EXTEND

Promising excerpts may function as the foundation and inspiration for larger pieces of music. Variants of these events can be developed and recorded. Events should be analyzed (see *Advice for Self-Criticism* in box 11.2 on page 202). Phrases and subsections can be made by extending shorter units.

IN RETROSPECT

At some point, it becomes important to look over the material that has been developed. It may be necessary to create contrasting sections or to enlarge one area while decreasing another. New material may be based on smaller elements and built up, or may be designed from the top, based on a new understanding of what is needed.

TOP-DOWN DESIGN

Sometimes, more coordination and planning is necessary to create well-structured works. A structured approach to composition can both limit choices and free the musician to be creative within these self-imposed limits. If the limits become too confining, they may be changed, or the composer may choose to honor the limits, and change the music. Often, the struggle with and against limits will lead to exciting musical results.

We may often feel that the music should just flow from the composer's pen or fingertips—and sometimes it does. Usually, years of formal and informal study of music and performance are the basis for any improvisation: music does not come out of thin air.

START AT THE TOP

As many elements of the composition as possible are determined and described before the actual composition process (notes on paper or in a sequencer, or instrument design, or various other studio procedures) begins. This includes determining the length of the work, its purpose, the general characteristics of its instrumentation, the general approach to creating sonic events (improvisation, acoustic or previously recorded material, tape music techniques, sequencing, notated score, or some combination of approaches).

DEFINE EACH SECTION

Specific information on the form of the piece must be worked out. This includes the number of sections, the length of each, the character of each—in fact, the same questions asked about the overall piece apply to each section and subsection. Out of this arises an understanding of the shape and style of the piece. With this information, it should become easier to plan how to complete the project.

DEVELOP INCREASINGLY FINER DETAIL

As the work proceeds, more documentation will be needed on the actual patches or instrument design parameters. What are the patches? How does each sound? Where in the work will they appear? Where on the tape or disk or synthesizer are they stored? Any notated score may be refined, including more notes as to types of sonic events, duration, loudness, rhythm, pitch (frequency), and character of each.

STRUCTURE

The intended result is to give a great deal of structure and organization to a musical project. Elements of free improvisation can exist in a work created through top-down design, but within a strong overall plan. In a MIDI environment, a sequencer can be a great tool, since it is possible to create and manipulate blocks of musical material, and explore different relationships of these blocks as music is being created. Mark of the Unicorn's *Performer* for the Macintosh, for example, has a special "chunks" window, which allows this type of compositional activity to be undertaken. Figure 7.11 on page 134 offers an example of the chunks window in use.

MODELING

There is a time-honored tradition among composers of borrowing musical ideas from previously written works. Some of this borrowing would today be considered plagiarism, especially in commercially successful music, since ideas, themes, and sometimes entire movements were used. Still, a theme can be borrowed, as in a theme and variation set, or one or more musical ideas can be quoted in the course of a work, whether for shock value, amusement, or because of simple musical appropriateness. Indeed, a new piece can be based on the procedures and form of an existing piece of music, to give the composer a beginning point for his or her creative efforts.

PARODY

The techniques mentioned here are but a few of the possibilities for using other composers' ideas as stimuli for creativity. In parody, a work is closely modeled on another, specific work. This is not as easy as it sounds, since the idea is to write or create a new piece,

BOX · 11.2

ADVICE FOR SELF-CRITICISM

Arnold Schoenberg (1874-1951) was an innovative composer. In his *Fundamentals of Musical Composition* (London: Faber and Faber, 1967) he discusses thoroughly a variety of important technical procedures and aesthetic concepts. His discussions of musical form, melody, accompaniment, and construction of themes focused on acoustic, traditional musical forces. Much of his advice is just as valid for electronic music.

In chapter 12, "Advice for Self-Criticism," he states "... but even a master may stray on to the wrong track. When such a deviation occurs, one has to discover where and why one erred, and which is the right track. And therefore, self-criticism is necessary to a composer, gifted or not."

Schoenberg offers seven guidelines.

• *Listen.* Does the piece accomplish what the composer intended? Is is stylistically coherent? If harmony and melody are important, are they well constructed?

• *Analyze.* Are there portions of the piece that merely occupy time without contributing to the overall effect? Even in a meditative work where events unfold slowly, there may be unneeded filler. On the other hand, perhaps more of a sense of direction and connection is needed, requiring reorganization of material and/ or the creation or insertion of more material.

• *Eliminate nonessentials.* Simplicity is often to be preferred to complexity. Sensory overload may be caused by excessively thick textures, too many contrasts of tone color, too many different melodic/rhythmic figures.

• *Avoid monotony.* The other side of the coin of the previous paragraph is that simplicity still requires appropriate structure. Inconsistent repetition of chords and tones, restricted use of register or tone color, unfolding material too slowly (or the absence of interesting material) may weaken the piece. Schoenberg comments on the need to "evaluate sensitively the endings of the phrases."

• *Watch the bass line.* In Schoenberg's approach, the bass line may function as a complementary melody to the principal melody, usually present in the soprano, or top, line. While electronic music requires a broader concept of "the melody," his advice is useful. All material, whether intended as the primary focus for the listener, for some effect, or as a traditional bass line or other countermelodic role, needs to be carefully constructed. Appropriate variety, contour, direction, and rhythmic vitality should be lavished throughout the piece.

• *Make many sketches.* While electronic music may not be notated until after the fact of its creation and recording, it is important in the case of tape or digital recording to record more than one version of a musical passage. One would like to achieve perfection on the first try, but this seldom occurs. In addition, backup copies are useful in order to avoid accidental loss of material.

• *Watch the harmony; watch the root progressions; watch the bass line.* In other words, do not stop listening, analyzing, and creating.

not merely rehash the old piece. Along these lines are the electronic performances of Wendy Carlos's *Well-Tempered Synthesizer* and *Switched-On Bach*. These often go beyond merely playing an existing piece to some quite sophisticated use of the synthesizer, thus adapting these works to a new medium.

QUOTATION

Short excerpts by other composers can be cited in the course of a piece of music. They may be the source of musical inspiration, may provide humor, may be suggested to the composer by the musical context he or she has created, or may provide an underlying structure for a piece.

The third section of Luciano Berio's *Sinfonia* (1968), based upon the third movement of Gustav Mahler's *Second Symphony*, is an excellent extended acoustic example of both parody and quotation. The composer used the original work as a structure within which works of many other composers are quoted.

HOMAGE

Stylistic elements and practices of a composer may be deliberately studied and imitated to create a retrospective work that may be in the style of the composer being honored, or that may be in an original style that allows respect to be paid to the composer. In electronic music, this could mean that either an acoustic or electronic composer or performing group could be the subject of homage.

Homage to an acoustic composer involves the challenge of translating acoustic practices into the electronic medium. Exploring the style of an electronic composer, a specific composition, or a performing group requires much listening and studio experimentation, since little in this medium is written down (whereas in acoustic music there are often study scores and analytical articles to aid the stylistic investigation).

Homage is a useful technique, since the initial intent is to imitate a successful style rather than to begin with blank tape or empty paper. Many composers have, perhaps unconsciously, begun their composing careers with this technique. After imitating or modeling the music they heard around them, they eventually developed their own sense of style and command of the compositional craft.

MODULATION AS A FORMAL ELEMENT

Frequency, formant, pulse width, and amplitude modulation are standard tools for the creation of interesting timbres and instruments. They are used mainly on local levels, having more effect on behavior within tones and single events. It is possible, however, to extend the concept of modulation or change to broader, global activities.

Modulation is defined by David Cope in his *New Music Composition* (page 238) as "a smooth transition from one state of being to another." This approach to modulation has formal implications. Like tone color melody, it is not itself a form, but is a useful procedure for the development of form.

Cope suggests five types of modulation: spatial, timbre, rhythmic, articulation, and dynamic. He further suggests that any parameter may be open to modulation and that interesting effects can result from the combination of these types.

Spatial modulation involves panning the sound from one location to another, as has been previously discussed. **Timbre** (or formant or pulse width) **modulation**, is one of the primary tools for the creation of electronic sonic material.

Rhythmic modulation involves the gradual change from one rhythmic idea to another. This can occur in a single melodic line, where a slight displacement is introduced as a rhythmic pattern keeps repeating. It can apply to the composite rhythm created when

Figure 11.3. Modulation. This portrays a gradual shift from the predominance of one element to another.

Λ •••• Λ • Λ ••• Λ ••• Λ • Λ •• Λ •• Λ • ΛΛΛ •

two or more melodic lines occur simultaneously, with one voice gradually altering its rhythm, causing still further changes, creating a richly evolving composite rhythm.

Composer Elliott Carter has explored the concept of **metric modulation.** This might be considered a variant of Cope's rhythmic modulation. By gradually changing tempo indications and note values, a shift from one meter to another takes place.

Articulation modulation involves the gradual shift from one kind of articulation to another. In electronic media, envelope settings or the amount of portamento or glide might be subject to modulation. The general manner of playing the keyboard can also be modulated, but may be less effective than envelope settings.

The process of modulating may not be a simple linear progression. Cope suggests that it should be "hidden by constant backstepping so that one is never sure of the direction." His example, portrayed in figure 11.3, is worth considering. Simple, periodic modulations and straightforward linear modulations may be too obvious at times. By setting a goal for a modulation but being a bit devious about reaching it, a more subtle, effective shift from one condition to another can be achieved.

SOUND AND SIGHT

Electronic music is quite effective as an accompaniment to film or other visual elements. With the visual element providing the primary sense of continuity, the composer is free to comment on the action and add a unique interpretive element to the project. As with live performers, there are problems of coordination, particularly in timing. Video tape and collaboration with dancers and actors offer opportunities for exploration.

AUDIO FOR VIDEO

Adding sound to a video or film project is beyond the scope of this book for the most part. Those who wish to pursue this avenue should be familiar with synchronization procedures (see the section on synchronization in chapter ten on pages 182 to 187). Audio can range from sound effects to enhancement of the sound initially recorded on video tape to the addition of acoustic and electronic music to the addition of dialog. Computer applications are available to assist in keeping track of cues, copyright information, and all the attendant bookkeeping.

A good beginning point is to work with a colleague who is interested in video or computer animation. Have your colleague produce a short work of no more than two to three minutes in length. Become familiar with the video, and develop a list of cue points where music or other sound seems appropriate.

Keep in mind that music can support or be in contrast with the image. It can respond to or seem to generate an image. It can appear to be produced by someone or something on the screen (a piano player; a record player) or can be offscreen. Use the same video product to develop several different soundtracks.

In a MIDI studio, a good sequencer can be very useful. Tracks or sequences can be assigned to the cues you've developed. Once the sequencer is synced to the video you can play back your work at any point, not worrying about those spots where nothing comes to mind right away. This combines the bottom-up and top-down approaches: the top-down, overall structure is provided by the video; you can develop your work from the bottom, developing local cues which fit and support this structure.

Composing for dance or theater offers similar challenges and promises. Each idiom requires that you learn the appropriate sense of timing. Video or film is very precise, down to 1/30th of a second. Other media are not quite as exacting.

Unless you are knowledgeable about dance, it is best to work with a choreographer. This can be very satisfying, with new musical ideas coming from movement, and movement coming from the unfolding music. The musical product can be a tape, or a score which will be performed live, or can be a combination of recorded or sequenced music with additional live performers. While all three have their advantages, the presence of a musical performer can allow the music to react to the performance in a way the pre-recorded material cannot.

A range of possibilities is available in combining music with drama. The work may be an opera or musical, in which music plays a key role. On the other hand, it may be a play, with the music providing incidental comments and atmosphere. In both cases, the book or script provides a strong structure.

As with dance, the musical product may take different forms. Totally recorded music will require consideration of how the music is to start and stop. Is the music continuous, or will someone have to operate the equipment? How are individual cues marked? What happens when someone forgets a line?

Collaboration between musicians and other performers (or visual artists, for that matter) is often overlooked by many composers. It forces you to learn something about another medium, and it is often necessary to learn how to work with, or for, people who don't know much about the musical forces you are using. The tradeoffs in terms of having an overall structure to fit music into, rather than starting from scratch, and the energy that comes from working with another creative person, are worth the effort.

COMPUTERS AND COMPOSITION

Various computer programs can assist the composer in the compositional process. This help can include the creation of simple **effects** patches that turn a straightforward MIDI performance into a much more complex and interesting piece, blurring the distinction between the design of an instrument and the score of a piece. It can also include the use of a program that can interact with the composer or that can take settings given by the composer and turn them into a piece, giving the composer more the role of the orchestral conductor, rehearsing or performing a score.

PROGRAMMING LANGUAGES

A number of computer programmers have developed sets or libraries of commands or procedures that can be added on to standard programming languages to allow them to process MIDI data. On the Macintosh these include Altech System's *MIDIPascal* and *MIDIBASIC* for Pascal and BASIC, and Nigel Redmon's *HyperMIDI* (available from Earlevel Engineering), which provides similar extensions to *Hypercard*. Some music applications also have programming extensions, such as Jim Miller's *Personal Composer* for the IBM PC, a sequencing and notation application that includes a LISP (LISt Processing) programming environment for those who wish to customize their software.

HMSL (Hierarchical Music Specification Language) offers a wide range of programming options for Amigas and Macintoshes. Where *Personal Composer* is designed for processing data in non-real time, *HMSL* is particularly good for real-time performance. Although *HMSL* is listed as a language, it requires a version of the Forth programming language: JForth for the Amiga, and Mach2Forth for the Macintosh.

Another Forth-based extension is *MASC* (Meta-language for Adaptive Synthesis and Control). Currently available without cost in **source code** (a listing on paper of the language: you enter it into the computer), it runs on Amiga, Apple II, Commodore 64 and 128, IBM-PC, and Macintosh computers. Although there are many approaches to MIDI programming, we will look at one that offers a basic set of procedures.

INPUT AND OUTPUT

Since features vary from program to program, and the purpose and focus of each program may be different, some generalizations must be made. Although program syntax and the exact means of use will vary, certain common commands or procedures can be expected to be found. There must be a means of setting a MIDI port and providing any necessary specifications; it must be possible to receive and send MIDI data; there must be some means of manipulating and using that data.

Most MIDI extensions rely on the host language for the bulk of the third criterion, and provide the means for the host to communicate with the MIDI network. *MIDIPascal* accomplishes this with a basic set of eleven commands, listed in table 11.3.

Basic MIDI communication is established by setting up input and output buffers with the command *InitMIDI* (InSize, OutSize: integer), where the information in the parentheses provides two integer values representing the size of input and output buffers that hold MIDI data before and after it is processed. It is also necessary to provide information about the port through which the data will flow with the *MIDIPort*. It needs one parameter: values 0, 1, and 2 set the interface speed at 0.5 MHz, 1 MHz, or 2 MHz; values 3 and 4 select the modem or printer port.

For a program to receive data from a synthesizer, for example, InitMIDI initializes the input and output buffers, MIDIPort sets the interface speed and port, and *MIDIIn* gets

Table 11.3. Summary of *MIDIPascal* routines. The discussion of these routines was helped by Steve DeFuria and Joe Scacciaferro's *MIDI Programming for the Macintosh.*

ROUTINE	VARIABLE	TYPE	VALUE	FUNCTION
InitMIDI	InSize	Integer	Maximum 32767 bytes	set input buffer size
	OutSize	Integer	Maximum 32767 bytes	set output buffer size
MIDIPort	parameterValue	Integer	0-4	set interface speed and select port
MIDIIn	byte	Integer	0-127	byte from input buffer
MIDIOut	byte	Integer	0-127	byte to output buffer
GetMIDI	theString	String	Length set before use	string from input buffer
	mode	Integer	0-2	format of data bytes
	count	Integer	Number of bytes taken	
	result	Integer	0-3	status of string, from full to empty
SendMIDI	theString	String	Length set before use	string to output buffer
	mode	Integer	0-2	format of data bytes
InCount	byteCount	Integer	Maximum 32767 bytes	report number of bytes in input buffer
OutCount	byteCount	Integer	Maximum 32767 bytes	report number of bytes in output buffer
MIDI	bufferStatus	Integer	0-6	set status of buffers
MIDIFilter	filterID	Integer	0-8	select or reset filters
	lower	Integer	0-127	low value to filter
	upper	Integer	0-127	high value to filter
	skipCount	Integer	0-127	skip bytes after filtering
QuitMIDI	none			disable MIDIPascal

Figure 11.4. Transposing with *MIDIPascal*

```
PROCEDURE TransposeUp;
  VAR
    MIDIByte: integer

  BEGIN
    MIDIIN (MIDIByte); {get a byte from the input buffer}
    IF (MIDIByte >127) AND (MIDIByte < 160) THEN {check for Note On or Off}
      BEGIN {if byte is Note On or Off status}
        MIDIOut( MIDIByte); {send out Note On/Off status byte}
        MIDIIN (MIDIByte); {get next byte, MIDI note value}
        IF MIDIByte < 116 THEN {check to see if range is ok}
          MIDIByte:= MIDIByte + 12; {if so,transpose up one octave}
        MIDIOut(MIDIByte) {send out transposed note}
      END; {transposition portion of procedure}
    ELSE {if first byte was not Note On or Off status}
        MIDIOut(MIDIByte); {send byte back out}
  END; {TransposeUp}
```

the first byte that enters the input buffer. To send data to a synthesizer or other MIDI device, *MIDIOut* sends a byte to the output buffer which immediately passes the byte into the MIDI data stream. It is also possible to get and send longer strings of data with *Get-MIDI* and *SendMIDI*, which each have variables specifying various aspects of the data they are receiving or sending.

PROCESSING DATA

Various operations can be done to the buffers. *InCount* and *OutCount* can be used to find out how many bytes are in the respective buffers. *MIDI* allows the buffers to be cleared and reset using a series of buffer status values: 0 causes a reset; a 1, 2, or 5 causes the input buffer to be enabled, disabled, or cleared; a 3, 4, or 6 does the same for the output buffer.

Two additional commands round out the basic set. Since not all MIDI data is necessarily desirable (active sensing messages, for example, can quickly fill up a buffer; pitch-bend information could get in the way when only MIDI note messages are being examined), the *MIDIFilter* command allows nine different filters to be set up, to look for and eliminate specified MIDI values. When all is said and done, *QuitMIDI* disables *MIDIPascal* when an application is finished.

This may seem fairly rudimentary, particularly in a chapter devoted to composition. Just as a piece of music may be built up from small units to larger, so may complex procedures be made from the simple commands of *MIDIPascal* or *MIDIBASIC*, when combined with the features of the host language. Procedures can be easily created to process and modify MIDI note data, creating compositionally-oriented special effects.

Figure 11.4, for example, presents a procedure that that transposes incoming notes up an octave and sends them back out. Since MIDI note-on and -off messages consist of a status byte followed by note number and on or off velocity, each incoming byte is examined. Once a status byte is detected, the following byte is transposed by adding 12 after checking to see that the result will not exceed 127. Each byte is sent to the output buffer and automatically into the MIDI data stream. Notice that the only actual MIDIPascal statements used for this procedure are *MIDIIN* and *MIDIOut*. Earlier in a complete program *InitMIDI* would set the size of the input and output buffers and *MIDIPort* would set the interface speed and select the serial port to be used.

Using other Pascal routines, transposition could be random, or a delay could be added by waiting a specified amount of time. If this procedure were part of a larger set of procedures, the input and output sections might well be separate procedures, and TransposeUp would return a variable value that could be used in other procedures. Also, rather than have the program operate on incoming data, procedures could be devised that would generate MIDI data, allowing development of programs that create musical material as well as process it.

BEYOND THE BASICS

These types of procedures may be designed to function in real time, or to process or generate data that will be sequenced and edited before being performed, or to process previously sequenced data before it is turned into audio. With the addition of **timestamping**, *MIDIPascal* and other language extensions can handle timed data, allowing the creation of sequencer-like procedures.

In addition to providing similar functionality, applications like *HyperMIDI* benefit from the Macintosh's graphical user interface by providing sliders and other means for the user to interact with the program. HyperCard, the host language, provides a set of tools that make it easy to design applications that look good and require somewhat less involvement with programming than Pascal (although **scripting**—HyperCard's version of programming—has its own special syntax). Asymetrix's *ToolBook* provides a similar programming environment on IBM PC-type platforms.

All MIDI extensions suffer and benefit from the capabilities of their host. Extensions like *MIDIPascal* require traditional programming skills, and a good deal of understanding of the host language. Extensions like *HyperMIDI* require less programming, but suffer from the limitations on speed and complexity that result from the heavy involvement with graphics. The compromises that result from such hybrid languages have led other programmers to develop more comprehensive environments that focus mainly on MIDI.

GENERAL-PURPOSE ENVIRONMENTS

General-purpose programming environments occupy a middle ground between straight programming languages with MIDI extensions and interactive compositional tools (discussed in the following section). They generally offer more immediacy of use, with less need to have formal programming training. This is a boon to the composer who is looking for tools to use in composition, not having the patience and/or time to learn how to create such things from scratch.

Although the focus here is on *Megalomania* and *Max*, two applications that run on the Macintosh (as of the early 1990s), the emphasis is on the functions they allow. It would be impossible to present any reasonable tutorial on such environments, given the rapid changes and developments in software and hardware. There are excellent programs available for all platforms that offer a range of involvement with MIDI and composition. They all have some form of MIDI input and output, just like *MIDIPascal*. They offer various approaches to creating and processing MIDI data, either with program modules similar to the ones described here, or with the capability of creating original modules to fill these functions, as well as being able to provide additional features.

A LIMITED ENVIRONMENT

Figure 11.5 shows a patch designed in *Megalomania*, a 1990's shareware program. Icons are used to represent the program modules which are reusable. This is an example of Object-Oriented Programming, since the programmer manipulates objects rather than actual computer code. In the figure, incoming notes are delayed and transposed up or down a fifth, so that a single incoming note produces a chain of outgoing notes.

Figure 11.5. *Megalomania* patch and icons (used by permission of author Eric Huffman)

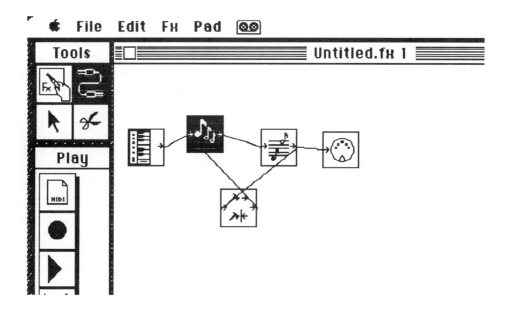

The first and last icons represent *Megalomania's MIDI In* and *MIDI Out* routines. They are comparable to *MIDIPascal's MIDIIn* and *MIDIOut* routines, although *Megalomania's* allows filtering of input data directly, rather than relying on an additional routine. This patch doesn't require any modules comparable to *InitMIDI*, *MIDIPort*, and *MIDI*, because the functions of those routines are contained in pull-down menu commands that are part of the shell of the environment. The highlighted icon represents a delay routine. Its output goes to the *Transpose* icon, whose output goes to the *MIDIOut* icon and to a *Velocity Filter* icon. The *Velocity Filter* feeds its ouput back to the *Delay*, so that a single note, as mentioned previously, will produce a series of ever-transposing notes that gradually get softer until some velocity limit is reached.

In at least one sense, an application like *Megalomania* is quite different from a *MIDIPascal*-type of program. Although they can both process MIDI data with compositionally useful procedures, the one is an environment with a somewhat fixed nature, while the other can be used to actually construct environments. This difference in approach exists throughout the electroacoustic medium and, for that matter, throughout music. Some composers prefer to rely on the expertise of performers, or the developers of patches, rather than create unique sounds and new timbres. Others find that their creativity works itself out partly in the development of instruments, whether physical or electronic.

It is important that you know what approach suits you best. Both programming languages and general-purpose environments offer a variety of options for modifying channel, note, velocity, duration, controller, and program change information. A program like *Megalomania* may not have opportunities for the user to create new modules, since the focus is on patching elements of a set of pre-designed modules in compositionally useful ways. Designing a patch is usually as simple as selecting modules from a list, placing the modules on the screen, connecting them in some fashion (*Megalomania* uses a patch cord tool), and specifying any available options (*Megalomania* requires double-clicking on an icon to call up an option window).

Each patch will begin with some form of MIDI input, and end with some form of MIDI output (*Megalomania* uses *MIDI In* and *MIDI Out* icons, as shown in figure 11.5). In *Megalomania* it is possible to have several patch windows on screen, and change active screens to shift from one patch to another in real time.

Table 11.4 lists the various modules currently available. This set is quite different than *MIDIPascal's*, largely because the focus is on manipulating MIDI data rather than on getting it in and out of Pascal. With appropriate thought, of course, any of the procedures represented in this program by an icon could be constructed in Pascal. In both cases, routines may be used as often as necessary, although the means of doing so differs.

A FULL-FEATURED ENVIRONMENT

With the power of the C programming language, and the ease of use of the Macintosh user interface, *Max* combines the programming flexibility of *MIDIPascal* with the ease of use of *Megalomania*. Effective patches can be easily created like *Megalomania's*, by placing icons on the screen and connecting them with patch cords.

Max's icons represent objects, of which there are more than one hundred. There were fourteen categories of objects, shown in table 11.5, as of 1991. In addition to these objects, *Max* also provides a palette of 18 more specialized objects, ranging from number boxes and buttons to various sliders and switches to LEDs, transparent buttons, and pop-up menus. When you place an object icon on the screen, the New Object List window is shown, with categories in one column, and the objects in the selected category in the other. This makes it easier to sort through the extensive list of options (of course, if you know what you want, you don't need to use the list).

Since *Max* is based on C, a programming language similar to Pascal, it is easy to create new, external objects, which can be added to *Max's* repertoire. As well, patches created in *Max* itself can become elements of of other patches. In acknowledgement of its complexity, *Max* comes with substantial documentation, and an excellent on-line help

Table 11.4. *Megalomania* program modules. Asterisked functions may be modified by a graph of time versus quantity, with amounts specified by the user, or by a controller using the range specified on the graph.

MODULE	FUNCTION
Channel Assign	Assign channel pressure, control, note, and pitch bend messages to specified MIDI channel
Channel Filter	Pass or filter channel pressure, control, note, and pitch bend messages on specified MIDI channel
Channel Hocket	Cycle output through specified series of MIDI channels
Control Envelope	Set envelope* of given controller on given MIDI channel
Control Map	Transfer control data to and from channel pressure, given controller, or pitch bend
Delay	Delay channel pressure, controller, or pitch bend, specifying delay time*, decay amount (velocity) and number of delays
Duration Assign	Set duration as percentage* of beat
MIDI In	May filter channel pressure, controllers, or pitch bend as well as assign MIDI channel(s) to incoming data
MIDI Out	Sends out MIDI data
MIDI Record	Records MIDI data
Note Cluster	Specify delay time and increment, decay amount and increment, and number of delays*
Note Filter	Pass odd or even notes or notes in given range; remove note off bytes
Note Filter (Single)	Only pass given note
Note Hold	Hold given number of notes
Note Map	Use one of four note maps to remap note data
Note Transpose	Transpose by specified interval*
Program Change	Remap given program number on given channel to specified program number on specified channel
Velocity Assign	Set velocity to percentage* or amount*
Velocity Filter	Pass odd or even velocities or range of velocities

system, which itself was created using *Max*. This makes it possible to option-click on an object to see an example patch containing the object, and copy that example into your patch, if it does what you want.

Just like any programming language, *Max* requires that a special syntax and vocabulary be learned. Most of the time, precedence is given to equal elements from right-to-left and top-to-bottom. This means that it is possible to have all the correct ingredients for a patch, but not obtain the expected results because something is placed in the wrong screen location. To make learning somewhat easier and give the user the opportunity to become familiar with *Max's* syntax, a 40-lesson tutorial is included.

As a full-featured environment, *Max* allows, on the one hand, all of the facility to create musically rich patches and composing environments that you would expect from a serious programming language; at the same time, it is flexible enough to provide for the creation of compositionally satisfying patches with a minimum of effort. It also contains on-screen features like sliders, dials, and hypertext-like invisible buttons, that allow the development of interactive compositional tools similar to the applications discussed in the following section.

COMPUTER-AIDED COMPOSITION

Programming language extensions and general-purpose environments usually leave note production up to the musician. In terms of the three-phase approach developed in chapter four these approaches center on a combination of instrument development and score construction, with the division between instrument and score somewhat vague. Programs focusing on note production center on a combination of the score production and rehearsal/performance phases, with the demarcation of the two again somewhat vague.

ALGORITHMIC COMPOSITION

Some programs explore options through algorithmic composition, where the program generates notes and related information using parametric information supplied by the user. *Tunesmith*, for the Atari ST or Mega (distributed by Dr. T's Software) fits into this category. *Sound Globs*, for the IBM PC and compatibles (Twelve Tone Systems) also fits, although it focuses on generating textures rather than the melodies of the former.

Another PC program, *MusicBox* (released as shareware in 1986 by John Dunn), offers a variety of user-controlled parameters used during playback, as the program calculates notes anew with each performance. According to the manual, "It is intended to be

Table 11.5. *Max* objects

CATEGORY	OBJECTS	FUNCTION
All Objects	106	A full list of all objects
Arithmetic/Logic	19	A full range of arithmetic and logic functions
Bitwise	4	Operations on the bit content of two numbers
Control	18	Control or change direction of data flow
Data	8	Store and manipulate data
Graphics	7	Create and manipulate graphic shapes
Keyboard/Mouse	2	Report when mouse button is pressed or released
Lists	3	Structure data lists
MIDI	20	Input and output of various MIDI messages
Notes	9	Operations on MIDI note messages
Patch Editors	4	Operations on patches, including bulk dumps
Right-to-Left	5	Operations relating to right-to-left ordering
System	11	System-level operations (as opposed to local)
Timing	7	Control timing of other functions

used with a large number of MIDI instruments playing simultaneously...In this context, MusicBox becomes both powerful and elegant, giving the composer the ability to quickly move from control of the overall sound of the electronic orchestra to an individual parameter of a single instrument."

INTERACTIVE COMPOSITION

Other programs take a more real-time interactive approach. Laurie Spiegel's *Music Mouse* (distributed by Dr. T's for Macintosh, Atari ST, or Amiga) creates musical material as the mouse moves across the monitor screen. *sYbil* (distributed by Scorpion Systems for Macintosh, Atari ST and PC) is another real-time program, allowing up to sixteen MIDI notes to be processed and operated upon. The operations can be fairly complex, and only occur when triggered by a performer.

Even some sequencers allow interactive operations. Opcode's *Vision* (Macintosh) and Dr. T's *KCS* (originally for Commodore C-64; also C-128, Apple II, Macintosh, Atari ST, and Amiga) allow events or sequences to be triggered by MIDI messages, essentially allowing the performer to improvise on relationships between sequences.

David Zicarelli and Joel Chadabe's *M* (distributed by Dr. T's for Macintosh, Atari, Amiga; distributed by Voyetra for IBM PC and compatibles running *Windows*) can also function as a partner in composition by combining pre-performance planning with real-time improvisation.

Figure 11.6 shows the Macintosh screen of version 2.0 of this program. Like *Music-Box* and *Tunesmith* its screen is full to the point of being confusing. Dividing the screen into rough quarters, the upper left contains a patterns window which controls the length and type of patterns as well as some input and output information. Up to six sets of four patterns may be stored. The upper right window, here titled "Beginnings," contains standard transport controls (play, record, and so on). There is also a conducting grid which can be used manually or automatically to control which variables or cyclic variables (the major portion of the rest of the screen) are active. The grid affects those variables whose arrow (to the left or above each group) is highlighted. The arrow may be pointed to the right, up, left, or down. As the mouse is dragged through the grid, variables will switch from set to set, depending upon their chosen direction.

Variables fall into three groups: standard variables (pattern group, note density, velocity range, note order, transposition, and time distortion), MIDI (sound choice and channel orchestration), and cyclic variables (patterns of accent, legato, and rhythm). By selecting different sets of variables, a large number of useful variants can be created. The results often seem to have a family relationship, and often seem somewhat meditative in character, since all patterns are looped.

Like *KCS* and other sequencers with interactive or algorithmic components, this program allows improvisation on the sequence level, although with the addition of an important difference. Pitch loops can have one length, velocity another, articulation (legato) yet another, and duration (rhythm) yet still another. Combine this with a level of randomness in note order and a constantly evolving fabric can be created. On the other hand, with the help of the conducting grid or the snapshot columns on the right of the screen, a piece with consistent results can be gradually developed. Program changes ("sound choice") can be coordinated with pattern group changes with transpositions with note density with cyclic variables. Where the conducting grid moves the changes from one cell to the adjoining cell, snapshots allow the screen to be reconfigured as you wish and then saved, allowing shifts from any configuration to any other configuration. With the help of the transport-like controls of the top of the third column in the snapshot area, snapshots can also be looped. Other features, such as the importation of MIDI files, make this program a challenging and creative compositional tool.

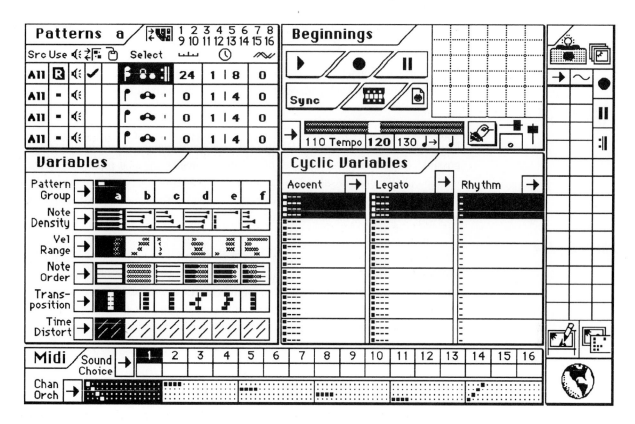

Figure 11.6. The screen display for *M* for the Macintosh.
Distributed by Dr. T's Music Software (used by permission).

FOR FURTHER STUDY

Chapter twelve presents a series of projects and exercises that explore the compositional use of MIDI sequencing software. Even in the absence of programming extensions, compositional environments, or interactive or algorithmic tools, the sequencer can be an extremely useful compositional aid.

EXERCISES

Most of these exercises are applicable to analog and digital synthesizers, since the focus is on musical parameters and compositional strategies. Beyond the exercises suggested here is the broad world of sound. One of the hardest assignments that might be given is "make something." Whether the approach is bottom-up, top-down, or freeform stream of consciousness, there must be limitations. The exercises given here attempt to offer a variety of models. Modify them as needed to fit the available hardware and software.

EXERCISE 11.1

With the help of a sequencer or by playing on the keyboard, develop a short melodic pattern that will be repeated. While it repeats, gradually alter timbre so that tension is increased. This may include envelope, filter, or waveform settings. Is it best to only alter one parameter or to alternate between several?

Do the same type of experimentation for pitch, duration, and tempo. This will result in the creation of four sequences, each focusing on one parameter. It may be possible to create a tension-producing sequence combining aspects of all four.

EXERCISE 11.2

Create a sequence of events that moves from tension to relaxation. Control as many different musical parameters as possible. After recording the sequence, listen critically and try to determine how each parameter contributed to the relaxation.

EXERCISE 11.3

Develop an interesting motive. Record it. Describe as many significant features of it as possible. Develop and record a set of variants, remembering that pitch and duration are not the only parameters subject to variation. Using a sequencer, organize the original and the variants so that the variants either seem to develop from the original, or the original seems to come out of the set of variants.

EXERCISE 11.4

Through improvisatory experimentation, develop a sonic library of at least 15 events ranging from a single note or chord to more complex events of 10-20 seconds in length. Use the library to create a two- to three-minute piece using the process of bottom-up design. How can the original material be extended? What contrasting ideas are suggested? How much influence do the available recording resources have on the type of piece that may be created.

EXERCISE 11.5

Plan and realize a two- to three-minute piece using top-down design. Plan as many aspects of the piece prior to using the studio. The form can be arbitrary, can explore the theme of "contrasts," or can fulfill the plan suggested by a story.

EXERCISE 11.6

Using top-down design, create and record a four-minute work for two-channel recorder. The work should have two or three sections. Title the work *Monkey See, Monkey Do*. The right channel should provide a varied imitation of material presented on the left channel. The material on the two channels should overlap at some points. Echo or tape delay does not qualify as imitation.

MIDI systems can either play back live, if two-channel output is possible, or can download the music to tape. This will be particularly effective for systems not capable of multitimbral performance, since the downloading process will allow timbral layering to take place on the tape recorder.

EXERCISE 11.7

Realize an existing short two-voice piano piece or other simple excerpt on synthesizer. Do not hesitate to electronically modify the original piece through the creative use of instrument design. In this parody-oriented process, the original piece should still be recognizable. The work may be monophonic or stereophonic.

EXERCISE 11.8

Using a familiar piece of music or song, create a 30- to 60-second segment based as much as possible on procedures from the given work. This parody/homage procedure requires analytical listening to first determine how the musical material is used. Provide a written explanation for your choices.

EXERCISE 11.9

Create a short piece entitled *The Children's Hour* in which one or more children's songs are quoted.

VOCABULARY

Many of the following terms were used for the first time in this chapter. A definition of each term may be found in the glossary.

articulation	articulation modulation	closure
effects	metric modulation	motive
polyphonic	register	rhythmic modulation
scripting	simultaneities	source code
spatial modulation	timbre modulation	timestamping

REVIEW QUESTIONS

QUESTION 11.1

Match related terms by writing the letter of the term in the second column in the blank of the term in the first column that most closely relates to it.

Conjunct	_____	A.	Distance
Duration	_____	B.	Loudness
Dynamics	_____	C.	Melody
Interval	_____	D.	Rhythm
Pitch	_____	E.	Speed
Tempo	_____	F.	Step
Timbre	_____	G.	Tone Color

QUESTION 11.2

Compare and contrast the following terms.

Duration — Rhythm

_____

_____

_____

_____

Musical Parameter — Digital Parameter

_____

_____

_____

_____

QUESTION 11.3

Provide the question for the given answer.

ANSWER	QUESTION
Gradual change from one thing to another	What is _____ ?
Citing short excerpts	What is _____ ?
General planning, then details	What is _____ ?

QUESTION 11.4

Define briefly.

Closure

_____

_____

_____

_____

Motive

_____

_____

_____

_____

CHAPTER · TWELVE

CREATIVE SEQUENCING

In this chapter a set of exercises exploring some of the creative uses of MIDI editing and sequencing is presented. The exercises are intended to follow up on the ideas presented in several of the preceding chapters, with particular emphasis on the editing procedures presented in chapter ten. Although most of the exercises are short and focussed, some may be developed into complete compositions.

There is an element missing from each exercise: the creativity provided by the composer. Without this, and without musical understanding, these exercises won't work. The results will be unique: there are many correct solutions. Be creative!

PARAMETERS

The exercises in this chapter are viewed from six different points of view: Pitch, Duration, Dynamics, Texture, Tempo and Meter, and Timbre. Through this procedure a set of related exercises is developed. Unlike the exercises sets in other chapters, these are placed throughout the chapter. Although it is possible to choose only those exercises that appear most interesting, try even those that at first glance appear to offer little: often there is more than initially suspected.

PITCH

Pitch is used here as synonymous with "key" or "note." Since MIDI records sonic events as a combination of note-on and note-off bytes (along with MIDI channel and attack and release velocity), these terms will be used interchangeably, even though they may have their own separate meanings. "Key" can also refer to one element of a keyboard or to the collection of sharps, naturals, and/or flats that form the background scale of a piece of music. Although there's an expectation that a synthesizer has a keyboard, other MIDI controllers can be used quite effectively here as well.

DURATION

Duration refers to the length of a note. Standard music notation operates in terms of divisions of a whole note: (= 2 half notes; = 4 quarter notes; = 8 eighth notes; = 16 sixteenth notes, and so on). Triplets (for example, 3 eighth notes in the space of 2) and other "tuplets" (5 sixteenths in the space of 4, for example), along with a range of other devices add flexibility to durational notation.

Articulation (the length of time a note actually sounds) further modifies duration and proves particularly troublesome in MIDI music, since written durations are seldom articulated with their full value (MIDI durations are usually given in terms of measure, beat, and subdivisions of the beat: the degree of subdivision or "resolution" depends on the individual sequencer). In the exercises presented here, the duration heading also includes *rhythm* which involves the ordering of durations into musically useful patterns.

DYNAMICS

Dynamics deals with the level of loudness of a note or a section of a piece of music. Traditional music notation uses a continuum of values from PP (pianissimo—very soft) through FF (fortissimo—very loud) with a variety of modifying symbols to indicate loudness. In MIDI music, the primary means of determining loudness is the attack velocity of a note (this assumes that the MIDI keyboard is responsive to velocity information). The higher the number (caused by pressing the key harder or more quickly) the louder the note. Sequencers with regional editing ability can scale velocities over a given number of notes to suggest a crescendo (increase in loudness) or decrescendo (decrease in loudness) or can create MIDI controller #7 (volume) information.

TEXTURE

Texture has both actual and apparent qualities. The actual texture of a passage of music refers to the number of notes occurring at more or less the same instant. It can also be thought of in terms of the number of active musical lines, where each line represents a musical instrument or section (as in first violins or second violins in an orchestra). Textures may be thick or thin or somewhere in between. Since this is somewhat subjective, it remains somewhat elusive.

Texture may also be simulated by horizontal activity: as a musical line has a number of skips that occur fairly close together the effect of multiple musical lines is simulated. The texture is apparently denser than it actually is "on paper." Texture may also be made to sound thinner than its notated appearance if the timbres or tone colors of the instruments involved interact in such a way that the ear hears a lighter texture.

TEMPO AND METER

Tempo and *meter* refer to the speed of a piece of music (tempo) and the organizing of the piece into measures of (usually) consistent numbers of beats (meter). A commonly occurring meter is 4/4, where there are four beats in a measure (shown by the upper 4) and the quarter note (shown by the lower 4) receives a beat. Standard performance practice has assigned a greater pulsation to the first beat of a measure.

TIMBRE

Timbre is a term referring to the tone color of an instrument. It applies here to the choice of a preset, or voice, or patch. Multi-timbral synthesizers are capable of responding to MIDI information over more than one MIDI channel at a time, allowing each channel to have its own active preset, or timbre.

EXERCISES

There are six topic areas into which the exercises are divided: Loops, Layers, Less is More, Motives and Variants, Modulation Procedures, and Modes. Within each area, one or more exercises focus on each of the musical parameters presented previously. Table 12.1 summarizes the relationship between the exercises, the six topic areas, and the six musical parameters.

Exercises 12.1 through 12.15 explore some of the uses of loops by modifying a short, simple monophonic melody. The next fifteen (Exercises 12.6 to 12.30) explore various layering techniques, using more complex melodic material. Exercises 12.31 through 12.36 deliberately use as simple a form of one of the six parameters as possible to explore the concept of "less is more," while relying on the other parameters to compensate for the lack of activity of the selected parameter.

Motives, discussed in chapter eleven (see page 196), are the focus of exercises 12.37 through 12.45. *Modulation*, also discussed in chapter eleven (page 203), is explored in exercises 12.46 through 12.55. *Modes*, presented earlier in chapter five on pages 95 and 96, are explored in exercises 12.56 through 12.65.

LOOPS

The loop is a mainstay of phase music and some minimalist music. Sequencer loop capability ranges from none, through all tracks looping, to user-defined loops of any length (this may even include the ability to"nest" loops). In the event that the sequencer has limited or no looping capability, the composer can simulate looping by copying the looped material as many times as needed.

The ability to loop all tracks can lead to interesting results if each track can be made to repeat independently, rather than waiting for the others to finish. In this case loops may

Table 12.1. Exercises organized by parameter

	Pitch	Duration	Dynamics	Texture	Tempo	Timbre
Loops	1, 2	3, 4	5, 6	7-10	11, 12	13-15
Layers	16-18	19, 20	21, 22	23, 24	25-27	28-30
Less is More	31	32	33	34	35	36
Motives	37	38, 39	40, 41	42	43	44, 45
Modulation	46, 47	48, 49	50	51, 52	53, 54	55
Modes	56-58	59, 60	61, 62	63	64	65

Figure 12.1. A short monophonic segment. The end of the segment is designed to flow into the beginning when the segment is looped.

a. In standard notation

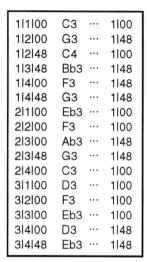

1	1	00	C3	⋯	1	00
1	2	00	G3	⋯	1	48
1	2	48	C4	⋯	1	00
1	3	48	Bb3	⋯	1	48
1	4	00	F3	⋯	1	48
1	4	48	G3	⋯	1	48
2	1	00	Eb3	⋯	1	00
2	2	00	F3	⋯	1	00
2	3	00	Ab3	⋯	1	48
2	3	48	G3	⋯	1	48
2	4	00	C3	⋯	1	00
3	1	00	D3	⋯	1	00
3	2	00	F3	⋯	1	00
3	3	00	Eb3	⋯	1	00
3	4	00	D3	⋯	1	48
3	4	48	Eb3	⋯	1	48

b. The same melody in an event list

EXERCISE 12.1

EXERCISE 12.2

be left unsynchronized, or may need to have endpoints adjusted so that they stay in sync. Sequencers which allow the user to specify where loop beginning and endpoints will be and how many times loops will occur add a level of flexibility to MIDI musical activities.

For the purposes of this section, develop a short monophonic melodic segment, similar to figure 12.1. Although "short" is left up to the actual musical context, around 10 seconds is a good maximum, with 5-6 seconds a good minimum (aim for the minimum if possible). Musical style, **register** (pitch placement) and other characteristics depend on taste and mood.

If possible, avoid closure. That is, make the segment open-ended, so that when it is looped it flows easily into the beginning. This can be done primarily by keeping the rhythm going, although pitch can also help by aiming toward the opening note. If your melodies all seem to have strong closure, just chop off the last measure. For ease of use in the following exercises, make the segment end with a complete measure.

The loop will be modified in the following exercises, grouped by parameter (pitch, duration, dynamics, texture, tempo and meter, timbre). Be sure to save a backup copy of the original material before beginning the exercises. Some exercises may require that the loop be "written out" or through-composed by linking copies to create a chain.

First put the melody into looping mode (consult the sequencer documentation). Listen to it several times. Does the end flow smoothly into the beginning? Can you tell where the beginning is? Take the segment out of loop mode, or remove the loop statements (again consulting sequencer documentation as needed). Copy the segment and paste it into the sequence directly following itself, so that the segment is now stated twice.

In the second statement of the segment, change one pitch, moving it an octave higher or lower. Choose an interval other than the octave if it seems more fitting. Copy this second statement and paste it to the end (see figure 12.2). In this statement, alter another note. Continue in the same fashion until all pitches have been altered. The result should be a loop that gradually changes into a different loop.

Develop a systematic approach to the pitch changes you'll make. Start at the beginning, or at the end, or alter every other note, for example. First shift up, then down, or perhaps lower all notes above C3, and raise all notes below C3. Flip a coin if you wish. But even in the midst of your system, listen to the unfolding piece (not too critically at first, since it may not sound like much for the first few modifications) and modify the modifications if your musical taste suggests something better (analyzing why such a change is necessary).

Use the copying approach of exercise 12.1. Rather than altering existing pitches, insert a new pitch (with an appropriate duration) in each successive statement. Rests may be added also. Make sure that the loop does not get longer, by "stealing" time from existing notes as new ones are added.

Sequencers handle the insertion of new durations differently. An insert mode may automatically shift the following values (see table 10.3 on page 177). Since the intent is

Figure 12.2. Copy-and-paste loops

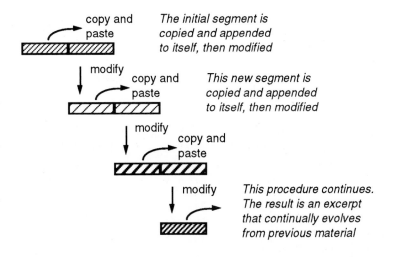

copy and paste — *The initial segment is copied and appended to itself, then modified*

modify → copy and paste — *This new segment is copied and appended to itself, then modified*

modify → copy and paste

modify → *This procedure continues. The result is an excerpt that continually evolves from previous material*

to add new notes without the loop getting longer, it may be best to shorten the duration preceding the location of the new note before inserting the new note.

As in exercise 12.1, a systematic approach is helpful. Try inserting one note between each of the original notes, such that the new note gets half the duration of the old note (in other words, it takes over half the space of the old note). Some experimentation with articulation may be necessary, since duration has two meanings in this context. One the one hand, a note lasts from its start time to the start time of the next note. On the other hand, the note lasts from its start time to its end time (where the end time equals start time plus duration), plus an undetermined release time, depending upon the characteristics of the patch. When altering durations, keep in mind that the space occupied by a note may be different than its written duration.

This approach shortchanges rests, since MIDI itself does not have a way to show rests. If you wish to insert a rest, merely alter durations and start times so that there is a longer silence between sounding events.

EXERCISE 12.3

Begin with a fresh statement of the original loop. In each statement of the loop alter one duration (use the copying procedures of the previous exercises). Effective techniques include adding a dot (half the value of the note), doubling the value, or halving the value. The main procedure used here, after altering a duration, is the "shift" function, moving everything after the alteration later or earlier in the piece by the amount of the addition or reduction. Unlike exercise 12.2, this exercise does alter the segment length.

Some striking effects can be achieved by adding values that give the loop a "limp." Adding the value of a sixteenth note to a quarter note, for example, displaces the rest of the loop by one sixteenth. Adding durations to the original loop will result in an evolution away from the starting meter (although it is possible to add enough material in such a way that the loop returns to the original meter). Rests may also be altered.

If material is not shifted in time, notes start overlapping. Although that was not the intent of this exercise, the development of texture through overlapping is worth exploring. It may prove interesting, as well as helpful in hearing the rhythmic alterations, to add a second track which loops a single pitch at a steady eighth-note pulsation.

EXERCISE 12.4

Combine elements of exercise 12.3 with elements of either pitch exercise (exercises 12.1 and 12.2). This allows more variety to be introduced sooner. Care should be exercised so as not to get too chaotic a result (unless that is the intent).

EXERCISE 12.5

Set the original melody into loop mode. Using the volume control of a synthesizer or mixer, create various dynamic curves with successive repetitions of the loop (crescendo, decrescendo, various combinations within one statement).

Using a velocity-sensitive synthesizer, develop a similar effect with the assistance of a sequencer. If the studio has a MIDI-controlled mixer or the sequencer has software faders, it should be possible to develop a control track that contains information on fader movement. With the ability to create continuous data, a sequencer should also be able to create a **control track** with volume data (MIDI controller #7).

If the sequencer has regional editing capabilities, another approach to altering volume is to develop velocity curves. First link copies of the original melody, repeating the copy-and-paste procedure as many times as needed. Then alter attack velocities on this non-looped version. If regional editing procedures aren't available, it will be necessary to change the velocity of each note separately to develop a curve.

EXERCISE 12.6

Alter, in several successive copied statements, the velocity of all notes so that they move from their original dynamic level to the opposite state (from soft to loud, or vice versa). Find the value midway between the softest and loudest velocity, and pivot the velocity value of each note around this midpoint. For example, if the attack velocity of a note was originally 40, and the midpoint is 64, shift it through intervening stages to 88. Do this in three or four statements of the loop, so that the changes are fairly obvious.

It may be useful to split the track into two tracks after lengthening it with the appropriate number of repetitions, one with all notes softer than the midpoint, the other with notes louder than the midpoint. Calculate the change needed for a note as it pivots, and make the changes as you move through the first segment. In the example given in the previous paragraph, the total distance to be covered is 48; if the change is to be made in three repetitions, this note will have the velocity 56 in the first statement (40 + 16), 72 in the second (40 + 16 + 16), and 88 in the third. It is best to do this for each successive note, rather than making one change on one note, a different change on the next, and trying to remember your changes when the loop repeats.

Check out your work by muting the original track and only playing the split tracks. Since they are on the same MIDI channel, the result should sound like one track. If the sequencer requires that each track be on a different MIDI channel, assign the same patch to each channel—assuming that the synthesizer is multi-timbral—or enjoy the effect of different timbres for soft and loud notes, if two synthesizers must be used. If the effect is too subtle (loud notes have become soft, soft notes have become loud), alter the velocities with a percentage curve (from 100% to 80% over the three or four repetitions for the loud notes, and from 100% to 120% for the soft notes). When you're done, merge the two tracks so that one track contains the full sequence.

EXERCISE 12.7.

Create a multi-layer texture with two or more versions of the loop differentiated by pitch. Transpose the loop into different registers (up or down an octave or more). Construct a backwards (retrograde) version of the loop for one layer. When reversing the order of notes, consider whether only pitches, or both pitches and durations, should be reversed.

This might be a regional editing feature, or may need to be done by hand. If it is automatic, and the result seems off a bit rhythmically, try quantizing durations by moving endpoints to the nearest grid point before retrograding.

This exercise allows exploration of the transposing and looping features of the sequencer. It should not be necessary to edit single events, except in the construction of a backwards loop.

To aim towards a more complex piece, try doubling or halving durations on one track (using the time scaling feature discussed in chapter ten and exercise 12.8). Also try varying volume, allowing layers to have different volume settings or to change volume over time (see exercise 12.9). If possible, explore setting different start times (a standard procedure for some sequencers; an advanced or unavailable feature on others).

EXERCISE 12.8.

Differentiate the layers of the multi-layer texture of exercise 12.7 by altering the time scale or tempo of layers of the loop. Try having one layer move half as fast as another. Have a third move twice as fast, or at some more complex ratio. On some sequencers this is a matter of selecting a track and altering its time scale. On other sequencers, it is necessary to edit each duration manually.

Editing durations or altering rhythms will not usually alter the time scale: the result will be notes with shorter or longer durations and the same distance between attack points as the original had. It will usually be necessary, when editing "by hand," to change the attack times as well to reflect the compression or expansion of time.

EXERCISE 12.9.

Differentiate the layers of a multi-layer texture (either using material from exercises 12.7 or 12.8, or developing a fresh texture) by altering dynamics. One layer may be louder than another; one may grow in volume while another gets softer; one may have fairly constant velocity values while another has erratic and ever-changing values. If all layers of the selected exercise were using the same MIDI channel, set each track to its own channel so that each musical line may respond independently to the volume information (MIDI controller #7) that you will be creating.

Exercises 12.5 and 12.6 should provide experience with the velocity and volume editing capabilities of the sequencer. It is recommended that one or both of those be done before doing this exercise.

EXERCISE 12.10.

Differentiate the layers of a multi-layer texture (exercises 12.7 through 12.9) through the control of timbre. This requires either a multi-timbral synthesizer, a synthesizer with several keyboard splits, or several synthesizers, each handling a layer. It may be wise to do exercise 12.13 to gain experience with timbral changes before doing this exercise.

The easiest approach is to assign each layer its own timbre. This gives each layer an additional unique element and develops a more colorful texture. To do so, assign each layer to a different MIDI channel and give each channel a different tone color (preset, voice, instrument, patch). For a more complex and interesting result, use a different timbral procedure for each layer. Have one layer change presets in an erratic and unpredictable way; have another layer change presets at the start of each statement of the loop; have another layer alternate between two or more timbres.

This exercise requires some understanding of the MIDI implementation on the available synthesizers, particularly if preset changes are sent, since presets may be given one name or number on the front panel display, yet be given a different MIDI program value.

Figure 12.3. Changing the timebase. Changing the timebase allows a piece to be slowed down more than the metronome may allow with the original timebase. Here, the metronome can only go as low as 20 beats per minute; switching to the sixteenth note gives an effective speed of 5 quarter notes per minute.

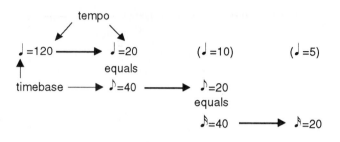

EXERCISE 12.11

Loop a copy of the original melody. Play the loop, trying it at different speeds. There will often be a change of character between slow and fast versions of a loop.

If tempo changes can be automated through use of a control track, explore this feature. Have the sequence gradually increase in tempo over several statements of the loop, then slow down as much as possible. If the timebase can be changed (the metronome click represents eighth notes rather than quarter notes, for example), it may be possible to slow the sequence even more (see figure 12.3).

Develop an interesting sequence of tempo changes, either automated or manual. Keep in mind that tempo can affect timbre. A slowly-developing sound will not function clearly in a fast tempo; short, crisp sounds that are great in faster tempi may sound empty in slow tempi. It may be necessary to adjust (tweak) a sound, perhaps developing several versions, each intended for a specific tempo range.

EXERCISE 12.12

Determine what meter the original melody is in. If it was recorded in real time, and hasn't been **quantized** (adjusted to fit the meter by moving attack times and possibly altering durations) do this before proceeding.

With a quantized version of the melody, explore the possibilities of deliberately changing the loop to some other meter (for example, change a 4/4 pattern to 11/8). Try different ways to make the loop fit: add extra notes; modify existing notes (lengthen, shorten, or even delete). Keep the pattern as recognizable as possible, but notice the types of changes you make. Try this procedure with several different meters.

Some sequencers will have automated procedures for changing meter in a given region. It may be possible to merely adjust barlines without affecting the content (it sounds the same in the new meter as it did in the old). It may be possible to realign the music, so that the content of old measure 1 fits into the new measure 1 (if your sequencer does that, what happens if the new measure is smaller than the old?).

The point of this exercise is not to just shift barlines, or alter the measure/beat location of a note. Rather, explore how melody defines meter (which helps define melody) by transforming your melody into a new melody with a new meter.

EXERCISE 12.13.

Set a copy of the original melody into loop mode. While the loop repeats try different presets on the available synthesizer(s). When a set of useful presets has been developed, record an interesting pattern of preset changes. It may be possible to do this by recording preset changes on an empty track. This control track may either stand alone or be merged with the track it is controlling.

It may be possible to indicate preset changes by editing an existing track, if the sequencer allows alphanumeric entry. This approach is especially appropriate for software

Figure 12.4. Control track
with program changes

1|1|00	#0
4|1|00	#1
4|2|00	#0
7|1|00	#1
7|2|00	#2
7|2|48	#0
10|1|00	#1
10|2|00	#2
10|2|48	#3
10|3|48	#0

46|1|00	#1
46|2|00	#2
46|2|48	#3
46|3|48	#4
46|4|00	#5
46|4|48	#6
47|1|00	#7
47|2|00	#8
47|3|00	#9
47|3|48	#10
47|4|00	#11
48|1|00	#12
48|2|00	#13
48|3|00	#14
48|4|00	#15
48|4|48	#0

1|1|00	C3	···	1|00
1|2|00	G3	···	1|48
1|2|48	C4	···	1|00
1|3|48	Bb3	···	1|48
1|4|00	F3	···	1|48
1|4|48	G3	···	1|48
2|1|00	Eb3	···	1|00
2|2|00	F3	···	1|00
2|3|00	Ab3	···	1|48
2|3|48	G3	···	1|48
2|4|00	C3	···	1|00
3|1|00	D3	···	1|00
3|2|00	F3	···	1|00
3|3|00	Eb3	···	1|00
3|4|00	D3	···	1|48
3|4|48	Eb3	···	1|48

*a. Starting the control
track*

*b. Nearing the end:
only the last event
is unchanged*

*c. The original melody
(from figure 12.1)*

sequencers based on a microcomputer. It is usually best to place patch changes between notes. This will minimize any delay caused by the transmission of too much MIDI data (not a problem with the textures used here, admittedly, but a good habit anyway) and will allow the change to be in place for the next note, avoiding any glitch that might happen if the synthesizer needs to process the information before it takes affect.

EXERCISE 12.14.

Introduce one new preset for one note with each new statement of the loop, until each note has its own preset (this is a timbral variant of exercise 12.1). This is especially effective if the new presets have different characteristics (some percussive, some orchestral, some frankly electronic), different tunings (this adds a pitch variant), and different registral placement.

This exercise requires the development of a control track to handle program change information. Notice that, as program changes are introduced, it is necessary to enter the new preset number and then return to the old number for the next note. Figure 12.4a shows the program change information for the first three iterations of the loop of figure 12.1. Notice that the return to the original patch is moved later and later in the loop, until, as in figure 12.4b, the entire loop has been modified.

EXERCISE 12.15.

A mono-timbral synthesizer may be able to simulate the multi-timbral layering presented in exercise 12.10 by modifying the loop so that a second statement of the loop, delayed or shifted slightly, only plays when the first layer isn't playing (this is a type of "hocket," a technique dating from medieval times). Preset changes may be sent either through a control track or by editing each track, with each note having a program change attached to it so that each layer maintains its own timbral identity. It will be necessary to shorten durations so that notes in one layer aren't cut off by the other layer. This is an example of a type of MIDI delay, involving timbral as well as temporal displacement. Those with patience may wish to try adding additional displaced loops, each with its own timbre.

LAYERS

Exercises 12.16 through 12.30 explore the development of multilayered, improvisational pieces, going beyond the multi-layer textures of several of the loop exercises. Where those exercises built layers out of a single loop, these consist of longer, more improvisational layers, not all of which need be loops (although the repetitive character of a loop builds an element of stability).

Begin by recording a rather freely improvised melodic segment. Try to make it at least one minute long. Determine meter, tempo, and key signature before beginning. Be sure that the segment does not modulate or have complex harmonies. After the segment is recorded, listen to it several times, and develop one or more additional layers as suggested in the following exercises. A metronome click or flash may prove helpful. Of course the segment should be saved to disk before any exercises are begun.

EXERCISE 12.16

Find a set of pitches, or an interesting melodic idea, present in the original layer, and develop a second layer based on some aspect of that set or idea. Keep the two layers basically an octave or two apart. Practice the new material against the old before recording the new material on a second track in real time. If you wish, try reacting spontaneously to the old material, imitating and commenting on the material as it unfolds.

Using common material promotes an underlying unity even when the material is treated differently. It also makes for a more successful improvisation, since the focus can be on melodic and rhythmic aspects, and less on choice of pitches, or on what the next harmony will be.

EXERCISE 12.17

Develop a bass line to the original layer. If the original was thought of as a bass line, try transposing it up and then creating a new lower part. Add a contrasting middle part. Don't be afraid to have the middle part rest from time to time. Also explore varying its thickness (occasional two- or three-note chords, or perhaps an ongoing two-note texture).

Do these layer exercises in real time (as opposed to step entry mode). If necessary, do the recording slowly and play back at a faster tempo. Avoid the temptation to edit or redo things too much. Improvisations are intended to be somewhat free, but not necessarily error-free (on the other hand, a little self-criticism is good).

EXERCISE 12.18

Construct at least two other layers without being overly concerned with relating them to the original (use the same key signature and meter). Start with either exercise 12.16 or 12.17. Although these layers are to be primarily separated by register, some timbral differentiation may suggest itself, particularly as the texture thickens.

Listen to the the entire piece at various tempi and edit pitches as needed to achieve a workable result. Also try repositioning the layers in relationship to each other. Put the top in the middle or bottom, for example, or see what happens when the bass line is transposed up a couple of octaves.

EXERCISE 12.19

Begin with a fresh copy of the original layer. Listen to it several times, making note of the types of durations used in it. Construct two or more new layers, each with some characteristic durations not prevalent in the other layers.

The idea in this exercise is that each layer should have its own durational identity, even if those values are present to some extent in other layers. For example, one layer might be generally slow-moving, while another is faster; one could primarily alternate slow and fast notes (dotted-eighth and sixteenth, or the triplet rhythm common in swing or blues) while another could feature a fairly regular walking bass. Try crossing layers: with a strong durational identity layers will often still stay separated.

EXERCISE 12.20

Construct a multi-layer structure in which each layer uses only one duration. Begin either by making a variant of your original layer, changing durations to the same value (quite easy with regional editing capability) or by making a new beginning layer for this exercise (based on only one duration).

Make at least three layers in this exercise. This idea is derived from species counterpoint which at one time was part of the study of every composer. The approach is somewhat different here, since in species counterpoint one could choose to develop several lines at the same time, in an attempt to follow fairly strict harmonic rules. The difficulty comes in trying to give the faster-moving lines a sense of direction and identity, rather than being mere finger exercises. This particular variant lends itself well to step entry or to recording at a slow tempo.

If step editing is used, a little may be entered in each layer, the piece may be played back, and decisions may then be made as to how to proceed next. This is only a minor contradiction to the stated aim of stressing improvisation in this chapter; many step entry systems allow automatic step advance: with only one duration value, step entry may be quite improvisatory, even if in quasi-slow motion.

Once the layers are created, listen for pitch clashes that may need some minor editing or revision. Also consider the need for modification of velocity. Step entry often results in uneven velocities. Global editing may be needed to soften down secondary lines and bring out primary melodic material, as well as to promote a sense of direction and dynamic climax. Local velocity editing may be needed if occasional notes were struck too hard or too soft for the context. Rather than controlling velocity by global editing, controlling volume by software or specialized hardware may solve weaknesses in dynamic structure. The following exercise specifically addresses velocity.

EXERCISE 12.21

Take the result of any other multi-layer exercise (exercise 12.20 is an especially good candidate) and add in dynamic differentiation. Make the bottom layer louder than the top; have middle layers change dynamic levels over the course of the piece. The actual procedure will depend to some extent on the sequencer. It may be possible to globally edit a track, changing all attack velocities to some specific value, or to reduce or increase all values by some percentage. With some sequencers, it may be necessary to change values one by one. Do exercise 12.5 before doing exercise 12.21, since they both deal with regional editing of velocity.

EXERCISE 12.22

Start with your original layer or any layer from exercises 12.16 through 12.20. Split it into two tracks, placing softer notes in one track and louder notes in the other (there should be a global or regional "split notes" function or an edit filter that can be set before performing a cut).

Play each of the new tracks by itself (using the sequencer's **solo** or **mute** function). Reduce the velocities of the soft track to 80% and increase the velocities of the loud track to 120%. Play the two together. There should be much less cohesion then in the original track. Now edit each track, supplying new notes to fill the gaps created by splitting the old track. Modify the dynamic separation if you wish, but try to make the two new tracks work together as a new, two-voice piece.

EXERCISE 12.23

Layers are often thought of as having only one note at a time. Begin this exercise with a fresh copy of the original layer. Record a new layer that is chordal in nature. It should probably move at a slower rate than the other layer. In fact, since these layers must work together, it may be wise to derive the chords from the existing material. Don't think so much in terms of standard harmonic progressions as of parallel structures that are more melodic than harmonic in nature. The chords can change type as you go along, with the notes sometimes close, sometimes more spread out.

Also don't get caught thinking that chords are always lower than the melody. It may be wise to set the track for this new material on a separate MIDI channel if the synthesizer can handle more than one channel at a time, since it allows for timbral differentiation if you wish, as well as avoiding any glitches when a previously recorded note is struck in the new material while the old note is sounding (the two note-off messages may have unexpected results).

EXERCISE 12.24

Consider the value of silence as a textural and musical element. Using exercise 12.20 or any completed multi-layer exercise, explore the results of removing pitches. How much silence can be "added" before the segment disintegrates? Notice how rhythmic patterns change and new relationships are created as silence is added.

Try this exercise several times, in different ways. One time, remove all notes on strong beats (beats 1 and 3 in 4/4, beat 1 in 2/4 and 3/4), leaving as many "off-beats" as possible. Another time, remove the off-beats and leave strong ones. Try one method with one layer and a different method with another layer, so that the composite activity stays constant. Or, deliberately go too far, leaving irregular holes of silence. Do patch changes affect your feeling for the results? Would changes to velocity or other parameters help?

MIDI does not actually record rests, but the onset of a note, its duration and velocity characteristics, and the onset and duration and velocity of the next note. Silence is the absence of a sounding note (remember that release values may make a note longer than its indicated MIDI value).

EXERCISE 12.25

Begin with a fresh copy of the original layer. Change its tempo, speeding it up at least double the original tempo. Record a new layer against the sped-up layer, trying to retain some of the flavor of the original. After saving the result, again increase the tempo, and record one final layer. Adjust the volume or velocities of the first two layers so that this final layer moves into the foreground. If a click is used during recording, the timebase may need adjusting, since it will get a bit frenetic at several times its initial speed. Play back your results at different tempi. How does tempo affect the character of the piece?

EXERCISE 12.26

Using exercise 12.17 or any other multi-layer exercise, alter the tempi of the various layers. This may involve changing the time scale, or may be a simple matter of adjusting individual track tempi. Speed up one track enough (at least double the tempo) so that it must be looped to maintain the texture while the other layers are playing. Slow down another layer. As a layer is slowed down, of course, either the other layers must be made longer (by adding new material or looping) or the slower layer must be made shorter or

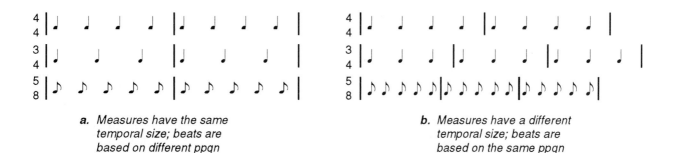

a. Measures have the same
   temporal size; beats are
   based on different ppqn

b. Measures have a different
   temporal size; beats are
   based on the same ppqn

Figure 12.5. Multiple meters

otherwise altered to maintain the texture. Along with changes in tempo may come the urge to change timbre or other parameters. Be creative, but notice what types of changes seem the right choice for a particular change of tempo.

EXERCISE 12.27

Begin with a fresh copy of the original layer. Construct additional layers that are deliberately set in different meters. Don't neglect angular meters such as 5/8 or 7/8. In developing this polymetric piece, decide how to emphasize the metric independence of each layer: should important beats be accented (higher velocity, more articulation), should there be more repetition, should the different meters coincide on first beats, should they share a common pulse or should each be totally independent of the others?

The sequencer may only be able to operate in one official meter. This should not stop the development of this polymetric exercise, although it may require a bit of calculation, the complexity of which will depend upon the resolution of the sequencer.

For example, if the sequencer divides the quarter note into 120 ticks, or **ppqn**, and the official meter is 4/4, there are 480 ticks per measure. If a layer has a different number of beats in the same space as the 4/4 measure, the beat, even if it is thought of as a quarter note, will have a different ppqn. If the piece were to be printed out, it might look a little strange, unless the notation program could compensate for the change in ppqn. Since the goal here is aural, the concept of "measure" is primarily a bookkeeping tool, and a beat can be any note or value. Alternatively, for the purposes of this exercise, the beat could stay the same, but be organized into different meters by accent and other musical means.

Figure 12.5 shows these two options. In figure 12.5a the measures in each layer are the same size and begin and end at the same time. Each beat is based on a different ppqn. If the standard is 120 ppqn, as suggested previously, the 3/4 measure will be based on 160 ppqn, and each eighth note in the 5/8 measure will contain 96 ticks, based on 192 ppqn (2-1/2 quarter notes per measure). In figure 12.5b all notes are based on 120 ppqn. This will cause barlines to be staggered and will set up a different kind of cross-accenting than figure 12.5a produces.

A simple and effective approach is to create short segments of two or so measures in each of the desired meters using either figure 12.5a or b as a model. Loop each segment the appropriate number of times to keep it going through the time span of the original layer. Make one of the new segments a bass line. After it's done, play it with the original layer. Assuming that there aren't too many harmonic clashes, notice how your perception of the original layer is altered. After the other segment is created, try it against each of the others, and then put all three together. Listen for the interplay of meters. Strengthen the sense of meter with appropriate editing, and provide endings for any looped layers.

EXERCISE 12.28

It's tempting to think of layers spatially, as in high—medium—low. Layers may to some extent overlap and intertwine, particularly if something other than register provides the sense of difference between them.

Begin with a fresh copy of the original layer. Make a second layer that is close to, sometimes above, sometimes below, the original layer. Make the new layer imitate the old layer where possible. If you can, have the new layer play a riff before the original layer does. Differentiate the two by choosing contrasting timbres for each layer. This does require some minimal multi-timbral capability.

EXERCISE 12.29

Using as many voices as possible, double the original layer at various intervals above the original layer to create a thick texture based on the one melodic line. This involves copying the layer to new tracks, then transposing the new tracks. If you wish, choose intervals in the harmonic series. Experiment with different timbres for the upper "harmonics" and consider altering velocity so that the notes farthest from the original are the softest (just as they tend to be in the harmonic spectra of acoustic instruments). Percussive timbres add crispness to the sound mass, while timbres with a long release or some delay, such as bell-like sounds, lend quite a different character to the sound.

EXERCISE 12.30

Using guidelines similar to exercise 12.29, develop a variant in which the original layer has harmonics and sub-harmonics: doublings of the original line that are lower than the original. Make the sub-harmonics softer, if only to allow the original to be heard as the fundamental pitch level and to avoid too muddy a texture. If you wish, start with your version of exercise 12.29 and modify it appropriately.

LESS IS MORE

The approach in the following six exercises is a little different than that of the previous exercises. Where the earlier exercises were organized by parameter, trying elaborations of an original idea or pattern, this set is based on the theme of limiting one parameter as much as possible, and using one or more of the other parameters to overcome the challenges created by this limitation.

Following each exercise statement is a set of comments on some of the possibilities offered by the various parameters to provide variety and musical interest. Use the comments to generate ideas but don't try to include everything that is discussed in your own solution to each exercise (after all, less is more!).

EXERCISE 12.31

Construct a piece built on a single pitch or, for textural variety, built on a single **pitch class** (for example, Cl, C2, C3, C4, CS, C6). Make the piece at least one minute long. As a general rule, this and the other "less is more" exercises benefit from starting simply and gradually developing complexity.

Pitch: This is the limiting parameter. The actual pitch chosen will have some effect on the piece: a high pitch will tend to be a little thin, lacking in harmonic content; a low pitch will be fuller, perhaps to the point of being muddy, with a fuller harmonic content; a middle-register pitch may offer the most flexibility in terms of available timbres.

Duration: This parameter can do much to create an interesting piece. A single-line, single-pitch piece with strong rhythmic content, combined perhaps with dynamics, could be quite interesting. Articulation is also important here: legato (smooth playing without a break between notes) is less effective than non-legato and even staccato (relatively short values) playing. See also the discussion of timbre.

Dynamics: Without pitch differentiation all other parameters need to be carefully considered. Juxtaposition of different velocity values in successive notes along with crescendos and decrescendos (in other words, making the line dynamic, rather than static) will give this exercise a sense of life. Consider both velocity and volume editing.

Texture: It is hard to achieve any thickness of texture with a single-pitch piece, although timbral thickness (the simultaneous use of two or more timbres) gives a sense of a thicker line. If one explores the pitch class variant discussed at the beginning of this exercise, the piece takes on quite a different aspect. It may now be spread over several octaves. Combined with variety of durations, timbre and dynamics, a striking multi-layer piece using only a single pitch class may be constructed.

Tempo and Meter: Meter tends to be a more utilitarian organizational device than tempo. A useful metric approach would be to explore a shifting metrical scheme, rather than the generally static approach of more conventional pieces. In this approach, for example, a measure of 4/4 could be followed by a measure of 3/4, followed by 6/8, then 7/8, then 4/4; and so on. Meter may either be organized into a regular pattern, or may be left free.

Tempo tends to be more expressive—or rather, the dynamic change in tempo, such as a rallentando (slowing down) or accelerando (speeding up) is expressive. This parameter is often overlooked, except for a slowing down at the end of a piece. In this exercise, dynamic tempo changes, particularly in conjunction with other parameters, will lead to an expressive piece.

Timbre: A multi-timbral synthesizer is well-suited to a single-pitch piece, since the focus can be on the interplay of tone colors. This actually involves combining duration and dynamics with timbre. Tone colors may alternate, or may be treated as separate durational layers, similar to the layers of exercise 12.20.

EXERCISE 12.32

Construct a piece built on a single duration value. The length of the piece will depend on the chose duration: 50 to 60 times the duration is appropriate.

Duration: This is the limiting parameter. Just as the choice of pitch has some effect on determining the character of the single-pitch piece, so does the choice of duration value have an effect on the character of the single-duration piece. This effect may be limited, however, since, unlike pitch, duration is highly relational in quality. A whole note in a tempo of quarter note=60 is 4 seconds long; a whole note in the tempo of quarter note=120 is only 2 seconds long. This is an excellent step record exercise.

There are at least three ways to define duration in electronic music: the length of time between attack points of successive notes; the written or stated duration of a note; the actual length of time a tone lasts as defined by its amplitude envelope. The main limitation here is on the distance between attack points (rests or silences may be some multiple of this distance). Clear articulation of successive notes may require some alteration of notated durations without altering the distance between attacks, or may require the choice of sounds with appropriate envelopes (or the modification of envelopes).

Pitch: In the face of limited durational variety, pitch takes on a very important role. It can provide direction, contrast, a sense of repetition or variation—these are procedures pitch is normally involved with, but usually in partnership with duration. Don't overlook silence (the rest) as a pitch. It will aid in organizing the duration chain into rhythmic units, which will be delineated by silence.

To get going with this exercise, try pitch and duration first. Using a fairly quick duration, repeat a pitch several times, touch on one new pitch, then return to the first pitch. Again play it several times, then go to a third pitch, followed by the first pitch. Notice that several new pitches can be linked into a melody as well as providing rhythmic articulation. Go to the other extreme, with little or no pitch repetition, and notice the difference in character. As an interesting combination of pitch and rhythm is developed, add in the other parameters.

Dynamics: This parameter becomes an essential part of a piece in the absence of rhythmic articulation (in fact it allows for the establishment of rhythms and meters, almost in the sense that a bass drum underlines the percussion). Try making higher pitches louder (or deliberately reversing the procedure, and making lower pitches louder). Make every fourth duration louder. Try other arbitrary schemes.

Texture: It is possible to be quite expressive with texture. Since the duration is statically repetitive, other elements need to be less static. Explore changing textures. Grow from a single note to thick chords. Contrast material in different registers (high versus low). Avoid 4-part chordal writing and work for more variety. Develop a thicker composite rhythmic texture by offsetting a layer by some fraction of a durational unit (for example, if the chosen duration is a quarter note, offset one layer by an eighth note to achieve a composite eighth-note rhythmic texture).

Tempo and Meter: The expressive use of tempo can make up greatly for the limitation of a single duration. Abrupt tempo changes contrasted with gradual tempo changes can lead to a rather fluid durational context. This can be exploited on a sequencer with good single-note and regional editing capability. If a tempo map or list of tempo changes can be made, it will be possible to modify the given duration almost at will.

Timbre: With a little work a rhythm of tone color changes may be created. Develop melody lines in which two or more presets work together to express a single line. Alternate between two presets. Give each layer its own timbral identity. On the other hand, avoid timbral chaos. It would take strong organization of the other parameters to have a piece in which each note had a different tone color (although the idea of each pitch class being associated with its own timbre has some attraction, especially with duration being reduced in importance).

EXERCISE 12.33

Construct a piece using only one dynamic level (velocity value). This piece should have a length of one minute.

Dynamics. This is the limiting parameter. Many pieces suffer from this limitation without the composer being aware of it. An attack velocity of 64 is most appropriate, since it is the value usually assigned to instruments that are not velocity-sensitive. This involves editing velocities after notes are recorded or entered. Do not use a volume controller for expression, but rely on other parameters for contrast and interest.

Pitch: Rising lines give a sense of dynamic increase, while descending lines suggest a decrease. Some timbres sound softer as they rise, so timbre will affect this sense of increase, and may even reverse it. Since durations are also free, there is much more choice than in the previous exercise. The problem here is to combine the elements that suggest dynamic change to avoid having a static, somewhat bland piece.

Duration: There is no limitation on duration. A mixture of values is useful. Longer values suggest points of rest, while shorter values give a greater sense of motion.

Texture: Changes in texture will actually give a sense of change in dynamic level. This parameter, in conjunction with changes in pitch register and timbral specifications, has been used quite effectively in pipe organ literature. If you wish, develop "loud" and "soft" textures, and use them thematically or structurally. As in exercise 12.32, avoid static textures, except as a contrast for more dynamic sections.

Tempo and Meter: After the piece is put together, explore tempo modifications, especially on a small scale. Can the beginning of a phrase speed up slightly? How about slowing down just a bit at the end of a phrase? Striking contrasts can draw attention away from the limited dynamic range.

Timbre: The selection of presets or the modification of presets allows for a means of getting around the limitation of dynamics or velocity values. Presets with dramatic attack or decay phases or various release slopes can aid in dynamic contrast. It is possible to develop a set of presets categorized by their relative loudness. Presets may then be assigned much as one would assign a dynamic level to some portion of a piece of music. Even without much dynamic contrast, timbral contrast can provide interest and expression.

EXERCISE 12.34

Construct a piece using only one textural density. This piece should have a length of about one minute. Since texture is a product of musical activity, more precompositional thought may be needed to develop a consistent density.

Texture: This is the limiting parameter. While it is not often consciously considered, it is important. Try developing a piece which constantly has five active lines with a maximum distance between top and bottom of about three octaves. The bottom line should never come closer to the next line than a sixth and no two lines should be more than a seventh apart. In essence: don't get the bottom lines so close that the sound gets muddy; keep all the lines roughly equidistant.

Pitch: Although there are no direct limitations on pitch, the choice of notes becomes to some extent dependent upon the placement of other notes in the texture. Don't make each line unique: imitate interesting pitch/duration ideas in other voices.

Duration: This parameter can assume more importance in a relatively static texture, since a composite rhythm (the sum of the rhythm of all attacks) can add an element of interest. A static texture does not mean that all lines have the same rhythm (try it, however - it can have an interesting effect, particularly if one line is out of sync with the others). Generally a certain level of rhythmic richness is to be desired.

Dynamics: Work for dynamic interest within each line as well as between lines. Dynamic variety actually can work to give a sense of textural variety, since the relationship between notes in chords can shift.

Tempo and Meter: In the face of a static texture, either a shifting metrical scheme or some angular meter (5/8, 7/8, 11/8, and so on) will provide greater rhythmic and metric interest and take attention away from the texture. Faster tempi will add to the effect of the meter, while slower tempi may be more contemplative and allow other parameters more opportunity to play a leading role.

Timbre: This parameter is always important, particularly in slower tempi. Texture can be made to appear to vary by changing tone colors, and will certainly be given character by the choice of timbres. A set of heavy, harmonically rich presets will make a texture fuller, while lighter sounds will make the texture both thinner and brighter.

1I1I00	4/4
2I1I00	7/8
3I1I00	3/4
4I1I00	5/8
5I1I00	2/4
6I1I00	4/4
7I1I00	2/4
8I1I00	5/8
9I1I00	3/4
10I1I00	7/8
11I1I00	4/4
12I1I00	5/4
13I1I00	6/4
14I1I00	7/4
15I1I00	13/8
16I1I00	11/8
17I1I00	9/8
18I1I00	7/8
19I1I00	4/4

a.

1I1I00	4/4		
	G3	⋯	0I48
1I1I48	E3	⋯	0I48
1I2I00	E4	⋯	0I48
1I2I48	C4	⋯	1I00
1I3I48	A3	⋯	0I48
1I4I00	D4	⋯	0I48
1I4I48	F3	⋯	0I48

b.

5I1I00	2/4		
	G3	⋯	0I48
5I1I48	E3	⋯	0I24
5I1I72	E4	⋯	0I24
5I2I00	C4	⋯	0I24
5I2I24	A3	⋯	0I24
5I2I48	D4	⋯	0I24
5I2I72	F3	⋯	0I24

c.

14I1I00	7/4		
	G3	⋯	1I00
14I2I00	E3	⋯	1I00
14I3I00	E4	⋯	0I48
14I3I48	C4	⋯	1I00
14I4I48	A3	⋯	1I00
14I5I48	D4	⋯	1I48
14I7I00	F3	⋯	1I00

d.

Figure 12.6. Organizing by meter. An arbitrary meter scheme is developed (*a*). A multi-layer measure is created for the first measure (one possible layer is shown in *b*). As meter causes the measure to shrink (*c*) or expand (*d*) the layer's durations are modified so that all pitches are used. Rhythmic characteristics are preserved when possible.

EXERCISE 12.35

Construct a piece using only tempo or meter as an important organizing tool. The length of the piece is open, depending to some extent on choice of tempo and meter. If you explored tempo or meter previously, this will allow you to build on that experience.

Tempo and Meter: Begin by developing a one-measure (4/4) musical unit with two or three layers. This material will repeat in each measure of your piece, but will be modified as needed to fit the changing tempo or meter.

If tempo is the organizing tool, loop the measure using either the looping capability of the sequencer or copy-and-paste procedures. Experiment with gradual and sudden changes of tempo to modify what could rapidly becoming a rather simple (and boring!) repetition of material. If it is possible, record these tempo changes or automate them so that the piece plays back according to the tempo scheme. If recording is not possible, save the results by writing down the tempo plan and realizing it in real time.

If meter is the organizing tool, develop an interesting sequence of meters and decide how the musical material may be altered to fit the space. Essentially what this exercise does is to vary the size of the "box" (the measure) into which a constant quantity of musical material (so many notes) must be fit.

One approach is to decrease or increase all durations by the percentage that represents the difference in size between 4/4 (the original meter) and the current meter. This is actually nothing more than a tempo change disguised as a meter change. Another approach is to alter various characteristics of the original musical material to fit the current metrical environment. The comments that follow address this approach.

Pitch: Don't feel that the order of pitches needs to remain the same. It may be interesting to swap pitches with another layer, perhaps changing the octave. This works well especially if the original material is strongly chordal in nature (revoicing chords keeps the repetition fresher and less obvious). Try not to drop out pitches as the space gets tight.

Duration: Duration values must certainly be altered to fit smaller or more expansive measures. Rather than just having material occupy space, try to have the rhythm give some sense of the meter. For example, 3/4 organizes material into multiples and portions of a quarter note while 6/8, even though it occupies the same amount of time, organizes material in units of a dotted quarter note. A combination of velocity (accentuate or strengthen the 1st, 3rd, and 5th eighth notes in 3/4; accentuate the 1st and 4th in 6/8) and articulation (a full-value note followed by one that lasts only a portion of its potential length will sound like the beginning of a rhythmic group, and hence stronger) will aid in the strengthening of metric feel.

Dynamics: This parameter will tend to be something of an afterthought, particularly since this exercise requires much step editing. Since there will be rapid changes of tempo or meter, the dynamics should support this activity by a greater degree of variety than in more metrically consistent pieces. Dynamics are also important because this exercise is likely to be fairly short. Longer works can be painted with a fairly broad dynamics brush; shorter works require more attention to detail.

Texture: As space gets smaller, texture will get thicker. A 1/4 measure, for example, will require either fairly rapid duration values or more layers (thicker chords) than 4/4. As the space expands, there is a tendency for texture to thin out. Avoid its getting too thin by adding additional notes or chords in larger measures.

Timbre: It may be easier to develop this exercise as a mono-timbral piece, to allow the creative focus to be on tempo and meter, and the response to these parameters. As the exercise proceeds, consider adding in more timbral elements, particularly if they can support the metrical structure. One possibility is to develop a different set of timbres for each different meter, so that as each meter reappears it has its own tone color or colors. This can be effective in combination with alterations to pitch and duration that support the choice of timbres (fanfares for brass sounds, arpeggios for harps, percussive activity for percussion, and so on).

EXERCISE 12.36

Construct a piece in which timbre is an important organizing tool. It should be no more than two to three minutes in length. Make it a free-form improvisatory, melodic segment. If possible make it a single layer with occasional chords as an outgrowth of the melodic material, rather than as a separate accompaniment.

Timbre: Begin by dividing the keyboard up into chunks, or zones, of six notes (C0-F0; F#0-B0; C1-F1; F#1-B1; and so on). Each zone will be assigned a different timbre. If the synthesizer allows for enough splits, this can be done live; for most of us, editing procedures or MIDI mapping software will be required.

One approach is to edit an existing piece to fit the timbral scheme. The results could be striking — and certainly will be different — since the piece was not conceived with this sort of orchestration in mind. The comments that follow speak to a second approach: the development of a new piece with this timbral restriction.

Pitch and Duration: There are no restrictions. Try developing a musical line (melody) in real time which changes timbre as a new timbral zone is entered. This will either require playing the keyboard with one hand and the front panel with another, or having an assistant who handles program changes. Keep in mind the advantage of digital technology in allowing one to record slowly and play back more quickly without changing pitch. Experiment with the melody to take advantage of the timbral zones: move back and forth between two zones; go to a third, and then return to the first two.

Should it not be possible to record timbre changes as the musical line is played, the material may be entered in either real or step time. Keep in mind the timbral zones and what the effect should be. After a few measures have been entered, add preset changes to a separate control track or to the melodic material itself. To make it easier to see when the changes take place, give them the same start time as the first note they affect. Listen to the work and modify as needed. Proceed further in the same fashion.

Dynamics: This parameter is to a great extent built in to the selection of timbres, and doesn't require much additional activity. It may be useful to edit velocities of a timbre that is too weak in relation to its neighbors, although in most cases this can be compensated for this by choosing timbres that balance better or by playing in such a way to avoid or exploit dynamic differences.

Texture: Since this exercise explores timbral zones, a thick texture would negate the procedure. Make no more than two layers or, preferably, one layer that occasionally gets thicker. Before adding patch changes to a thick layer, deflam chords if you wish and use separate tracks for the additional notes so that each note in a chord may have its own timbre if that is called for by the zone scheme (each track will also have its own MIDI channel as well). Musical lines or layers are easily identified with registral placement and tone color; since the idea here is to encourage the listener to hear timbre as an aspect of melody, the use of a single layer minimizes distractions.

Tempo and Meter: As with texture, since this piece is exploring timbral relationships, tempo and meter can be kept in the background. In fact, the tempo may do well to be on the slower side. Some metric flexibility may enhance the movement from one zone to another, or the movement from zone to zone may be made at metrically important moments. The general rule is not to be intrusive with a high degree of parametric activity, but to allow timbre and pitch to interrelate as they will.

MOTIVES AND VARIANTS

One of the identifying characteristics of much Classical music is the use of the motive: a short, recognizable musical idea that can be repeated, altered, or developed in a variety of ways. Although motives are often created on paper using music notation, motives can be developed as well using a MIDI sequencer and one additional piece of equipment: the ear. While musical ideas are often conceived in terms of pitch and duration (the primary elements in melody), motives are shaped and influenced by other parameters as well.

First develop an interesting musical idea. It may be monophonic, chordal, or a combination of the two. It should be fairly short. Listen to the motive and see if there might be smaller motivic ideas inside the original motive. If so, first try this exercise using one of the smaller motives, then use the larger motive.

EXERCISE 12.37

Leaving the other parameters of the motive unchanged, only vary the pitch. First try changing just one note, then two or three. Save the more successful motives and organize them into a chain, moving from the original motive to less recognizable versions.

Chaining variants works best if there is a way to organize tracks or sequences by time. This may involve either setting different start times or using a graphic editing window to put the variants in a useable order. Lacking these alternatives, develop each variant on its own track, then use a new track to copy and paste variants in the desired order.

In changing notes when developing variants, experiment with different amounts of displacement. Notice that if the displaced note gets too far from the rest of the motive it may not fit well with the rest of the motive. When this happens, either reduce the amount of displacement or deliberately displace a few more notes so that they either lead to or from the displaced note, or increase the angularity of the variant.

EXERCISE 12.38

Using the original motivic material, develop durational variants. Without changing the other parameters, modify durations. First try changing just one duration (this may make the motive lopsided), then try altering several. Repeat pitches if desired, but don't add new ones (it is possible, of course, to develop variants by leaving material out, as done in exercise 12.24 on page 228). Save the more successful variants and, using the procedures of exercise 12.37, organize them into a chain, moving from the strangest or least recognizable one to the original motive.

Variants may be developed in either real or step time. In either case, it is important to listen critically to them to identify important characteristics. Edit as needed, particularly if the material is too long.

EXERCISE 12.39

Develop several variants of the motive by combining pitch and duration modifications. In many cases, rhythm gives a stronger sense of "family" identification than pitch. This exercise is best done after doing exercises 12.37 and 12.38. Develop a chain of variants that moves from less recognizable to the motive back to less recognizable. If variants are different lengths develop a chain that has variants beginning on the same beat of the measure. This will make it necessary to have silence between some variants. (If you were already doing this, make your second chain have little or no silence between variants.)

EXERCISE 12.40

Dynamics tends to generally have less effect on either the motive or its variants, probably because motives are rarely developed with dynamics as a primary component. Explore the effect of dynamics as a motivic modifier, using the original motive. Can changes in character be caused by dynamics? What about a different dynamic level (velocity) on each successive note? What about a strong crescendo or decrescendo, or, upon each repetition, strong dynamic changes on only two or three notes (different ones each time)?

EXERCISE 12.41

Apply dynamics to one of your solutions to exercises 12.37 through 12.39. Dynamics may be used to strengthen various aspects of your variant chain, or may be imposed in a way that actually contrasts with your material.

EXERCISE 12.42

Using material developed in earlier exercises, develop a piece with at least three layers that explores the technique of imitation. In this technique, material may be stated in one layer and then restated (either literally or with some degree of variation) in other layers.

One approach to restatement involves using one of the variant chains as the first layer, and creating a second by offsetting a different ordering of the same material. Figure 12.7 shows an arrangement of variants developed in exercise 12.37 and an offset retrograde ordering of the same material. Notice that the top row doesn't present variants in their developed order, since the focus was on going from the motive to less recognizable variants rather than on merely presenting material as it was developed.

Figure 12.7. Layering motivic chains

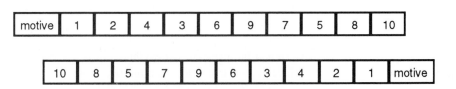

There are several advantages in combining material with itself as done in figure 12.7 Familiar material is presented in fresh ways. There is an underlying sense of unity (a plus for the listener). Material gets reused (a plus for the composer).

Material may be restated on any pitch, either by transposition or intervallic alteration. Although the motive has been approached as a succession of pitch/duration pairs (notes) it may also be thought of as a succession of intervals (distance up or down the keyboard from one note to the other). In transposition, the pitch of a musical unit is altered (shifted by a common interval). In intervallic alteration, some intervals are altered (only selected pitches are moved).

Try at some point taking one statement and making it two or more times longer (augmentation). This gets musical material working at different speeds and encourages independence of line as well as a richness of texture. The opposite approach (diminution, or reducing the duration of each note) is also useful, particularly with the aid of looping or copy-and-paste techniques, since a motive may be compacted and then repeated several times As much as possible, derive the musical material used in this exercise from the original motive or some variant of it.

EXERCISE 12.43

Fit variants of the original motive into different meters, changing pitch and duration values as needed. While material from earlier exercises may be used and altered, it would be good to also create new variants directly in new meters. Organize the variants into a chain. If the sequencer doesn't allow independent units to have their own time signature, it may be necessary to develop an arbitrary metric scheme or meter map, such as the one shown in figure 12.6a on page 234, before developing variants.

EXERCISE 12.44

Timbre is usually overlooked in discussions of motives. Using an original motive and several pitch/duration variants (either new or from exercise 12.39), develop variants based on changing timbres. This can take several forms: change on each successive pitch; change only when the direction of the musical line changes; follow some other arbitrary criterion. Keep a timbre for several pitches, and overlap with a new timbre for one or two notes when changing (this creates three timbres out of two: the first, the second, and the combination of both). Either develop a control track, record preset changes while playing the motive, or use editing procedures to add in preset changes.

Be sparing in the number of timbres you work with: two or three are sufficient. Put the more successful variants in an appropriate order. Select one to function as a refrain, and bring it into play after every three or four variants.

EXERCISE 12.45

As was done with dynamics in exercise 12.41, develop a more complex motivically-based piece by combining changes in tone color with changes in pitch, duration, and other parameters. Develop a piece with two or more layers that combines the techniques discussed in this section with timbral creativity.

If you wish, rather than creating a new piece, add in timbre to one of the chains developed in exercises 12.37 through 12.39. In so doing, keep in mind that more than one layer should be involved. If the chain you select is primarily a single layer, create one new layer, either using the same motivic techniques of earlier exercises, or through an improvisation based on the original motive of this section. Add other layers to provide rhythmic interest, a bass line, or other needed features. Keep the focus on timbre.

MODULATION PROCEDURES

The term "modulation" has several appropriate meanings, all of which involve the constructive use of changing from one state or set of conditions to another. Chapter twelve presents a discussion of modulation procedures which are explored in exercises 12.46 through 12.55. These exercises have been inspired by a chapter on modulation in David Cope's *New Music Composition* (New York: Schirmer Books, 1977).

Record a short melody in any style. It should not be more than about a dozen notes long (roughly equivalent to two measures of 4/4). Save it to disk before using it in many of the exercises in this section.

EXERCISE 12.46

Use the melody in this exercise. Examine the track list or whatever means the sequencer has of showing what notes were played when. Determine which of the twelve pitch classes were not used in the melody.

Loop the melody by the appropriate copy-and-paste procedures, gradually substituting the unused pitch classes for melodic notes until the melody consists primarily of the originally unused pitch classes. Be fairly free in the substitution process so that the style of the original melody doesn't get lost in the process. Substituting notes a half step up or down makes a fairly smooth effect. Should all statements of a pitch class be handled the same way, or changed at the same time?

Continue "modulating' the melody once all or most of the pitches have been substituted. The purpose now is to turn the modified melody into a transposed version of the original melody. Each note in the final product should be transposed the same interval above or below its original note as the first note is. As in the first half of this exercise, the substitution process should be freely applied so that the melody gradually shifts on each repetition, rather than changing abruptly.

EXERCISE 12.47

Using the original melody, make one note move one step closer to the beginning in each statement of the copy-and-paste loop until it reaches its initial position (i.e. it makes a full circle). Choose a note that is prominent in some sense, so that its movement will be noticeable. The final note is an excellent candidate, since all but the first and last statements will sound less finished, since the "correct" last note will be passing through the loop, rather than acting to close the melody.

Editing procedures should allow easy editing of note names (the combination of letter-name and octave number described in the MIDI specification). Each statement of the loop requires that the moving note name trade places with the previous note name.

EXERCISE 12.48

Modify the original melody, if necessary, so that there is a range of articulation values (the duration occupies varying percentages of the time between its attack and the attack of the next note). Make sure that differences in articulation are quite noticeable. Repeat this melody several times using copy-and-paste procedures, shifting articulations one or more notes forward (those at the end wrap around to the beginning). This means that the pitches repeat exactly, and the order of durations remains the same, but pitches are given different duration values with each repetition.

EXERCISE 12.49

Using the modified melody of exercise 12.48, repeat the melody, shifting durations around so that eventually their order is reversed. More than one duration may be shifted in each copy-and-paste repetition, but durations may move either to an adjacent note or may skip one note.

While this sounds like a simple variant of exercise 12.48, it is quite different. In the previous exercise, *articulation* was shifted. In musical terms, articulation is determined by a combination of MIDI note duration (the time interval between Note On and Note Off messages) and envelope. In standard music notation, duration has both a written and an aural meaning, with the MIDI analog of written duration being the distance between two successive Note On messages (this ignores the concept of the rest, or notated silence, which is not used in MIDI). This exercise, therefore, involves shifting both MIDI duration (musical articulation) and notated duration (the time interval between adjacent MIDI note start points).

Consider that the last note has a notated duration that continues to the end of the measure. Durations may wrap around to the beginning to the melody. Careful use of the shift feature of the sequencer will aid in reassigning note start times.

EXERCISE 12.50

Add three layers to the original melody, each with its own dynamic level. Try to give each layer some variety in dynamics as well. Loop the material, causing dynamic levels to shift from layer to layer or from note to note (in other words, both horizontal and vertical shifting, with the emphasis on vertical movement).

Using controller #7 (volume), cause volumes to shift so that the loudest layer becomes the softest and vice versa. In lieu of controller #7, loop the layers using copy-and-paste procedures. Shift one or two prominent velocities from the lowest-pitched layer to the highest (passing through the intermediate layers) and vice versa.

EXERCISE 12.51

Develop an interesting chord progression or multi-layer segment based on the original melody. Develop variants of the progression by experimenting with different chord voicings. Gradually, for example, shift lower notes higher as higher notes are shifted lower. Not all chords need be revoiced at the same time. This procedure allows musical material to have a different feel while containing basically the same material. Try placing several variants into a sequence and creating a free melodic part against the sequence.

EXERCISE 12.52

If stereo sound output is possible, create a two-voice segment in which each voice begins at one output and gradually moves to the other. Against this spatial modulation other material that does not change its output location may occur. Review exercises 12.5, 12.6, and 12.22 before doing exercise 12.52.

The effectiveness of this exercise depends on the features of the available synthesis equipment. The ability to receive controller #8 (balance) or #10 (pan) will make it much easier, since location can be determined by sending different values. If a patch can be placed in a stereo field, multiple versions, each with its own location, may be created. By sending program changes, a melody may be shifted from one location to another.

EXERCISE 12.53

On a sequencer with the capability of editing tempo curves it is easy to cause the music to speed up or slow down by editing a region of previously recorded music. To explore this feature, record a segment which expands the original melody in real time. As you play, gradually slow down by about 50%. Edit this segment using the tempo editing features of the sequencer so that over the course of the slowdown the tempo doubles, rather than slowing, as the original actually does. Listen to the result. Can it be smoother? Make additional versions as needed. Style, texture, and other parameters may be freely selected, depending upon what seems the appropriate means of expanding on the original melody.

EXERCISE 12.54

If the sequencer allows tempo or meter maps (sequences of tempo or meter settings), develop an arbitrary sequence of meter(for example, 4 measures of 4/4, 8 measures of 3/4, 4 measures of 7/8, and so on). Set the metronome and/or flash feature and try playing freely into the changing metric sequence, using the original melody as the point of departure. Don't ignore the changes, but adjust your playing style to fit them.

Also develop a sequence of tempo changes and experiment with it. This exercise will either confirm one's low opinion of metronomes or may allow the development of some flexibility. Take advantage of the metronome and start slowly and simply.

Record several of your versions of the tempo and meter sequences, and save any that seem to work well. If a particular meter or tempo change causes trouble, look at the display of your work to determine the nature of the problem. Does your work convincingly portray the changes in tempo and/or meter when the metronome is off?

EXERCISE 12.55

Create a melodic segment involving the use of several timbres, based on the original melody (review exercises 12.13 and 12.14). Have the melody repeat and shift tone colors from one note to another (use a control track to minimize copying and pasting). This may be either random or purposeful. In the latter case, determine some scheme that timbre changes will follow. Have one tone color move from one end of the melody to the other with a slow rate of change. Have several timbres change, each with its own rate, even if several notes end up with more than one timbre at a time.

MODES

Over the last few centuries there has been a move away from the richness offered by the resources of the system of church modes (a set of scales discussed in exercise 12.56). The loss of the modes—at least in the mainstream of musical development—has been compensated for by the development of the major-minor scale system. This system is so pervasive that many people are not even aware of the earlier modal system.

Pitch is not the only parameter that may be ordered into different scale patterns. The exercises in this chapter explore some of the possibilities offered by developing "scales" of duration, dynamics, texture, and the other parameters. Although the idea of ordering parameters may seem somewhat cerebral and unmusical, a close look at any piece of music should show that there is a great deal of calculating—even if it occurs on an unconscious level—regardless of style.

EXERCISE 12.56

The standard modes can be found by playing scales using only the white keys of the keyboard. The Ionian mode (the major scale) goes from C(n) to C(n+1); the Dorian mode from D(n) to D(n+1); the Phrygian starts on E, the Lydian on F, the Mixolydian on G, the Aeolian (pure or natural minor) on A, and the Locrian on B (see figure 5.14 on page 96). By examining the distance between notes a pattern of intervals—the mode—may be discerned. This allows each mode to start on any note.

Compose melodies or thicker textures in various of the standard modes. In order to allow the modal character to predominate, use no notes not determined by the mode (without this limitation modal writing too easily reverts to major or minor).

EXERCISE 12.57

Compose a piece which begins in one mode, moves or modulates to another mode using the same home note, and returns to the first mode. This exercise requires the application of modal interval patterns to determine the family of modes that share the same home note.

EXERCISE 12.58

Composer Olivier Messiaen developed or collected a set of modes. One of them involved alternating whole and half steps (C-C#-D#-E-F#-G-A-A#-C). Because it stated eight notes before returning to the home note name it is an octotonic scale. Use it in this exercise, or develop an original octotonic scale.

Compose a piece that explores both the melodic and chordal implications of the chosen octotonic scale. Since the chords are likely to be a bit unusual, make the piece meditative in character and develop interesting chord progressions before adding melodic material. It would be appropriate to loop a chord progression.

EXERCISE 12.59

Develop a scale of durations. Since a pitch scale commonly rises in frequency, should a duration scale increase, or decrease, in duration? Should the durations follow standard notation (whole note, half note, various dotted values) or should it be strictly numeric, taking advantage of the resolution of the sequencer? Should the scale have more than one octave? How is that handled? Create a single-pitch piece that explores the duration scale.

EXERCISE 12.60

Use the same duration scale developed in exercise 12.59. Create a thicker texture using percussive timbres for the various layers. Use the scale in a fashion analogous to the handling of a pitch scale: there should be a home value; there should be some sort of cadential or closing pattern; there should be some way to modulate to or stress secondary values; and so on.

EXERCISE 12.61

Develop a scale of dynamic values. Since there are more gradations in velocity values than in standard notation, find out how small a velocity change can be while still being perceived. Check to be sure that the velocity range is valid for your synthesizer.

Create a segment with one or more melodic layers. Make a backup copy before modifying it. Apply the dynamic scale to each layer, determining either intuitively ("now seems like a good point") or arbitrarily (throw a die) how many notes to enter before changing velocity values. If the piece has more than one layer, apply the scale of values differently in each layer.

Rather than editing velocity values, set them all to 64 and introduce level changes with controller #7 data. If there are several layers, each will require a separate MIDI channel to benefit from this procedure.

EXERCISE 12.62

Split the keyboard into six-note groups (C0-F0; F#0-B0; C1-F1; and so on). Assign each group a different velocity or dynamic value.

Use a fresh copy of the segment developed in Exercise 12.61. If it consisted of only one layer, add additional material or use an earlier multi-layer piece. Edit the selection according to the velocity scheme. Does the scheme work? What can be done (short of throwing it out!) to revise and refine it?

EXERCISE 12.63

Develop modes, or orderings, of pitch, duration, dynamics, and timbre on paper. Set each parameter into a repetitive pattern, making sure that each pattern has a different number of events or a different total time. Combine these parameter cycles into a piece by creating one or more layers (or by editing an existing piece).

The pitch and duration may be entered in step time. The dynamic cycle will involve editing the pitch/duration information. Timbre may either be edited in or entered in real time on a control track.

Since this procedure is rather arbitrary, there is no way to know the full results ahead of time. It is unlikely that these procedures will lead to any commercial masterpieces; the ability to control parameters is highly useful, however.

EXERCISE 12.64

Develop a scale of meters. Organize it into a sequence that has some of the aspects of a pitch scale (see also the comments on duration scales given in exercise 12.59). Use this scale in developing a piece of music. Be free in the number of measures the piece stays in a meter before going on to the next. Feel free to change the sequence of meters in response to the musical material. Just as melodic or rhythmic segments are repeated, repeat segments of meters.

EXERCISE 12.65

Develop a timbral scale. Have it move from one sort of timbre to another. That may be as simple as moving from flute-like to brass-like (sweet to harsh) or it could be more subtle, as a scale involving different brass-like timbres, or a scale of flute-related tone colors (this depends to a great deal on the available sonic material).

Apply the timbral scale to a piece of music. Shadings of timbres within a timbre family could be applied from low to high (in much the same way that orchestral instruments are organized into families whose members operate in different registers) or gradually over time during the course of a piece. This latter approach could be worth exploring in a multi-layer piece where each layer uses one family of timbres. Timbres may be expressively juxtaposed or may be overlapped to gradually shift tone colors.

FOR FURTHER STUDY

Appendix E suggests ideas for further reading on page 265.

VOCABULARY

Terms important to this chapter are listed below. The italicized terms were not highlighted in the chapter, but have been included because of their importance. A definition of each term may be found in the glossary.

articulation	control track	deflam
duration	*dynamics*	*meter*
mode	*modulation*	*motive*
mute	*pitch*	pitch class
ppqn	quantize	register
retrograde	*rhythm*	*tempo*
texture	*timbre*	solo

REVIEW QUESTIONS

QUESTION 12.1

Match related terms by writing the letter of the term in the second column in the blank of the term in the first column that most closely relates to it.

Deflam	_____	A.	Articulation
Duration	_____	B.	Beat
Meter	_____	C.	Chord
Mute	_____	D.	Quantize
PPQN	_____	E.	Solo
Speed	_____	F.	Tempo

QUESTION 12.2

Compare and contrast the following terms.

Mode—Scale

_____

_____

_____

_____

Pitch—Pitch Class

_____
_____
_____
_____

Velocity—Volume

_____
_____
_____
_____

QUESTION 12.3

Define briefly.

Copy-and-paste editing

_____
_____
_____
_____

Motive

_____
_____
_____
_____

QUESTION 12.4

Provide the question for the given answer.

ANSWER	QUESTION
MIDI volume controller	What is _____ ?
MIDI pan controller	What is _____ ?
The G above C3	What is _____ ?
The range of velocity values	What is _____ ?

APPENDIX · A

WAVEFORMS AND HARMONIC SPECTRA

Waveform: **Sine**

Harmonic Content: **Only one partial (fundamental)**

Amplitude of Harmonics: **Amp (fundamental) = 100%**

Waveform: **Sawtooth**

Harmonic Content: **All integer multiples**

    Freq (partial *n*) = Freq (fundamental) times *n*

Amplitude of Harmonics: **Amp (partial *n*) = Amp (fundamental) times 1/*n***

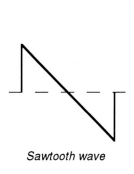

Sawtooth wave

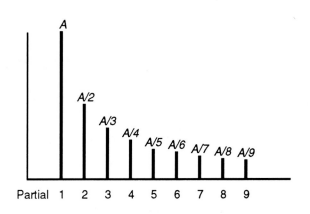

Waveform: **Square**

Harmonic Content: **Odd integer multiples**

> Freq (partial n) = Freq (fundamental) times n

Amplitude of Harmonics: **Amp (partial n) = Amp (fundamental) times $1/n$**

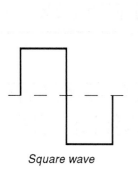

Square wave

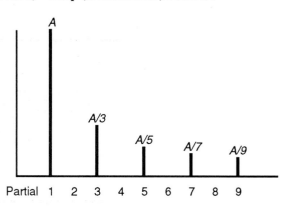

Waveform: **Triangle**

Harmonic Content: **Odd integer multiples**

Amplitude of Harmonics: **Amp (partial n) = Amp (fundamental) times $1/n^2$**

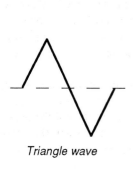

Triangle wave

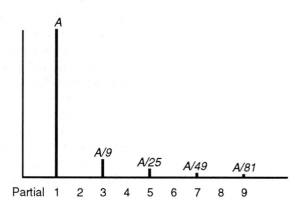

Waveform: **Pulse**

Harmonic Content: **Varies** (see amplitude formula)

Amplitude of Harmonics: **Amp (partial n) = $1/n$ times sin (n times pi times d/T)**

> When d/T (d = pulse width, T = period) equals $1/a$ (where a is any integer value) each ath partial has an amplitude of essentially zero (the square wave is a pulse wave with $d/T = 1/2$).

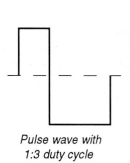

*Pulse wave with
1:3 duty cycle*

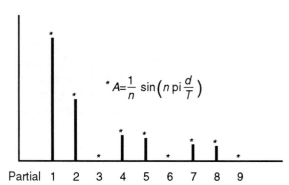

$$* A = \frac{1}{n} \sin\left(n\, pi\, \frac{d}{T}\right)$$

APPENDIX · B

FREQUENCIES OF EQUAL-TEMPERED SCALES

The frequency for any equal-tempered scale can be found easily by applying the formula $F(a) = F(0)$ times $2^{a/n}$. Since the increase in pitch of one octave represents a doubling of frequency, any tone within the octave may be found by multiplying the starting frequency $F(0)$ by $2^{a/n}$, where n indicates the number of tones into which the octave is divided (conventionally 12) and a indicates how many tones (half steps) above the starting tone the desired pitch is located.

In addition to the standard 12 tones per octave, frequencies in Hertz for a scale containing 19 tones per octave are given in the following table. In both cases, decimal values have been rounded off, and both scales start from the piano's "middle c." The values for the 12-tone scale have been apportioned to show the approximate relationship between the two sets. To find values for higher or lower octaves, multiply or divide by 2^n, where n indicates the octave displacement.

Letter names	C	C#	D	D#	E	F	F#	G	G#	A	A#	B	C
12-tone scale	262	277	294	311	330	349	370	392	415	440	466	494	524
19-tone scale	262 271	281	292 303	314 326	338 350	363 377	391 405	420 436	452	469 486	505		524

Several tones in the two tunings are within a few Hertz of each other. A 12-tone melody played in a 19-tone tuning will clearly not sound the same, however. Just as an instrument demands, in many cases, its own playing style, so does a scale, whether a subset of the 12-tone system (major or minor) or a different tuning, require some investigation into the best means of its musical application.

APPENDIX · C

MORE ABOUT MIDI

The full MIDI specification includes the material presented here and in chapter three as well as additional information on channel mode messages, system messages, including system exclusive codes, the sample dump standard, and MIDI time code. There is also a schematic diagram of the basic circuits used in sending and receiving MIDI messages. Given the rapidity with which things change and evolve in the music technology field, the focus here is on basic information. For further details, contact the International MIDI Association. A full version of the MIDI 1.0 specification may be obtained from

> the International MIDI Association
> 5316 W. 57th St.
> Los Angeles, CA 90056 USA

The information presented in this appendix is intended as a supplement to chapter three (pages 35-47). Section I presents the full list of controller numbers, expanding on table 3.4 (page 45). Section II discusses channel voice messages in more detail. Section III presents a summary of the various system messages.

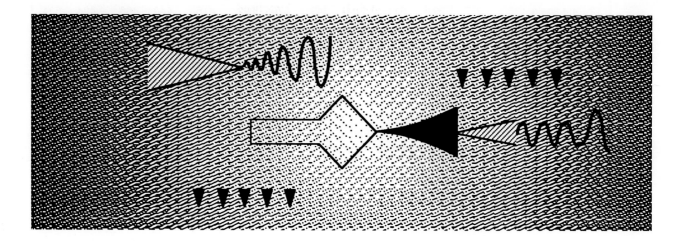

I. CONTROLLER NUMBERS

Many MIDI devices can send or receive controller information. Some devices, and most MIDI sequencers and similar software, can send out or receive controller information for controllers they don't actually have, by remapping the controller numbers. For example, a modulation wheel (controller number 1), might be able to function as a sustain pedal (controller number 64) or as a controller of pan amount (controller number 10).

With software, of course, no physical device is needed to generate information. There will generally be some procedure to select a controller number with an accompanying data value and specify the time for this information to be sent during a sequence. Data values are discussed in chapter three on pages 39-40.

CONTROL NUMBER		CONTROL FUNCTION
Decimal	Hex	
0	00H	Undefined
1	01H	Modulation wheel or lever
2	02H	Breath Controller
3	03H	Undefined
4	04H	Foot Controller
5	05H	Portamento time
6	06H	Data entry MSB
7	07H	Main volume
8	08H	Balance
9	09H	Undefined
10	0AH	Pan
11	0BH	Expression Controller
12-15	0C-0FH	Undefined
16-19	10-13H	General-Purpose Controllers (#1-4)
20-31	14-1FH	Undefined
32-63	20-3FH	LSB for values 0-31
64	40H	Damper pedal (sustain)
65	41H	Portamento
66	42H	Sostenuto
67	43H	Soft pedal
68	44H	Undefined
69	45H	Hold 2
70-79	46-4FH	Undefined
80-83	50-53H	General-Purpose Controllers (#5-8)
84-90	54-5AH	Undefined
91	5BH	External Effects depth
92	5CH	Tremolo depth
93	5DH	Chorus depth
94	5EH	Celeste (Detune) depth
95	5FH	Phaser depth
96	60H	Data increment
97	61H	Data decrement
98	62H	Non-Registered Parameter Number LSB
99	63H	Non-Registered Parameter Number MSB
100	64H	Registered Parameter Number LSB
101	65H	Registered Parameter Number MSB
102-120	66-78H	Undefined
121-127	79-7FH	Reserved for Channel Mode Messages

II. CHANNEL VOICE MESSAGES

Most MIDI activity involves the use of channel voice messages. There are also channel mode messages and a variety of system messages. For further, current information contact the International MIDI Association, whose detailing of the MIDI specification has provided the background for the information presented here. Figure 3.3 (page 38) lists the status bytes for these messages.

NOTE ON

This message is sent whenever a key is pressed or some analogous event is initiated on a non-keyboard MIDI device. The three bytes of the message convey four pieces of information. The first, or status, byte states that a Note On message is being sent on a particular MIDI channel. The second byte states the note number (see figure 3.5 on page 39) affected by the message. The third byte gives the velocity, or hardness, with which that note is played or struck (instruments may respond differently to this information; some may allow the selection of different tables for velocity response, either for receiving or sending). Instruments that are not sensitive to velocity will generally default to a value of 64, based on the 0-127 velocity range allowed by the MIDI specification.

NOTE OFF

Every note event must be turned off at some point. The basic Note Off message has the same 3-byte format as note-on messages: a note-off status byte with MIDI channel assignment, a note number byte, and a velocity byte. Release velocity is as yet not widespread in its implementation.

A number of devices send a Note On message with a velocity of 0, rather than a specific Note Off message. Although instruments have a physical maximum number of notes that they can produce, they also have an algorithm for handling new information received when they are at their maximum, usually involving releasing the softest notes still being held. This allows the Note On message to effectively function as a Note Off message as well.

The advantage of this scheme is that instruments may function in running status. When a status byte is received, it is put into a buffer and reused until a new status byte arrives. This has the potential of reducing data overload. Devices that use this approach must still be able to handle the standard Note Off message. For many users, therefore, the type of Note Off message is not important.

CONTROL CHANGE

These messages, like Note On and Note Off messages, involve three bytes. The first states that the message is a control change message (see figure 3.3 on page 38). The second gives the controller number (listed in the table in section I of this appendix), while the third provides some appropriate data value.

Many controllers produce a continuous range of values. This range is often satisfied by the 0-127 range allowed by a single data byte. Where this is not sufficient, a second byte (the LSB or Least Significant Byte) may be added to increase the range of values from 128 to 16,384. If extremely fine adjustments are needed, the LSB message can be sent by itself.

Some controllers have switch, rather than continuous, functions. Although 0 should be "off," and 127 should be "on," receivers should recognize 0-63 for "off" and 64-127 for "on," since this allows continuous controllers to function as switches.

Normally 0 is considered to indicate minimum or no effect, while 127 indicates maximum or full effect. Balance (controller number 8) and Pan (controller number 10) use the center value (64) as a neutral point, with 0 indicating left and 127 indicating right.

PROGRAM CHANGE

This messages involve two bytes: a status byte indicating the nature of the message and its assigned MIDI channel, and a data byte indicating the number of the program, or patch, requested. Since there is no specific meaning involved with a program number, some understanding of the patches of the receiving device is necessary. This holds true, even as the industry works to establish standards for the type of patches one can expect for a given range of program values, since the actual sound will vary from manufacturer to manufacturer.

AFTERTOUCH

Polyphonic Key Pressure and Channel Pressure messages offer two approaches to aftertouch, which itself involves moving or pressing a key as it is being held down or by increasing breath pressure on a wind controller or some similar effect. Aftertouch may be used to modify virtually any aspect of a tone, or even to cause a crossfade from one patch to another.

Polyphonic messages are three bytes long: status (including MIDI channel), pressure level, and note to be affected. This differs from Channel Pressure, which does not have the third byte, since the whole channel is affected rather than only individual notes. As with any MIDI feature, if the receiving instrument is not equipped to reproduce the effect, the message is ignored.

PITCH BEND

Like many of the continuous controllers listed in the table in section I, pitch bend involves an LSB and an MSB. Unlike the other controllers, both are sent in every message, which consists of a status byte (including MIDI channel) followed by LSB, followed by MSB. Bend ranges from a maximum negative value of 00, 00 through the midpoint or off position of 00, 64 to the maximum positive value of 127, 127. Sensitivity to pitch bend (typically ranging from no sensitivity to covering the span of an octave) is set on the receiving device, although Registered Parameter Number 00 00 can be used for this task on synthesizers which have been so constructed.

III. SYSTEM MESSAGES

There are three categories of system messages: exclusive, common, and real time. Since they affect an entire network or system, they generally do not have any channel designation. System Exclusive messages may be used to transmit information about patch parameters, sample information, and any other information a manufacturer wishes to implement. System Common and System Real Time are used by devices that handle location and timing information.

The System Common Quarter Frame message is part of a set of messages that implements MIDI time code. This set, which includes special System Exclusive messages, allows the transmission of the same information found in SMPTE time code. It takes eight Quarter Frame messages to provide full temporal location information. See the full MIDI specification for further details.

| STATUS BYTE | | DATA | FUNCTION |
Binary	Hex		
System Exclusive			
11110000	F0H		Start of system exclusive message
		0iiiiiii	iiiiiii: Manufacturer's identification (involves 2 additional bytes if the first is 0)
		0ddddddd	ddddddd: Data (any number of bytes may follow)
11110111	F7H		End of system exclusive message
System Common			
11110001	F1H	0nnndddd	MIDI time code Quarter Frame nnn: Message type dddd: Values
11110010	F2H		Song Position Pointer
		0lllllll	lllllll: LSB
		0hhhhhhh	hhhhhhh: MSB
11110011	F3H		Song Select
		0sssssss	sssssss: Song number
11110100	F4H		Undefined
11110101	F5H		Undefined
11110110	F6H		Tune request
System Real Time			
11111000	F8H		Timing clock
11111001	F9H		Undefined
11111010	FAH		Start
11111011	FBH		Continue
11111100	FCH		Stop
11111101	FDH		Undefined
11111110	FEH		Active Sensing
11111111	FFH		System Reset

APPENDIX · D

MUSIC HARDWARE
AND SOFTWARE

Given the rapid rate of development of both hardware and software, any listing of products or manufacturers will necessarily be incomplete. There is an increasing richness of available choices in equipment, augmented in the area of digital technology by a rapidly growing music software industry and advances in digital recording.

The following listing was culled from advertisements in various periodicals and visits to various showrooms. For more specific information on current products, write to the manufacturers. In addition to magazines like *Keyboard* and *Electronic Musician*, consult periodicals dealing with specific brands of microcomputers. Information may also be obtained through electronic bulletin board services like Compuserve, Genie, The Well, and, for the latest in information in the digital music industry, Pan.

I. KEYBOARDS, SYNTHESIZERS, TONE MODULES, AND CONTROLLERS

Products by these manufacturers include analog and digital synthesizers, tone modules, strap-on keyboards, samplers and sample players, and non-keyboard MIDI controllers. In some cases, onboard effects and sequencers allow a unit to function as a stand-alone music workstation.

Akai	Hammond Suzuki	Peavey
Bachman	Kawai	Roland
Casio	Korg	Steinberg/Jones (Waldorf)
E-mu	Kurzweil	Stick
Elka	Lync	Voce
Ensoniq	Oberheim	Yamaha
Fatar		Zeta

II. OTHER HARDWARE

Products range from cards for digital signal processing (DSP) intended for use in a specific brand of computer to MIDI interface devices, hardware sequencers, time code synchronizers, and various effects devices.

Adams-Smith	Eventide	Peavey
Ad Lib	Key	Rane
Altech	KMX	Roland
Alesis	Korg	Sony
Applied Research	Lexicon	Spectral Synthesis
C-Lab	Mark of the Unicorn	SunRize
Covox	MediaVision	Symbolic Sound
Creative Labs	Meridian	Tascam
dbx	Midiman	Turtle Beach
Digidesign	Music Quest	Voyetra
Digitech	Nady	Yamaha
Dolby	Opcode	Zoom
Dr. T's		

III. NOTATION PROGRAMS

In addition to scoring and printing functions, most of these programs have MIDI input and output, integrating some of the functions of a sequencer. These programs focus on scoring, page layout, and printing, rather than on sequencing.

MANUFACTURER	PRODUCT	AM*	AT*	MAC*	PC*
alla breve	*Musicad*				x
C-LAB	*Notator*		x		
Cerl Sound Group	*Lime*			x	
Coda	*Finale*			x	x
	Music Prose			x	
Dr. T's	*Copyist DTP*	x	x		x
	Copyist Apprentice	x	x		x
Dynaware	*DynaDuet*				x
Electronic Arts	*Deluxe Music*				
	Construction Set	x		x	
Errato	*Music Manuscripter*				x
Grandmaster	*MusicEase*				x
Great Wave	*ConcertWare MIDI*			x	
Hybrid Arts	*EZ Score Plus*		x		
Mark of the Unicorn	*Professional Composer*			x	
Music Publisher	*Music Publisher*			x	
Passport	*NoteWriter II*			x	
	Encore			x	x
	Score				x
Pygraphics	*Music Writer*			x	x
SongWright	*SongWright V*				x
Steinberg-Jones	*Masterscore*		x		
Temporal Acuity	*MusicPrinter Plus*				x
Teach Services	*Laser Music Processor*				x
Theme Software	*Theme*				x
Thoughtprocessors	*The Note Processor*				x

*AMiga, ATari, MACintosh, IBM PC and compatibles

IV. SEQUENCING PROGRAMS

Some sequencers have notation features which may eventually allow them to function as notation programs also. The focus in most of these programs is on recording, performance, and timecode-related functions.

MANUFACTURER	PRODUCT	AM*	AT*	MAC*	PC*
Big Noise	Cadenza				x
Blue Ribbon	Bars and Pipes	x			
C-LAB	Creator		x		
Circa	Orpheus				x
Covox	MIDI Maestro				x
Dr. T's	Beyond			x	
	KCS	x	x		
	MRS	x	x		
	Prism				x
	RealTime		x		
	Tiger Cub	x	x		
Dynaware	Ballade				x
Eclipse	PC MusicMaker				x
Electronic Arts	Deluxe Recorder			x	
Freq Sound	One Step			x	
Green Oak	Rhapsody			x	
Hybrid Arts	Edit Track		x		
Keller	64 Track PC				x
Key Electronics	Keynote 16				x
LTA	Forte II				x
Magnetic Music	Texture				x
Mark of the Unicorn	Performer			x	
Microillusions	Music X	x			
Midisoft	Studio		x		x
Musicator	Musicator				x
Opcode	EZ Vision			x	
	Vision			x	
Passport	Trax	x	x	x	x
	Pro 4			x	
	Master Tracks Pro	x	x		x
Softelligence	Personal Composer				x
Steinberg/Jones	Pro 24	x			
	Cubase		x	x	
Twelve Tone	Cakewalk				x
The Disc Company	Harmoni	x			
Voyetra	Sequencer Plus				x

*AMiga, ATari, MACintosh, IBM PC and compatibles

V. OTHER PROGRAMS

The programs listed here are representative of those for Amiga, Atari, Macintosh, and IBM PCs and compatibles. There are also similar programs for the Apple II and Commodore families. Algorithmic/interactive programs (**ALG**) have some degree of computer participation in the creative process; multimedia-oriented programs (**M**) provide for some form of interaction of music with other performing media; patch editor/librarian programs (**ED**) offer computer-assisted patch storage and editing; programming languages or environments (**PLE**) allow the creation of patches, effects, and a wide range of customized programming options for those who wish to more directly use the computer as a creative tool; sampling and digital signal processing programs (**DSP**) offer the ability to create and/or edit samples.

MANUFACTURER	PRODUCT	TYPE	AM*	AT*	MAC*	PC*
Big Noise		ED				x
C-Lab		ED		x		
cMIDI	cMIDI	PLE				x
Cool Shoes	Sound Globs	ALG				x
Digidesign	Softsynth	DSP		x		
	SoundDesigner	DSP		x	x	
	Turbosynth	DSP			x	
Dr. T's	Fingers	ALG		x		
	Jam Factory	ALG	x	x	x	
	M	ALG	x	x	x	
	Music Mouse	ALG	x	x	x	
EarLevel	HyperMIDI	PLE			x	
Frog Peak	HMSL	PLE	x		x	
Hip Software	Harmony Grid	ALG			x	
	HookUp!	PLE			x	
Hybrid Arts		ED		x	x	
Metsan	MidiText	ALG	x	x	x	x
Opcode	Cue	M			x	
		ED			x	
	Max	PLE			x	
		DSP			x	
Passport	Alchemy	DSP			x	
PG Music	Band-in-a-box	ALG		x	x	x
Richmond Sound	Stage Manager	M	x			
Sound Quest		ED	x	x	x	x
Symbolic Sound	Kyma	PLE			x	
Turtle Beach	Sample Vision	DSP				x
	Wave/Windows	DSP				x
Voyetra	M for the PC	ALG				x

*AMiga, ATari, MACintosh, IBM PC and compatibles

VI. ADDRESSES OF MANUFACTURERS

Ad Lib, Inc.: 50 Staniford St., Boston MA 02114

Adams-Smith: 34 Tower St., Hudson, MA 01749-1721

Akai: PO Box 2344, Fort Worth, TX 76113

Alesis Corporation: 3630 Holdrege Avenue, Los Angeles, CA 90016

alla breve: Suite 111, 1105 Chicago Ave., Oak Park, IL 60302

Altech Systems: 122 Faries Industrial Park Dr., Shreveport, LA 71106

Applied Research & Technology: 215 Tremont Street, Rochester, NY 14608

Bachman: General Music, 1105 North Ellis Avenue, Bensonville, IL 60106

Big Noise Software: 3827 Pizarro Rd., Jacksonville, FL 32217

Brown-Wagh: 130-D Knowles Drive, Los Gatos, CA 95030

C-LAB Software: PO Box 750, Nevada City, CA 95959

Casio: Professional Products Division, 570 Mt. Pleasant Avenue, Dover, NJ 07801

Cerl Sound Group: University of Illinois, 252 ERL, 103 S. Mathews, Urbana, IL 61801

Circa Industries: PO Box 3751, Reston, VA 22090

cMIDI: PO Box 11586, Lynchburg, VA 24506-1586

Coda Music Software: 1401 E. 79th St., Minneapolis, MN 55425-1126

Cool Shoes Software: 116 Churchland Drive, Winston-Salem, NC 27101

Covox: 675 Conger St., Eugene, OR 97402

Creative Labs: *See* Brown-Wagh

dbx Professional Products: 1525 Alvarado Street, San Leandro, CA 94577

digidesign: 1360 Willow Rd., #101, Menlo Park, CA 94025

Digitech: DOD Electronics Corp., 5639 South Riley Lane, Salt Lake City, UT 84107

Dolby Laboratories, Inc.: 100 Potrero Avenue, San Francisco, CA 94116

Dr. T's Music Software: 100 Crescent Road, Needham. MA 02194

Dynaware: 950 Tower, #1150, Foster City, CA 94404

EarLevel Engineering: 21213-B Hawthorne Blvd., Ste 5305, Torrance, CA 90509-2881

Eclipse Technologies, Inc.: 1221 West Campbell Rd., Suite 125, Richardson, TX 75080

Electronic Arts: 1820 Gateway Dr., San Mateo, CA 94404

Elka: *See* Music Industries

E-mu Systems, Inc.: 1600 Green Hills Road, Scotts Valley, CA 95066

Eventide: One Alsan Way, Little Ferry, NJ 07643

Ensoniq: 155 Great Valley Parkway, Malvern, PA 19355

Errato Software: PO Box 526278, Salt Lake City, UT 84152-6278

Fatar: *See* Music Industries

Freq Sound: 5451 Watercress Place, Columbia, MD 21045

Frog Peak Music: Box A36, Hanover, NH 03755

Grandmaster, Inc.: PO Box 2567, Spokane, WA 99220-2567

Great Wave Software: 5353 Scotts Valley Dr., Scotts Valley, CA 95066

Green Oak Software: 4446 Salisbury Dr., Carlsbad, CA 92008

Hammond Suzuki: 1121 N. Main St., Lombard, IL 60148

Hip Software: 117 Harvard St., Suite 3, Cambridge, MA 02139

Hybrid Arts: 8522 National Blvd., Culver City, CA 90232

Kawai America Corporation: 2055 E. University Drive, Compton, CA 90224

Keller Designs: 2920 Jefferson, Eugene, OR 97405

Key Electronics: 7515 Chapel Ave., Fort Worth, TX 76116

KMX: 67 W. Easy Street, #134, Simi Valley, CA 93065

Korg USA: 89 Frost St., Westbury, NY 11590

Kurzweil Music Systems: 13336 Alondria Blvd., Cerritos, CA 90701

Lexicon, Inc.: 100 Beaver St., Waltham, MA 02154

Lync Systems, Inc.: 14 Walker Way, Albany, NY 12205

LTA Productions: PO Box 6623, Hamden, CT 06517

Magnetic Music: 6 Twin Rocks Rd., Brookfield, CT 06804-1910

Mark of the Unicorn: 222 Third St., Cambridge, MA 02142

Media Vision: 47221 Fremont Blvd., Fremont, CA 94538

Meridian Data, Inc.: 5615 Scotts Valley Rd., Scotts Valley, CA 95066

Metsan Corporation: PO Box 681272, Schaumburg, IL 60168

Microillusions: PO Box 3475, Grenada Hills, CA 91394

Midiman: 30 North Raymond Avenue, Suite 505, Pasadena, CA 91103

Midisoft: PO Box 1000, Bellevue, WA 98004

Music Industries Corp.: Dept. KC, 99 Tulip Ave., Floral Park, NY 11001

Music Publisher: 2-1645 E. Cliff Dr., Santa Cruz, CA 95062

Music Quest: 1700 Alma Drive, Suite 330, Plano, TX 75075

Musicator: PO Box 410039, San Francisco, CA 94141

Nady Systems, Inc.: 6701 Bay St., Emeryville, CA 94608

Oberheim: 13345 Saticoy St., North Hollywood, CA 91605

Opcode Systems, Inc.: 3641 Haven Dr., Suite A, Menlo Park, CA 94025-1010

Passport Designs, Inc.: 625 Miramontes St., Half Moon Bay, CA 94019

Peavey Electronics Corporation: 711 A Street, Meridian, MS 39301

PG Music, Inc.: 111-266 Elmwood Avenue, Buffalo, NY 14222

Pygraphics: PO Box 639, Grapevine, TX 76051

Richmond Sound Design, Ltd.: 1234 W. 6th Avenue, Vancouver, BC V6H 1A5

Roland Corporation US: 7200 Dominion Circle, Los Angeles, CA 90040-3696

Softelligence: 3213 West Wheeler St., Suite 140, Seattle, WA 98199

SongWright Software: 7 Loudoun St. SE, Leesburg, VA 22075

Sony Professional Audio: 1600 Queen Anne Rd., Teaneck, NJ 07666

Sound Quest: 66 Broadway Ave., Suite 1207, Toronto, ON, Canada M4P 2T4

Steinberg/Jones: 17700 Raymer, Suite 1001, Northridge, CA 91325

Stick Enterprises, Inc.: 6011 Woodlake Ave., Woodland Hills, CA 91367

SunRize Industries: 2959 S. Winchester Blvd., Suite 204, Campbell, CA 95008

Symbolic Sound Corporation: PO Box 2530, Champaign, IL 61825-2530

Tascam: TEAC America, Inc., 7733 Telegraph Rd., Montebello, CA 90640

Teach Services: 182 Donivan Rd., Brushton, NY 12916

Temporal Acuity Products: 300-120th Ave. NE, Bldg 1, Ste 200, Bellevue, WN 98005

The Blue Ribbon Soundworks, Ltd.: 1293 Briardale NE, Atlanta, GA 30305

The Disk Company: PO Box 67713, Los Angeles, CA 90067

Theme Software Company: PO Box 8204, Charlottesville, VA 22906

Thoughtprocessors: 584 Bergen Street, Brooklyn, NY 11238

Turtle Beach: PO Box 5074, York, PA 17405

Twelve Tone Systems: PO Box 760, Watertown, MA 02272

Voce Inc.: 111 Tenth Street, Wood-Ridge, NJ 07075

Voyetra: 333 Fifth Avenue, Pelham, NY 10803

Waldorf: *See* Steinberg/Jones

Yamaha Corporation of America: PO Box 6600, Buena Park, CA 90622-6600

Zeta Systems: 2230 Livingston Ave., Oakland, CA 94606

Zoom Corporation: 385 Oyster Point Blvd., Suite #7, South San Francisco, CA 94080

APPENDIX · E

REFERENCES AND SUGGESTED READING

By its very nature, a bibliography is a work-in-progress. Bibliographies are available in many of the books cited, for those who wish to delve further. In the area of microcomputing there are many off-the-shelf periodicals pertaining to specific systems; given the volatility of this market, citations have been severely limited.

The following material is divided into two major sections. In the suggested reading list, accessibility of the works cited, their usefulness as follow-up or companion readings, and a certain eclecticism on the part of the author were primary selection criteria. In the reference section additional material is listed.

SUGGESTED READING

Following is an annotated listing of books and periodicals that offer opportunities for further study or for interesting side-trips. It is organized into five parts, the first four listing books following the division of the text, the fifth listing useful periodicals.

INTRODUCTION

Backus, John. *The Acoustical Foundations of Music*, 2nd ed. New York: W. W. Norton, 1977.
An exposition of the physics of music, covering physics and acoustics, reception of sound, the environment, and the production of musical sounds by the various classes of musical instruments, including electronic sound production. Highly recommended.

Christie, Linda Gail, and Christie, John. *The Encyclopedia of Microcomputer Terminology*. Englewood Cliffs, NJ: Prentice-Hall, 1984.
Brief, clear definitions of a wide range of microcomputer-related terminology.

Keane, David. *Tape Music Composition*. New York: Oxford University Press, 1980.
An exposition of the tape studio and its use in composition. Useful insights are offered in spite of the out-of-date nature of the topic.

Milano, Dominic, ed. *Mind over MIDI*. Milwaukee, WI: Hal Leonard Books, 1987.
A compilation of articles from *Keyboard Magazine* which specifically address MIDI and MIDI-related topics. Includes a listing of the MIDI 1.0 Specification.

Partch, Harry. *Genesis of a Music*. New York: Da Capo Press, Inc., 1974.

A fascinating look at the philosophy and approach to music of this unorthodox musician. This book offers interesting excursions beyond the strictly electronic, particularly for those who wish to explore scalar resources.

Schrader, Barry. *Introduction to Electro-Acoustic Music*. Englewood Cliffs, NJ: Prentice-Hall, 1982.

Covers a broad range of introductory topics, including a series of interviews with composers.

Strange, Allen. *Electronic Music: Systems, Techniques and Controls*. Dubuque: Wm. C. Brown, 1983.

A broad exposition of electronic music hardware and procedures. Particularly useful in studios with a variety of equipment, including older analog synthesizers.

INSTRUMENT DESIGN

Appleton, Jon H. and Perera, Ronald C., eds. *The Development and Practice of Electronic Music*. Englewood Cliffs, NJ: Prentice-Hall, 1975.

The editors have assembled a series of articles ranging from the history of electronic music (Otto Leuning) through live-electronic music (Gordon Mumma).

Blackwood, Easley, as told to Jim Aiken. "Easley Blackwood: Discovering the microtonal resources of the synthesizer," *Keyboard* 8, no. 5 (May 1982), pp. 26-38.

A report on a series of microtonal etudes by this composer.

Chamberlin, Hal. *Musical Applications of Microprocessors*. Rochelle Park, NJ: Hayden Book Company, 1983.

The first three chapters discuss synthesis, sound modification, and voltage control in setting the background for discussions of microprocessors and music. A look at the material of parts I and II of this text from a slightly different perspective. Recommended for those exploring analog synthesis.

De Furia, Steve, and Scacciaferro, Joe. *The Sampling Book*. Pompton Lakes, NJ: Third Earth Publishing Inc., 1987.

A practical exploration of sampling, including 29 experiments that are generic in nature. Recommended.

De Furia, Steve. *The Secrets of Analog & Digital Synthesis*. Pompton Lakes, NJ: Third Earth Productions Inc., 1986.

Excellent beginning-level discussions of synthesis concepts, including Yamaha's FM synthesis. A video tape is also available (DCI Music Videos, New York, NY).

Devarahi. *The Complete Guide to Synthesizers*. Englewood Cliffs, NJ: Prentice-Hall, 1982.

Includes 99 experiments with flowcharts that explore the use of a variety of analog synthesizer modules.

Kostka, Stefan. *Materials and Techniques of Twentieth-Century Music*. Englewood Cliffs, NJ: Prentice-Hall, 1990.

A survey of compositional and analytical approaches, including chapters on both acoustic and electronic timbre and texture.

Strange, Allen. *Electronic Music: Systems, Techniques and Controls*. Dubuque: Wm. C. Brown, 1983.

A broad exposition of electronic music hardware and procedures. Particularly useful in studios with a variety of equipment, including older analog synthesizers.

Wells, Thomas. *The Technique of Electronic Music*. New York: Schirmer Books, 1981.

A technical approach to electronic music equipment. Advanced, with some good insight into analog equipment and its use.

Wilkinson, Scott R. *Tuning in: Microtonality in Electronic Music*. Milwaukee, WI: Hal Leonard Books, 1988.

Subtitled "A Basic Guide to Alternate Scales, Temperaments and Microtuning Using Synthesizers," this book offers a clear, detailed look at this little used aspect of electronic music. Highly Recommended.

Yasser, Joseph. *A Theory of Evolving Tonality*. New York: Da Capo Press, Inc., 1975 (reprint of 1932 edition).

A discussion of the history of tonality and its possible evolution.

SCORE CONSTRUCTION

Boretz, Benjamin and Cone, Edward T., eds. *Perspectives on Notation and Performance*. New York: W. W. Norton, 1976.

One of a series of books reprinting articles from *Perspectives on New Music*. Brian Fennelly's "A Descriptive Language for the Analysis of Electronic Music" (pages 117-33), although dated and somewhat cumbersome, offers a systematic approach to analysis of electronic music.

Cooper, Jeff. *Building a Recording Studio*. Calabasas, CA: Synergy Group, Inc., 1984.

Although somewhat peripheral to the topics presented here, this book offers much insight into the music environment. Highly recommended.

Cope, David. *New Music Notation*. Dubuque: Kendall-Hunt, 1976.

A brief but useful overview of notation is given.

Cope, David. *New Directions in Music*. Dubuque: Wm. C. Brown, 1989.

In this survey of avant garde trends in music, many notational examples and ideas for further study are presented, as well as a series of "vectoral analyses," which offer a three-dimensional examination of selected works.

Dwyer, Terence. *Composing with Tape Recorders*. London: Oxford University Press, 1971.

An early, somewhat personal, look at the use of tape recorders in a musical way. Although the technology has changed, and resources have increased, his attitude toward what is musical and his attempt to systematize the wealth of available sounds offer valuable models.

Karkoschka, Erhard. *Notation in New Music: A Critical Guide to Interpretation and Realization*. Translated by Ruth Koenig. New York: Praeger, 1972.

A survey of notation with fascinating examples. Not as well organized as other resources, it has a wealth of material worth examining.

Langer, Suzanne. *Philosophy in a New Key*, 3d ed. Cambridge, MA: Harvard University Press, 1976.

Subtitled "A Study in the Symbolism of Reason, Rite, and Art." For those who wish to delve into the world of notation or explore the significance of musical gesture, this book offers fascinating insights. Highly recommended.

McIan, Peter, and Wichman, Larry. *The Musician's Guide to Home Recording*. New York: Linden Press/Fireside, 1988.

An extensive look at this topic, with many excellent insights. Audio cassettes are also available. Recommended.

Meyer, Leonard. *Explaining Music*. Chicago: University of Chicago Press, 1978.

An advanced look at music structure. Requires a background in music theory.

Risatti, Howard. *New Music Vocabulary*. Champaign: University of Illinois Press, 1975.

A more extensive look at contemporary notational practices than Cope's *Notation*, although its organization is less concise.

Whitney, John. *Digital Harmony*. Peterborough, NH: Byte Books, 1980.

Subtitled "On the Complementarity of Music and Visual Art," this book offers fascinating images and concepts.

Woram, John. *Sound Recording Handbook*. Indianapolis, IN: Howard W. Sams & Company, 1989.

An exhaustive investigation of sound recording, including basic acoustical concepts, psychoacoustics, and all the systems that are part of the recording process. An excellent reference volume. Highly recommended.

ELECTRONIC COMPOSITION

Appleton, Jon H. and Perera, Ronald C., eds. *The Development and Practice of Electronic Music*. Englewood Cliffs, NJ: Prentice-Hall, 1975.

Chapter 5, "The Uses of Digital Computers in Electronic Music Generation" (John E. Rogers) is particularly germane, although it is pre-MIDI in outlook.

Conger, Jim. *C Programming for MIDI*. Redwood City, CA: M&T Publishing, Inc.,

A look at MIDI is combined with an introduction to the C programming language in developing to simple MIDI applications. A disk is available (MS-DOS only).

Conger, Jim. *MIDI Sequencing in C*. Redwood City, CA: M&T Publishing, Inc.,

A followup to *C Programming*, this book looks extensively into the functioning of sequencers by developing a sequencing program. A disk is available (MS-DOS).

Cooper, Grosvenor, and Meyer, Leonard. *Rhythmic Structure in Music*. Chicago: University of Chicago Press, 1960.

A background in music theory is required. Since electronic music is not the focus, concepts need to be translated into the medium (but useful concepts make the effort worthwhile).

Cope, David. *New Music Composition*. New York: Schirmer Books, 1977.

Compositional techniques for a variety of musical media, including electronics and computers, are explored in this practical survey.

Dallin, Leon. *Techniques of Twentieth Century Composition*. Dubuque: Wm. C. Brown, 1974.

Subtitled "A Guide to the Materials of Modern Music." One of only a few books on composition, there is little on electronic composition, although there are expositions of 12-tone and serial technique, microtones, and other relevant topics.

De Furia, Steve, and Scacciaferro, Joe. *MIDI Programming for the Macintosh*. Redwood City, CA: M&T Publishing, Inc., 1988.

A look at the MIDI specification is combined with a discussion of programming the Macintosh. Altech *MIDIBASIC* and *MIDIPascal* routines are explored and used in developing applications. A disk is also available.

De Furia, Steve, and Scacciaferro, Joe. *The MIDI Programmer's Handbook*. Redwood City, CA: M&T Publishing, Inc., 1989.

A detailed look at the MIDI specification and MIDI messages. The process of writing MIDI software is examined, with examples given in both English and Pascal code. A disk (MS-DOS, Macintosh, or Atari) of MIDI functions is also available.

Erickson, Robert. *Sound Structures in Music*. Berkeley: University of California Press, 1975.

A look at the psychoacoustical properties of music from the point of view of the musician. This work may prove too advanced for many readers—provocative insights are the reward for the persistent.

Rona, Jeffrey. *Synchronization from Reel to Reel*. Milwaukee, WI: Hal Leonard Publishing Corporation, 1990.

An extensive look at synchronization, time codes, film, video, and music. Highly recommended.

Score: An Anthology of New Music, commentaries by Johnson, Roger. New York: Schirmer Books, 1980.

A collections of scores for various musical forces. Some may be adapted for electronic ensembles; others may be used as models for electronic scores.

Whorinen, Charles. *Simple Composition*. New York: Longman, 1979.

Although the book explores 12-tone composition, part I offers some general concepts worth examining and relating to electronic music composition.

PERIODICALS

Byte. Peterborough, NH: McGraw-Hill Inc.

Monthly issues with articles on a variety of microcomputing topics and an encyclopedia of product advertisements. A good entree to the wealth of microcomputing.

Computer Music Journal. Cambridge, MA: The MIT Press.

Quarterly issues on computer music and related topics. Oriented toward larger systems, but with useful articles on small systems as well.

Electronic Musician. Berkeley: Mix Publications, Inc.

This monthly periodical has a slight technical orientation, with a variety of useful electronic music topics. Highly recommended. Mix publishes other magazines and also maintains the *Mix Bookshelf*, a catalog with books and other publications covering the whole spectrum of electronic music.

Keyboard. Cupertino, CA: GPI Publications.

Monthly issues covering a wide range of keyboard-related topics. An excellent publication for those interested in synthesizers and MIDI topics. Highly recommended. GPI publishes other magazines and also issues a series of books, mainly reprinting *Keyboard* articles.

REFERENCES

The following material offers opportunities for further study in the areas indicated at the end of each citation. Nine categories are included, as listed below:

A: Aesthetics, nature of sound
C: Composition and musical form
H: History (music, electronics, computers)
M: Microcomputers, computers, and MIDI
N: Notation (music)
P: Physics and acoustics
O: Other
R: Recording and tape music topics
S: Synthesizers and electronics

Anderton, Craig. *Electronic Projects for Musicians*. New York: Music Sales Corp. (S)

Armbruster, Greg, ed. *The Art of Electronic Music*. Cupertino, CA: GPI Books, 1985 (H, S)

Beaver, Paul, and Krause, Bernard. "The Nonesuch Guide to Electronic Music." New York: Nonesuch Records HC 73018, 1968. (S, R)

Ceely, Robert. *Electronic Music Resource Book*. Denver: Multi-media Publishing, 1981. (R, S)

Davis, Don, and Davis, Carolyn. *Sound System Engineering*. Indianapolis, IN: Howard W. Sams & Co., 1989. (R)

De Furia, Steve, and Scacciaferro, Joe. *The MIDI Implementation Book*. Pompton Lakes, NJ: Third Earth Publishing Inc., 1986. (M, S)

Dodge, Charles, and Jerse, Thomas A. *Computer Music*. New York: Schirmer Books, 1985. (C, M, O)

Eimert, Herbert, and Stockhausen, Karlheinz. *Electronic Music (Die Reihe I)*. Totowa, NJ: European American Music, 1958 (German edition 1955). (C, H)

Helmholtz, Hermann. *On the Sensations of Tone*. New York: Dover Publications, Inc., 1954 (reprint of 1885 second edition). (P)

Hiller, Lejaren, and Isaacson, Leonard M. *Experimental Music: Composition with an Electronic Computer*. Westport, CT: Greenwood, 1979 (reprint of 1959 edition). (C, H)

International MIDI Association. *MIDI 1.0 Detailed Specification*. Los Angeles: the International MIDI Association, 1989. (M)

Keyboard Magazine Staff. *Synthesizer Basics*. Cupertino, CA: GPI Books, 1984. (S)

Keyboard Magazine Staff. *Synthesizer Technique*. Cupertino, CA: GPI Books, 1984. (S)

Keyboard Magazine Staff. *Synthesizers and Computers*. Cupertino, CA: GPI Books, 1984. (S, M)

Kohs, Ellis B. *Musical Composition: Projects in Ways and Means*. Metuchen, NJ: Scarecrow Press, 1980. (C)

Krause, Bernhard. *The New Nonesuch Guide to Electronic Music*. New York: Nonesuch Records NB-78007, 1980. (S, R)

Naumann, Joel, and Wagoner, James D. *Analog Electronic Music Techniques*. New York: Schirmer Books, 1985. (C, R, S)

Read, Gardner. *Music Notation*. New York: Taplinger Publishing Co., Inc., 1979. (N)

Roederer, Juan G. *Introduction to the Physics and Psychophysics of Music*. New York, Heidelberg, Berlin: Springer-Verlag, 1980. (P)

Schafer, R. Murray. *Creative Music Education*. New York: Schirmer Books, 1976. (A, C, N)

Schoenberg, Arnold. *Style and Idea*. Edited by Leonard Stein, translated by Leo Black. Berkeley: University of California Press, 1984. (A, C, H)

Schwartz, Elliott. *Electronic Music: A Listener's Guide*. New York: Da Capo Press, Inc., 1985 (reprint of 1975 edition). (H)

Schwartz, Elliott, and Childs, Barney. *Contemporary Composers on Contemporary Music*. New York: Da Capo Press, Inc., 1978 (reprint of 1967 edition). (A, C, H)

Seashore, Carl E. *Psychology of Music*. New York: Dover Publications, Inc., 1967 (reprint of 1938 edition). (P)

Stone, Kurt. *Music Notation in the Twentieth Century*. New York: W. W. Norton, 1980. (N)

Winckel, Fritz. *Music, Sound and Sensation*. Translated by T. Binkley. New York: Dover Publications, 1967. (P)

Wittlich, Gary, with Schaffer, John, and Babb, Larry. *Microcomputers and Music*. Englewood Cliffs, NJ: Prentice-Hall, 1986. (M)

GLOSSARY

Italicized terms are also defined.

AA': Descriptor for a form involving the varied repetition of previously stated material.

AB: Descriptor for *binary* form.

ABA': Descriptor for *ternary* form.

ABACA: Descriptor for *rondo* form.

AC: Alternating current.

ACCELERANDO: Becoming faster.

ACOUSTIC: Relating to the science of sound (acoustics). Acoustic sound sources are differentiated from electronic or synthesized instruments or voices in that the former generate tone using various physical systems such as strings, columns of air, or membranes, rather than relying on electronic circuitry.

ADC: *Analog-to-digital converter.*

ADDITIVE RHYTHM: The organization of musical durations into rhythmic structures whose time values do not fit into a regular hierarchy. Basic time values are added together to create irregular groupings and successions of durations. This differs from divisive rhythm that organizes durations with the aid of standard metric schemes such as 4/4, 3/4, 6/8 (and so on). This latter organization of time encourages a certain periodic organization of material not necessarily found in additive structures. *See also* meter, architectonic hierarchy, rhythm.

ADDITIVE SYNTHESIS: The process of developing audio signals by combining, or adding, less complex signals. These signals, usually sine waves, may be related by the harmonic series.

ADSR: *Attack, Decay, Sustain, Release. See also* envelope.

AFAP: As Fast As Possible.

AFTERTOUCH: A MIDI message generated by further pressure on a key that is already pressed down. It may be a *Channel Pressure* or *Polyphonic* message.

ALEATORY: Depending upon dice or other random event generators for the determination of structure or the choice of various aspects of a musical composition.

ALGORITHM: The process or plan used to solve a problem.

ALGORITHMIC COMPOSITION: Essentially, the use of a computer in developing a musical score. The computer may or may not help turn the piece into sound.

ALIASING: *See* foldover.

ALPHANUMERIC: Any member of the set of all numbers, letters, and other characters used by a computer; the keyboard used to produce alphanumeric characters.

ALTERNATING CURRENT: Electric current which periodically reverses direction.

AM: *Amplitude modulation.*

AMPLIFIER: A device that controls the volume or loudness of a signal. A voltage-controlled amplifier may have its gain controlled by the application of one or more control voltages applied to its control voltage inputs.

AMPLITUDE: Volume or loudness of a sound or signal; the peak value of an alternating current.

AMPLITUDE MODULATION: A variance of the amplitude of one signal (the *carrier*) in accordance with the frequency and amplitude of a second signal (the *program*).

ANALOG: A quality or characteristic of something that is analogous to a quality or characteristic of something else. In an analog synthesizer, voltage is an analog for sound waves.

ANALOG-TO-DIGITAL CONVERTER: A device capable of converting an analog signal into a series of digital values representing the signal. This representation may then be stored or processed by digital devices.

AR: *Attack, Release. See also* envelope.

ARCHITECTONIC HIERARCHY: A systematic organization of aspects of music into higher and lower categories or levels, such that activity on the lower levels may be more or less consistently grouped into increasingly larger structures. For example, in traditional rhythmic notation two quarter notes (or equivalent sums of other duration values) equal one half note, and two half notes (or equivalent values) equal one whole note. On yet larger levels, small groupings of measures may form single elements in a section of a composition, and sections in their turn can be grouped to form either larger elements, or complete compositions.

ARPEGGIO: The rapid performance, either ascending or descending, of *chords* or chord-like structures one tone at a time (from the Italian "arpa": harp).

ARRAY: A means of organizing related data. Computer languages make use of arrays to allow for efficient manipulation of data. Rather than having variables A, B, C, for example, one may use the array A(1), A(2), A(3). This suggests that the data in the array are related and allows more generalized program loops to be constructed, since only the index value needs changing to find a particular element.

ART MUSIC: A term for music often grouped under the loose appellation "classical music." The term is an extension of "art song," a work of artistic intent written by a composer (that is, not a "folk song").

ARTICULATION: The shaping of a musical *tone* or *phrase*. Tones can be accented or emphasized, performed smoothly, crisply, or in other ways; phrases can be connected or separated. In electronic music the process of articulation depends on the combination of envelope settings with playing style on a keyboard or other controller.

ARTICULATION MODULATION: The process of gradually shifting from one articulation type to another.

ASCII: American Standard Code for Information Interchange, an information processing industry standard that defines how characters are encoded.

ASSEMBLY LANGUAGE: A low-level computer language using mnemonic symbols. A program called an assembler translates an assembly language program into machine language.

ATTACK: The initial phase of a sound; one segment of an amplitude *envelope* used to control the gain of a *VCA* or various characteristics of other synthesizer modules.

ATTENUATION: The reduction in level of some parameter of a signal.

ATTENUATOR: A device that controls the strength of some parameter of a signal. Also called a potentiometer, or "pot."

AUDIO-FREQUENCY RANGE: The range of frequencies perceived by humans as sound: from roughly 16-20 Hz to 20 kHz.

BAND-PASS FILTER: A filter that passes a given range, or band, of frequencies, attenuating frequencies on either side of this passband. *See also* VCF.

BAND-REJECT FILTER: A filter that attenuates a given range, or band, of frequencies, allowing frequencies on either side of the stopband to be passed relatively unattenuated. *See also* VCF.

BANK SWITCHING: A means of increasing the amount of memory available to a microcomputer, used with some 8-bit microprocessors. Although there are a limited number of addresses, by switching from one bank of memory to another the apparent memory size appears to be greater than it actually is at any one instant.

BASIC: Beginners All-purpose Symbolic Instruction Code, a high-level computer language developed at Dartmouth College.

BATCH PROCESSING: An approach to computer use that involves loading many programs or jobs in a single batch, rather than allowing the apparent individual interaction of timesharing.

BAUD: A term used in measuring the rate of transmission of data, usually in terms of bits per second.

BAUD RATE: *See* baud.

BEAT: The regular pulsation defined by conventionally notated time signatures ("4/4" signifies "four beats per measure and the quarter note gets one beat"); the pulsation shown by a conductor's beat pattern; the pulsing resulting from the difference in frequency of two waveforms that are fairly close in frequency.

BIAS: A circuit on a tape recorder that compensates for distortion caused by the nature of the tape medium. This circuit may often be adjusted for various brands of tape.

BINARY: Referring to a base-two numbering system; a situation that can only have two states of being.

BINARY FORM: The organization of a musical composition into two sections, the second of which usually acts as a necessary continuation and completion of the first.

BINAURAL: Referring to the use of both ears to perceive sound, such that sound travels over two paths.

BIT: A binary digit or integer, denoted in arabic numerals as either 0 or 1.

BLOCK: A group of words or a set of locations handled as a unit.

BOOLEAN VARIABLE: A byte whose bits are used to signify the state of a condition or set of conditions (on-off, true-false, for example).

BOOT: When a microcomputer is turned on, the operating system is "booted," or loaded into memory. The term comes from the phrase "to pull oneself up by the bootstraps," referring to the fact that the process is initiated by the computer itself from a set of instructions contained in permanent memory. *See also* DOS, ROM.

BREATH CONTROL: A controller type allowed for in the MIDI specification, found on the Yamaha FM synthesizers.

BUFFER: A digital information storage area. Computers make use of buffers to store information before and after it is transmitted to and from various devices (*alphanumeric* keyboards and printers, for example). Digital synthesizers use a buffer to store parameter values during the process of instrument design.

BUTT SPLICE: Joining together two samples such that they butt up against each other with no overlapping. *See also* crossfade.

BYTE: A group of adjacent bits (typically eight). All *alphanumeric* characters are represented by one byte.

CADENCE: A progression of musical harmonies that helps to round off the motion for a *phrase* or other musical unit. *See also* closure.

CARRIER: An audio-frequency range signal whose amplitude or frequency is modulated by another signal (the *program* or *modulator*).

CARTESIAN COORDINATES: A set of numbers which locate a point in relation to a collection of mutually perpendicular axes. Objects may be plotted on computer monitor screens through the application of some version of this system. Graphs may use cartesian coordinates to plot the change in one parameter as another is varied, as amplitude over time, or frequency versus voltage.

CENTER FREQUENCY: The central point of a given frequency band.

CENT: One one-hundredth of a half step. There are 1200 cents per *octave*.

CENTRAL PROCESSING UNIT (CPU):   The part of a computer that interprets and executes instructions.

CHAINING: A procedure used in some microcomputer music editors in which one musical passage is chained or connected to the end of another passage.

CHANNEL: One track of a tape recorder; one of 16 logical "lines" of MIDI data transmission.

CHANNEL PRESSURE: A form of *aftertouch* in which all notes on the given MIDI channel are affected.

CHART: A term for a musical score, common in commercial and jazz musics.

CHIP: An integrated circuit, containing many logic circuits. Used in computers and in most synthesizers.

CHORD: A set of three or more tones. Chords may have a "root" or home position and various rearrangements, or inversions. Conventional harmonies use chords whose root positions involve successive elements normally at a distance of three or four half steps. *See also* cluster.

CHORUS EFFECT: Combining the main, direct, signal with several delayed versions of the signal (so called because it replicates the effect of a chorus singing a single note).

CHORUSING: *Chorus effect.*

CHROMATIC: The scale formed by the successive playing of all 12 tones of a 12-tone-per-octave set of pitches; a piece of music with chromatic characteristics. *See also* diatonic.

CHROMATICISM: The use of chromatic procedures in a composition.

CLASSIC STUDIO: A tape music studio that relies on tape splicing and other tape techniques for the primary development of electronic music.

CLICK TRACK: A recorded click used as an aid in synchronizing material to be recorded. The click track is not part of the material heard by the audience.

CLOCK MESSAGE: One of 24 messages sent per quarter note in MIDI. Unlike *MIDI Time Code*, MIDI clock messages contain no temporal location information.

CLOSURE: A sense of ending, respite, or completion caused by the interaction of various musical parameters. Closure may be partial, or momentary, at *phrase* and section endings, and fuller at the end of major subdivisions or at the close of a musical work.

CLUSTER: A simultaneous set of usually more than three tones in which successive elements are adjacent to their neighbors, producing a somewhat harsh effect.

COARSE TUNE: A potentiometer or parameter that provides a rough adjustment in frequency for an oscillator or other tone-generating module.

COLD BOOT: The process of booting a computer by turning the power on. *See also* boot, warm boot.

COMPRESSOR: An amplifier with a variable *gain* that causes the level of the output signal to be less than that of the input signal. Compression varies from 1:1 to 10:1. *See also* expander, limiter.

COMPUTER MUSIC: Music produced on or by a computer, including the actual production of sound.

CONJUNCT: An interval of a *half step* or *whole step. See also* disjunct.

CONTINUE: A MIDI message that asks all clock-based devices to continue from the point at which they stopped, rather than returning to the beginning.

CONTROL: A key on the *alphanumeric* keyboard used in conjunction with other characters for the generation of nonprinting command sequences.

CONTROL INPUT: The means by which control voltage signals are input into a voltage-controllable module. Control inputs may be hard-wired, digitally programmable, or accessed through the use of patch cords.

CONTROL CHANGE: A MIDI message containing a new value for a specified MIDI controller.

CONTROL TRACK: A sync code used by some devices to control tape speed; a sequencer track that contains controller information.

CONTROL VOLTAGE: Any voltage used to control the output characteristics of a synthesizer module. *See also* control input, voltage control.

CONTROLLER: A synthesizer module or function which controls some aspect of another module or function; a keyboard or other electronic music instrument that generates MIDI information used to control tone modules or other MIDI synthesizers.

COPY: Placing selected data into a buffer without destroying the original data. *See also* cut.

CORNER PEAKING: *Resonance.*

CPU: *Central Processing Unit.*

CRESCENDO: Increasing volume; getting louder.

CROSSFADE: Joining two samples together such that a portion of the resulting sample contains material from both samples. *See also* butt splice.

CURSOR: A character or symbol on the monitor screen that indicates where the next character will appear.

CUT: Placing selected data into a buffer, destroying or removing the original data in the process. *See also* copy.

CUTOFF FREQUENCY: The frequency at which a filter has attenuated the signal 3 dB. This frequency is adjusted by attenuator, and usually subject to various *voltage control* procedures.

D: *Decay. See also* envelope.

DAC: *Digital-to-analog converter.*

DATA BYTE: A byte in a MIDI message whose *MSB* is set, allowing a value range of 0-127.

DATA ENTRY: A slider or other device allowing data to be entered into a synthesizer; also a MIDI controller.

dB: *Decibel.*

dbx: A noise reduction system used in magnetic tape recording. Like *Dolby*, processing is required before both recording and playback. *See also* HX Pro.

DC: *Direct current.*

DCO: Digitally Controlled Oscillator. In function, essentially a digital version of a *VCO.*

DEBUG: To fix errors in a computer program.

DECIBEL: A standard unit of loudness; one tenth of a Bel (named after Alexander Graham Bell).

DECAY: A decrease in signal amplitude. One of the elements in the standard attack, decay, sustain, release *envelope.*

DECRESCENDO: A musical term involving a gradual reduction in volume.

DEFAULT: A standard or start-up condition.

DEFLAM: An averaging of attack times in a chord so that all notes occur at the same time, and not one after the other.

DEGAUSS: To demagnetize.

DEGREE (scale):   An element in a musical scale: "c" is the first degree in the scale of C major.

DIATONIC: Those tones in a piece of music that are "in the key." Diatonic tones in the key of C major include the traditional white keys of the piano, with the other tones being *chromatic*.

DIGITAL: Referring to a computer or synthesizer which uses information stored in binary format. *See also* analog.

DIGITAL DELAY: A device that creates effects based on varying the number and amplitude of, and time between, the echoes of a signal.

DIGITAL-TO-ANALOG CONVERTER: Used to convert digital information into analog voltages.

DIMENSION: The number of elements in an *array*; the process of setting aside memory space for an array.

DIN: Deutsche Industrie Normen; a cylindrical, five-prong plug used in hi-fi and MIDI applications (DIN plugs are available in many different configurations).

DIRECT CURRENT: A steady, unfluctuating voltage that flows in only one direction. *See also* alternating current.

DIRECT MODE: Any situation in which a command or procedure results in an immediate, rather than delayed, response. *See also* indirect mode.

DIRECTORY: An area within a computer system assigned to a particular user; a file that lists all available files within a directory area or on a disk.

DISK: Computer storage medium, ranging in size from 3-1/2 inch minis through 14-inch Winchester hard disks. The 5-1/4 and 3-1/2 inch disks, or diskettes, used on many systems, are flat plastic disks located within a square envelope used to store data and programs from a computer. Also referred to as "floppies."

DISK OPERATING SYSTEM: A set of system commands that allows a computer to use one or more disk drives for storage and retrieval of files.

DODECAPHONIC: A term for music based on twelve-tone or *serial music* procedures.

DOLBY: One of several noise reduction systems named for their inventor. Like *dbx*, processing is required before both recording and playback. *See also* HX Pro.

DOMINANT: A term for the fifth *degree*, or for the chord built on the fifth degree, of major and minor scales.

DOS: *Disk Operating System.*

DOWN-BEAT: The first beat in a measure; more generally, an area or point of emphasis in a composition that has down-beat-like importance.

DURATION: The time value of a tone or other musically useful event. This latter category includes silence. Duration may be determined absolutely (1 second long) or relatively (1 quarter note).

DUTY CYCLE: The "on" or positive portion of a pulse wave, expressed as a fraction of the *period*. A square wave is a pulse wave with a 1:2 duty cycle.

DYNAMIC: Not static; referring to an electronic instrument or modulation process that involves elements that are always changing.

DYNAMICS: A set of symbols used in music to define relative loudness, using various combinations of *f* (forte—loud), *m* (mezzo—medium), and *p* (piano—soft).

EARLY REFLECTION: The first reflections of a sound that are heard by the listener.

ECHO: A single reflection of a sound.

ECHO CLUSTER: A group of echoes, usually separated from other sounds by silence.

EDITING: In tape music, the process of developing compositions through splicing and/or stop-start recording. In various computer music applications, editing is subject to the capabilities and limitations of an editor.

EDITOR: A computer program or part of a program that allows data to be entered into the computer for storage and further manipulation. These data are often in the form of text (word processing), computer code (developing computer programs), or music (recording or transcription).

EFFECTS: *Echo*, *Chorus*, *digital delay*, *reverb*, and other modifications produced by passing a sound or audio signal through an effects processor.

ELECTROACOUSTIC: A term sometimes used to indicate electronic music, since it involves the use and conversion of both electrical and acoustic forms of energy.

ELEKTRONISCHE MUSIK: A German term for electronic music which relied on electronic sound sources. *See also* musique concrete.

ENTER: A key on an *alphanumeric* keyboard (often called the "Carriage Return" or just "Return") which causes data typed on the keyboard to be entered into memory.

ENVELOPE: The amplitude history of a sonic event; a multi-segmented voltage curve or series of digital levels and rates. The most common envelopes have *attack* time, *decay* time, *sustain* level, and *release* time (ADSR) segments.

ENVELOPE GENERATOR: A device that generates an envelope. Often referred to as an "ADSR." *See also* gate.

EQUAL TEMPERAMENT: The division of the *octave* into equal parts. Most often refers to the 12-part division of traditional music, based on the 12th root of 2 ($2^{n/12}$). Other divisions are possible, particularly with computers and analog synthesizers.

EQUALIZATION: The use of an equalizer, usually to compensate for a nonuniform amplitude response in a sound system or for the response in the room.

EQUALIZER: A device, usually a filter or a bank of filters, that can alter the frequency response of a sound system.

ESCAPE: A key on the *alphanumeric* keyboard usually used to indicate that one or more characters are to be interpreted with some meaning other than their usual one.

EVENT: Any musically useful sound or occurrence. An event may consist of a single tone, or of several tones occurring simultaneously, or of more complex sounds of tones (and silences) that are treated more as a single event than as a succession of events. Examples of the last type include tape loops and various sequences used as bursts or layers of sound; the emphasis is more on the generalized nature of the activity than on the importance of each consecutive element in the event.

EVENT CHASING: A sequencer procedure in which a sequencer, upon starting in the middle of a piece, searches for the previous statement of one or more parameters before continuing.

EXPANDER: An amplifier with a variable *gain* that causes the level of the output signal to be greater than that of the input signal. Expansion varies from 1:1 to 1:10 or more. *See also* compressor, limiter.

EXPONENTIAL: Involving the use of algebraic exponents; a relationship used in describing frequency and amplitude that corresponds to the way the ear works. For example, if the pitch of an event rises one *octave*, its frequency is doubled. Frequency changes from F to F times 2 ($Fx2^0$ to $Fx2^1$). A second octave increase brings the frequency to F times 4 ($Fx2^2$). *See also* linear.

F: Frequency; forte. *See* dynamics.

FADER: A potentiometer or slider that varies the value of some parameter or signal.

Fc: *Cutoff frequency*.

FFF: Fortississimo (very loud). *See* dynamics.

FILE: A computer program or other collection of information stored on disk.

FILTER: A device capable of passing one range of frequencies while attenuating others. Commonly found in low-, high-, band-pass and band-reject formats.

FIRMWARE: Software (programs and procedures) stored permanently in read-only memory (ROM).

FLANGING: A tape music procedure involving the application of pressure to the edge, or flange, of a tape reel; electronic simulation of the tape music procedure.

FLAT: A symbol that lowers the pitch of a music note by a half step.

FLOPPY DISKETTE: *See* disk.

FLOWCHART: A chart using specialized symbols to indicate the patch, or interconnection of modules and parameter settings, of an electronic instrument; a graphic aid in computer programming for the definition of an *algorithm.*

FM: *Frequency modulation.*

FOLDOVER: *Aliasing* or distortion caused in digital synthesis when frequencies higher than one-half the sample rate are created. They fold over, or generate lower frequencies, which are usually not desired.

FORMANT: A portion of the harmonic spectrum of a tone in which there is a concentration of energy.

FORMANT MODULATION: A varying of the frequency of a *formant* in one signal caused by another, often periodic, signal.

FORMAT: The process of initializing, or structuring system information on, a disk so that the computer disk operating system can store and retrieve files.

FORTE: Loud. *See* dynamics.

FRAME NOTATION: The use of boxes, brackets, or other devices to outline, or frame, a set of notated musical events. The composer usually provides performing instructions that give the performer some flexibility in structuring the order or other aspects of the events.

FREQUENCY: The number of cycles per unit time of a periodic waveform, usually measured in *Hertz* (Hz).

FREQUENCY MODULATION: A variation in the frequency of one signal caused by another, often periodic, signal.

FSK: Frequency Shifted Keying, a clock-based audio synchronization approach. Smart FSK includes temporal location information.

FULL MESSAGE: A complete *MIDI Time Code* message describing the temporal location of the system.

FUNCTIONAL TONALITY: A term for the network of relationships that have developed around the chords based on the major-minor scale system (including both *diatonic* and *chromatic relationships).*

FUNDAMENTAL: The primary component of a waveform, usually the lowest in frequency or strongest in amplitude; the first *partial* of a harmonic spectrum.

GAIN: The loudness or volume of a signal.

GATE: A voltage produced by a device such as an analog keyboard. A gate voltage is typically in the +5 to +10 volt range. It is used in the operation of an envelope generator: while the gate is high, the *attack* and *decay* segments occur. Any additional duration beyond these times allows the *sustain* voltage level to determine the envelope.

GESTURE: A musical action; the sense of a series of musical events.

GLIDE: *Portamento.*

GLISSANDO: The rapid execution of ascending or descending scales by sliding the nail of a finger up or down the music keyboard. This term is often used in place of *portamento*, which involves a glide from one pitch to another.

GRAND STAFF: *See* staff.

GRAPHIC NOTATION: Scores that communicate pitch and other musical information by the use of visual images that are evocative of the desired effect, rather than symbolic, as in traditional notation.

HALF-POWER POINT: *Cutoff frequency.*

HALF STEP: On a music keyboard, from any key to its nearest upper or lower neighboring keys; a semitone.

HARDWARE: The components of a computer system,

HARD-WIRED: Referring to analog synthesizers in which connections between modules have been built into the system by the manufacturer.

HARMONIC: A sine wave component of a waveform; its frequency is an integral multiple of the *fundamental* frequency of the waveform; also referred to as a "harmonic partial."

HARMONIC SPECTRUM: The set of harmonic *partials* that comprise a waveform.

HARMONY: Used loosely as synonymous with chord; more properly the study and practice of *functional tonality*.

HERTZ: The unit of measurement of frequency equal to one cycle of a periodic waveform per second. Abbreviated Hz.

HEXADECIMAL: Referring to a base-16 numbering system. Following the digits 0 through 9 are the letters A through F. $10 ("$" indicates a hexadecimal value) means "one 16 and zero ones;" $1F means "one 16 and 15 ones," or 31 (decimal).

HIERARCHY: *See* architectonic hierarchy.

HIGH-LEVEL LANGUAGE: A computer programming language that uses words and expressions that resemble English usage. A high-level language must be translated into machine language code to be "understood" by the computer.

HIGH-PASS FILTER: A filter that attenuates frequencies below the *cutoff frequency* while passing those frequencies above the cutoff frequency with relatively little attenuation.

HX PRO: A noise reduction system developed by Dolby/Bang & Olufsen, except that no special processing is needed on playback. *See also* dbx, Dolby.

HYBRID SYSTEM: An electronic music system that combines elements of analog synthesis with computer control of some processes.

Hz: *Hertz*.

IBM: International Business Machines Corporation.

ICON: A symbol used in computer software (associated often with the Macintosh) to indicate a particular action or choice.

IMITATION: In *polyphonic* music, this procedure involves the repetition of events or gestures in more than one line.

IMPEDANCE: Resistance to AC current, measured in ohms. Professional microphones and other studio equipment use low impedance, which allows long cable runs.

IMPROVISATION: An approach to music composition that involves a high degree of relatively spontaneous performer involvement in the creation of the musical material to be performed.

INDICATIVE NOTATION: Symbols or other information that indicate musical actions to be taken without specifying the timbre or other features of the sonic result.

INDIRECT MODE: Any situation in which the desired response occurs after a delay. *See also* direct mode.

INIT: *Initialize*.

INITIAL DECAY: *See* decay.

INITIAL GAIN: The amplitude attenuator on a VCA.

INITIALIZE: The process of formatting a disk in some computer systems. *See also* format, disk operating system.

INSTRUMENT: A generic term for a *patch* or set of *parameter* values; *preset*; *voice*.

INSTRUMENT DESIGN: One of three phases used in this book to structure the creative process, focussing on the creation of *instruments*. *See also* Score Construction, Rehearsal/Performance.

INSTRUMENTATION: The process of selecting timbres for a piece of music.

INTEGRATED CIRCUIT: A chip used in digital circuitry that itself contains a large number of circuits.

INTENSITY: The amount of power in a sound, often measured in *decibels.*

INTERFACE: A device or point where two or more instruments or procedures meet and communicate. Digital-to-analog and analog-to-digital converters allow computers and analog signal sources to be interfaced. *See also* MIDI.

INTERVAL: The distance between two tones. In 12-tone *equal temperament* an interval may be stated in terms of *half steps* or *whole steps*, or may be further refined in conjunction with letter names. In this system D to E is a major second (a distance of two half steps), but E to F is a minor second (only one half step). Intervals using this nomenclature may be diminished, minor, major, perfect, or augmented, depending on convention.

INVERSION: The reversal of the direction of some process. A positive-going voltage may be inverted into a negative-going voltage; descending or ascending musical gestures may be inverted, as well as chords and other musical structures.

INVERT: To turn over; create an *inversion.*

IPS: Inches per second, a measure of magnetic tape speed.

IRCAM: Institute de Recherche et Coordination Acoustique/Musique (Paris, France).

JAM SYNC: Live replacement or regeneration of damaged or missing time code.

JUST INTONATION: One approach to tuning or tempering musical tones (or more properly, the intervals between tones). In just intonation, as many diatonic scale degrees are tuned perfectly, or "justly," as is possible. This leads to some tuning problems with certain intervals, which equal temperament is designed to eliminate. *See also* diatonic, equal temperament.

K: Thousand; also kilobyte, which is actually 1024 bytes.

Kbaud: One thousand bits per second.

KEYBOARD SPLIT: Dividing a keyboard into two or more timbral regions.

KLANGFARBENMELODIE: A melodic line in which tone color (klangfarben) plays a major role. *See also* timbre.

LAYERING: Playing two or more timbres with one key; creating a piece with two or more discrete layers.

LEAD SHEET: *Chart.*

LEADER TAPE: Blank tape (either plastic or paper) intended for use with magnetic tape. It may lead or follow a portion of music, or may be inserted into an excerpt to add silence. Timing marks on some leader tape aid in determining length of the tape.

LEAST SIGNIFICANT BYTE: In 14-bit MIDI controller values, the 7 bits that give the values 0-127. *See also* data byte.

LEGATO: Connected; the smooth playing or singing of a musical line.

LFO: *Low Frequency Oscillator. See also* Voltage-Controlled Oscillator.

LIBRARIAN: A computer program designed to transfer patches to and from a synthesizer. May be combined with patch editor which allows creation and modification of patches. *See also* patch.

LIMITER: An amplifier with a variable *gain* that causes the level of the output signal to remain constant for any input signal level; a *compressor* with a ratio of at least 10:1. *See also* expander.

LINEAR: A relationship in which a change of value in one parameter produces a consistent change of value in another parameter. Compare with *exponential.* Linear also has a musical connotation (*see* melody).

LIVE ELECTRONICS: The use of synthesizers and other equipment in a concert or live performance setting, as opposed to using them in a tape studio setting.

LOCAL CONTROL: A parameter or switch on a digital switch which determines if the keyboard output controls the local tone generating circuitry.

LOCATION CUE: Localization, or the ability of the listener to determine the direction and distance of a sound.

LOGICAL OSCILLATOR: An oscillator based on digital, or logical, circuits.

LOUDNESS: The volume or amplitude of a sound, measured somewhat subjectively.

LOW FREQUENCY OSCILLATOR: A device that generates sub-audio and low-range audio frequencies, sometimes voltage-controllable. *See also* VCO, voltage control.

LOW-PASS FILTER: A filter that attenuates frequencies above the *cutoff frequency* of the filter while passing lower frequencies with relatively little attenuation.

LTC: *See* SMPTE Time Code.

MACHINE LANGUAGE: Data interpreted as instructions that are to be executed by a computer's *central processing unit*; the lowest level of programming languages, most accessible to the computer and least accessible to the programmer. *See also* assembly language, high-level language.

MAINFRAME: A large computer system that is usually capable of serving many users at once through the use of remote terminals.

MAPPING: Changing a range of values to another range, often according to a predetermined map, or list.

MEASURE: The space between two vertical lines on a musical staff. This notational device allows musical time to be easily measured (thus the term "measure"). Successive measures need not be the same length, although they often are. Measures are used in MIDI software, again as a timing device, although the performer is free to disregard it, as long as the notational aspect of the piece is not important.

MELODY: Conventionally, a succession of musical tones. Melodies are often thought of as being located in the upper voice or instrumental line. In electronic music this concept is expanded to include successions of events.

MERGE: Combine material with previously existing material such that the two overlap in the merge region. *See also* paste.

METER: The (generally regular) subdivision of a measure into beats, notated as a meter or *time signature* at the beginning of a musical score or wherever the meter changes. The actual musical material sometimes supports and sometimes works against the meter, although ultimately the relationship between meter and music is a tautology: the meter is the result of the various interactions of musical material, while the material may be molded to express the meter.

METRIC MODULATION: The process of moving from one tempo to another through the use of various *meters* and other music notational devices. *See also* modulation.

METRONOME: A device that measures musical tempo in beats per minute; often with a click or flash.

MEZZO: Medium; a modifier for *forte* and *piano*.

MICROCOMPUTER: Either an entire computer system on a single chip or a small computer consisting of *microprocessor* and associated chips; a personal computer.

MICROPROCESSOR: The *central processing unit* of a *microcomputer*.

MICROTONE: A member of a scale based on a division of the *octave* into more than 12 parts. On most electronic equipment, such divisions will be equal-tempered. *See* equal temperament.

MIDI: Musical Instrument Digital Interface. MIDI is a hardware and software specification intended to allow interconnection of various digital synthesizers, computers, and other digital equipment.

MIDI CLOCK: *See* Clock Message.

MIDI FILE FORMAT: A standard file format for transmission and storage of sequenced material that can be read and written by many MIDI applications.

MIDI TIME CODE: A MIDI version of *SMPTE Time Code*.

MILLISECOND: One thousandth of a second.

MINICOMPUTER: A computer system larger in memory and faster than a *microcomputer* but smaller than a *mainframe* computer.

MINIFLOPPY: A term for a 5-1/4 inch disk. *See* disk.

MIT: Massachusetts Institute of Technology.

MIX: To combine two or more streams of musical material; in a mixdown material from a multitrack recording is combined and balanced while being transferred to the master recorder (usually *monophonic* or *stereo*).

MODAL: Music written in a particular *mode*; a computer program that isolates its various functions, so that only one mode of operation is available at a time.

MODE: A particular set of characteristics or conditions. Computer editors may have "insert" or "change" modes (allowing material to be inserted into a file either without changing what is already there or by overwriting—thus changing—previous entries). Musical scales are modes, since they impose conditions and establish special relationships among the various *diatonic* and *chromatic* tones; major and minor are but two of many possible musical modes.

MODEM: Modulator-demodulator; a device used for data transmission.

MODULAR: Consisting of modules; referring to a synthesizer consisting of independent modules, usually interconnected by the user with the aid of patch cords. *See also* patch.

MODULATION: The process of controlling characteristics of a wave, often frequency or amplitude, according to the amplitude and frequency of another, modulating, wave; the process, in *functional tonality*, of moving from one *tonic* area to another. It is also possible to modulate from one set of durations, or timbres, or attack types, or any other parameter, to another, different set.

MODULATION INDEX: Used to determine the number of sidebands produced by audio-range frequency modulation. The index equals the *peak frequency deviation* divided by the program frequency.

MODULATION SYNTHESIS: Any approach to synthesis relying on *modulation* processes to develop waveforms.

MODULATION WHEEL: A manual controller, typically used to control *LFO* amount.

MODULATOR: Any signal that modulates some aspect of another signal; in FM synthesis, the audio-range signal combined with the *carrier* to produce *sidebands*. *See also* modulation.

MODULE: A unit in a synthesizer or a computer program.

MONITOR: A system program providing basic utility routines for a computer; the display screen for a microcomputer.

MONOPHONIC: One sound. Monophonic synthesizers only allow one key on a music keyboard or one signal path to be active at a time. Monophonic compositions have essentially only one melodic line. A monophonic tape recorder has only one channel. *See also* polyphonic, melody, event.

MOST SIGNIFICANT BIT: The leftmost bit in a byte.

MOTIVE: A short succession of sounds that occurs more than once in a piece, with subsequent statements often having various aspects altered (faster, slower, inverted, extended, truncated, in different registers, with changes in timbre or other parameters). *See also* event, inversion.

MPU401:   The de facto MIDI-IBM PC interface standard developed by Roland.

MSB: *Most Significant Bit.*

MULTIPHONICS: The production of two or more sounds simultaneously, especially on woodwind instruments (which officially produce only one sound at a time). This requires special fingerings or other special performance techniques.

MULTISAMPLE: One of a set of samples used in *multisampling*; a set of samples with registral separation intended to function together to create a single *instrument*.

MULTISAMPLING: The process of creating a *multisample*; developing multiple samples, each in its own register, which function together to create an *instrument*.

MULTI-TIMBRAL: A synthesizer or tone module capable of producing more than one timbre at a time, with each timbre on a separate MIDI channel.

MULTITRACK: A tape recorder with four or more tracks in the same direction (a stereo recorder has four tracks, but only two in a given direction).

MUSIQUE CONCRETE: Music produced by recording and altering acoustic sounds. *See also* classic studio, tape music.

MUTE: A switch or control that zeroes out, or turns off, the audio from a track; a device used by various acoustic instruments as an aid to playing softer. *See also* solo.

NIBBLE: A grouping of 4 *bits*, as opposed to a *byte* (8 bits).

NOISE: Sound that is not appropriate for a given situation; also nonperiodic sound complexes in which individual frequencies cannot be discerned. White noise has constant power per bandwidth and pink noise has constant power per octave.

NOISE GENERATOR: A device that generates random noise. It may be able to produce white and/or pink noise and is often used in conjunction with a sample and hold module for the production of random stepped control voltages. *See also* noise.

NOISE REDUCTION: The process of increasing the signal-to-noise ratio of a signal. *See also* dbx, Dolby, HX Pro.

NORMALLED: Referring to a jack wired so that a normal signal path is established without the use of a patch cord. The insertion of a plug breaks this connection.

NOTCH FILTER: *See* band-reject filter.

NOTE: The written symbol for a musical tone. *See also* tone.

NOTE OFF MESSAGE: A 3-byte MIDI message that terminates the gated portion of a MIDI note. A Note On message with a velocity of 0 may act as a Note Off message.

NOTE ON MESSAGE: A 3-byte MIDI message that initiates the gated portion of an audio signal. *See also* Note Off message.

NYQUIST THEOREM: Signals with frequencies up to a little less than half the sample rate can be sampled by an *ADC* or generated by a *DAC* without distortion.

OBJECT-ORIENTED PROGRAM: An application in which portions of code can be used (and reused) as blocks, or objects. In graphic environments the user may deal more with icons representing code segments than with the actual code.

OCTAVE: A relationship between two frequencies such that one is twice the other. On a music keyboard the octave is the point at which the pattern of black and white keys repeats.

OFFSET VOLTAGE: A DC voltage created by adjusting a *potentiometer* on an analog synthesizer module. This voltage can be added internally to any control voltages to modify various characteristics of a signal.

OPERATOR: In FM synthesis, a module functioning as either *carrier* or *modulator*.

OSCILLATOR: *See* voltage-controlled oscillator.

OSTINATO: A melodic and/or rhythmic pattern of pitches (often a bass line) which is constantly repeated ("ostinato" can be translated from Italian as "obstinate").

OVERDUB: The addition of material to a recording after the initial session.

OVERTONE: A term for "harmonic partial." In this nomenclature the first overtone is the second *partial*, while the first partial is called the *fundamental*.

P: *Piano*.

PAGE: A standard amount of memory; on an 8-bit microcomputer a page is 2^8, or 256, consecutive bytes.

PANNING: Placing a signal in a stereo field; may be under voltage or MIDI control.

PANPOT: A *potentiometer* used in panning, or causing a signal to appear to have vertical or horizontal movement.

PARALLEL: The transmission or other manipulation of data one word at a time; musical lines may also operate in parallel fashion. *See also* serial.

PARAMETER: A variable; the values stored in a digital synthesizer which create or modify an *instrument*; some aspect or characteristic of musical time or space which may be identified and used to control or articulate the flow of music.

PARTIAL: A sine wave component of a complex waveform. *See also* fundamental, harmonic, harmonic spectrum.

PASSBAND: The band of frequencies that will pass through a filter relatively unattenuated.

PASTE: Combine material with previously existing material such that the new material replaces the old in the paste region. *See also* merge.

PATCH: The interconnection of synthesizer modules to create an electronic *instrument*. Although patches formerly relied on patch cords, the term may still be applied to instruments designed by setting switches to determine signal routing or by digital programming techniques.

PATCH PANEL: A panel, often rack-mounted, consisting of a set of jacks which allow various equipment and circuits to be easily interconnected.

PC: Personal computer. The term is somewhat generic, although it is also used to refer to IBM's PC family. Also abbreviation for "printed circuit."

PEAK FREQUENCY DEVIATION: The maximum variation in the frequency of a carrier signal from its unmodulated state.

PEDAL POINT: A tone, usually in a low *register*, that is sustained while activity continues in other musical lines.

PENTATONIC SCALE: Literally, a scale consisting of five *pitch classes*. The most common form consists of the black keys on the music keyboard.

PERIOD: The time required to complete one cycle of a periodic waveform. For a waveform to be periodic, it must repeat itself exactly at some regular time interval.

PERIOD, MUSICAL: A musical unit consisting of two or more *phrases* with some type of conclusive harmonic *cadence*.

PERIPHERAL: Any piece of computer equipment that may be connected to the central processing unit; used here to refer primarily to hardware added to the basic microcomputer system.

PHASE DISTORTION: A synthesis procedure involving phase modification used by Casio in its CZ series.

PHASE SHIFTER: A device that creates an electronic version of flanging, in which a copy of a signal has its phase shifted by the application of a short delay. *See also* flanging, digital delay.

PHRASE: A musical unit, often corresponding to the length performed in one breath by a singer, defined by a combination of harmonic and melodic activity.

PIANO: The musical term for "soft." MP (mezzopiano) and PP (pianissimo) allow "piano" to be modified to indicate medium soft and very soft respectively. *See also* dynamics.

PINK NOISE: *See* noise.

PITCH: A musical term for a tone or a note; the perceived highness or lowness of a sound.

PITCH BEND: Manual alteration of the pitch of a note through use of a pitch bend device (often a wheel); a MIDI message affecting pitch in a similar fashion.

PITCH CLASS: The set of all pitches sharing the same letter-name designation (members of a pitch class are related by *octave* transposition).

PIXEL: A picture element, or dot on certain monitor screens.

PL/I: Programing Language/One, designed for the Intel 4004 microprocessor.

POINTILLISTIC: A term borrowed from the visual arts, in which a musical composition is considered to be a collection of discrete points, rather than a succession or progression of events.

POLYPHONIC: More than one tone occurring simultaneously; music keyboards which may control more than one signal path at a time; compositions containing two or more musical lines with some degree of independence.

PORT: The entry/exit point for data on a computer. *See also* parallel, serial.

PORTAMENTO: A glide from one pitch to another. This term is often used in place of *glissando*.

POSITIONAL NOTATION: Music notation in which the placement of a symbol on the page indicates pitch.

POSTEMPHASIS: Compensation at a recorder's output for pre-recording *equalization*.

POT: *Potentiometer*.

POTENTIOMETER: A variable resistor, used to control amplitude and other signal characteristics.

PPP: Pianississimo (very, very soft). *See* dynamics.

PPQN: Pulses Per Quarter Note. *See* tick.

PREEMPHASIS: *Equalization* applied at a recorder's input, usually of specific frequency bands. Often followed by *postemphasis*.

PRESET: An electronic *instrument* or voice that has been previously designed, often by the manufacturer; an instrument or set of instruments (a preset bank) created and stored digitally; an analog synthesizer whose signal path options have been restricted by hard-wiring or other hardware or software design constraints.

PRINT-THROUGH: The leakage of a magnetically recorded signal from one portion of tape to another.

PROGRAM: A set of instructions to the computer; a *patch* or electronic *instrument*; a *program signal*.

PROGRAM CHANGE: A MIDI message causing a change in the selected *preset*.

PROGRAM, MUSICAL: A non-musical source, such as a story or other literary work, which inspires the composition (and often structure) of a piece of music

PROGRAM SIGNAL: A signal that modulates another signal. See *modulation, carrier.*

PROGRESSION: A succession of harmonies whose underlying structure involves motion from *dominant* to *tonic*, considered to be the primary progression in *functional tonality*. By extension, a progress in music that doesn't rely on functional tonality would be a succession whose structure involves a sense of completion, or closure. *See also* succession.

PULSE WAVE: A basic analog synthesizer waveform. The width of the pulse (the *duty cycle*) is usually adjustable, either manually or through voltage control.

PULSE WIDTH: The width of the *duty cycle* of a *pulse wave*.

PULSE WIDTH MODULATION: A variation in the *duty cycle* of a pulse wave caused by another, often periodic, signal. *See* pulse wave, modulation, voltage control.

PWM: *Pulse Width Modulation*.

Q: *Resonance*.

QUANTIZATION: The production of a series of discrete values, as opposed to a continuous function.

QUANTIZED: Measured in discrete values. *See* quantization.

QUARTER FRAME MESSAGE: One of a set of eight *MIDI Time Code* messages that specify temporal location.

QUARTER-TONE: The distance of one half of a *half step*, created by the division of the octave into 24 equal parts. Some acoustic instruments, synthesizers which can attenuate keyboard control voltage, digital synthesizers with preset and user-programmable tunings, and microcomputer-controlled and computer-based music systems can produce quarter-tones and other microtonal intervals.

R: *Release* time.

RAM: Random access memory. A portion of computer memory in which data and programs may be temporarily stored; a computer's working memory. *See* ROM.

RANDOM NOISE: A type of noise produced by analog noise generators used for control functions and unusual effects.

READ-WRITE HEAD: The device on a disk drive which is used for data transfer to and from a disk.

REAL-TIME COMMAND: Any command issued during a process; MIDI messages used by clock-based equipment for synchronization purposes.

REGISTER: A pitch region; a one-*word* portion of memory used by a microprocessor to hold or process instructions or data.

REHEARSAL//PERFORMANCE: One of three phases used in this book to structure the creative process, focussing on real-time recording and playback in the studio along with presentation of the work to its intended audience. *See also* Instrument Design, Score Construction.

RELEASE: The final segment of an amplitude *envelope* used to control the gain of a VCA or various characteristics of other synthesizer modules. The release segment begins when the gate voltage drops (usually by releasing a key on a music keyboard). *See also* attack, decay, sustain.

RESERVED WORD: Keywords or symbols with special significance in BASIC.

RESET: To return a device to an initial state or condition; the switch or key which triggers such a procedure.

RESOLUTION: The level of detail allowed on a monitor screen or printer; in music, the completion of a harmonic progression or logical release of musical tension.

RESONANCE: A concentration of energy at a filter *cutoff frequency*; the reinforcing of a sound by vibration or reflection of the sound.

REST: Measured musical silence; a symbol denoted measured silence.

RETROGRADE: The reversal of a sequence of musical events.

RETURN: *See* enter.

REVERB: An effect utilizing the principle of *reverberation*. *See also* digital delay.

REVERBERATION: Persistent *echoes* so closely spaced that they are not individually identifiable.

RF: Radio frequency.

RGB: Red, Green, Blue; the monitors equipped to handle these signals which produce high quality color.

RHYTHM: The organization of musical time, often of the durations of musical sounds and silences. Other parameters may be subject to rhythmic perception, or may in turn affect rhythm.

RHYTHMIC MODULATION: Gradually shifting from one set of rhythms to another.

RING MODULATOR: An *amplitude modulation* device whose output contains the sum and difference frequencies of its two input waveforms.

RITARDANDO: Gradually becoming slower.

ROM: Read-only memory. A computer or microprocessor may read information stored in this type of memory but may not overwrite it.

RONDO FORM: A standard musical form, in which the periodic return of opening material is essential. A typical rondo may have the form ABACA, in which B and C represent different and contrasting material from A.

RUBATO: An expressive, flexible varying of *tempo*.

S: *Sustain*.

SAMPLE: A numerical value representing a voltage. The more samples per second used by a computer, the more accurately an analog signal may be digitally stored and reproduced.

SAMPLE-AND-HOLD: A device that regularly outputs the frequency at its input, creating a *quantized* version of the input waveform or, if the input is a noise source, a random sequence of frequencies or voltages.

SAMPLE RATE: The rate at which a computer samples a waveform. The sample rate should be at least twice the highest desired frequency, to avoid *foldover* error. To produce a 20 kHz signal, the sample rate should be at least 40 kHz.

SAMPLER: A digital device that records audio input; a music keyboard that samples. *See also* sample.

SAMPLING: The process of recording *samples*.

SAMPLING RATE: *Sample rate.*

SAWTOOTH WAVE: A basic waveshape containing all integer *partials*. The amplitude of a partial is defined as $1/n$ times the amplitude of the fundamental, where n is the partial number.

SCORE: Material which enables the organization and expressive use of musical resources, usually involving written material.

SCORE CONSTRUCTION: One of three phases used in this book to structure the creative process, focussing on assembling basic musical materials through notation and step recording. *See also* Instrument Design, Rehearsal/Performance.

SCRIPTING: Writing program code in HyperCard, a Macintosh programming tool.

SCROLL: The effect caused when lines of text appear to move up and off the monitor screen while new ones enter at the bottom, simulating the unrolling of a scroll.

SECTOR: A segment of a track of a floppy disk, usually consisting of 256 bytes. Although various disk operating systems have different procedures, a sector is the amount of material moved to or from the disk by a microcomputer in one operation.

SEL-SYNC: A circuit or switch on a tape recorder which allows recorded material and source material to be synchronized by allowing the recorded material to be played back via the record head. *See* sound-with-sound.

SEMITONE: Another term for *half step*.

SENSITIVITY LEVEL: A setting that determines a sampler's response to audio input. *See also* sampler, sample.

SEQUENCER: A device or software which allows recording and playback of music keyboard information. In a MIDI environment, sequencers handle a wide range of MIDI data, and are not restricted to keyboards and note data.

SERIAL: A means of handling digital data in which digital *words* are transmitted one bit at a time. MIDI protocol requires serial data transmission. *See also* parallel.

SERIAL MUSIC: Music in which parameters are organized into series, or rows. Various operations may be carried out upon these rows to create a piece of music.

SHARP: A symbol that raises the pitch of a note by a half step.

SIDEBAND: A frequency generated by modulation. *See also* carrier, program.

SIGNAL: The electrical analog of a sound wave.

SIGNAL PATH: The route taken by an audio signal through a synthesizer.

SIGNAL TO NOISE RATIO: A ratio between signal strength and the ambient noise level, with high ratios being preferred.

SIMULTANEITY: Events consisting of two or more tones. *See also* chords, clusters.

SINE WAVE: A basic waveshape containing only the *fundamental* frequency.

SMART FSK: *See* FSK.

SMPTE TIME CODE: Developed by the Society of Motion Picture & Television Engineers, this is the standard code used to synchronize sight and sound.

SOFTWARE: Programs, both user-supplied and commercial, which allow the computer to perform specialized applications. *See also* hardware.

SOLO: A switch or device that isolates and monitors a single track in a recording studio; a similar function provided by a MIDI sequencer. *See also* mute.

SONG POSITION: A MIDI message that asks clock-based devices to find a particular temporal location.

SONG SELECT: A MIDI message that specifies which song should be selected.

SOUND-ON-SOUND: A tape recording procedure in which recorded sound and incoming audio signals are mixed and recorded on a second track.

SOUND-WITH-SOUND: A tape recording procedure in which each track has its own source material. *See also* sound-on-sound.

SOURCE CODE: The code written by a computer programmer.

SPATIAL MODULATION: The process of controlling the spatial location of a signal, generally according to the amplitude and frequency characteristics of another signal.

SPECTRUM: The set of *partials* or frequencies which create a complex waveform.

SQUARE WAVE: A pulse wave with equal positive and negative segments. A square wave contains only odd integer *partials*, with the amplitude $1/n$ times the amplitude of the fundamental, where n is the partial number.

STAFF: The system of five parallel horizontal lines used to notate pitch (plural: staves). The "grand staff" is the two-staff system used to notate piano and other keyboard music.

START TIME: The time at which a note or sequence is scheduled to begin.

STATUS BYTE: A byte used in MIDI data transmission to signify the status or function of the MIDI message it begins.

STAVES: *See* staff.

STEP RECORDING: In MIDI practice, the sequencing of material one event at a time, with duration being specified rather than being a function of the performance.

STOPBAND: The band of frequencies attenuated by a filter.

STOP-START EDITING: The ordering of material on magnetic tape by recording one event then stopping, setting up for the next event and recording it, and so on.

STRENGTH (QUANTIZATION):   The percentage of the distance that notes are moved to grid nodes when quantized (at 50% notes would be moved half the distance from their present location to the nearest grid node). *See also* quantization.

SUBROUTINE: A module of a computer program, called from the main portion of the program. Following execution of all statements in the subroutine, the program continues with the statement following the one which called the subroutine.

SUBTRACTIVE SYNTHESIS: The process of developing audio signals by filtering more complex signals. The low-pass filter is most commonly used to filter triangle, sawtooth, square, and pulse waveforms. Other, more complex, signals may also be filtered.

SUCCESSION: A sequence of harmonies or other musical material which does not provide a sense of *closure*; successions may elaborate or extend aspects of a piece but tend to be more ornamental than essential to the structure of a piece.

SUSTAIN: One element in the standard amplitude envelope. The sustain setting indicates a voltage level (analogous to an amplitude level), while the other elements indicate the amount of time for an envelope segment to either increase or decrease in amplitude. *See also* attack, decay, release.

SYNC: Synchronize.

SYNTHESIZER: A set of electronic modules or devices used for the generation and modification of sound. Either voltage is used as an analog for sound, or, increasingly, digital means are used. Most digital synthesizers are built in accordance with the MIDI specification, allowing for their combination into MIDI networks or systems.

SYSTEM COMMON: MIDI messages that apply to all equipment in a network.

SYSTEM EXCLUSIVE: MIDI messages that apply to a particular synthesizer or piece of equipment.

SYSTEM REAL TIME: MIDI messages that are used in real-time activities.

TAILS-OUT: A method of magnetic tape storage which requires that tape be rewound before playback or recording.

TAPE MUSIC: A generic term for electronic material produced and recorded in a studio setting. This material generally falls into the *art music* category.

TEMPERAMENT: Any system of tuning or tempering intervals which causes them to deviate from acoustically pure ratios. *See also* equal temperament, just intonation.

TEMPO: The speed of a composition or of a portion thereof.

TERNARY FORM: The organization of a musical composition into three sections, with the second providing contrast and the third providing some form of restatement of the opening material. *See also* binary form.

TEXTURE: The grain or density of activity of a musical composition, often defined in terms such as "thin" or "thick."

THEME: A musical idea used as the basis for further musical activity.

THROUGH-COMPOSED: A composition that is completely written or composed out, without substantial restatement of material.

TICK: A unit of division of a quarter note by a sequencer, generally much smaller than *MIDI clocks*. *See also* ppqn.

TIMBRE: The tone color or character of a sound or musical tone. Each acoustic instrument has a unique timbre—actually a set of related timbres, since *register*, playing technique, fingering, and loudness of the tone all have an effect on timbre. Timbre also depends on the relative intensity and frequency of the set of harmonic *partials* which combine to produce the musical tone.

TIMBRE MODULATION: Modulation processes in which the harmonic content of a waveform is subject to change. *Formant* and *pulse wave modulation* both produce timbre modulation.

TIME CODE: Any system for synchronizing clock-based devices that includes temporal location information. *See also* FSK, MIDI Time Code, SMPTE Time Code.

TIMESHARING: The simultaneous use of a computer from more than one terminal.

TIMESTAMPING: A procedure by which MIDI sequencers keep track of the time between incoming MIDI events.

TONE: A discrete musical pitch. Although "tone" and "note" are often used interchangeably, "note" refers to the written symbol which the musician translates into a tone. "Tone" may also be used to indicate the interval of a *whole step*, although that usage is avoided in this book.

TONE COLOR: Another term for *timbre*.

TONIC: A term for the first *degree*, or for the chord built on the first degree, of major and minor scales.

TOUCH SENSITIVITY: The ability of a MIDI keyboard or other controller to produce or respond to velocity information based on how hard or quickly keys are struck. Some devices may respond to velocity information without producing it.

TRACK: A channel on a tape recorder; the portion of magnetic tape which is used to record one channel; one of a set of concentric circles on a floppy disk, used for data and program storage.

TRANSIENT: Any portion of an instrument's sound when its amplitude envelope is not in a (more-or-less) steady state; the characteristic attack of an instrument (the initial transient).

TRANSISTOR: An electronic substitute for the vacuum tube. Transistors were developed in the late 1940s.

TRANSPOSE: To uniformly raise or lower the pitch of some portion of a piece of music. Transposition may be *chromatic* or *diatonic*.

TREMULO: A subtle low-frequency (6-8 Hz) amplitude modulation of an audio signal; a variation in intensity, as opposed to a *vibrato*, a variation in frequency.

TRIANGLE WAVE: A waveform consisting of odd integer harmonic *partials*. The amplitude of a partial is defined as $1/n^2$ times the amplitude of the *fundamental*, where n is the partial number.

TRIGGER: A device or voltage that causes a module or process to start.

TRUE PITCH: The actual pitch range produced by MIDI tone circuitry; notes outside this range will be transposed up or down by octaves into the actual playing range.

TUNE REQUEST: A MIDI message requesting the tuning of analog oscillators.

TUPLET: Triplets, quintuplets, and similar rhythmic units.

UART: The Universal Asynchronous Receiver/Transmitter, part of the MIDI circuitry that receives and transmits MIDI information.

UP-BEAT: The final beat in a measure; a *gesture* or *event* that has the quality of leading to a goal (evocative of the raising of a conductor's arms prior to the *down-beat*).

UTILITY: A computer program that carries out some specific "housekeeping" function such as program debugging and verification, file copying, disk file maintenance, and other functions.

VCA: *Voltage-Controlled Amplifier.*

VCF: *Voltage-Controlled Filter.*

VCO: *Voltage-Controlled Oscillator.*

VIBRATO: A generally subtle low-frequency (6-8 Hz) frequency modulation of an audio signal; a variation in frequency, as opposed to a *tremulo*, which involves a variation in amplitude.

VIRTUAL MEMORY: Using a hard disk as an extension of computer memory.

VITC: *See* SMPTE Time Code.

VOICE: A musical line (*see* melody); a *patch* or *preset* or *instrument*.

VOLTAGE: A measure of electrical pressure. Voltage is used in analog synthesizers as an analog for air pressure.

VOLTAGE CONTROL: The process of controlling one analog module by another through the use of voltage. *Control voltages* produced by a module are sent to a control voltage input, and added to any other control voltages and *offset voltages* created by potentiometer settings to cause changes to one or more of the characteristics of a signal produced by the module being controlled.

VOLTAGE-CONTROLLED AMPLIFIER: A synthesizer module capable of modifying the amplitude characteristics of a signal through *voltage control* procedures.

VOLTAGE-CONTROLLED FILTER: A synthesizer module allowing voltage-controlled *subtractive synthesis*; often used to indicate a low-pass filter. *See also* voltage control.

VOLTAGE-CONTROLLED OSCILLATOR: An analog module that generates audio range waveforms whose frequencies are subject to *voltage control* procedures. A Low Frequency Oscillator (*LFO*) generates sub-audio and low-range audio frequencies, sometimes voltage-controllable. Some VCOs also produce low-frequency waveforms.

VOLUME: The loudness or amplitude of a sound.

VOLUME PEDAL: A *volume* controller.

WAVEFORM: One means of describing an electrical or sound pressure wave by showing how the amplitude of a signal varies over time. *See also* harmonic spectrum, pulse wave, sawtooth wave, sine wave, square wave, triangle wave.

WAVEFORM SYNTHESIS: The creation of waveforms on a computer through setting up and manipulating tables of numbers.

WAVE TABLE: A series of digital values representing a waveform.

WELL-TEMPERED: *See* equal temperament.

WHITE NOISE: Non-periodic, random sound with constant power over its bandwidth. Pink noise has constant power per octave. *See also* noise.

WHOLE STEP: Used in the twelve tone division of the *octave* to describe the distance from one *pitch class* to another in which there is but one intervening available pitch class; two half steps. Also called a whole tone (two semitones). *See also* half step.

WORD: The organization of digital data into a group of 4, 8, 16, or 32 bits.

WRAP-AROUND: A feature of many monitor screens, in which a line of text, upon reaching the right margin, is automatically continued or wrapped around to the left margin on the next, lower, screen line.

WRITE-ENABLE NOTCH: A notch on a 5-1/4 inch diskette which, when open, allows information to be transferred to disk. Eight-inch and 3-1/2 inch disks use this notch in reverse fashion. *See also* disk.

INDEX